Modeling Monetary Economies

Too often monetary economics has been taught as a collection of facts about institutions for students to memorize. By teaching from first principles instead, this advanced undergraduate textbook builds on a simple, clear monetary model and applies this framework consistently to a wide variety of monetary questions. Starting with the case in which trade is mutually beneficial, the book demonstrates that money makes people better off, and that government money competes against other means of payments, including other types of government money. After developing each of these topics, the book tackles the issue of money competing against other stores of value, examining issues associated with trade, finance, and modern banking. The book then moves from simple economies to modern economies, addressing the role banks play in making more trades possible, concluding with the information problems plaguing modern banking, which result in financial crises.

Bruce Champ was a Senior Research Economist at the Federal Reserve Bank of Cleveland, and passed away in 2013. Earlier he taught at Virginia Polytechnic Institute, the Universities of Iowa and Western Ontario, and Fordham University. Dr. Champ's research interests focused on monetary economics and his articles have appeared in the *American Economic Review; Journal of Monetary Economics*; *Canadian Journal of Economics*; and *Journal of Money, Credit, and Banking*, among other leading academic publications. He coauthored the first and second editions of *Modeling Monetary Economies* with the late Scott Freeman.

Scott Freeman was a Professor of Economics at the University of Texas, Austin. He taught earlier at Boston College and the University of California, Santa Barbara. Professor Freeman died in 2004 after struggling with Amyotrophic Lateral Sclerosis for several years. Professor Freeman specialized in monetary theory, and his articles appeared in the *Journal of Political Economy*; *American Economic Review*; *Journal of Monetary Economics*; and *Journal of Money, Credit, and Banking*, among other eminent academic journals.

Joe Haslag is Professor and Kenneth Lay Chair in Economics at the University of Missouri. Professor Haslag received his PhD in Economics from Southern Methodist University in 1987. Professor Haslag spent 12 years in the Research Department at the Federal Reserve Bank of Dallas, teaching graduate and undergraduate courses at Southern Methodist University. He visited the Economics Department at Michigan State University in 2000 and the Department of Monetary Economics at Erasmus University in 1994. He has published his research in such prestigious academic journals as the *Journal of Monetary Economics; Journal of Money, Credit, and Banking; The Review of Economics and Statistics; International Economic Review; and Review of Economic Dynamics*, among other leading academic journals.

Modeling Monetary Economies

Fourth Edition

BRUCE CHAMP

SCOTT FREEMAN

JOSEPH HASLAG
University of Missouri-Columbia

CAMBRIDGE
UNIVERSITY PRESS

One Liberty Plaza, 20th Floor, New York, NY 10006, USA

Cambridge University Press is part of the University of Cambridge.

It furthers the University's mission by disseminating knowledge in the pursuit of education, learning, and research at the highest international levels of excellence.

www.cambridge.org
Information on this title: www.cambridge.org/9781316508671

First published 2016
3rd printing 2019

Printed in the United Kingdom by TJ International Ltd. Padstow Cornwall

A catalog record for this publication is available from the British Library.

Library of Congress Cataloging in Publication Data
Names: Champ, Bruce, author. | Freeman, Scott, author. | Haslag, Joseph H., author.
Title: Modeling monetary economies / Bruce Champ, Scott Freeman, Joseph Haslag.
Description: Fourth edition. | New York : Cambridge University Press, 2016. | Revised edition of the authors'
Modeling monetary economies, 2011. | Includes bibliographical references and index.
Identifiers: LCCN 2016000897| ISBN 9781107145221 (hardback) | ISBN 9781316508671 (paperback)
Subjects: LCSH: Money–Mathematical models.
Classification: LCC HG221 .C447 2016 | DDC 339.5/301–dc23
LC record available at http://lccn.loc.gov/2016000897

ISBN 978-1-107-14522-1 Hardback
ISBN 978-1-316-50867-1 Paperback

Additional resources for this publication at www.cambridge.org/champ4

I dedicate this book to Bruce Champ, a generous friend and a skilled economist. Bruce was loved by many and is missed every day. I am writing this edition to honor his love for economics and his love for friends. He taught me a great deal and I hope to carry on his legacy.

Contents

Preface

Monetary economics is the branch that seeks to explain how people execute trades with one another. In particular, why would a person be willing to accept a colored piece of paper, willingly giving up something valuable? The answer is compelling.

In this fourth edition, we build an undergraduate-level exposition about economies in which these colored pieces of paper are a means of executing trade. The backdrop is the overlapping generations models. Money, with a record-keeping friction, expands the set of allocations that a person can acquire during their lifetime. Once this door is open, the student can begin to dig deeper and deeper into world in which we live. The goal here is to develop a toolkit so that undergraduates can address important questions. After more than 20 years in publication, these models are well within the reach of undergraduates at the intermediate and advanced levels. These elegantly simple models strengthen our fundamental understanding of the most basic questions in monetary economics. How does money promote exchange? What should serve as money? What causes inflation? What are the costs of inflation?

This approach to teaching monetary economics follows the professions general recognition of the need to start building the microeconomic foundations. More directly, our observation is that economists explain aggregate economic phenomena as the implications of the choices of rational people who seek to improve their welfare within their limited means. The use of microeconomic foundations makes macroeconomics easier to understand because the performance of such abstract economic processes as gross domestic product and inflation is linked to something understood by all – rational individual behavior. It brings powerful tools such as indifference curves and budget lines to bear on questions of interest. Finally, the joining of micro- and macroeconomics offers symmetry; instead of studying microeconomics and macroeconomics as independent entities with different tools, there is just economics.

When the first edition of this book was published, inertia and tradition could account for teaching monetary economics as a swamp of institutional details. It was as if monetary economies were only an unchanging set of facts to be memorized. The rapid pace of change in the financial world belies this view. Undergraduates need a way to analyze a wide variety of monetary events and institutional arrangements because the events and institutions of the future will not be the same as those the students learned in the classroom. The teaching of analysis, the heart of a liberal education, is best accomplished by having students learn clear, explicit, and internally consistent models. In this way, students may uncover the links between the assumptions underlying the models and the performance of the model economies and thus apply their lessons to new events or changes in government priorities or policies.

This book implements our goals by starting with the simplest model – the basic overlapping generations model – which we analyze for insights into the most basic questions of monetary economics, including the puzzling demand for intrinsically worthless pieces of paper and the costs of inflation. Of course, such a simple model will not be able to discuss all the issues of monetary economies. Therefore, we proceed in successive chapters by asking which features of actual economies the simple model does not address. We then introduce those neglected features into the model to enable us to discuss the more advanced topics. We believe that this gradual approach allows us to build, step by step, an integrated model of the monetary economy without overwhelming the students.

The book is organized into three parts of increasing complexity. Part I examines money in isolation. Here we take the questions of the demand for fiat money, a comparison of fiat and commodity money, inflation, and exchange rates. In Part II, we add capital, to study money's interaction with other assets, banking, the intermediation of these assets into fiat money, and alternative arrangement of central banking. In Part II, we look at money's effects on saving, investment, output, and non-monetary government debt.

This book is written for undergraduates. Its requirements are no more advanced than the understanding of basic graphs and algebra; calculus is not required. (Those who want to use calculus can find an exposition of this approach in the appendix to Chapter 1.) While the book may prove useful to graduate students as a primer in monetary theory, the main text is pitched at the undergraduate level. This has kept us from a few demanding topics, such as nonstationary equilibria; we hope the reader will be satisfied by the wide range of topics we have been able to discuss within a single, simple framework. Material that is difficult but within the grasp of undergraduates is set apart in appendices and can be easily skipped or inserted. The appendices also have many extensions, such as the model of credit, which instructors may wish to use but are not essential to the main topics.

The references display the most tension between the undergraduates and the technical base in which this approach originated. Whenever possible, we reference material written for undergraduates or general audiences; these references are marked by asterisks. Finally, where undergraduate references were not available, we supply references to academic articles and surveys to offer graduate and advanced undergraduates some places to start with more advance work. This is not intended as a full survey of the advance literature.

The choice of topics to be covered was also difficult. We make no claim to encyclopedic coverage of every topic or opinion related to monetary economics. We limited coverage to the topics most directly linked to money, covering banking (but not finance in general) and government debt (but not macroeconomics in general). We insisted on models with rational agents operating in explicitly specified environments. We also selected topics that could be addressed in the basic framework of the overlapping generations model. In our view, the selected topics are tractably teachable, promoting unity and consistency. We also selected what we best know and understand. We hope that instructors can build on our foundations to fill in any gaps.

To reduce these gaps we added material to examine the 2007 Financial Crisis in the fourth edition. Not since the Great Depression has there been such widespread failure among the set of financial institutions. Liquidity and sudden withdrawals played very big roles during this (hopefully) once-in-our-lifetime event. Monetary economics is uniquely situated to develop models that help us understand financial crises. More important, by building models from first principles, we can examine which policies will help when such events occur. We have greatly expanded our presentations of data and have added new exercises.

In addition, we have updated many of the graphs. We have divided the first chapter into two chapters. By doing so, the student is forced to understand money as a means of overcoming a record-keeping friction that exists in the world. To show how money serves this role, it is important to start with a chapter in which money is not needed in an economy with perfect record keeping. Here, intergenerational credit arrangements develop because trading histories are maintained without using up any resources.

Many have contributed to the development of this book. We owe Neil Wallace a tremendous intellectual debt for impressing upon us the importance of microeconomic theory in monetary economics. Many others have provided helpful suggestions, criticisms, encouragement, and other help during the writing of this book. These include David Andolfatto, Leonardo Auernheimer, Robin Bade, Richard Barnett, Valerie Bencivenga, Joydeep Bhattacharya, Jerry Brozek, Mike Bryan, John Bryant, Douglas Dacy, Siverio Foresi, Greg Hess, Christian Gilles, Paul Gomme, Dennis Jansen, Kam Liu, Mike Loewy, Finn Kydland, Antoine Martin, Helen O'Keefe, John O'Keefe, David Laidler, Michael Parkin, Dan Peled, Pedro Gomis-Porqueras, Guillaume Rocheteau, Steve Russell, Tom Sargent, Pierre Silos, Bruce Smith, Ken Stewart, Dick Tresch, Francois Velde, Paula Hernandez-Verme, Warren Weber, and Steve Williamson. In addition, Rebecca Whitworth,

Sumittra Ganguli, Nicholas Pretnar, Lucas Nathe, and Dean Crader were especially helpful on this edition. Overall, we would like to thank the large number of students at Boston College, the University of California at Santa Barbara, the University of Western Ontario, Fordham University, the University of Texas at Austin, Southern Methodist University, Michigan State University, and the University of Missouri-Columbia, who have persevered through the development of this book.

Bruce Champ
Scott Freeman
Joseph Haslag

Part I

Money

Chapter 1

Trade without Money:
The Role of Record Keeping

1 Roadmap

In this chapter, the aim is to develop a model of the economy in which trade makes people better off. A model description has four main parts: (i) there is a description of the physical environment, which consists of things like how long does the economy last, who lives there, how long each person lives, what goods are present, and what meetings occur between people; (ii) there is a description of how people get goods, such as things they are endowed with over their lifetime or the ways in which they can produce things; (iii) we need to know what kinds of goods people like and be able to compare different bundles of goods; and (iv) we need a way to combine the different actions that people want to take so that the quantity supplied is equal to quantity demanded. With all four pieces together, we have a model economy.

This is a book that uses a model economy to explain why anyone would be willing to value colored pieces of paper with portraits of famous people. In the remainder of this book, fiat money is what we will call those colored pieces of paper with famous people depicted. Before we offer a view into an economy in which fiat money is valued, we start with a model economy in which information is not hidden and the economy can keep records of every interaction.

There are two main goals. First, we develop the basic framework for studying monetary economics. To analyze problems in which self-interested people trade with one another, it is very useful to build a model of the economy. And in this book you will see that you only need to invest in one framework – the overlapping generations economy – to analyze lots of different problems in monetary economics. Second, we use the model economy to study a case in which money is not present. Here, our aim is to show that trade can occur in economies without money, provided that records of trade histories exist. With a complete history of previous transactions, people can offer and receive gifts. The records keep track of who participates and who should be shunned. Such trades are efficient. This is a good place to start.

2 Beginnings

In this book we will try to learn about monetary economies through the construction of a series of model economies that replicate essential features of actual monetary economies. All such models are simplifications of the complex economic reality in which we live. Model economies are descriptions of the physical environment in which people live, a description of the technology that produces goods and services, what people are endowed with by nature, a description of what people want, and a description of how to solve all these simultaneous problems. The solution is called equilibrium. Model economies are useful because they are able to illustrate key elements of the behavior of people who choose to hold money and to predict the reactions of important economic variables such as output, prices, government revenue, and public welfare to changes in policies that involve money. We start our analysis with a model economy in which information is complete and there is a technology that is costless to operate that records every transaction. If people want to trade with one another – and they do – then it is useful to see how mutually beneficial trade can be accomplished when there are no barriers keeping them from doing so. We will learn what we can from this simple model and then ask how the model fails to adequately represent reality; in particular, what is missing from this idealistic model so that we can match the observation that people value colored pieces of paper. Throughout the book we try to correct the model's oversights by adding, one by one, the features it lacks.

We concentrate on the overlapping generations model. This model, introduced by Paul Samuelson (1958), has been applied to the study of a large number of topics in monetary theory and macroeconomic theory. Among its desirable features are the following:

- Overlapping generations models are easy to solve. Although they can be used to analyze quite complex issues, there are equilibria that are easy to characterize and to find. Many of their predictions may be described on a simple two-dimensional graph.
- Overlapping generations models provide an elegantly parsimonious framework in which to introduce the existence of money. Money in overlapping generations models dramatically facilitates exchange between people who otherwise would be unable to trade.
- Overlapping generations models are dynamic. They demonstrate how behavior in the present can be affected by anticipated future events. They stand in marked contrast to static models, which assume that only current events affect behavior.

We begin this chapter with a very simple version of an overlapping generations model. As we proceed through the book, we introduce extensions to this basic model. These extensions allow us to analyze a variety of interesting issues.

Other model economies share the same three characteristics we identified in the bullet points. Our aim is not to be all encompassing and cover all of these alternatives. Rather, our approach is more topic driven. After building the basic framework, the extensions we introduce are tied to questions. By focusing on the overlapping generations model, we are able to utilize its flexibility. Over time, other model economies with the same three characteristics will likely exhibit the same flexibility, and coverage of the same broad set of topics will be made available.

Therefore, let us turn to the development of the basic overlapping generations model.

3 The Environment

You will quickly see why we call this an overlapping generations economy. Time is divided into equal-sized bits, which we will call periods. For simplicity, we can always call the starting period 1, the next period 2, and so on. When needed, we use the notation t to stand for the time period. People in this economy, however, do not live forever. Indeed, they live for two periods. Anyone born in period $t = 1$ lives in period 1 and period 2, a person born in period $t = 2$, lives in periods 2 and 3, and so on.[1] Generally speaking, anyone born in period $t \geq 1$, is "young" in period t and "old" in period $t + 1$. In each period $t \geq 1$, N_t people are born. Note that we index time with a subscript. For example, in period $t = 2$, N_2 is our notation for the number of people born in period 2. The people born in periods $t = 1, 2, 3, \ldots$ are called the "future generations" of the economy. In addition, in period 1, there are N_0 people that live for just one period. These people are called the "initial old."

Next, we describe the population living in each period. In each period $t \geq 1$, there are N_t young people who were just born and there are N_{t-1} old people. It is the fact that two generations coexist that gives rise to the name overlapping generations. For example, in period t, there are N_{t-1} old people and N_t young people living. Two generations always overlap with each other every period.

For simplicity, there is only one good in this economy. The good is perishable, meaning that it cannot be stored from one period to the next. In this basic setup, each person receives an endowment of the consumption good when young in the first period of life. The amount of this endowment is denoted as y. When old, no one receives any quantity of the consumption good. This pattern of endowments is illustrated in Figure 1.1.

Of course you might think that this simplification is way too costly to help us understand the wide variety of goods and services available in today's economy. But it is also easy to see that if you want to include work effort in this economy, it is easy. Suppose people are endowed with one unit of work time when young. Let

---

[1] Or, put another way: the number of old period in any date t is the same as the number of young people born at date $t - 1$.

Period Generation	1	2	3	4	5	6	7
Initial old 0	**0**						
1	y	**0**					
2		y	**0**				
3			y	**0**			
4				y	**0**		
5					y	**0**	
						…	…

Figure 1.1. The pattern of endowments. In each period t, generation t is born. Each person lives for two periods. People are endowed with y units of the consumption good when young and 0 units when old. In any given period, one generation of young people and one generation of old people are alive. The name of this model, the overlapping generations model, follows from this generational structure.

people use that time productively, using a technology to transform effort into units of the consumption good. Now, we can interpret the endowment as an endowment of labor – the ability to work. By using this labor endowment (by working), each person is able to obtain a real income of y units of the consumption good. To be even more concrete, consider an economy in which the only consumption good is coconuts. Each young person is capable of climbing the coconut tree and harvesting the edible nut. Old people, however, cannot climb the tree. You could imagine that young people would harvest nuts, storing the harvest in their hut. Unfortunately, coconuts are perishable, going bad before an old person can eat stored nuts.

4 Preferences

People consume the economy's sole commodity and obtain satisfaction – or, in the economist's jargon, utility – from having done so.

4.1 Future Generations

Members of future generations in an overlapping generations model consume both when young and when old. Each person's utility therefore depends on the combination, or bundle, of personal consumption when young and when old. We make the following four assumptions about a person's preferences regarding consumption. The first two assumptions allow you to see that we can assign a consistent numerical value to a bundle of consumption. The second pair of assumptions helps us to draw a picture of a young person's preferences over consumption when young and consumption when old. Based on the consistent numerical value associated with each bundle, the picture is a great device for characterizing the *solution* to each person's lifetime decision problem.

It will be useful to have some notation. We denote the amount of the good that is consumed in the first period of life by a person born in period t with the notation $c_{1,t}$. Similarly, $c_{2,t+1}$ denotes the amount the same person consumes in the second period of life. It is important to note that $c_{2,t+1}$ is consumption that actually occurs in period $t + 1$, when the person born at time t is old. When the time period is not crucial to the discussion, we denote first- and second-period consumption as c_1 and c_2. Let (c_1^a, c_2^a) stand for a bundle of lifetime consumption referred to as Bundle A. Similarly, let (c_1^b, c_2^b) stand for a bundle of lifetime consumption referred to as Bundle B.

Assumption 1 (Completeness) When facing two bundles, a person can provide valid response to two statements. A valid response is either true or false. The two statements are: (1) I get at least as much happiness from Bundle A as I get from Bundle B and (2) I get at least as much happiness from Bundle B as I get from Bundle A.

What do these two true/false answers tell us? If a person says Statement 1 is true and Statement 2 is false, then I can tell that this person gets more happiness from Bundle A than from Bundle B. If the person says Statement 1 is false and Statement 2 is true, then I know that person gets more happiness from Bundle B than from Bundle A. If the person says Statement 1 and Statement 2 are both true, then I know that the person gets the same level of happiness from Bundle A and Bundle B. Thus, Assumption 1 offers a complete description of the happiness obtained from any two bundles. There are three options: Bundle A is preferred to Bundle B, Bundle B is preferred to Bundle A, or the person is indifferent between Bundle A and Bundle B.

Assumption 2 Preferences are transitive.

To illustrate this assumption, I create a third bundle. Let Bundle D be (c_1^d, c_2^d). Transitivity is just an assumption to guarantee consistency. We ask a person to provide valid responses to Statements 1 and 2 for Bundles A, B, and D. Suppose that Bundle A is preferred to Bundle B. Furthermore, suppose Bundle B is preferred to Bundle D. We can ensure that nothing screwy happens insofar as a person satisfying Assumption 2 will prefer Bundle A to Bundle D.

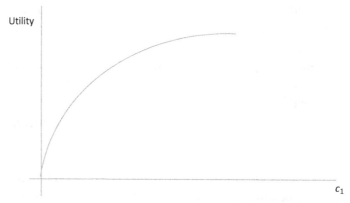

Figure 1.2. Assumptions 3 and 4 are captured. First, the slope of the utility curve is positive, showing that an increase in consumption when young results in greater utility; more is preferred to less. Second, the slope is getting flatter and flatter and the quantity of c_1 increase. Diminishing marginal utility assumes that the marginal utility gain is decreasing as the quantity of the good increases.

Armed with Assumptions 1 and 2, we can define a relationship that assigns a numerical value to each bundle and that numerical value is consistent with the preference ranking obtained from valid responses to Statements 1 and 2. In other words, if Bundle A is preferred to Bundle B, the numerical value assigned to Bundle A – that is, its utility – is greater than the numerical value assigned to Bundle B. If a person is indifferent between Bundle A and Bundle B, for example, the numerical values assigned to each bundle must be equal. The relationship that assigns a numerical value to bundle is called a utility function.

Assumption 3 (More is preferred to less) Suppose Bundle A and Bundle B are constructed so that $c_1^a = c_1^b$ and $c_2^a > c_2^b$. This person is comparing bundles with the same quantity of consumption when young, but when old, Bundle A gives a greater amount of consumption than does Bundle B. According to Assumption 3, this person will always prefer Bundle A to Bundle B.

Assumption 4 (Diminishing marginal utility) The purpose of this assumption is to put some curvature into relationship between bundles. You will know why this is so useful after everything is put together. The simple overview of Assumptions 3 and 4 is that each extra unit you get makes you happier, but extra happiness is getting smaller and smaller with each extra unit. Figure 1.2 graphically depicts the meaning of Assumptions 3 and 4. Figure 1.2 plots the utility value of each extra morsel of consumption when young. Hopefully, from your previous economics classes you remember that marginal utility is defined as the difference between the utility you receive from consuming two different quantities, holding everything else constant. For example, suppose you hold the quantity of consumption when old fixed, call it $\bar{c}_2$ then the marginal utility is the difference in utility value associated with consuming c_1^a and that associated with consuming c_1^b, where $c_1^a > c_1^b$.

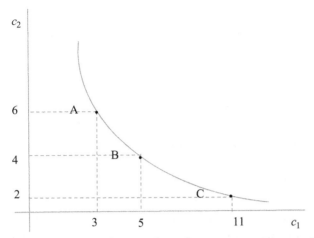

Figure 1.3. An indifference curve. A person's preferences are represented by indifference curves. The figure portrays an indifference curve for a typical person. Along any particular indifference curve, utility is constant. Here, the person is indifferent between Bundles A, B, and C.

Figure 1.2 tells us two things. First, the slope of the utility function is positive, indicating that this person receives greater utility by consuming more of the consumption good when young. Second, the slope is declining, telling us that the marginal value is getting smaller with each additional unit that this person consumes when young.

With Assumptions 1 through 4, we are able to assign a numerical value to every bundle. The utility function is the mathematical representation of a person's preferences over all the bundles. It will be extremely useful to portray a person's preferences graphically. We do this by introducing an indifference curve. An indifference curve connects all the consumption bundles such that there is equal utility. In other words, our young person is saying that for every point on the indifference curve, she responds true to Statements 1 and 2. Figure 1.3 displays a typical indifference curve.

To illustrate the indifference curve, suppose we offer a person the following consumption choices:

- Bundle A, which consists of three units of the consumption good when a person is young and six units of the consumption good when a person is old. We denote this bundle as $c_1 = 3$ and $c_2 = 6$.
- Bundle B, which consists of five units of the consumption good when a person is young and four units of the consumption good when a person is old ($c_1 = 5$ and $c_2 = 4$).

By Assumptions 1 through 4, this person has assigned a numerical value to these bundles by the utility function. On this indifference curve, we show the two points A and B. We also illustrate a third point, C, representing the bundle $c_1 = 11$ and

$c_2 = 2$. Because C lies on the same indifference curve as points A and B, point C yields the same level of utility as points A and B for the person.

Note some features of the indifference curve. The first is that the curve becomes flatter as we move from left to right. This is how indifference curves represent Assumption 4. Note that the slope of the indifference curve is called the marginal rate of substitution. Hence, the curvature of the indifference curve is called the "assumption of diminishing marginal rate of substitution" and diminishing marginal utility can explain this property. To illustrate this assumption, start at point A, where $c_1 = 3$ and $c_2 = 6$. Suppose we reduce the person's second-period consumption by two units. The indifference curve tells us that, to keep the person's utility constant, we must compensate him or her by providing two more units of first-period consumption. This places the person at point B on the indifference curve. Now suppose we reduce second-period consumption by another two units. Our person will remain indifferent if six more units of first-period consumption are provided. In other words, we must compensate a person with ever-increasing amounts of first-period consumption as we successively cut second-period consumption. This should make intuitive sense; people are more reluctant to give up something they do not have much of to begin with.

Consider food and clothing as an example. A person who has a large amount of clothing and very little food would be willing to give up a fairly large amount of clothing for another unit of food. Conversely, this person would be willing to give up only a small amount of food to obtain another unit of clothing.

We demonstrate this assumption of diminishing marginal rate of substitution by drawing an indifference curve that becomes flatter as we move downward and to the right along the curve.

We also assume that the indifference curves become infinitely steep as we approach the vertical axis and perfectly flat as we approach the horizontal axis. The curves never cross either axis. This might be justified by saying that consuming nothing in any one period would mean horrible starvation, to which consuming even a small amount is preferable. This is Assumption 3.

It is also important to keep in mind that the indifference curves are dense in the (c_1, c_2) space. This means that if you pick a combination of first- and second-period consumption, there is an indifference curve running through that point. However, to avoid clutter, we normally show only a few of these indifference curves. A group of indifference curves shown on one graph is often called an "indifference map." Figure 1.4 illustrates an indifference map that obeys our assumptions.

Note that utility is increasing in the direction of the arrow. How do we know this? Compare points A, B, and C. Each of these bundles gives the person the same amount of second-period consumption. However, moving from point A to B to C, the person receives more and more first-period consumption. Hence, the person will prefer point B to point A. Likewise, point C will be preferable to points A and B. This is Assumption 2.

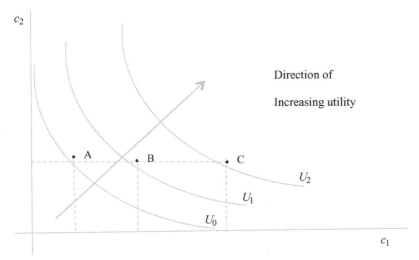

Figure 1.4. An indifference map. An indifference map consists of a collection of indifference curves. For a constant amount of consumption in one period, people prefer a greater amount of consumption in the other period. For this reason, people prefer Bundle C to Bundle B and Bundle B to Bundle A. Utility increase in the general direction of the arrow.

It is often useful to draw an analogy between an indifference map and a contour map that shows elevation. On an indifference map, the curves represent points of constant utility; on a contour map, the curves represent points of constant elevation. Extending the analogy, if we think of traversing the indifference map in a northeasterly direction, we would be going uphill. In other words, utility would be increasing. In fact, an indifference map, like a contour map, is merely a handy way to illustrate a three-dimensional concept on a two-dimensional drawing. The three dimensions here are first-period consumption, second-period consumption, and utility.

One other important concept is that our person's rankings of preferences are transitive. If a person prefers bundle B to bundle A and bundle C to bundle B, then that person must also prefer bundle C to bundle A. Graphically, this implies that indifference curves cannot cross. To do so would violate this property of transitivity and Assumption 2 (see Figure 1.5). This figure portrays two indifference curves that cross at point A. We know that indifference curves represent bundles that give a person the same level of utility. In other words, the person whose preferences are represented by Figure 1.5 is indifferent between Bundles A and B because they lie on the same indifference curve U_0. Similarly, the person must be indifferent between Bundles A and C on indifference curve U_1. We see, then, that the person is indifferent between all three bundles. However, if we compare Bundles B and C, we also observe that they consist of the same amount of second-period consumption but that C contains more first-period consumption than B. According to Assumption 3, the person must prefer C to B. But this contradicts our earlier statement about

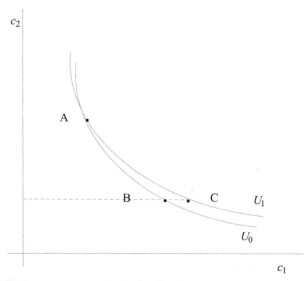

Figure 1.5. Indifference curves cannot cross. By Assumption 3 about preferences, the person preferences are represented by these indifference curves prefers Bundle C over Bundle B because Bundle C consists of more consumption when young and the same amount of consumption when old compared with Bundle B. However, because the person must be indifferent between all three bundles, A, B, and C, a contradiction arises. Our assumptions rule out the possibility of indifference curves that cross.

indifference when comparing the three bundles. For this reason, indifference curves that cross violate our assumptions about preferences.

4.2 The Initial Old

The preferences of the initial old are much easier to describe than those of future generations. The initial old live and consume only in the initial period and thus simply want to maximize their consumption in that period.

4.3 The Never-Ending Economy

You may wonder why time never ends in the physical environment. Actually, inifinity plays an important economic role. Because young people have goods and old people do not, there is a possibility that trade across generations could result in higher lifetime welfare. Indeed, we will show that is true later in the chapter. In this model economy, meetings are one-time interactions between the young and the old. Therefore, any mutually beneficial trade actually requires a never-ending future. Suppose, for example, the economy has a known end date. The young born in the last period will never trade with the old. The reason is simple, the young will never get anything in return. There is nothing mutually beneficial to the young born in the last period to induce them to give up any of their goods. Let's work backward one period. The young born in the next-to-last period know that no young person born next period will trade any goods with them. It follows that young people born in the next-to-last period will not trade with any old people because no trades will occur in the last period. The same decision problem faces people born in the second-to-last period. With knowledge that no young person will trade with them in the next-to-last period, the young born in the second-to-last period will not trade with the old. By applying backward induction over and over, we can see that trade between young and old ceases in *every* period.

Though it may a technical device, the economics of infinity actually ensure that a future of one-time meetings will result in trade.

5 The Economic Problem

The problem facing future generations of this economy is very simple. They want to acquire goods they do not have. Each has access to the nonstorable consumption good only when young but wants to consume in both periods of life. They must therefore find a way to acquire consumption in the second period of life and then decide how much they will consume in each period of life.

We examine, in turn, two solutions to this economic problem. The first, a centralized solution, proposes that an all-knowing, benevolent planner will allocate the economy's resources between consumption by the young and by the old.[2] In the second, decentralized solution, we allow people to use money to trade for what they want. We then compare the two solutions and ask which is more likely to offer people the highest utility. The answer helps provide a first illustration of the economic usefulness of participating in the transfers across generations.

5.1 Feasible Allocations

Imagine for a moment that we are central planners with complete knowledge of and total control over the economy. Our job is to allocate the available goods among the young and old people alive in the economy at each point in time.

As central planners, under what constraint would we operate? Put simply, at any given time, we cannot allocate more goods than are available in the economy. Recall that only the young people are endowed with the consumption good at time t. There are N_t of these young people at time t. We have

$$\text{(total amount of consumption good)}_t = N_t y. \tag{1.1}$$

---

[2] No one believes that such a benevolent central planner exists. For one thing, it is costly to redistribute goods among people. Economists use the "central planner" device to understand what allocations are economically efficient in our model economies. Under the best circumstances, we can gauge how well an economy is doing by comparing the equilibrium in a decentralized economy with the efficient allocation chosen by the fictitious central planner.

Suppose that every member of generation t is given that same lifetime allocation $(c_{1,t}, c_{2,t+1})$ of the consumption good (our society's view of equity). In this case, total consumption by the young people in period t is

$$(\text{total young consumption})_t = N_t c_{1,t}. \tag{1.2}$$

Furthermore, total old consumption in period t is

$$(\text{total old consumption})_t = N_{t-1} c_{2,t}. \tag{1.3}$$

Let us make sure the notation is clear. Recall that the old people in time t are those who were born at time $t - 1$. There were N_{t-1} of these people born at time $t - 1$. Furthermore, recall that $c_{2,t}$ denotes the second-period (time t) consumption by someone who was born at time $t - 1$. This implies that total consumption by the old at time t must be $N_{t-1} c_{2,t}$.

Total consumption by young and old is the sum of the amounts in Equations 1.2 and 1.3. We are now ready to state the constraint facing us as central planners: Total consumption by young and old cannot exceed the total amount of available goods (Equation 1.1). In other words,

$$N_t c_{1,t} + N_{t-1} c_{2,t} \leq N_t y. \tag{1.4}$$

For simplicity, we assume for now that the population is constant ($N_t = N$ for all t). In this case, we rewrite Equation 1.4 as

$$N c_{1,t} + N c_{2,t} \leq N y.$$

Dividing through by N, we obtain the per-capita form of the constraint facing us as central planners:

$$c_{1,t} + c_{2,t} \leq y. \tag{1.5}$$

For now, we are also concerned with a stationary allocation.[3] A stationary allocation is one that gives the members of every generation the same lifetime consumption pattern. In other words, in a stationary allocation, $c_{1,t} = c_1$ and $c_{2,t} = c_2$ for every period $t = 1, 2, 3,$ and so on. However, it is important to realize that a stationary allocation does not necessarily imply that $c_1 = c_2$. With a stationary allocation, the per-capita constraint becomes

$$c_1 + c_2 \leq y. \tag{1.6}$$

This represents a very simple linear equation in c_1 and c_2, which is illustrated in Figure 1.6.

The set of stationary, feasible, per-capita allocations – the "feasible set" – is bounded by the triangle in the diagram. We refer to the triangular region as the

---

[3] Nonstationary equilibria have been studied by Azariadas (1981) and by Cass and Shell (1983).

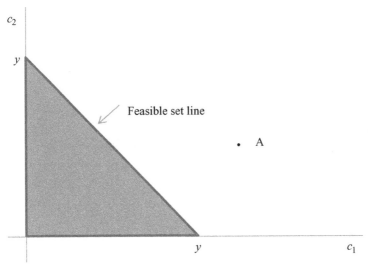

Figure 1.6. The feasible set. The feasible set, the triangle, represents the set of possible allocation that can be attained given the resources available in the economy. Points outside the feasible set, such as Bundle A, are unattainable given the resources of the economy.

feasible set. The thick diagonal line on the boundary of the feasible set is called the "feasible set line." The feasible set line represents Equation 1.6, evaluated at equality.

5.2 The Golden Rule Allocation

If we now superimpose a typical person's indifference map on this diagram, we can identify the preferences of future generations among feasible stationary allocations. This is shown in Figure 1.7.

The feasible allocation a central planner selects depends on the objective. One reasonable and benevolent objective is the maximization of the utility of future generations, an objective we call the "golden rule." The golden rule in Figure 1.7 is represented by point E, which offers each person the consumption bundle (c_1^*, c_2^*). This combination of c_1 and c_2 yields the highest feasible level of utility during a person's entire lifetime. Note that the golden rule occurs at the unique point of tangency between the feasible set boundary and an indifference curve. Any other point that lies within the feasible set yields a lower level of utility. For example, points B and C are feasible because they lie on the boundary of the feasible set. However, they lie on an indifference curve that represents a lower level of utility than the one on which point A lies. Point D is preferable to point A, but it is unattainable. The endowments of the economy simply are not large enough to support the allocation implied by point D.

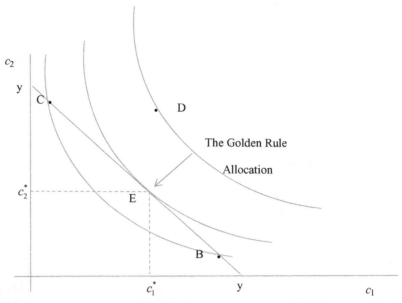

Figure 1.7. The golden rule allocation. The golden rule allocation is the stationary, feasible allocation of consumption that maximizes the welfare of future generations. It is located at a point of tangency between the feasible set line and an indifference curve (Bundle E). This is the highest indifference curve in contact with the feasible set. As drawn, the golden rule allocation E allocates more goods to people when young than when old ($c_1^* > c_2^*$) but this is arbitrary. The tangency point can just as easily have been drawn at a point where $c_2^* > c_1^*$.

5.2.1 The Initial Old

It is important to consider the welfare of all participants in the economy – including the initial old – when considering the effects of any policy. Although the golden rule allocation maximizes the utility of future generations, it does not maximize the utility of the initial old. Recall that the initial old's utility depends solely and directly on the amount of the good they consume in their second period of life. The goal of the initial old is to get as much consumption as possible in period 1, the only period in which they live. (You may want to imagine that the initial old also lived in period 0, however, because this period is in the past, it cannot be altered by the central planner, who assumes control of the economy in period 1.) If the central planner's goal were to maximize the welfare of the initial old, the planner would want to give as much of the consumption good as possible to the initial old. This would be accomplished among stationary feasible allocations at the vertical intercept of the feasible set line in Figure 1.7, which allocates y units of the good for consumption by the old (including consumption by the initial old) and nothing for consumption by the young.

This stationary allocation, which implies that people consume nothing when young, would not maximize the utility of the future generations. They prefer the more balanced combination of consumption when young and old, represented by

(c_1^*, c_2^*). Faced with this conflict in the interests of the initial old and future generations, an economist cannot choose among them on purely objective grounds. Nevertheless, the reader will find that, on subjective grounds (influenced by the fact that there are an infinite number of future generations and only a single generation of initial old), we tend to pay particular attention to the golden rule in this book.

6 Decentralized Solutions

In the previous section, we found the feasible allocation that maximizes the utility of the future generations. However, to achieve this allocation, in each period the central planner would have to take away c_2^* from each young person and give this amount to each old person. Such redistribution requires that the central planner have the ability to reallocate endowments costlessly between the generations. Furthermore, to determine c_1^* and c_2^*, this central planner also must know the exact utility function of the subjects.

These are strong assumptions about the power and wisdom of central planners. This leads us to ask if there is some way we can achieve this optimal allocation in a more decentralized manner, one in which economy reaches the optimal allocation through mutually beneficial trades conducted by the people themselves. In other words, can we let a market do the work of the central planner?

Before we answer this question, we need to define some terms that are used throughout the book. First, we discuss the notion of a competitive equilibrium. A "competitive equilibrium" has the following properties:

1. Each person makes mutually beneficial trades with other people.
2. People act as if their actions have no effect on prices (rates of exchange).
3. Supply equals demand in all markets. In other words, markets clear.

In a sense, the definition of competitive equilibrium tells us how to solve for the equilibrium prices and quantities. Each person maximizes lifetime welfare subject to their budget constraint when determining whether to trade with another person. There is no collusion in the sense that people do not get together to set prices. Rather, each person takes the price as given and maximizes lifetime utility. So a utility-maximizing person chooses the quantity of consumption when young and consumption when old that maximizes lifetime utility, treating the price as given. This solves for the quantities of lifetime consumption as a function of the price. To pin down the price, the definition of competitive equilibrium tells us it is the price that equates the demand for the consumption good with the supply.

We assume there are no frictions in this economy. This means that every young person can observe what trades each old person conducted when they were young. Because no resources are used to see trading histories, record keeping is referred to as perfect. Because young people have goods and old people do not, the key question is whether there is a pattern of mutually beneficial trade that can be sustained. In other words, what kind of trades, if any, will occur between young and old in an economy with perfect record keeping.

6.1 A Record-Keeping Equilibrium

Let us now examine how a person will decide how much to consume when young and how much to consume when old. To answer, we must first establish the constraints on the choices of the person – why he cannot simply enjoy infinite consumption both when young and when old. As was the case for the entire society, the constraints on each person are that he cannot consume more goods than he has. We will refer to the limitations on a person's consumption as his "budget constraints." In this section, we treat the trades "as if" they occur in a market. Unfortunately, there is no mutually beneficial trade between people. Literally, a young person is giving up goods to an old and receiving a record of this transfer. Next period, the now old person has a record of the gift provided when young that everyone can see. Does this record provide any consumption when the person is old?[4] For now, we will pretend that such a sequence of trades over a person's lifetime occurs and solves for the competitive equilibrium.

When young, each person has an endowment of y goods. The person can do two things with these goods – consume them or transfer them to an old person. By perfect record keeping, any goods transferred to an old person are tallied. The quantity of the consumption given to an old person at time t is denoted by Φ_t. We can therefore write the budget constraint facing the person in the first period of life as

$$c_{1,t} + \Phi_t \leq y. \tag{1.7}$$

The left-hand side of Equation 1.7 is the person's total uses of goods (consumption and transfer). The right-hand side of Equation 1.7 represents the total sources of goods (the person's endowment).

When old, no person receives an endowment. Hence, when old, a person only acquires consumption goods by receiving a transfer. This means that the constraint facing the person in the second period of life is

$$c_{2,t+1} \leq \Phi_{t+1}^R \tag{1.8}$$

where Φ_{t+1}^R denotes the goods received as transfer when old. Note that when you are young, the person decides how to transfer to an old person. In contrast, the quantity transferred to an old person is taken as given; that is why we need two separate

---

[4] The record is not a tangible item, like an IOU. Throughout this book, an IOU is a piece of paper that says Henry, for example, will receive goods from Charles today. The IOU says when Henry will pay Charles back. In the overlapping generations economy, Henry does not meet with Charles in the future because Henry is dead.

pieces of notation. In this model economy, Φ_t is something that each young person decides while Φ_{t+1}^R is, strictly speaking, something that is outside the person's lifetime decision. We will deal with this complication in the next section. But, for now, it is easy to think about the record as a measure of the quantity a young person gave up. With that quantity in the record, the old person can use that as if were something they can trade for consumption goods. Thus, perfect record keeping offers a connections between two people in two different generations who will never meet again.

Suppose a young person would pay Φ_t goods when young in order to obtain Φ_{t+1}^R goods when old. In this hypothetical market, the relationship between the transfer when young and the transfer received when old is represented by an equation that converts the period $t+1$ goods into what they are worth as period t goods. We could formalize this conversion rate, denoted x_{t+1}, as the rate at which a person can exchange units of the consumption good at period t for units of the consumption good in period $t+1$. In equation form, $\Phi_t x_{t+1} = \Phi_{t+1}^R$. Armed with this conversion rate and the market, we can rewrite Equation 1.8 as

$$c_{2,t+1} \leq x_{t+1}\Phi_t. \tag{1.9}$$

We are creating a relationship between the gift given when young and the gift received when old. Each person takes the price, x_{t+1}, as given. This trick allows us to write down each young person's lifetime budget constraint. By definition, $x_{t+1} > 0$ for all t, so that we can rewrite the old-age constraint as $\Phi_t \geq (c_{2,t+1})/(x_{t+1})$ and substitute it into the first-period constraint (Equation 1.7) to obtain

$$c_{1,t} + \frac{c_{2,t+1}}{x_{t+1}} \leq y. \tag{1.10}$$

Equation 1.10 expresses the various combinations of first- and second-period consumption that a person can afford over a lifetime. In other words, it is the person's "lifetime budget constraint."

We can graph this budget constraint as shown in Figure 1.8. We can easily verify that the intercepts of the budget line are as illustrated.

The budget line represents Equation 1.10 at equality. If nothing is consumed in the second period of life ($c_{2,t+1} = 0$), then the constraint implies that $c_{1,t} = y$. This is the horizontal intercept of the budget line. On the other hand, if nothing is consumed in the first period of life ($c_{1,t} = 0$), so that the entire endowment of y is used to provide gifts to old people, the constraint implies that $c_{2,t+1}/x_{t+1} = y$ or $c_{2,t+1} = yx_{t+1}$. This represents the vertical intercept of the budget line.

Note that x_{t+1} can be considered as the "(real) rate of return to gifting" because it expresses how many goods can be obtained in period $t+1$ if one unit of the good is presented as a gift to an old person in period t.

For a given rate of return of money, x_{t+1}, we can find the $(c_{1,t}^*, c_{2,t+1}^*)$ combination that will be chosen by people who are seeking to maximize their utility.

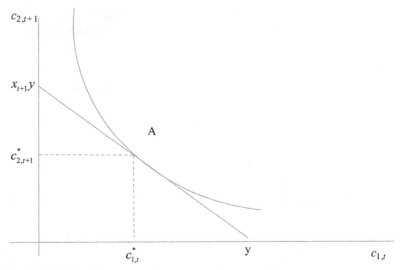

Figure 1.8. The choice of consumption with perfect record keeping. At Bundle A, a person maximizes utility given their lifetime budget constraint in a perfect record keeping equilibrium. Bundle A is found by locating a point of tangency between an indifference curve and the person's lifetime budget set line. The conversion rate on transfers determines the slope of the budget set line.

This point is shown in Figure 1.8. It is the point along the budget line that touches the highest indifference curve. This must occur at a point where the budget line is tangent to an indifference curve.[5]

6.2 Finding the Conversion Rate

How can we determine the rate at which transfers by young people can be converted into transfers received when old? In this setup, the hypothetical market for transfers clears when the supply of transfers by young people is equal to the demand for transfers by old people. In this economy, the conversion rate serves as a two-piece transaction. The young person gives up so many goods to an old person, receives a tally in the record-keeping system, and trades that record in for a transfer when old.

We start by focusing on a case in which the conversion is the same for every generation. This assumption is reasonable because in this basic model, every generation faces the same problem: endowments, preferences and population are the same for every generation. If views about the future are also the same across generations, then each person will react in the same manner each period, choosing $c_{1,t} = c_1$ and

---

[5] There are other ways for a decentralized economy to build credit arrangements similar to how our old people take their "participation record" to young people in order to get goods. One could imagine a social norm in which people are shunned – not allowed to consume – if they do not participate. In this model economy, the key distinction is that this is not a social norm imposed on people but a market for trade that requires a record of past performance.

$c_{2,t+1} = c_2$ for each period t. We call such equilibria "stationary equilibria." Notice that because each person faces different circumstances, depending on whether they are young or old, we are not imposing c_1 equal to c_2 in a stationary equilibrium. People may choose to consume more when young than when old or vice versa. It turns out that the relative mix of consumption when young and consumption when old depends on people's preferences and on the conversion rate.

We also assume that people in our economy form their expectations of the future rationally. In this nonrandom environment, where there are no surprises, "rational expectations" means that the person's expected values of future variables will be equal to the actual values of these future variables. In this special case, we say that people have perfect foresight. With perfect foresight, there are no errors in a person's forecast of important economic variables that affect their decisions. In the context of our model, this assumption means that a person born in period t will perfectly forecast the conversion rate in the next period, x_{t+1}. The person's expectation of this conversion rate will be exactly realized. This assumption would be less credible in an economy buffeted by random shocks than in our model economy, where preferences and the environment are unchanging and therefore are perfectly predictable.

To see the importance of perfect foresight, consider the alternative in a nonrandom economy – that people always expect a conversion rate greater or less than the conversion rate that actually occurs. People with wrong beliefs about the conversion rate will not choose the transfers that maximize their utility. They therefore have an incentive to figure out the conversion rate that actually will occur.

Let us now employ the assumptions of stationarity and perfect foresight to find an equilibrium time path for the conversion rate. In perfectly competitive markets, the price (or value) of an object is determined as the price at which the supply of the object equals its demand. This applies to the determination of the price (value) of money as well as the price of any good.

The supply of transfers by people is the number of goods each young person offers, which equals the goods of the endowment that the person does not consume when young, $y - c_{1,t}$. The total transfer supply by all people in the economy in period time t is therefore $N_t(y - c_{1,t})$.

The total demand for transfer, measured in units of the young person's consumption good is $N_{t-1}x_t\Phi_{t-1}$, implying that the total supply of transfers is the product of the number of current old people and the value of goods transferred when they were young. Equality of supply and demand therefore requires that

$$N_{t-1}x_t\Phi_{t-1} = N_t(y - c_{1,t}). \tag{1.11}$$

This, in turn, implies that

$$x_t = \frac{N_t(y - c_{1,t})}{N_{t-1}\Phi_{t-1}}, \tag{1.12}$$

which states that the conversion rate for transfers is given by the ratio of the real supply of transfers to the aggregate transfers from the previous period. Since $\Phi_{t-1} = y - c_{1,t-1}$, can write Equation 1.12 as

$$x_t = \frac{N_t(y - c_{1,t})}{N_{t-1}(y - c_{1,t-1})}.$$ (1.13)

To simplify this, we look for a stationary solution, where $c_{1,t} = c_1$ and $c_{2,t} = c_2$ for all t. Because all generations have the same endowments and preferences and anticipate the same future pattern of endowments and preferences, it seems quite reasonable to look for a stationary equilibrium. Then, after some cancellation, Equation 1.13 becomes

$$x_t = \frac{N_t}{N_{t-1}}.$$ (1.14)

Because we are assuming a constant population ($N_{t+1} = N_t$), the terms in Equation 1.14 cancel out and we find that

$$x_t = 1$$ (1.15)

implying a one-for-one conversion rate.

Notice that the conversion rate is also a constant (1) in the stationary record-keeping equilibrium. Identical people who face the same conversion rate will choose the same consumption and transfers over time, a stationary equilibrium.

Using the information that $x_t = 1$ and recalling that the budget line in a stationary record-keeping equilibrium is represented by $c_1 + \frac{c_2}{x_t} = y$, we determine that $c_1 + c_2 = y$. Our graph of the budget line therefore becomes the one depicted in Figure 1.9.

Be aware that the stationary record-keeping equilibrium may not be a unique equilibrium. There also may exist more complicated nonstationary equilibria. In this text, however, we confine our attention to stationary equilibria because there is much that can be learned from these easy-to-study cases.

6.3 The Game and the Enforcement

In the decentralized solution, the mechanism used was the competitive market. To characterize this equilibrium, we had to pretend that a young person received a marker that was maintained in the record keeping system. By trading with an old person, the record-keeping system costlessly kept information on the quantity traded by each young person. In doing so, the young person could then trade that information for consumption goods next period when they are old.

In this section, we relax the competitive market mechanism. Instead, suppose there is a game young people decide to play, taking what future young people will do as given. In this way, the game does not require an old person to physically

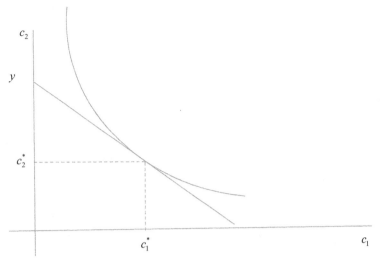

Figure 1.9. A person's choice of consumption when the population is constant. With perfect-record keeping, the conversion rate is 1, implying the lifetime budget constraint of the diagram.

exchange anything with a young person that is mutually beneficial. Here, a young person takes an action, which is a trade with an old person, and then waits, taking the action by next period's young person as given. If you are familiar with the prisoner's dilemma game, you are familiar with the description of a person's best response to the rules of the game. When each person's action is a best response, and there is no unilateral incentive for a person to deviate, we have a Nash equilibrium.

So our goal in this section is to characterize a young person's best response in a world in which perfect record keeping is present. To keep matters simple, suppose we consider a case in which there are two actions; a young person can either not transfer any goods to an old person or transfer $\Phi = c_2^*$ to an old person. Such an action depends on the payoff to the young person next period. If, for example, the young person takes $\Phi^R = c_2^*$ as the action chosen by next period's young person, then the transfer when young is justified as a best response. Indeed, the lifetime welfare for the young person would be strictly lower if any other action were taken.[6]

What role does perfect record keeping play in this game? Here, perfect record keeping is a means of holding a young person accountable. There is no way to hide your actions when young, so the actions each generation takes are costlessly verifiable. Consider a case in which there is a friction and perfect record keeping is absent. Now, suppose a young person decides not to transfer any goods to an old person. In this case, future generations cannot observe this person's actions, lessening the chance that next period's young will offer any transfers to them. Through the perfect record-keeping device, future generations can punish a person who does not

---

[6] People cannot trade directly in this model because they are separated in time. The same absence of trade would result if they were separated by space, as in the models of Robert Townsend (1980).

participate in the intergenerational transfer program. Now, from the person's utility function, we know they like to consume when old. So the perfect record keeping acts as a kind of contract; basically, if a young person transfers, they will receive some transfer when old. In this way, the game that a person plays requires a best response, understanding that choosing not to transfer results in a punishment in which no transfers are provided when old.

Thus, young people are held accountable by the social accounting system. The records show that you participated when young so that you get goods when old. If you deviate, the records are free for everyone to see and you are excluded from any old-age transfer. We refer to the costless record keeping as being consistent with a frictionless world. Therefore, nothing impedes the smooth process of intergenerational transfers. And it rests squarely on the idea that perfect record keeping means there are no resources needed to enforce the intergenerational transfers.

7 Is the Record-Keeping Equilibrium the Golden Rule?

We have seen that record keeping can provide for old-age consumption, improving the welfare of people otherwise unable to trade. We would like to make the people in our economy not just better off but as well off as possible. It remains to ask, therefore, whether the record-keeping equilibrium results in the best possible allocation of goods. In particular, we would like to see whether the stationary record-keeping equilibrium we have just found maximizes the welfare of future generations. In other words, does the record-keeping equilibrium reach the golden rule?

Compare the budget line of Figure 1.9 with the feasible set line of Figure 1.7. They are identical. The choice of consumption in this record-keeping equilibrium will be identical to the one we found when we were looking at the stationary allocation that was dictated by a central planner who wanted to maximize the utility of the future generations. This implies that the stationary record-keeping equilibrium obeys the golden rule. The introduction of decentralized trade with perfect record keeping not only allows them to reach their maximum feasible utility through trade but, in this case, also allows them to reach their maximum feasible utility. This will not always be the case. The budget set and the feasible set answer different economic questions. The budget set depicts the constraint on a person, whereas the feasible set describes the constraint on the society as a whole.

The initial old are also better off in the record-keeping equilibrium than they were with the autarkic equilibrium. In the record-keeping equilibrium, everyone was among the initial old will receive Φ^R units of the consumption good. This means their consumption will be positive. In the autarkic equilibrium, their consumption would be zero. They are certainly better off in record-keeping equilibrium.

Because we concentrate on stationary record-keeping equilibria in this book, it may be useful to summarize the features of such equilibria. A stationary consumption bundle of a record-keeping equilibrium satisfies two basic properties:

- It provides the maximum level of utility given the person's budget set. It is found where an indifference curve lies tangent to the person's budget set.
- It lies on the feasible set line, with the boundary of the set representing all feasible per-capita allocations.

8 Summary

In this overlapping generations economy, each person has a pair of one-time meetings over their lifetime. When young, a person meets with an old person. Next period, our old person meets with a young person. Each meeting offers an opportunity for trade. The sticking point is that young people have goods but old people do not. Why would a young person give up any goods to someone they will never meet again?

In a world where record-keeping does not cost anything, trading history is a record that can provide an incentive to trade with an old person. The quantity you offer this old person is recorded so that other people, like next period's young, can see whether you participated or not. The key is that there is punishment; no young person will trade with an old person that does not have a record of offering goods when they were young. Each generation compares lifetime welfare when they offer a quantity of goods to each old person with lifetime welfare when they do not. Because giving up goods when young is best for every current and future generation, people get to consume when young and when old. And the absence of any friction associated with keeping these records enables punishment to be applied, thus creating a kind of discipline that keeps the meet-and-trade sequence going forever between the young and old at these one-time meetings.

9 Exercises

1.1. Consider an economy with a constant population in which each person is endowed with y_1 when young and y_2 when old. Assume that y_2 is sufficiently small so that everyone wants to consume more that y_2 in the second period of life. Bear in mind that under the new assumptions, the equations and graphs you use may differ from the ones in this chapter.
   a. Apply the Equations 1.1 through 1.6 to find the feasible set.
   b. Assume that all people within a generation will be treated alike and graph the set of stationary per-capita feasible allocations. Draw arbitrarily located, but correctly shaped, indifference curves on your graph and point out the allocation that maximizes the utility of the future generations.

1.2. Suppose a person faces the following two bundles: Bundle A, which consists of 6 units of the consumption good when a person is young and 12 units of the consumption good when a person is old ($c_1 = 6$ and $c_2 = 12$); and Bundle B, which consists of 4 units of the consumption good when a person is young and 10 units of the consumption good when a person is old ($c_1 = 4$ and $c_2 = 10$). Which bundle would this person prefer? Which assumption on preferences did you use to draw this conclusion?

1.3. Consider an economy in which the population follows the rule $N_t = 1.1N_{t-1}$. In addition, suppose that endowments per young person grow each period according to $y_t = 1.05y_{t-1}$. Assume old people do not receive any endowments. Assume that a young person's preferences are such that they want to consume one-half of their endowment so that $c_{1,t} = 0.5y_t$. Compute the rate at which transfers by young people can be converted into transfers received when old, that is, the conversion rate for this economy.

1.4. Consider two economies, labelled A and B. In each one, let every two-period-lived person be endowed with 20 units of the consumption when young and nothing when old. In Economy A, each young person chooses to consume 10 units of the consumption good. In Economy B, each young person chooses to consume 8 units of the consumption good. In each economy, the young person's choice is the one that maximizes lifetime welfare.

    a. What, if anything, can you infer about the welfare level of the current and future generations from this information? Specifically, is one on an indifference curve representing greater welfare than the other?

    b. What, if anything can you infer about the welfare of the initial old from the description given for Economies A and B?

1.5. Suppose a person has constant marginal utility over both goods instead of diminishing marginal utility for consumption when young and consumption when old.

    a. Draw an indifference curve for constant-marginal-utility preferences.

    b. If the marginal utility of consumption when young were greater than the marginal utility of consumption when old, how would this affect the equilibrium level of consumption over a person's lifetime?

    c. What if the marginal utility of consumption when old were greater than the marginal utility of consumption when young?

Chapter 2

A Simple Model of Money

1 Roadmap

Now that we know how people execute trades in a pair of one-time meetings without money, we add a friction into the model that can account for valued fiat money. The key friction is that record keeping is costly. Suppose, for example, that the cost of maintaining such a record-keeping device is prohibitively high. Now young people can fake trading with an old person in order to get goods when they are old. Faking means that there is no way to punish non-participating young people. What should people do in the economy with such a friction?

There are three goals for this chapter. First, we want to demonstrate that the only equilibrium in the decentralized economy results in no trade between the young and the old. We call this non-participating equilibrium autarky. In other words, old people want to use the credit they earned by trading when they were young. If there is no way to verify that an old person did indeed trade when young, such credit arrangements will not be granted. Not surprisingly, autarky is not the efficient equilibrium. Second, we propose valued fiat money as a government policy that can attempt to deal with the friction. Third, it important to show that the stationary equilibrium is efficient in an economy with a constant money stock over time.

Thus, the chief purpose of this chapter is to create a friction and incorporate that into the overlapping generations economy. As we did in the previous chapter, we compare the equilibrium quantities with what a planner would choose for the current and future generations. Even with perfect social memory absent, and the externality associated with this friction, the equilibrium quantities are efficient in an economy with valued fiat money. Because the equilibrium in the monetary economy and in the perfect record-keeping economy is identical, we use this equivalence to say that money is memory.[1]

---

[1] Memory is an important device in trade. To illustrate the importance, there is a story about two people who commit to having dinner with each other every Saturday night. Neither person can remember whose turn it is

2 The Environment

To arrive at the simplest possible model of money, we must ask ourselves which features are essential to monetary economies. The demand for money is distinct from the demand for the goods studied elsewhere in economics. People want goods for the utility received from their consumption. In contrast, people do not want money in order to consume it; they want money because money helps them get the things they want to consume. In this way, money is a medium of exchange – something acquired to make it easier to trade for the goods whose consumption is desired.

A model of this distinction in the demand for money therefore requires two special features. First, there must be some "friction" to trade that inhibits people from directly acquiring the goods they desire in the absence of money. One of the main messages from Chapter 1 is that people want to smooth their consumption over lifetime. If there are no frictions, they can accomplish this feat through the discipline imposed by social memory; that is, if, when young, Andy participates by giving goods to an old person, then next period, a young person will redeem that memory by giving goods to Andy. Moreover, the level of giving is part of that memory and determines how much is given when young and received when old. Social memory is necessary because trading partners only meet once in their lifetime.[2] So what happens if there is no social memory. To make this point more concrete, let Ψ_t represent the cost of keeping societal records at any date t. We assume that $\Psi_t > N_t y$ so that keeping perfect memory is not feasible in this economy. With the desire to trade, but without memory, the question is whether some other means can be developed that can support trade.

Second, we propose a model in which fiat money is used to deal with social amnesia. Someone must be willing to hold money from one period to the next for this to be even possible. This is necessary because money is an asset held over some period of time, however short, before it is spent. The overlapping generations model makes it possible for people to acquire money when young and use when they are old.

The model economy has the same physical environment as the model we studied in Chapter 1 with the addition of no record keeping. Each period there are young people born. Each person lives for two periods, except for a group that is alive in the first period of the economy, whom we refer to as the initial old. There is a single, perishable consumption good. And each young person receives an amount of that good. Each young person wants to consume when young and when old.

---

to cook the meal. So they devise a plan to let a stone serve as the memory device. Whoever has the stone is the cook and the other person takes the stone with them at the end of the evening.

[2] The modifier "social" applied to memory is very important. We are not talking about people suffering amnesia. What is crucial to social memory – and therefore, to credit – is that the set of all possible interactions between people can be observed. Individually, you are not an amnesiac, but socially, you are incapable of keeping track of every person's trading history, especially the times they reneged.

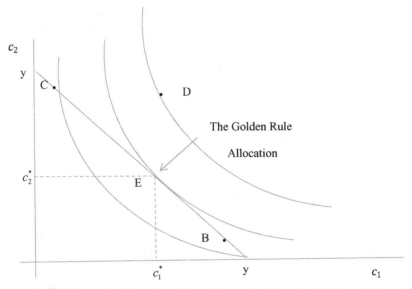

Figure 2.1. The golden rule allocation. The golden rule allocation is the stationary, feasible allocation of consumption that maximizes the welfare of future generations. It is located at a point of tangency between the feasible set line and an indifference curve (Bundle E). This is the highest indifference curve in contact with the feasible set. As drawn, the golden rule allocation E allocates more goods to people when young than when old ($c_1^* > c_2^*$) but this is arbitrary. The tangency point can just as easily have been drawn at a point where $c_2^* > c_1^*$.

3 The Economic Problem

The problem facing future generations of this economy is very simple. They want to acquire goods they do not have. Each has access to the nonstorable consumption good only when young but wants to consume in both periods of life. They must therefore find a way to acquire consumption in the second period of life and then decide how much they will consume in each period of life.

We examine, in turn, two solutions to this economic problem. The first, a centralized solution, proposes that an all-knowing, benevolent planner will allocate the economy's resources between consumption by the young and by the old. In the second, decentralized solution, we allow people to use money to trade for what they want. We then compare the two solutions and ask which is more likely to offer people the highest utility. The answer helps provide a first illustration of the economic usefulness of money.

3.1 Feasible Allocations

Imagine for a moment that we are central planners with complete knowledge of and total control over the economy. We studied this case in Chapter 1 and remind you what the Golden Rule allocation is for comparisons that are useful in this chapter. The Golden Rule allocation is represented in Figure 2.1 for a case in which population is constant over time.

The feasible allocation that a central planner selects depends on the objective. One reasonable and benevolent objective is the maximization of the utility of future generations, an objective we call the "golden rule." The golden rule in Figure 2.1 is represented by point E, which offers each person the consumption bundle (c_1^*, c_2^*). This combination of c_1 and c_2 yields the highest feasible level of utility during a person's entire lifetime.

What if the planner's objective was to maximize the consumption by the initial old? With this objective, the planner would allocate y units of the consumption good to the old and nothing for the consumption by the young. This stationary allocation would not maximize the utility of the future generations. All two-period-lived people would prefer the more balanced combination of consumption when young and old, represented by (c_1^*, c_2^*). Faced with this conflict in the interests of the initial old and future generations, an economist cannot choose among them on purely objective grounds. Nevertheless, the reader will find that, on subjective grounds (influenced by the fact that there are an infinite number of future generations and only a single generation of initial old), we tend to pay particular attention to the golden rule in this book.

4 Decentralized Solutions

In the previous section, we found the feasible allocation that maximizes the utility of the future generations. However, to achieve this allocation, in each period the central planner would have to take away c_2^* from each young person and give this amount to each old person. Such redistribution requires that the central planner have the ability to reallocate endowments costlessly between the generations. Furthermore, to determine c_1^* and c_2^*, this central planner also must know the exact utility function of the subjects.

These are strong assumptions about the power and wisdom of central planners. This leads us to ask if there is some way we can achieve this optimal allocation in a more decentralized manner, one in which economy reaches the optimal allocation through mutually beneficial trades conducted by each person. In other words, can we let a market do the work of the central planner?

We consider an economy in which perfect record keeping is not feasible. So we apply the notion of a competitive equilibrium to such an economy. Before offering money as way to achieve the optimal allocation, we consider the equilibrium outcome without any store of value.

4.1 Equilibrium without Money

Let us consider the nature of the competitive equilibrium when there is no money in our economy of overlapping generations. Recall that agents are endowed with some of the consumption good when young. Their endowment is zero when old. Their utility can be increased if they give up some of their endowment when they are young in exchange for some of the goods when they are old. Without the presence of an all-powerful central planner, we must ask ourselves if there are trades between people in the economy that could achieve this result.

No such trades are possible. Remember in Figure 1.1, there is a pattern of endowments described by young having goods and old people having nothing. A young person at period t has two types of people with whom to trade potentially in period t – other young people of the same generation or old people of the previous generation. However, trade with fellow young people would be of no benefit to the young person under consideration. They, like him, have none of the consumption good when they are old. Trade with the old would also be fruitless; the old want the good the young have, but they do not have what the young want (because they will not be alive in the next period). The source of the consumption good at time $t + 1$ is from the people who are born in that period. However, in period t, these people have not yet come into the world and so do not want what young people have to trade. This lack of possible trades is the manner in which the basic overlapping generations model captures the "absences of double coincidence of wants" (a term introduced by the 19th century economist W. S. Jevons [1875] to explain the need for money). Each generation wants what the next generation has but does not have what the next generation wants.

The resulting equilibrium is "autarkic" – people have no economic interaction with others. Unable to make mutually beneficial trades, each person consumes his entire endowment when young and nothing when old. In this autarkic equilibrium, utility is low. Both the future generations and the initial old are worse off than they would be with almost any other feasible consumption bundle. A member of the future generations would gladly give up some of his endowment when young in order to consume something when old. A member of the initial old would also like to consume something when old.

Figure 2.2 depicts the autarkic equilibrium in an economy with no record keeping and no money. In autarky, all the consumption is done when young and nothing is consumed by old people. It is easy to see how the record-keeping friction has bite when we see the autarkic equilibrium. When young, no one will unilaterally give up goods to an old person. Every old person will say that they gave goods when they were young. Social amnesia, however, keeps a young person from verifying the old person did participate. Such one-time meetings, therefore, result in no trade since a young person cannot establish a record of giving when young and will not trade with when they are old.

4.2 Equilibrium with Money

To open up a trading opportunity that might permit an exit from this grim autarkic equilibrium, we now introduce fiat money into our simple economy. "Fiat money"

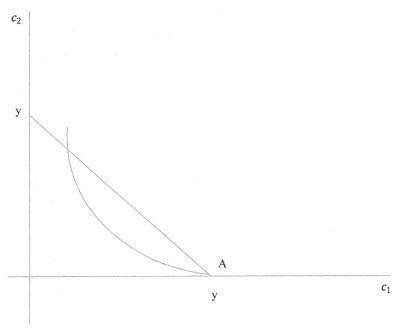

Figure 2.2. The autarkic equilibrium. It is located at a point where the indifference curve touches the budget line on the c_1-*axis* (Bundle A). The autarkic equilibrium results in all the consumption when young and nothing when old.

is a nearly costlessly produced commodity that cannot itself be used in consumption or production and is not a promise for anything that can be used in consumption or production.

For the purposes of our model, we assume the government can produce fiat money costlessly but that it cannot be produced or counterfeited by anyone else. Fiat money can be costlessly stored (held) from one period to the next and is costless to exchange. Pieces of paper distinctively marked by the government serve as fiat money.

Because people derive no direct utility from holding or consuming money, fiat money is valuable only if it enables people to trade for something they want to consume.

A "monetary equilibrium" is a competitive equilibrium in which there is a valued supply of fiat money. By valued, we mean that the fiat money can be traded for some of the consumption good. For fiat money to have value, its supply must be limited, and it must be impossible (or very costly) to counterfeit. Obviously, if everyone has the ability to print money costlessly, its supply will rapidly approach infinity, driving the value of any one unit to zero.

We began our analysis of monetary economies with an economy with a fixed stock of M perfectly divisible units of fiat money. We assume that each of the initial old begins with an equal number, M/N, of these units.

The presence of fiat money opens up a trading possibility. A young person can sell some of his endowment of goods (to old persons) for fiat money, hold the money until the next period, and then trade the fiat money for goods (with the young of that period).

5 Finding the Demand for Fiat Money

Of course, this new trading possibility exists only if fiat money is valued – in other words, if people are willing to give up some of the consumption good in trade for fiat money and vice versa. Because fiat money is intrinsically useless, its value depends on one's view of its value in the future, when it will be exchanged for the goods that do increase a person's utility.

If it is believed that fiat money will not be valued in the next period, then fiat money will have no value in this period. No one will be willing to give up some of the consumption good in exchange for it. That would be tantamount to trading something for nothing.

Extending this logic, we can predict that fiat money will have no value today if it is known with complete certainty that fiat money will be valueless at any future date T. To see this, first ask what the value of fiat money will be at time $T - 1$; in other words, ask how many goods you would be willing to give for money at $T - 1$ if it is known that it will be worthless at time T. The answer, of course, is that you would not be willing to give up any goods at time $T - 1$ for money. In other words, fiat money would have no value at time $T - 1$. Then what must its value be at time $T - 2$? By similar reasoning, we see that it will also be valueless at time $T - 2$. Working backward in this manner, we can see that fiat money will have no value today if it will be valueless at some point in the future.

Now let us consider a more interesting equilibrium in which money has a positive value in all future periods. We define v_t as the value of 1 unit of fiat money (let us call the unit a dollar) in terms of goods; that is, it is the number of goods that one must give up to obtain one dollar. It is the inverse of the dollar price of the consumption good, which we write as p_t. For example, if a banana costs 20 cents, $p_t = 1/5$ dollars and the value of a dollar, v_t, is five bananas. Note also that because our economy has only one good, the price of that good p_t can be viewed as the price level in this economy.

5.1 A Person's Budget

Let us now examine how people will decide how much money to acquire (assuming that fiat money will have a positive value in the future). To answer, we must first establish the constraints on the choices of the person – why he cannot simply enjoy infinite consumption both when young and when old. As was the case for the entire society, the constraints on a person are that he cannot give up more goods than he has. We will refer to the limitations on a person's consumption as his "budget constraints."

In the first period of life, a person has an endowment of y goods. The person can do two things with these goods – consume them and/or sell them for money. Notice that no one in the future generations is born with fiat money. To acquire fiat money, a person must trade. If the number of dollars acquired by a person (by giving up some of the consumption good) at time t is denoted by m_t, then the total number of goods sold for money is $v_t m_t$. We can therefore write the budget constraint facing each person in the first period of life as

$$c_{1,t} + v_t m_t \leq y. \tag{2.1}$$

The left-hand side of Equation 2.1 is the person's total uses of goods (consumption and acquisition of money). The right-hand side of Equation 2.1 represents the total sources of goods (the person's endowment).

In the second period of life, the person receives no endowment. Hence, when old, a person can acquire goods for consumption only by spending the money acquired in the previous period. In the second period of life (period $t + 1$), this money will purchase $v_{t+1} m_t$ units of the consumption good. The only use for these goods is second-period consumption. This means that the constraint facing the person in the second period of life is

$$c_{2,t+1} \leq v_{t+1} m_t. \tag{2.2}$$

In a monetary equilibrium in which, by definition, $v_t > 0$ for all t, we can rewrite this constraint as $m_t \geq (c_{2,t+1})/(v_{t+1})$ and substitute it into the first-period constraint (Equation 2.1) to obtain

$$c_{1,t} + \frac{v_t c_{2,t+1}}{v_{t+1}} \leq y \tag{2.3}$$

or

$$c_{1,t} + \left[\frac{v_t}{v_{t+1}} \right] c_{2,t+1} \leq y. \tag{2.4}$$

Equation 2.4 expresses the various combinations of first- and second-period consumption that a person can afford over a lifetime. In other words, it is the person's "lifetime budget constraint."

We can graph this budget constraint as shown in Figure 2.2. We can easily verify that the intercepts of the budget line are as illustrated. The budget line represents Equation 2.4 at equality. If nothing is consumed in the second period of life ($c_{2,t+1} = 0$), then the constraint implies that $c_{1,t} = y$. This is the horizontal intercept of the budget line. On the other hand, if nothing is consumed in the first period of life ($c_{1,t} = 0$), so that the entire endowment of y is used to purchase money, the constraint implies that $[(v_t)/(v_{t+1})]c_{2,t+1} = y$ or $c_{2,t+1} = [(v_{t+1})/(v_t)]y$. This represents the vertical intercept of the budget line.

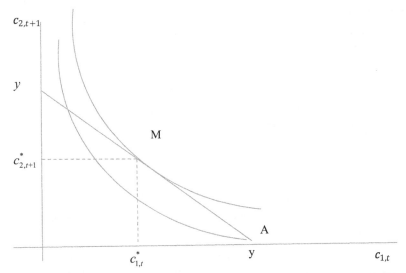

Figure 2.3. The choice of consumption with perfect record keeping. At Bundle M, a person maximizes utility given their lifetime budget constraint in a monetary equilibrium. Bundle M is found by locating a point of tangency between an indifference curve and the person's lifetime budget set line. The rate of return on money determines the slope of the budget set line.

Note that $(v_{t+1})/(v_t)$ can be considered as the "(real) rate of return of fiat money" because it expresses how many goods can be obtained in period $t + 1$ if one unit of the good is sold for money in period t.

For a given rate of return of money, $(v_{t+1})/(v_t)$, we can find the $(c^*_{1,t}, c^*_{2,t+1})$ combination that will be chosen by a person who is seeking to maximize their utility. This point is shown in Figure 2.3. It is the point along the budget line that touches the highest indifference curve. This must occur at a point where the budget line is tangent to an indifference curve.

5.2 Finding Fiat Money's Rate of Return

But how can we determine the rate of return on intrinsically useless fiat money? The value that a person places on a unit of fiat money at time t, v_t, depends on what that person believes will be the value of one unit of money at $t + 1$, v_{t+1}. By similar logic, the value of a unit of fiat money at time $t + 1$ depends on a person's beliefs about the value of money in period $t + 2$, v_{t+2}. And so on. We see that the value of fiat money at any point in time depends on an infinite chain of expectations about its future values. This indefiniteness is not due to any peculiarity in our model but rather to the nature of fiat money, which, because it has no intrinsic value, has a value that is determined by views about the future.

Whatever the views of the future value of money, a reasonable benchmark is the case in which these views are the same for every generation. This is plausible because in our basic model, every generation faces the same problem; endowments, preferences, and population are the same for every generation. If views about the future are also the same across generations, then people will react in the same manner in each period, choosing $c_{1,t} = c_1$ and $c_{2,t} = c_2$ for each period t. We call such equilibria "stationary equilibria." Notice that because each person faces different circumstances, depending on whether they are young or old, c_1 will not in general be equal to c_2 in a stationary equilibrium. People may choose to consume more when young or more when old. It turns out that the relative mix of first- and second-period consumption depends on preferences and on the rate of return of fiat money.

We also assume that people in our economy form their expectations of the future rationally. In this nonrandom economy, where there are no surprises, "rational expectations" means that a person's expectations of future variables equal the actual values of these future variables. In this special case, we say that people have perfect foresight. With perfect foresight, there are no errors in people's forecast of the important economic variables that affect their decisions. In the context of our model, this assumption means that a person born in period t will perfectly forecast the value of money in the next period, v_{t+1}. The person's expectation of this value will be exactly realized. This assumption would be less credible in an economy buffeted by random shocks than in our model economy, where preferences and the environment are unchanging and therefore are perfectly predictable.

To see the importance of perfect foresight, consider the alternative in a nonrandom economy – that people always expect a value of money greater or less than the value of money that actually occurs. A person with wrong beliefs about the future value of money will not choose the money balances that maximize their utility. They therefore have an incentive to figure out the value of money that actually will occur.

Let us now employ the assumptions of stationarity and perfect foresight to find an equilibrium time path of the value of money. In perfectly competitive markets, the price (or value) of an object is determined as the price at which the supply of the object equals its demand. This applies to the determination of the price (value) of money as well as the price of any good.

The demand for fiat money of each person is the number of goods each chooses to sell for fiat money, which equals the goods of the endowment that the person does not consume when young, $y - c_{1,t}$. The total money demand by all people in the economy at time t is therefore $N_t(y - c_{1,t})$.

The total supply of fiat money, measured in units of the consumption goods, is $v_t M_t$, implying that the total supply of fiat money measured in goods is the number of dollars multiplied by the value of each dollar, or $v_t M_t$. Equality of supply and demand therefore requires that

$$v_t M_t = N_t(y - c_{1,t}). \tag{2.5}$$

This, in turn, implies that

$$v_t = \frac{N_t(y - c_{1,t})}{M_t},$$

(2.6)

which states that the value of a unit of fiat money is given by the ratio of the real demand for fiat money to the total number of dollars. Similarly, at time $t + 1$,

$$v_{t+1} = \frac{N_{t+1}(y - c_{1,t+1})}{M_{t+1}}.$$

(2.7)

Using Equations 2.6 and 2.7 together, we have

$$\frac{v_{t+1}}{v_t} = \frac{\frac{N_{t+1}(y - c_{1,t+1})}{M_{t+1}}}{\frac{N_t(y - c_{1,t})}{M_t}}.$$

(2.8)

To simplify this, we look for a stationary solution, where $c_{1,t} = c_1$ and $c_{2,t} = c_2$ for all t. Because all generations have the same endowments and preferences and anticipate the same future pattern of endowments and preferences, it seems quite reasonable to look for a stationary equilibrium. Then, after some cancellation, Equation 2.8 becomes

$$\frac{v_{t+1}}{v_t} = \frac{\frac{N_{t+1}(y - c_1)}{M_{t+1}}}{\frac{N_t(y - c_1)}{M_t}} = \frac{\frac{N_{t+1}}{M_{t+1}}}{\frac{N_t}{M_t}}.$$

(2.9)

Because we are assuming a constant population ($N_{t+1} = N_t$) and a constant supply of money ($M_{t+1} = M_t$) the terms in Equation 2.9 cancel out and we find that

$$\frac{v_{t+1}}{v_t} = 1 \quad \text{or} \quad v_{t+1} = v_t,$$

(2.10)

implying a constant value of money. Because the price of the consumption good p_t is the inverse of the value of money, it too is constant over time.

Notice that the rate of return on fiat money is also a constant (1) in the stationary equilibrium. Identical people who face the same rate of return will choose the same consumption and money balances over time, a stationary equilibrium. Therefore, the stationary equilibrium is internally consistent.

Using the information that $(v_{t+1})/(v_t) = 1$ and recalling that the budget line in a stationary monetary equilibrium is represented by $c_1 + [(v_t)/(v_{t+1})]c_2 = y$, we determine that $c_1 + c_2 = y$. Our graph of the budget line therefore becomes the one depicted in Figure 2.3.

Be aware that the stationary equilibrium may not be a unique monetary equilibrium. There also may exist more complicated nonstationary equilibria. In this text, however, we confine our attention to stationary equilibria because there is much that can be learned from these easy-to-study cases.

5.3 The Quantity Theory of Money

The simplest version of the "quantity theory of money" predicts that the price level is exactly proportional to the quantity of money in the economy. We would like to investigate whether this theory holds in our basic overlapping generations model.

Recall that, in Equation 2.6, we found that the value of money is determined by

$$v_t = \frac{N_t(y - c_{1,t})}{M_t}.$$

In a stationary equilibrium with a fixed population and a fixed stock of fiat money, this equation simplifies to

$$v_t = \frac{N(y - c_1)}{M}. \tag{2.11}$$

As we have seen, the value of money is constant in this simple economy. This is evident from the lack of time subscripts on the right-hand side of Equation 2.11.

Because the price level is the inverse of the value of money ($p_t = 1/v_t$), we can write an expression for the price level as

$$p_t = \frac{1}{v_t} = \frac{M}{N(y - c_1)}. \tag{2.12}$$

This illustrates that the price level in our model is, in fact, proportional to the stock of fiat money, M. As an example, suppose that the initial stock of fiat money in the economy M is doubled but remains constant from then on. (This is referred to as a once-and-for-all increase in the fiat money stock.) Equation 2.12 tells us that the price level in every period will also be twice as high. This demonstrates that our model is indeed consistent with the quantity theory of money.

5.4 The Neutrality of the Fiat Money Stock

The nominal (measured in dollars) size of the stock of fiat money M has no effect on the real (measured in goods) values of consumption or money demand ($y - c_1$) of this monetary equilibrium. We see from Figures 2.2 and 2.3 that a person's choices of consumption and real money balances do not depend on the total number of dollars but do depend on the rate of return of money. The rate of return of money is unaffected by the size of the constant stock of fiat money (notice in Equation 2.10 that the money stock terms canceled each other out). This property of the monetary equilibrium is referred to as the "neutrality of money."

5.5 The Role of Fiat Money

The introduction of valued fiat money into the basic overlapping generations model improves the welfare of the people of the economy. In Figure 2.3, Bundle M in Figure 2.3 is on a higher indifference curve than Bundle A. Why is this the case? All we have done is introduce intrinsically worthless pieces of paper into an economy. How can this improve welfare? We hinted at the answer earlier. Without fiat money, people are unable to trade for the good they desire, c_2, because they do not own anything that the owners of these goods, the next generation, desire. With fiat money, however, people are able to trade for the goods they desire despite this absence of a double coincidence of wants. People sell some of the goods they have for fiat money and then use the money to buy the goods they want. In this model economy, therefore, fiat money serves as a medium of exchange. It is not consumed, nor does it produce anything that can be consumed. It is valued nevertheless because it helps people acquire goods they otherwise could not have acquired.

Second-period consumption is a market good in the sense that a person must trade to obtain more of it. In contrast, first-period consumption is a nonmarket good; people already possess first-period consumption without needing to trade for it. We can say then that fiat money provides a means for people to purchase market goods.

6 Is This Monetary Equilibrium the Golden Rule?

We have seen that fiat money can provide for second-period consumption, improving the welfare of people otherwise unable to trade. We would like to make the people in our economy not just better off but as well off as possible. It remains to ask, therefore, whether the monetary equilibrium results in the best possible allocation of goods. In particular, we would like to see whether the stationary monetary equilibrium we have just found maximizes the welfare of future generations. In other words, does the monetary equilibrium reach the golden rule?

Compare the budget line of Figure 2.3 with the feasible set line of Figure 2.1. They are identical. The choice of consumption in this monetary equilibrium will be identical to the one we found when we were looking at the stationary allocation that was dictated by a central planner who wanted to maximize the utility of the future generations. This implies that the stationary monetary equilibrium obeys the golden rule. The introduction of fiat money not only allows the future generations to increase their utility through trade but, in this case, also allows them to reach their maximum feasible utility. This will not always be the case. The budget set and the feasible set answer different economic questions. The budget set depicts the constraint on a person, whereas the feasible set describes the constraint on the society as a whole. We will later find cases in which these two constraints differ and the monetary equilibrium does not obey the golden rule.

The initial old are also better off in the monetary equilibrium than they were with the autarkic equilibrium. In the monetary equilibrium, everyone among the initial old will receive $v_1 m_0 = (v_1 M)/N$ units of the consumption good when they trade their initial holdings of money for goods with the young of period 1. This means their consumption will be positive. In the autarkic equilibrium, their consumption would be zero. They are certainly better off in the monetary equilibrium.

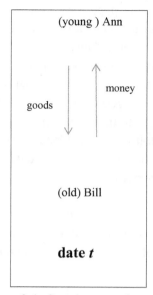

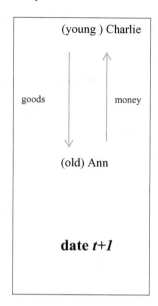

Figure 2.4. One-time meetings with valued fiat money. In the left-hand box, we see the one-time meeting between a young Ann and an old Bill at date *t*. At this meeting, Ann accepts money in exchange for some of her endowment. The right-hand-side box, shows a one-time meeting at date *t* + 1 between Ann, who is now old, and a young Charlie. Ann offers money to Charlie, receiving goods in exchange. This pattern illustrates the pair of one-time meetings that over each member of the current and future generations.

Because we concentrate on stationary monetary equilibria in this book, it may be useful to summarize the features of such equilibria. A stationary consumption bundle of a monetary equilibrium satisfies two basic properties:

- It provides the maximum level of utility given the person's budget set. It is found where an indifference curve lies tangent to the person's budget set.
- It lies on the feasible set line, with the boundary of the set representing all feasible per-capita allocations.

After considering how fiat money is valued in equilibrium, we can take a step back and see the big picture. Money solves a problem that is present when people face some one-time meetings during their lifetime. In the overlapping generations model, each person will have two opportunities to trade with someone from another generation. Figure 2.4 offers a picture of the pair of one-time meetings that members of current and future generations have during their lifetime, offering money as a store of value between those two meetings. Though money itself is intrinsically useless, its finite supply means that it serves as a placeholder – that is what store of value means – as people execute trades across generations. The young are willing to accept money and give up some of their endowment, knowing that the money can be exchanged for goods next period. In Figure 2.4, even though Ann will never meet Bill again, she is willing to accept fiat money from him because the pieces of paper represent future consumption goods for her. Ann knows what the supply of fiat money will be in the future and its future value so that when she offers money to Charlie next period, it will purchase the amount of goods that Ann desires to consume when old. In the endless carousel of one-time meetings, Charlie accepts Ann's money balances because he knows someone will accept the money when he is old.

7 A Monetary Equilibrium with a Growing Economy

In the example we just considered, we found that a constant value of money (constant prices) led to an equilibrium that maximized the welfare of future generations. Is this always the case? Are there cases in which a changing value of money maximizes the utility of future generations? To answer these questions, we now complicate our example by allowing the economy to grow over time. We accomplish this by assuming that the population is increasing over time. This implies that the total amount of the consumption good available in the economy will grow over time. In a monetary equilibrium, the assumption of a growing population also implies a growing demand for fiat money.

Specifically, we assume that the population of this economy is growing so that $N_t = nN_{t-1}$ for every period t, where n is a constant greater than 1. This says that the number of people born in any period is always n times the number born in the previous period. For example, if $n = 1.05$, then the number of people born in each period is growing by 5 percent from generation to generation. Five percent is the net rate of population growth; $n = 1.05$ is the "gross rate." The gross rate is the net rate plus 1. To test your understanding of population growth rates, try Example 2.1.

Example 2.1 Suppose there are 100 initial old in an economy ($N_0 = 100$) and that the number of young born in the economy is changing according to $N_t = nN_{t-1}$ in each period t, where $n = 1.2$. Trace out the number of young and old people alive in periods 1 and 2. What is the growth rate of the total population?

7.1 The Feasible Set with a Growing Population

First, as before, consider the case of an all-powerful central planner who determines allocations of the available goods in each generation. We consider the case of a monetary equilibrium later. As we determined earlier, the total amount of goods available for allocation in period t is $N_t y$. Assuming that all persons within a generation will have identical consumption, total consumption in each period t consists of aggregate consumption by the young ($N_t c_{1,t}$) and aggregate consumption by the old ($N_{t-1} c_{2,t}$). We then consider the stationary case where $c_{1,t} = c_1$ and $c_{2,t} = c_2$. The constraint describing feasible allocations is the same as before:

$$N_t c_1 + N_{t-1} c_2 \leq N_t y. \tag{2.13}$$

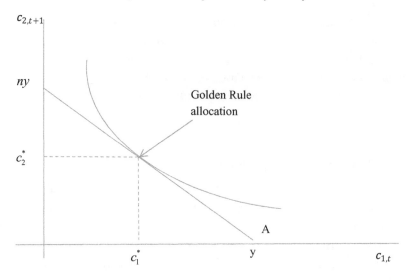

Figure 2.5. The Golden Rule allocation with a growing population. When the population grows at the rate, n, the feasible set line has a horizontal intercept of y and a vertical intercept of ny. As before, the Golden Rule allocation is determined at a point of tangency between the feasible set line and an indifference curve.

When we considered the case of a constant population ($N_t = N_{t-1}$), the N terms canceled out in the previous expression. Although this will not occur here, we can simplify Equation 2.13 by dividing through both sides of the inequality by N_t:

$$\left[\frac{N_t}{N_t}\right] c_1 + \left[\frac{N_{t-1}}{N_t}\right] c_2 \leq \left[\frac{N_t}{N_t}\right] y. \tag{2.14}$$

If we recall that ($N_t = nN_{t-1}$), we can simplify this expression to

$$c_1 + \left[\frac{N_{t-1}}{nN_{t-1}}\right] c_2 \leq y$$

or

$$c_1 + \left[\frac{1}{n}\right] c_2 \leq y. \tag{2.15}$$

We can easily graph this constraint, as is done in Figure 2.5. We leave the problem of verifying that the intercepts are as shown in the diagram for the end of chapter.

Note that if the two axes are scaled the same, then because $n > 1$, the vertical intercept lies farther from the origin than does the horizontal intercept. Why is this vertical intercept greater than it was in the case of a constant population? With a growing population, there are n young people for each old person. Therefore, if we divide the entire endowment of the young equally among the old, there will be ny goods for each old person. It is easier for the planner to provide for consumption by the old because they are relatively few in number.

If we superimpose a typical person's indifference curves on the graph with the feasible allocations line, we can find the stationary allocation that maximizes the utility of future generations. As always, this occurs at a point of tangency between the feasible allocations line and an indifference curve. This yields the point (c_1^*, c_2^*), which is illustrated in Figure 2.4. If the central planner were to give this combination of c_1 and c_2 to each member of future generations, his welfare would be maximized.

7.2 The Budget Set with a Growing Population

Now that we have determined the optimal allocation for future generations, let us turn to the case of a stationary monetary equilibrium. As before, we eliminate the central planner and introduce fiat money into the economy. We again require that markets clear. In particular, the total demand for money must equal the aggregate supply. Earlier (see Equation 1.12) we found that this condition implies that

$$v_t = \frac{N_t(y - c_1)}{M_t}. \tag{2.16}$$

Note that the numerator of Equation 2.16 is the total real demand for fiat money, and the denominator is the total fiat money stock. The equation tells us that the value of fiat money in any period is determined by the relative demand for fiat money and its supply. A higher real demand for fiat money will raise its value, and a higher supply of fiat money will lower its value.

If we update the time subscripts in Equation 2.16 by one period, we find that an expression for the value of fiat money in period $t + 1$ is

$$v_{t+1} = \frac{N_{t+1}(y - c_1)}{M_{t+1}}. \tag{2.17}$$

If we now look at the rate of return on money $(v_{t+1})/(v_t)$, we have

$$\frac{v_{t+1}}{v_t} = \frac{\frac{N_{t+1}(y-c_1)}{M_{t+1}}}{\frac{N_t(y-c_1)}{M_t}} = \frac{\frac{N_{t+1}}{M_{t+1}}}{\frac{N_t}{M_t}}. \tag{2.18}$$

If we assume a constant money supply, the M terms cancel. Previously, with a constant population, the N terms also canceled. However, with a growing population, we know that $N_{t+1} = nN_t$, so that Equation 2.18 becomes

$$\frac{v_{t+1}}{v_t} = \frac{N_{t+1}}{N_t} = \frac{nN_t}{N_t} = n. \tag{2.19}$$

The rate of return on money is merely equal to the rate of population growth n. Because $n > 1$, the value of money is increasing over time. This implies that the price of the consumption good is falling over time. Note that our earlier constant population example is merely a special case of the one just considered. With a constant population, n is equal to 1. We therefore conclude that the rate of return on money is also equal to 1 in that case.

Now if we recall the person's lifetime budget constraint (Equation 2.4), we find that

$$c_1 + \left[\frac{v_t}{v_{t+1}}\right] c_2 \leq y \quad \Rightarrow \quad c_1 + \left[\frac{1}{n}\right] c_2 \leq y. \tag{2.20}$$

This turns out to be the same constraint that faced our central planner (Equation 2.15). Therefore, the best allocation in the budget sets of future generations must also be the golden rule, the best allocation in the feasible set for future generations. This implies that an omnipotent, omniscient, and benevolent central planner could do no better than people acting within their budget sets.

You should note that our analysis also applies to a shrinking economy, where $n < 1$. In such a case, the value of money falls over time, implying a rising price level. However, the previous analysis would still apply. The monetary equilibrium with a constant fiat money stock would still attain the golden rule.

8 Summary

In this chapter, we introduced the basic overlapping generations model. We found that fiat money, intrinsically worthless pieces of paper, can have value by providing a means for people to acquire goods they do not possess. In addition, we saw that the introduction of a fixed stock of fiat money into an economy enables future generations to attain the maximum possible level of utility given the resources available.

So far, we have concentrated on factors that affect the demand for money. We found that, in a growing economy where the demand for money increases over time, a constant fiat money stock enables people to attain the golden rule. We might also be interested in knowing what effects a growing supply of fiat money has on an economy. We turn our attention to the case of an increasing fiat money stock in Chapter 4. Before doing so, in Chapter 3 we consider two alternative trading arrangements to using fiat money – the uses of barter and commodity money.

9 Exercises

2.1. Consider an economy with a constant population of $N = 100$. Each person is endowed with $y = 20$ units of the consumption good when young and nothing when old.

    a. What is the equation for the feasible set of this economy? Portray the feasible set on a graph. With arbitrarily drawn indifference curves, illustrate the stationary combination of c_1 and c_2 that maximizes the utility of future generations.

    b. Now look at a monetary equilibrium. Write down equations that represent the constraints on first- and second-period consumption for a typical person. Combine these constraints into a lifetime budget constraint.

c. Suppose the initial old are endowed with a total of $M = 400$ units of fiat money. What condition represents the clearing of the money market in an arbitrary period t? Use this condition to find the real return of fiat money.

For the remaining parts of this exercise, suppose preferences are such that each person wishes to hold real balances of money worth $\frac{y}{1+\frac{v_t}{v_{t+1}}}$ goods.

(In the appendix to this chapter, it is verified that this demand for fiat money comes from the utility function $[c_{1,t}]^{1/2} + [c_{2,t+1}]^{1/2}$.)

d. What is the value of money in period t, v_t? Use the assumption about preferences and your answer in part c to find an exact numerical value. What is the price of the consumption good p_t?

e. If the rate of population growth increased, what would happen to the rate of return of fiat money, the real demand for fiat money, the value of a unit of fiat money in the initial period, and the utility of the initial old? Explain your answers. (*Hint:* Answer these questions in the order asked.)

f. Suppose instead that the initial old were endowed with a total of 800 units of fiat money. How do your answers to part d change? Are the initial old better off with more units of fiat money?

2.2. Consider two economies, A and B. Both economies have the same population, supply of fiat money, and endowments. In each economy, the number of young people born in each period is constant at N, and the supply of fiat money is constant at M. Furthermore, each person is endowed with y units of the consumption good when young and zero when old. The only difference between the economies is with regard to preferences. Other things being equal, people in economy A have preferences that lean toward first-period consumption; individual preferences in economy B lean toward second-period consumption. We will also assume stationarity. More specifically, the lifetime budget constraints and typical indifference curves for people in the two economies are represented in the following diagram.

a. Will there be a difference in the rates of return of fiat money in the two economies? If so, which economy will have the higher rate of return of fiat money? Give an intuitive interpretation of your answer.

b. Will there be a difference in the value of money in the two economies? If so, which economy will have the higher value of money? Give an intuitive interpretation of your answer.

2.3. Consider an economy with a growing population in which each person is endowed with y_1 when young and y_2 when old. Assume that y_2 is sufficiently small that everyone wants to consume more than y_2 in the second period of life. Bear in mind that under the new assumptions, the equations and graphs you find may differ from the ones found previously.

a. Find the feasible set.

b. Assume that all people within a generation will be treated alike and graph the set of stationary per-capita feasible allocations. Draw arbitrarily located, but correctly shaped, indifference curves on your graph and point out the allocation that maximizes the utility of the future generations.

c. Turning now to the monetary equilibrium, find the equation representing the equality of supply and demand in the market for money.

Economy A

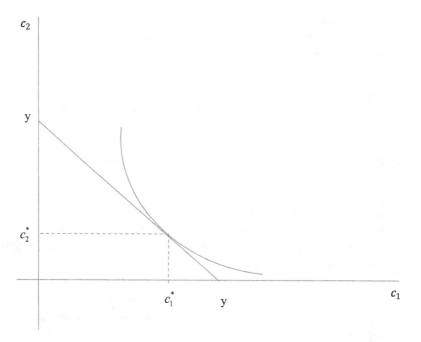

Economy B

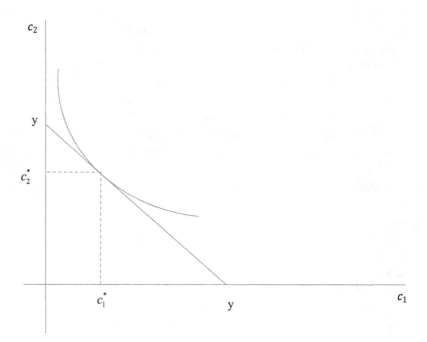

    d. Assume a stationary solution and a constant money supply. Use the equation in part c to find v_{t+1}/v_t.

    e. Draw the budget set for a person in this monetary equilibrium. Does this monetary equilibrium maximize the utility of future generations? Explain.

2.4. In this chapter, we modeled growth in an economy by a growing population. We could also achieve a growing economy by having an endowment that increases over time. To see this, consider the following economy: Let the number of young people born in each period be constant at N. There is a constant stock of fiat money, M. Each young person born in period t is endowed with y_t units of the consumption good when young and nothing when old. The person's endowment grows over time so that $y_t = \alpha y_{t-1}$ where $\alpha > 1$. For simplicity, assume that in each period t, people desire to hold real money balances equal to one-half of their endowment, so that $v_t m_t = y_t/2$.

    a. Write down equations that represent the constraints on first- and second-period consumption for a typical person. Combine these constraints into a lifetime budget constraint.

    b. Write down the condition that represents the clearing of the money market in an arbitrary period t. Use this condition to find the real rate of return of fiat money in a monetary equilibrium. Explain the path over time of the value of fiat money.

2.5. Suppose that population increases at a fixed rate n. For this model economy, verify that the horizontal intercept of the feasible set line is equal to y and that the vertical intercept of the feasible set line is equal to ny.

2.6. In each of the four cases, please tell me the unit of measure, or in the case of a price, the rate at which two goods are traded for one another (in other words, describe both the numerator and the denominator).

    a. $v_t m_t$

    b. M_t

    c. v_t

    d. p_t

10 Appendix: Using Calculus

With the use of simple calculus, we can derive mathematical representations of the demand of fiat money from specific utility functions. In the main body of the text, we have simply assumed certain demand-for-money functions to illustrate monetary equilibria. In this appendix, we demonstrate that these functions can be derived from utility functions that satisfy our basic assumptions about preferences. The appendix also serves as an illustration of a way to solve explicit examples of monetary equilibria. Following similar steps, advanced students may be able to solve examples of their own creation based on the simple model of this chapter or on the more complex economies of succeeding chapters.

If you do not know calculus, simply skip this appendix. It is not a prerequisite for any material in the succeeding chapters.

The problem facing a young person born at t is to maximize utility, which is a function, $U(c_{1,t}, c_{2,t+1})$, of consumption in each period of life. We assume that the function is continuous in each argument. Each person is constrained by his budget constraints

$$c_{1,t} + v_t m_t \leq y, \tag{2.21}$$

$$c_{2,t+1} \leq v_t m_t. \tag{2.22}$$

We want to solve for a young person's real demand for fiat money $v_t m_t$, which we write as q_t. We can now write the person's budget constraints (solved at equality) as

$$c_{1,t} + q_t \leq y \tag{2.23}$$

$$c_{2,t+1} \leq v_{t+1} m_t = \frac{v_{t+1}}{v_t}[v_t m_t] = \frac{v_{t+1}}{v_t}[q_t]. \tag{2.24}$$

If we use the budget constraints to substitute for $c_{1,t}$ and $c_{2,t+1}$ in the utility function, we can write utility as the following function of q_t:

$$U\left(y - q_t, \frac{v_{t+1}}{v_t}[q_t]\right). \tag{2.25}$$

If we graph utility as a function of q_t, we find a function, like that in Figure 2.5, with a single peak. (That there is a single peak is ensured by our assumption of a diminishing marginal rate of substitution.) Maximum utility is reached at q_t^*, where the slope of the utility function is zero.

Figure 2.5. Utility as a function of a person's real demand for fiat money. A person's utility can be expressed as a function of real fiat money holdings. Utility is maximized by hold real fiat money balances equal to q_t^*.

The derivative of a function is its slope. Therefore, we find maximum utility at the value of q_t, where the derivative of $U\left(y - q_t, \frac{v_{t+1}}{v_t}[q_t]\right)$ with respect to q_t equals zero. Let U_i denote the derivative of utility with respect to c_i. Then the utility maximizing demand for money, q_t^* is defined by

$$\frac{\partial U\left(y - q_t, \frac{v_{t+1}}{v_t}[q_t]\right)}{\partial q_t} = 0$$

$$\implies -U_1\left(y - q_t^*, \frac{v_{t+1}}{v_t}[q_t^*]\right) + \left[\frac{v_{t+1}}{v_t}\right] U_2\left(y - q_t^*, \frac{v_{t+1}}{v_t}[q_t^*]\right) = 0 \tag{2.26}$$

$$\implies \frac{U_1\left(y - q_t^*, \frac{v_{t+1}}{v_t}[q_t^*]\right)}{U_2\left(y - q_t^*, \frac{v_{t+1}}{v_t}[q_t^*]\right)} = \frac{v_{t+1}}{v_t}.$$

Equation 2.26 states that the utility maximizing demand for money occurs where the marginal rate of substitution between first- and second-period consumption equals the rate of return on money.

The marginal rate of substitution U_1/U_2, which is the ratio of the marginal utilities in the two periods of life, represents -1 times the slope of the indifference curve at the combination of $c_{1,t}$ and $c_{2,t+1}$ that corresponds to a given value of q_t. Because the slope of the budget set is -1 times the rate of return of fiat money, Equation 2.26 is simply a mathematical expression of the statement that utility is maximized where an indifference curve is tangent to the budget line.

10.1 An Example

Suppose that utility is given by $(c_{1,t})^{1/2} + (c_{2,t+1})^{1/2}$. If we use the budget constraints to substitute for $c_{1,t}$ and $c_{2,t+1}$, we can find utility as the following function of q_t:

$$(y - q_t)^{1/2} + \left(\frac{v_{t+1}}{v_t} [q_t] \right)^{1/2}. \tag{2.27}$$

Now differentiate this function with respect to q_t and set the derivative equal to zero:

$$-\frac{1}{2} (y - q_t^*)^{-1/2} + \frac{1}{2} \left(\frac{v_{t+1}}{v_t} \right)^{1/2} [q_t^*]^{-1/2} = 0. \tag{2.28}$$

Now solve this for q_t^*. (To start, take the first term over to the right-hand side and square both sides.) You should find the money demand function that we used in Exercise 2.1.

$$q_t^* = \frac{y}{1 + \frac{v_t}{v_{t+1}}}. \tag{2.29}$$

11 Appendix Exercise

2.7. Suppose utility equals $\ln(c_{1,t}) + \beta \ln(c_{2,t+1})$ where $\ln(c)$ represents the natural logarithm of c, whose derivative equals $1/c$. The parameter β is a positive number.

    a. Prove that real money balances are

$$q^* = \frac{\beta y}{1 + \beta}.$$

    b. Derive expressions for the lifetime consumption pattern $c_{1,t}^*$ and $c_{2,t+1}^*$.

    c. What effect does an increase in β have on real money balances and the lifetime consumption pattern? Give an intuitive interpretation of the parameter β.

Chapter 3

Barter and Commodity Money

1 Roadmap

In this chapter, we extend the basic overlapping generations model so that we can examine other ways in which people pay for things. We know that fiat money can be used to execute trades between people from different generations. So we consider what happens if there is trade amongst people of the same generation. We introduce multiple types of consumption goods so that there could be a reason for people to trade. Within a generation, the friction here is the cost associated with each meeting, known also as search costs. For trade to occur, there must be a double coincidence of wants; I have what you want and you have what I want. In the first comparison, we examine whether money or barter is the least costly way to execute trades. Even with consumption goods being allowed to be storable, money can reduce lifetime search costs compared with barter for economies with lots of different goods. With money as the generally accepted medium of exchange, every meeting between young person with goods and an old person with money means that in every meeting a young is offered something they want. Hence, the search costs associated are reduced. In a double-coincidence problem, the probability that you have what I want and I have what you want is difficult when there are lots of different consumption goods. However, when money is involved, the double-coincidence problem now requires that if you want what I have and I have money, we will always trade because you accept money.

The next comparison is between fiat money and commodity money. Human history has predominantly relied on commodity money – either actual precious metals or paper money that stands for a specified amount of precious metal – as a means of payment. It is easy to understand why we would not want to use anything that has intrinsic value as a means of payment. It is true that the monetary value cannot be less than the intrinsic value of the commodity. But it is generally better to free up the commodity and use intrinsically useless fiat money to conduct trades. In this

50

way, everyone gets to enjoy the commodity's intrinsic qualities by substituting an intrinsically useless good as the means of exchange.

2 Barter and Commodity Money

Exchange solves a mismatch problem for people. Often, a person produces goods but wants to consume other goods. In Chapter 2, we modeled this problem by assuming that people had goods when young but also wanted to consume when old. Because of the model's simplicity, we use it as the foundation on which we build more complicated models.

The simple model, however, provides no alternatives to fiat money – fiat money is used in exchange because there is no other way to trade what one has for what one wants. The model has only a single type of good in every period, so trading goods for goods is ruled out. In this chapter, we consider models of two historically important alternative trading possibilities – direct barter and commodity money. In a fiat monetary system, goods trade for fiat money, but goods trade directly for goods in an economy with barter or commodity money. We distinguish between the two in the following way: In a direct barter economy, the goods one owns are exchanged for the goods one desires. In a commodity money economy, the goods one owns may be traded for a good that is not consumed but is traded, in turn, for the good one desires.

In each case, we compare the performance of the model economy using fiat money with the alternative trading device. The first model illustrates how direct barter may be more costly than monetary exchange, the trading of goods for money and, subsequently, money for goods. In the second model, real commodities (not just pieces of paper) serve as money; people trade for commodities they do not want to consume in order to trade later for the goods they do want to consume. We then compare economies using commodity monies with those using fiat money to determine whether one is preferred to the other.

3 A Model of Barter

If we look at primitive economies, we find that they were typically barter economies. A **barter economy** is one which the goods one owns are traded directly for the goods one wants to consume. In a barter economy, no particular good is used as a medium of exchange. For small economies with few goods, barter does not present many problems for the typical trader. However, as soon as an economy begins to produce a greater variety of goods and specialization in production develops, barter becomes increasingly inefficient. This is because trade in barter economies requires a "double coincidence of wants." For a successful trade in a barter economy, the person with whom you wish to trade must not only have what you want but also want what you have. The inefficiency is apparent; a great deal of time is spent merely finding someone with whom to trade. We turn now to a model that illustrates the advantages of using fiat money to facilitate trades when many types of goods exist.[1] Consider a model economy like the overlapping generations model of Chapter 2, but in which there are J different types of goods. Each person is endowed with y units of one type of good when young and nothing when old. Equal numbers of the young are endowed with each type of good. When young, people wish to consume the type of good with which they are endowed. When old, they will wish to consume one of the other types of goods. However, young people do not know what type of good they will want to consume when old.

There exists a fixed stock of M units of fiat money, which is also costlessly stored. In the first period, the stock of fiat money is owned by the initial old. To provide an alternative to fiat money, we assume that goods can be stored costlessly over time.

People live on a large number of spatially separated islands. Everyone on a given island has the same endowment and tastes. Hence, all young people on a given island will be endowed with the same type of good. For example, on island 1, young people are endowed with good 1, on island 2, each young person is endowed with good 2, and so on. When old, all people on a given island will desire to consume the same type of good, but it is a good other than the one with which they were endowed when young.

People who want to trade must travel in a group to a trading area, where a group from one island is matched at random with a group from another island seeking to trade. When the people from a pair of islands meet, they can reveal to each other the type of good they are carrying and the type of good they want. If the groups agree to trade, they do so and go home. If they do not both wish to trade, they split, and each is matched again with some other island. We assume that islands searching for trading partners can choose to search among the young or the old.

Exchange is costly in the following way. Each time a group from one island is matched with a group from another island, each person in the group loses α units of utility. This represents the bother of searching for a suitable trading partner.

Let us now identify patterns of trade through which people in this economy may acquire the goods they desire. Our goal is to answer the following question: Which method of payment has the lowest expected cost? It is that measure that we will use to pick the most preferred means of executing trades.

3.1 Direct Barter

The most direct way for these people to get what they want is to store some of their endowment until they are old and then trade what they have for what they want

---

[1] The model is taken from Freeman (1989). Kiyotaki and Wright (1989) and Maeda (1991) offer other interesting recent models for the use of money when there are many different goods.

Endowment / Goods Desired	a	b	c
a		*	*
b	*		*
c	*	*	

Figure 3.1. Endowments and desired goods. When old, no one wants to consume the same goods with which they are endowed. Only those combinations of endowments and goods desired marked by "*" are possible meetings where trade could occur.

to consume. Recall that, until they are old, they do not know what they want to consume.[2] When they know what they want, they can go out and seek a trade.

Let us now determine the probability on any given attempt that they will meet someone who has what they want and wants what they have. Figure 3.1 presents every possible combination of the good with which a person is endowed and the good that person wants to consume for $J = 3$, labeling the goods a, b, and c. The asterisks in Figure 3.1 represent the possible combinations of endowments and desires. If it were possible to desire when old the good with which one is endowed, there would be $J^2 = 9$ possible combinations. Because we rule out possibilities in which a person wants the same good when young and when old, three combinations are excluded, there are $J^2 - J = 6$ possible combinations. Assuming that each group is equally likely to meet any of the possible combinations at any given meeting, the probability of finding a match in which your trading partner has what you want and wants what you have is only $1/(J^2 - J)$ on any given attempt. If there are many types of goods (if J is large), $1/(J^2 - J)$ is a small number. For example, if there are 100 goods, the probability of a successful trade for a given encounter is only $1/(10,000 - 100) = 1/(9,900)$.

The small probability of finding someone who has what you want and wants what you have is a good illustration of Jevons' double coincidence of wants. The average (mean) number of attempts before finding a double coincidence of wants is $J^2 - J$, the inverse of the probability of success on any single try.[3] Given that each

---

[2] These people will not want to barter when young because they do not yet know what they will want to consume.

[3] Students of statistics know that the number of attempts before a success follows a geometric distribution. The mean of the geometric distribution is the probability of failure on any single trial (here, $1 - 1/[J^2 - J]$) divided by the probability of success on any one try, $1/(J^2 - J)$. Hence, in this problem, the average number of failures before a success is

$$\frac{1 - \frac{1}{J^2 - J}}{\frac{1}{J^2 - J}} = \left[1 - \frac{1}{J^2 - J}\right](J^2 - J) = (J^2 - J) - 1.$$

Because this number represents the average number of failures before a success, success will occur in the next search. Hence, the average number of searches (including the last successful one) is $J^2 - J$. In this problem, the

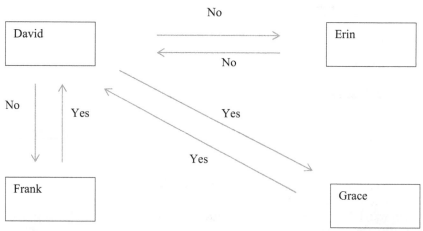

Figure 3.2. Direct barter meetings and double coincidence. The picture depicts three possible meetings that David could have in a barter economy. Everyone in this picture is old. The arrow points to a person who has a good. The "yes" or "no" indicates whether the person wants the good or not. With Frank, there is a single-coincidence meeting since David does not want Frank's good, but Frank does want David's good. With Erin, neither person wants what the other person has. With Grace, there is a double-coincidence meeting as each person wants what the other person has.

search costs α units of utility, the average search costs under barter are therefore $\alpha(J^2 - J)$.

Instead of having one-time meetings over your lifetime, we allow multiple meetings. In this setup, it is better to wait until you are old to meet since you do not know what you want. So any young meetings are costly without any expected benefit. Figure 3.2 shows the outcome of random meetings between David, who is old, and three other old people: Erin, Frank, and Grace. If David is matched with Erin, there is no trade because neither person wants what the other person has. If David is matched with Frank, David refuses to trade even though Frank wants the good that David has. If David is matched with Grace, barter exchange occurs because each person wants what the other person has. Overall, the direct barter dictates that an old person continues being matched, or searches, until the double coincidence occurs. By letting the consumption good be stored, the dominant strategy is for only old people to trade with one another. There is no intergenerational trade.

3.2 Monetary Exchange

An alternative pattern of trade uses fiat money as a medium of exchange. Suppose young people seek to trade their goods to the old for fiat money and then, when old, use fiat money to buy the goods they want.

---

number of attempts before a success approximates a geometric distribution because the probability of finding a match will rise as soon as almost everyone else has found a match. However, the difference is small in a large population of people seeking matches.

In this pattern of trade, people undertake two searches and exchanges over their lifetimes. Nevertheless, average lifetime search costs may be less with monetary exchange. In a single try, a young person's probability of finding an old person who wants what he is selling is $1/J$. The young person wants fiat money and does not care which type of old person is encountered, because all old people carry what the young person wants, fiat money. In other words, the double coincidence requires that the old person wants what the young person has since money is the generally accepted means of exchange. Therefore, the probability of a match on any given attempt is only $1/J$, which is greater than the probability of a match under barter, $1/(J^2 - J)$, where each side of the transaction cared about the type of good carried by the other side. With fiat money, it takes J searches on average for a successful trade.[4] Because each person undertakes two such searches, one when young and one when old, lifetime search costs will average $2\alpha J$ when people use money.

In the economy with money, young people do meet with old people. Instead of holding onto the consumption good, young people give up some of their endowment, just like in Chapter 2, in order to acquire money. There is still a double-coincidence problem, but money is generally accepted, meaning that anyone with money will always offer something that someone else wants. So trades occur as soon as the old person with money meets a young person who has the desired consumption good.

We see how money affects the frequency of exchange in Figure 3.3. In this setting, David is young while Erin, Frank and Grace are old. Both Frank and Grace want to consume the good David has, just as in the barter setting. (Erin does not want the good David has.) Compared with the direct barter case, there will be two successful meetings in the monetary economy. Because Frank and Grace offer money for David's goods, the meetings are successful. So we see that money gives rise to more *frequent* trades compared with direct barter.

Ultimately, we are interested in whether the expected search costs are lower in a monetary economy compared with a direct barter economy. Money allows successful meetings to occur more frequently. When there are enough different goods in the economy, expected search costs are lower in a monetary economy. To see this, we compare the search costs associated with using barter $[\alpha(J^2 - J)]$ with those when money is used $(2\alpha J)$. We find that the search costs when using barter are greater than those when using money if

$$\alpha \left(J^2 - J \right) > 2\alpha J \iff J > 3.$$

---

[4] As in the previous footnote, we compute the mean of the geometric distribution (mean number of failures before a success) as

$$\frac{probability\ of\ failure}{probability\ of\ success} = \frac{1 - \frac{1}{J}}{\frac{1}{J}} = \left(1 - \frac{1}{J} \right) J = J - 1.$$

Hence, on average, the first successful search occurs on the Jth attempt.

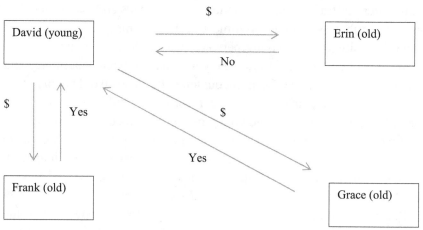

Figure 3.3. Money meetings. The picture depicts three possible meetings that David could have in a barter economy. In this setting, David is young and the other three people are old. The arrow points to a person who has a good. The "yes" or "no" indicates whether the person wants the good or not. In each meeting, the old person brings money indicated by an arrow with a "$." With Frank, there are two meetings that would yield a trade in this set of meetings. Both Frank and Erin want David's good while the meeting Grace depicts an unsuccessful meeting.

If there are more than three types of goods (if $J > 3$), average lifetime search costs are lower using money than barter. Although people must trade twice when using money, average search costs are lower (if $J > 3$) for a monetary exchange because people do not have to search until they find a double coincidence of wants. It is easier to find someone who wants to buy the endowment good with money, and then, when old, find someone who has the desired good and will accept money. The key to money's usefulness is that everyone accepts money in trade, whereas people who barter accept only the goods they desire.

Notice that the search cost advantage of money grows with the complexity of the economy. Figure 3.4 graphs the search costs associated with barter and money for different numbers of goods. As the number of types of goods J increases, search costs increase faster for barter $[\alpha(J^2 - J)]$ than for money $(2\alpha J)$; with barter, it becomes more and more difficult to find someone who has what you want and wants what you have. If goats and spears are the only two tradable commodities in a primitive village economy, it does not take very long for a goatherd to find a hungry spear maker with whom to trade. In contrast, in a complex modern economy, it may take some time for a hungry economist to find a restaurant owner who wants a lesson in monetary economics.

4 What Should Be Used as Money?

Nothing in our model of money and barter requires that the medium of exchange be fiat money. A commodity also can be used as a medium of exchange. Note

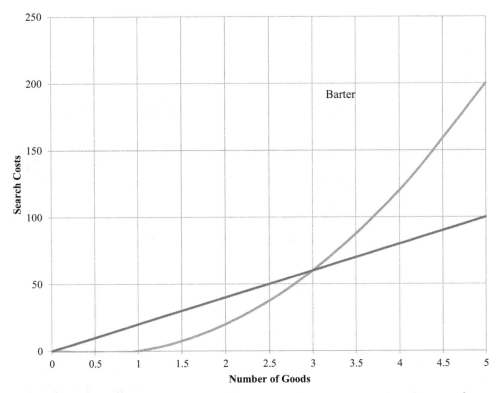

Figure 3.4. Search costs for barter and money. The plot shows that when there are fewer than three goods in the economy, the expected search costs associated with using barter are less than those associated with using fiat money. When there are more than three goods, however, the expected search costs associated with using fiat money are lower than those associated with using barter. The expected search costs associated with using barter rise exponentially with the number of goods.

that, as economies develop and a greater variety of goods are produced, the search costs associated with barter rise exponentially. As the number of wants and goods expands, people might come to accept one particular good in exchange for others even if they do not wish to consume that good. This can occur if people believe that it will then be possible to trade that good for one they want to consume. Once most people in the economy come to accept this special good, these barter economies essentially become monetary economies – more specifically, commodity money economies. An often-cited modern example of a commodity money is the cigarettes that circulated in prisoner-of-war camps in World War II.[5] Lacking any government currency, even nonsmoking prisoners of war came to accept cigarettes in trade, aware that the cigarettes could be used later to bribe guards or to trade for desired

---

[5] This example was introduced to economists by Radford's (1945) "The Economic Organization of a P.O.W. Camp." This nontechnical article still makes interesting reading.

goods. The example demonstrates that money is a natural economic phenomenon not dependent on government for its existence.

A good which everyone accepts in payment for goods is called a commodity money. More precisely, a "commodity money" is a good with intrinsic value (at least some people derive utility from consuming this good directly) that is used as a medium of exchange. A commodity money stands in contrast to fiat money, which has no intrinsic value.

In humankind's long history, the use of fiat monies is a rarity. Most economies either have used some valuable commodity as their medium of exchange or have backed their paper currency with a promise that it can be exchanged for some specified amount of a valuable commodity.

Which commodities will surface as media of exchange? The usefulness of a commodity or fiat money as a medium of exchange depends on its exchange costs.

4.1 Exchange Costs

Monetary exchange involves two trades – goods for money, then money for goods – whereas barter requires only one trade. If a money is costly to exchange, its advantage in reducing search costs may be offset by the costs of the second trade.

To be more precise, assume that there is an exchange cost of λ units of utility per person each time goods are accepted. This represents the bother of verifying the quantity and quality of goods exchanged or some other cost of transferring the goods from one island to another. Let λ denote the exchange cost of goods per person, and let λ_m denote the exchange cost associated with using money. An exchange cost is incurred whenever goods or money are accepted.

The lifetime exchange costs of barter are equal to λ because each person accepts delivery of goods once in a lifetime. Remember that in the barter economy people only trade when old since any consumption by young people is from their own endowment. In contrast, the exchange costs of monetary exchange equal $\lambda_m + \lambda$ because each person accepts money when young and goods when old. The average costs associated with money and barter are summarized in Table 3.1.

When the exchange cost of money λ_m is zero, barter and monetary exchange have the same lifetime exchange costs. Monetary exchange is then superior to barter because of money's lower search cost (if $J > 3$). If, however, money has an exchange cost, its advantage over barter in search costs may be offset by the extra cost of exchange occurred by making two trades instead of one.

It follows that people will want to use something easy to exchange as money. What makes something easy to exchange? It must be easy to recognize and measure. Fiat money tends to possess these properties. Hence, exchange costs for fiat money λ_m are approximately zero.

However, exchange costs with a commodity money system are typically not equal to zero. In fact, exchange costs with commodity money systems may be quite

Table 3.1. *Search and exchange costs for barter and money. Every meeting in which a trade occurs may also involve the costs of insuring the buyer is getting what they expected. This is what λ represents. In addition, we consider the case in which people accepting money must also verify the money is not counterfeit, which costs λ_M. The objective is to use the means of payment with the lowest expected total cost.*

	Expected Search Cost	Exchange Cost	Total Cost
Barter	$\alpha(J^2 - J)$	λ	$\alpha(J^2 - J) + \lambda$
Money	$2\alpha J$	$\lambda + \lambda_M$	$2\alpha J + \lambda + \lambda_M$

high. For example, early examples of commodity money took the form of chunks of precious metals called *bullion*.[6] People typically accepted these chunks of metal as payment for goods and services. A merchant who accepted bullion in exchange for goods had to assay the quality of the metal. Furthermore, accurate scales were needed to determine the weight of the metal. This process of verifying the quality of the money was costly. In the context of our model, λ_m, the exchange costs associated with using bullion as money were quite high relative to those that would be associated with using fiat money. This, as stated before, at least partially offset the lower search costs associated with the use of metals as money.

In an attempt to lower the exchange costs associated with commodity money, governments soon entered the picture by assaying metals and stamping them with their own insignia. This led to the minting of the metals into regular shapes (coins) stamped with their value.[7] The value that was stamped on the face of the coin was appropriately called the *face value* of the coin.

5 A Model of Commodity Money

Gold has two possible uses in this economy – consumption and trade. It follows that there are two possible equilibria – one in which gold is traded and not consumed and another in which gold is consumed. Let us look first at an equilibrium in which gold is traded but never consumed.

For purposes of this analysis, we modify the model economy so that there are two types of consumption good. Just as we did in Chapter 1, we assume there is a single, perishable type of consumption good. In addition, there is gold that can be consumed each period or used as money. Gold is not perishable. When

---

[6] For example, the Babylonians began using silver bullion as money in approximately 2000 BC.

[7] Herodotus attributes the origin of coinage to the kings of Lydia in the eighth century BC, although evidence exists that suggests coinage may have existed in India prior to this time.

young, a person is endowed with units of the perishable consumption good.[8] In each period, the young people consume a portion of their endowment and use the remainder to purchase gold. In this way, gold will be used to trade for second-period consumption. Given our notation, the number of units of the consumption good that will be used to purchase gold will be $v_t^g m_t^g$. This implies that the constraint facing each person in the first period of life is

$$c_{1,t} + v_t^g m_t^g \leq y. \tag{3.1}$$

When old, each person will trade holdings of gold for some of the consumption good. Therefore, the constraint facing each person in the second period of life is

$$c_{2,t+1} \leq v_{t+1}^g m_t^g. \tag{3.2}$$

Substituting Equation 3.2 into Equation 3.1, we find the combined budget constraint for a person born at time t:

$$c_{1,t} + \left[\frac{v_t^g}{v_{t+1}^g} \right] c_{2,t+1} \leq y. \tag{3.3}$$

We know that the market for gold must clear in each period. Recall that the supply of gold in each period is fixed at M^g. From Equations 3.1 and 3.2, we can see that each young person's demand for gold in period t is

$$m_t^g = \frac{y - c_{1,t}}{v_t^g}, \tag{3.4}$$

so that the total demand for gold is $[N(y - c_{1,t})/v_t^g]$. Equating the total supply of gold to the total demand for gold, we see that

$$M_t^g = \frac{N\left(y - c_{1,t}\right)}{v_t^g} \implies v_t^g = \frac{N\left(y - c_{1,t}\right)}{M_t^g}. \tag{3.5}$$

As usual, we restrict our attention to the stationary case where $c_{1,t} = c_1$ and $c_{2,t+1} = c_2$ for all t. In this case, we find that the value of gold in each period is

$$v^g = \frac{N\left(y - c_1\right)}{M^g}. \tag{3.6}$$

Note that in this stationary equilibrium, the value of gold is constant over time. This means that the rate of return of gold is 1 in every period ($v_{t+1}^g/v_t^g = 1$ for all t).

We have assumed in this equilibrium that gold is not consumed; the entire initial stock of gold is used as a medium of exchange. For this to represent the behavior of rational people, there must be no incentive for any person to consume gold. What condition ensures that this gold consumption does not take place? If people can obtain greater utility by trading gold for the consumption good, then they will

---

[8] You are likely to ask what happens to gold an old person has in possession. If used as money, the gold is transferred to young people as a means of payment. If used as a consumption good, an old person enjoys the consumption good. When an old person dies, we assume that it is distributed lump sum to young people next period.

not choose to consume their gold. In this case, the trading value of a unit of gold exceeds $\tilde{v}$, which is its intrinsic value. In other words, we must have that

$$v^g = \frac{N(y - c_1)}{M^g} > \tilde{v}. \tag{3.7}$$

In this case, trading 1 unit of the gold will give a person v_t^g units of the consumption good, which will generate a certain amount of utility. If people consumed gold, they would obtain the amount of utility associated with consuming $\tilde{v}$ units of the consumption good. Clearly, then, if $v_t^g > \tilde{v}$, the amount of utility obtained by trading gold for the consumption good is higher than that obtained by consuming the gold. This, in turn, implies that people will choose to trade their gold, utilizing it as a medium of exchange.

5.1 The Consumption of Gold

The other possibility is worth noting. Suppose that the trading value of gold is less than $\tilde{v}$. This will occur if

$$v^g = \frac{N(y - c_1)}{M^g} < \tilde{v}. \tag{3.8}$$

In this case, the initial old will choose to consume gold rather than trade it. If they sell their gold for some of the consumption good, their utility will be less than if they consume gold for its intrinsic value.

Will they consume all the gold? As they consume gold, the total stock of gold in the economy begins to fall. From Equation 3.6, we see that the price of gold will begin to rise. As long as the price of gold is less than $\tilde{v}$, this process will continue and the price of gold will increase. Eventually, the price of gold must rise to its intrinsic value. At this point, the consumption of gold will stop and then be used as a medium of exchange from that point forward in time. If we denote the amount of gold used for monetary purposes (not consumed) as M^{g*}, this variable is determined by

$$v_t^g = \frac{N(y - c_1)}{M^{g*}} = \tilde{v} \implies M^{g*} = \frac{N(y - c_1)}{\tilde{v}}. \tag{3.9}$$

The amount of gold in monetary use will be equal to the initial stock of gold minus the amount demanded for personal use (the amount consumed). More precisely, the real value (in units of the consumption good) of gold used as a medium of exchange, $\tilde{v}M^{g*}$, will be a quantity that will just equal $N(y - c_1)$. The amount of gold consumed by the initial old will be $M^g - M^{g*}$.

Because commodity money may be consumed, the quantity theory of money may not hold in quite the same way for commodity money that it did for fiat money. Recall that the quantity theory predicts that if two economies are identical except that the fiat money stock in one is twice as large as in the other, the price level will be twice as high (the value of money will be half as high) in the economy with the larger money stock. Prices adjust to the stock of money. Now consider two economies that are identical except that the gold stock in one is twice as large as in the other. If gold is never consumed but serves solely as a commodity money, prices simply will be twice as high in the economy with the larger stock of gold, just as they were in the case of fiat money. But if gold is consumed at the margin in both countries, with a trading value just equal to its intrinsic value, then the economy with a larger gold stock will consume gold until gold's trading value equals gold's intrinsic value. After the consumption of gold, the amount of gold used as money will be the same in the two economies. The intrinsic value of gold sets a minimum value for the trading value of gold, preventing higher nominal prices. If we consider the *initial* stock of gold in the two economies, the quantity theory does not hold because the price level in the economy with the larger initial stock of gold is not twice as high as the price level in the economy with the smaller gold stock. However, if we consider the stocks of gold actually *used as money* in the two economies, then the quantity theory does hold. In this case, the quantity theory holds because the stock of gold used as money adjusts to the price level and not because the price level adjusts to the stock of gold.

We see, then, that the price of gold will equal or exceed its intrinsic value if it is used as a medium of exchange – in other words, as a commodity money. This is a general feature of monetary systems, including commodity money systems; the trading value of a money may exceed its intrinsic value. This is not puzzling in light of the conclusions in Chapter 1. In the monetary equilibrium of that chapter, we saw that fiat money is valued even though it has an intrinsic value of zero. Like gold, fiat money, when used as a medium of exchange, may also have a price in excess of its intrinsic value. Money – whether fiat money or commodity money – may have value in excess of its intrinsic value because it provides a means of trading for goods desired (c_2) but otherwise unattainable.

Because the use of a commodity as money may raise its value, what serves as a medium of exchange in an economy has implications for the distribution of wealth. For example, if a commodity money system with $v_t^g > \tilde{v}$ were replaced with a fiat money system, the price of gold would fall to its intrinsic value of $\tilde{v}$. For this reason, owners of gold or other possible commodity monies are very interested in the medium of exchange used in their economy.

5.2 The Inefficiency of Commodity Money

Economists have often stated that commodity monies are inefficient.[9] What is meant by this statement? From the development of this chapter, we can gain useful insights into this claim.

---

[9] See, for example, Friedman (1960).

It is useful to compare the economy developed in this chapter with the fiat money economy in Chapter 2. In that chapter, we considered a monetary equilibrium in which there was a constant population and a constant money supply. Hence, the environment was similar to the environment of the commodity money economy of this chapter.

Recall the combined budget constraint governing individual choices in our commodity money economy (Equation 3.3, with a stationary equilibrium):

$$c_1 + \left[\frac{v_t^g}{v_{t+1}^g} \right] c_2 \leq y. \tag{3.10}$$

We found that, in this economy, the price of gold is constant over time, which implies a rate of return on gold of 1 ($v_{t+1}^g / v_t^g = 1$). Substituting this result, we find

$$c_1 + c_2 \leq y. \tag{3.11}$$

This represents the budget set available to future generations. Equation 3.11 shows that the budget set in the commodity money economy is identical to that in the comparable fiat money economy. The choices open to people of future generations are the same. Given identical preferences between the two economies, we expect people to choose the same (c_1^*, c_2^*) combination. With regard to future generations, the commodity money regime provides no advantages (or disadvantages) relative to the fiat money regime. All consumption possibilities that are attainable in the commodity money economy are also available in the fiat money economy. From the viewpoint of future generations, the inefficiency of commodity money systems is not apparent.

It is the initial old who are better off if our commodity money economy is switched to the use of fiat money as a medium of exchange. The initial old could use their holdings of fiat money to purchase some of the consumption good. The amount of the consumption good they could purchase with fiat money would be identical to the amount that could be purchased in the commodity money regime. In addition, they could consume all their holdings of gold, which gives them even more utility. Clearly, then, the consumption and utility of the initial old are higher in the fiat money regime than in the commodity money regime. It is important to keep in mind that this accomplished without diminishing the welfare of future generations.

The intuition is that with a commodity money system, resources that have intrinsic value are tied up to provide a medium of exchange. The fiat money system utilizes intrinsically worthless resources to provide the same services. In the case of a gold standard, precious metal that could be used to make jewelry or aeronautical equipment is used as money and is unavailable for these purposes. In this way, commodity money systems are inefficient. A fiat money system allows for the same trading patterns while freeing up a commodity that is useful for nonmonetary purposes.

6 Summary

The major goal of this chapter was to compare the efficiency of trade using barter or commodity money with that of trade using fiat money. This analysis is interesting because of the historical importance of barter and commodity money.

We found that search costs of barter exceed those of money when many types of goods are present in the economy. Intuitively, money facilitates trade by solving the double-coincidence-of-wants problem that is inherent in barter. The search cost advantage of using money expands as the number of types of goods becomes larger.

It is important to remember that the search cost advantage of money over barter holds whether the money we are considering is fiat money or commodity money. However, search costs are only part of the story. The use of money (trading goods for money and money for goods) requires twice as many exchanges as barter (trading goods for goods). Therefore, the exchange costs associated with using money may be higher than those associated with barter, partially offsetting money's lower search costs. To minimize exchange costs, a medium of exchange should be easily recognized and measured.

In the last part of the chapter, we compared welfare under two different monetary standards – a commodity money system and a fiat money system – assuming identical costs of search and exchange. We found that a commodity money system needlessly reserves as a medium of exchange goods that would give people utility if consumed. The switch to a fiat money system improves welfare by freeing those goods for individual consumption.

7 Exercises

3.1. Consider a fiat money/barter system like that portrayed in this chapter. Suppose the number of goods J is 100. Each search for a trading partner costs a person 2 units of utility.

    a. What is the probability that a given random encounter between people of separate islands will result in a successful barter?

    b. What are the average lifetime search costs for a person who relies strictly on barter?

    c. What are the average lifetime search costs for a person who uses money to make exchanges?

        Now let us consider exchange costs. Suppose it costs 4 units of utility to verify the quality of goods accepted in exchange and 1 unit of utility to verify that money accepted in exchange is not counterfeit.

    d. What are the total exchange costs of someone utilizing barter?

    e. What are the total exchange costs of someone utilizing money?

3.2. Consider a commodity money model economy like the one described in this chapter but with the following features: There are 100 identical people in every generation. Each person is endowed with 10 units of the consumption good when young and nothing when old. To keep things simple, let us assume that each young person wished to acquire money balances worth half of his endowment, regardless of the rate of return. The initial old own a total of 100 units of gold. Assume that people are indifferent between consuming 1 unit of gold and consuming 2 units of the consumption good.

a. Suppose the initial old choose to sell their gold for consumption goods rather than consume the gold. Write an equation that represents the equality of supply and demand for gold. Use it to find the number of units of gold purchased by each person, m_t^g, and the price of gold, v_t^g.

b. At this price of gold, will the initial old actually choose to consume any of their gold?

c. Would the initial old choose to consume any of their gold if the total initial stock of gold were 800? In this case, what would be the price of gold and the stock of gold after the initial old consumed some of their gold? Compare your answer in this part with your answer in part a. Does the quantity theory of money hold?

d. Suppose it is learned that a gold discovery will increase the stock of gold from 100 units to 200 units in period t^*. Assume the government uses the newly discovered gold to buy bread that will not be given back to its citizens. Find the price of gold at $t^* - 1$ and at t^*. Also find the rate of return of gold acquired at $t^* - 1$.

3.3. Consider a fiat money/barter system like that portrayed in this chapter. Suppose the number of goods J is 4. Each search for a trading partner costs a person 3 units of utility. In addition, suppose the exchange cost of goods is 2 units of utility. What is the maximum value of the exchange cost for money, λ_m, such that expected lifetime utility with money is at least as great as the expected lifetime utility under barter?

3.4. (advanced) Suppose the consumption of gold offers people a marginal utility that diminishes as that person consumes more gold. Assume also that gold can be mined in unlimited amounts at the constant marginal costs, χ, units of the nongold consumption good.

a. Can the trading value of gold exceed χ in equilibrium? Explain. What is the effect on gold consumption and mining of an increased use of gold as money?

b. Suppose instead that the marginal mining cost increases with the amount mined. What is now the effect on gold consumption and mining of an increased use of gold as money?

3.5. (advanced) Consider again the model economy described in Exercise 3.2, but suppose there is a second storable good, silver. Silver is as easy to exchange and store as gold. The initial old own a total of 50 units of silver. There can be no additions to the stock of silver. People are indifferent between consuming 1 unit of silver and 1 unit of the consumption good. Let v_t^s denote the trading value of a unit of silver.

a. Find the market-clearing condition if both silver and gold are used as money. Can there be an equilibrium in which both silver and gold are used only as money (are not consumed) and $v_t^s = 1.5? \ldots v_t^s = 2$? In each case, use the market-clearing condition to find the corresponding trading value of gold. For what range of values of v_t^s is there an equilibrium in which both silver and gold are used only as money (are not consumed)?

b. What would happen to the value of silver if the government passed a law banning the use of gold as money?

   c. If one member of the initial old owned the entire stock of silver, would that person prefer that gold alone, silver alone, or both gold and silver be used as money? Explain.

   d. If each member of the initial old owned 1/2 unit of silver and 2 units of gold, would the initial old prefer that gold alone, silver alone, or both gold and silver be used as money? Explain.

Chapter 4

Inflation

1 Roadmap

So far, we have shown that money is memory, it reduces transaction costs compared with barter and frees up resources compared with a commodity money economy. In Chapter 2, we focused on the demand for money. The next step is consider how changes in money supply affect economic decisions.

In this chapter, we learn that increasing the stock of fiat money represents a form of revenue for the government. Seigniorage is the name given to value of resources collected by the government from money creation. Revenues collected by the government also represent taxes paid by people; from taxpayer's perspective, the revenues are known as the inflation tax. Therefore, we have to specify how the government spends this revenue. In other words, just like people face a lifetime budget constraint, there is a government budget constraint. Our focus is to analyze the effect which this government policy has on people's welfare. In addition, we examine the revenue implications associated with different money growth rates.

2 Inflation

We have seen that we can find a role for money with either the simple, single-good model of Chapter 2 or the more complex multiple-good model of Chapter 3.[1] It can be verified that both models have essentially the same implications for the subject of this chapter, inflation, and for the subjects of later chapters. If two models have the same implications for a topic of interest, then it is generally preferable to work with the simpler model. For this reason, we use the single-good model of Chapter 2 as the framework for this and following chapters.

---

[1] See Freeman (1989).

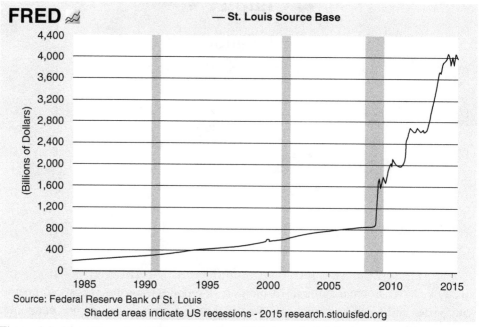

Figure 4.1. Money supply changes over time. This is a plot of the quantity of base money over the period 1985 through 2015. Recessions are identified by gray shaded bars. By this measure, the quantity of fiat money is not constant over time.

There is a very simple, compelling reason to examine the effects which changes in the fiat money supply have on economic decisions. Figure 4.1 plots the quantity of base money – the sum of currency in the hands of the nonbank public and total reserves – over the period 1985 through 2015. We use base money as the measure of the fiat money supply in our model economy. Base money is issued by the government. Certainly, there has been a dramatic increase in the quantity of base money since 2008. Even if you could look over the period from 1985 through 2007, you would see that the quantity of base money changed over time. This observation alone is sufficient to motivate our analysis of the effects that such changes have on economic decisions.

We begin in a very simplified version of the model economy in which money is the only store of value. In this way, we can see how changes in the money growth rate affects consumption when young versus consumption when old, welfare, and the demand for money.

3 A Growing Supply of Fiat Money

Let us now study the effects of an expansion of the supply of fiat money. First we consider money supply expansion in the simplest overlapping generations model with a constant population and a nonstorable consumption good. Contrary to what we saw in Chapter 2, no commodity money is present in the economy.

Let the money supply growth be such that

$$M_t = zM_{t-1} \tag{4.1}$$

for each period t where z, the gross rate of money supply expansion, is greater than 1. This implies that

$$M_t - M_{t-1} = M_t - \frac{M_t}{z} = \left(1 - \frac{1}{z}\right)M_t \tag{4.2}$$

units of new fiat money are printed each period. This new money is introduced into the economy by means of lump-sum subsidies (transfers) to each old people in every period t worth a_t units of the consumption good; that is,

$$N_{t-1}a_t = \left(1 - \frac{1}{z}\right)v_t M_t$$

or

$$a_t = \frac{\left(1 - \frac{1}{z}\right)v_t M_t}{N_{t-1}}. \tag{4.3}$$

To find a_t, we multiplied the new created money by the value of money to find its real value and then divided it by the number of old people among whom it will be distributed to find its value per old person.

Equation 4.3 is our first example of the "government budget constraint," an equilibrium condition that will prove essential in the analysis of government policy. The government budget constraint y says that the government (like a person) cannot spend more than it takes in. In this case, the expenses of government are its gifts to old people, and its revenue is the new fiat money it has printed.

It is important that these subsidies be made in a lump-sum fashion so that we can study the effect of money supply expansion in isolation. A subsidy (or tax) is "lump sum" if the amount given to (or taken away) from any person does not depend on any decision made by that particular person. The subsidy returns the new money to the public. In this way, we ensure that the expansion of the money stock does not represent a transfer of resources from the public to the government, a case we will consider later in this chapter.

We start with a person's budget constraints. When young, each person receives an endowment worth y units of the consumption good. The resources are used to consume when young and to acquire money balances. So we write,

$$c_{1,t} + v_t m_t \le y. \tag{4.4}$$

When old, each person has the date $t + 1$ value of money balances plus a lump-sum transfer provided by the government worth a_{t+1} units of the consumption good.

$$c_{2,t+1} \le v_{t+1}m_t + a_{t+1}. \tag{4.5}$$

After solving Equation 4.5 for the value m_t we substitute into Equation 4.3, obtaining the lifetime budget constraint as

$$c_{1,t} + \frac{v_t}{v_{t+1}} c_{2,t+1} \leq y + \frac{v_t}{v_{t+1}} a_{t+1}. \tag{4.6}$$

The equality of supply and demand in the market for money is

$$v_t M_t = N_t (y - c_{1,t}). \tag{4.7}$$

Using stationarity,[2] we can solve this for v_t to get

$$v_t = \frac{N_t (y - c_1)}{M_t}. \tag{4.8}$$

The rate of return of fiat money is given by

$$\frac{v_{t+1}}{v_t} = \frac{\frac{N_{t+1}(y-c_1)}{M_{t+1}}}{\frac{N_t(y-c_1)}{M_t}} = \frac{M_t}{M_{t+1}} = \frac{M_t}{zM_t} = \frac{1}{z}. \tag{4.9}$$

Because the population is constant, the N terms in Equation 4.9 cancel out.

Equation 4.9 tells us that when $z > 1$, the value of money declines over time. Furthermore, the larger the value of z, the lower the rate of return on money. In other words, expansion of the money supply creates inflation as more dollars (for example) bid for the same number of goods. The resulting inflation is easily seen by recalling that $p_t = 1/v_t$ and analyzing how the price level evolves over time. This is done by looking at the ratio of next period's price level to this period's price level (this ratio is the "gross inflation rate") and using the results of Equation 4.9:

$$\frac{p_{t+1}}{p_t} = \frac{\frac{1}{v_{t+1}}}{\frac{1}{v_t}} = \frac{v_t}{v_{t+1}} = z \tag{4.10}$$

$$\implies p_{t+1} = zp_t. \tag{4.11}$$

When $z > 1$, Equation 4.11 predicts that the price level increases over time at the same rate as the fiat money stock. For example, if $z = 1.05$, the price level grows at the same 5 percent net rate at which the fiat money stock is growing. In this way, the price level remains proportional to the size of the money stock, as predicted by the quantity theory of money.

3.1 The Budget Set with Monetary Growth

We found in Equation 4.9 that the rate of return of fiat money (v_{t+1}/v_t) in a stationary equilibrium is $1/z$. Substituting this into the lifetime budget set (Equation 4.6),

---

[2] In Equation 3.32 of the appendix, it is verified that a stationary equilibrium is consistent with a constant subsidy, a.

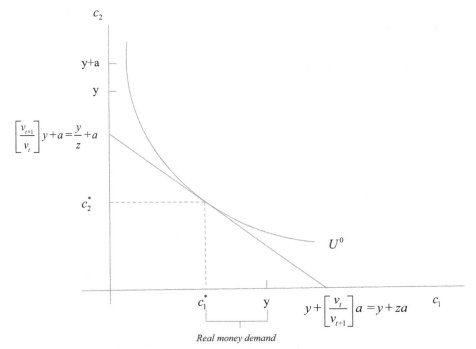

Real money demand

Figure 4.2. Equilibrium with growth of the money supply. The lifetime budget line is drawn for the case in which the fiat money stock is growing at rate z and the newly printed money is given to old people in the form of a lump-sum transfer. People chose the consumption bundle where the budget line is tangent to the indifference curve labelled U^0. For each young persons, the real money demand is marked in the diagram.

we find

$$c_1 + zc_2 \leq y + za. \tag{4.12}$$

In Figure 4.2, the budget set with inflation is graphed with a typical indifference curve that indicates the monetary equilibrium (c_1^*, c_2^*). Note that inflation $(z > 1)$ has altered our graph of the budget set in two ways. First, the budget line is flatter. This means that to get a unit of good when old, a person must give up more units when young than when there was no inflation. This reflects the lower rate of return offered by money when new money is being created. Second, the budget set intercepts the horizontal axis at $y + za$ instead of y, because a person's income now includes both the endowment and the subsidy.[3]

Common sense tells us that in order to make gifts (subsidies) to people, a government that owns no goods can raise revenue for the gifts only by taking goods

---

[3] Note that the budget line from $c_1 = y$ to $c_1 = y + za$ (the intercept) is dashed. For people to consume more than y when young $(c_1 > y)$, they must hold no money balances and also borrow from others, promising to repay the loan from the subsidy they will receive when old. Although any single person has this choice, no one is willing to lend when everyone is alike, so this option is never actually used. Therefore, although we mention this option here for completeness, we hereafter ignore it when presenting the budget equations and lines.

from private citizens (i.e., through taxation). Money creation may seem to be the way to raise revenue without taxation. Is this really so? The government can create that money out of thin air (or cheap paper), but the real value of government subsidy must come from somewhere. The feasible set is not magically expanded when the government decides to print additional intrinsically useless pieces of paper. Because the total number of goods in the economy is fixed at the total endowment $(N_t y)$, the gifts to old people can come only from losses sustained by them or by others.

Who loses goods when the government expands the fiat money stock? When the government expands the stock of fiat money, the stock of money currently held by private citizens falls in value. The new money competes with the old to purchase the goods of the young and drives down the value of all money. The loss sustained by the owners of the old money works as a tax on their money holdings.

Note that the value lost to the "tax" effected by the expansion of the money stock is proportional to the amount of money held (the more money held, the more one loses through inflation). In other words, the expansion of the money stock lowers the rate of return on fiat money. To reduce one's exposure to this tax on money balances, one can reduce one's use of money. In this way, inflation induces people to conserve on their use of money; the incentive for holding money is reduced.

3.2 The Inefficiency of Inflation

Let us return to the question of the optimality of expanding the money stock. To judge whether the equilibrium with inflation is optimal, we must compare it with the other possible alternatives. As in Chapter 2, this translates into comparing the budget set, which shows the options available to people in a monetary equilibrium, with the feasible set, which details the consumptions allocations that are feasible for the economy. If the budget set coincides with the feasible set, as it did in Chapter 2, then the golden rule allocation is attainable under the monetary equilibrium.

The government's expansion of the fiat money stock should have no effect on what is feasible in this economy. Merely printing more pieces of paper does not alter the stock of goods available for distribution between the consumption of the young and old. The feasible set is therefore exactly the one we found in Equations 1.4 to 1.6 of Chapter 1:

$$N_t c_{1,t} + N_{t-1} c_{2,t} \leq N_t y,$$

which, for a constant population and a stationary allocation, simplifies to

$$N c_1 + N c_2 \leq N y$$

or

$$c_1 + c_2 \leq y.$$

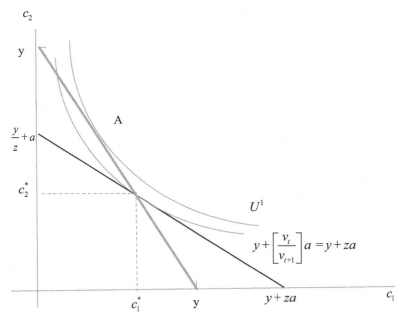

Figure 4.3. The inefficiency of inflation. Compare the budget line (thin line) and the feasible set line (thick line). The monetary equilibrium with a growing money stock results in lower welfare; in other words, inflation is inefficient. Point A yields the higher level of utility for both future generations and the initial old compared with the monetary equilibrium represented by the bundle (c_1^*, c_2^*) Point A is feasible but unattainable in the monetary equilibrium with inflation because it lies outside the budget set. Point could be attained in a monetary equilibrium with a constant fiat money stock.

To compare the monetary equilibrium with its feasible alternative allocations, in Figure 4.3 we superimpose the feasible set line on the monetary equilibrium graphed in Figure 4.2.[4] In this diagram, the feasible set line is represented by the thick line and the budget line is represented by the thin line. The feasible set line starts at y on the vertical axis and intersects the budget line at (c_1^*, c_2^*), as shown in Figure 4.3. If (c_1^*, c_2^*) lay in the interior of the feasible set, it would imply that someone was throwing goods away, an action not consistent with utility maximization. If it lay outside the feasible set, people would be consuming more goods than exist, which is impossible. Therefore, the equilibrium consumption bundle (c_1^*, c_2^*) must lie on the edge of the feasible set; that is, the feasible set line passes through (c_1^*, c_2^*).

In examining Figure 4.3, recall that, because (c_1^*, c_2^*) represents the maximum utility possible in the budget set, the consumption bundle (c_1^*, c_2^*) is located where some indifference curve (U^0 in Figure 4.3) is tangent to the budget line at (c_1^*, c_2^*).

Note also that the absolute value of the slope of the budget line is $1/z$ and that the absolute value of the slope of the feasible set is 1. Given that $(1/z) < 1$, the budget

---

[4] This graph and its proof of the inefficiency of inflation are taken from Wallace (1980).

line is flatter than the feasible set. Because the feasible set line goes through (c_1^*, c_2^*) but at a different slope, it cannot also be tangent to the indifference curve U^0 but must intersect it. This tells us that in the feasible set there are points of higher utility for the future generations than the monetary equilibrium (c_1^*, c_2^*). One such point is A on indifference curve U^1.

Point A is preferred by the future generations over (c_1^*, c_2^*) because it lies on a higher indifference curve. Furthermore, because second-period consumption is higher at point A than at (c_1^*, c_2^*), the initial old also prefer point A over (c_1^*, c_2^*).

Because point A is preferred by future generations over (c_1^*, c_2^*), why did the future generations not choose it? The answer is that point A is not in their budget set. The rate of return on fiat money is too low for future generations to be able to consume at point A. If a person were to consume the amount of first-period consumption associated with point A, their money holdings would be too small to afford the level of second-period consumption associated with that point. This is because of the low rate of return on fiat money. We know that the best the future generations can do, given this policy of monetary expansion, is to choose (c_1^*, c_2^*) where their budget line is tangent to an indifference curve.

Recall from Chapter 1 (Figure 1.8) that, in the absence of money creation, the budget set was identical to the feasible set. To see this, realize that if there is no expansion of the money stock, $z = 1$ and $a = 0$. For these values of z and a, the budget set is identical to the feasible set drawn in Figure 4.3. Therefore, when the fiat money stock is fixed, people are free to choose A, the best feasible point for future generations. It follows that future generations prefer the monetary equilibrium without an expanding money supply.

Figure 4.3 can help us uncover the welfare cost of expanding the money stock. The inflation caused by money creation does not destroy any goods; people still consume at the boundary of the feasible set. However, they consume a different combination of c_1 and c_2 with inflation than they would consume without it. They choose to consume less of good c_2, whose purchase requires use of fiat money (and more of the other good, c_1) because of the lower rate of return on fiat money. In other words, the tax on money balances induces future generations to reduce their demand for money $(y - c_1)$ to a level below the quantity each person would hold in the efficient equilibrium. Moreover, the drop in the demand for fiat money reduces the value of the initial money balances owned by the initial old, thus also reducing their utility.

We should be careful about interpreting this model. A literal interpretation may lead us to conclude that the cost of inflation is that people are induced to consume too much when young and not enough when old.

What, then, is the cost of inflation? People are induced by fiat money's low rate of return to consume needlessly less of goods that require the use of money. In our model, c_2 represents a market good whose acquisition requires the use of fiat money and c_1 is a nonmarket good that can be acquired without the use of money (leisure is a good real-world example).

To better understand, one can interpret the model as follows: Let the endowment in the first period of life be an endowment of time, which can be spent in any combination of leisure or labor. Leisure is that part of the time endowment consumed immediately, c_1 in the notation we have been using. Each unit of labor produces 1 unit of goods, which can be sold to the old for fiat money. The worker then spends the money in the second period of life. In this interpretation, the key economic decision of the model is not one of a person saving for retirement but of a person who works during the week to acquire money to spend on the weekend.

What is the cost of inflation under this interpretation of the model? Inflation discourages the consumption of the market good c_2 in favor of the consumption of leisure c_1, which a person can acquire without the use of money. By discouraging the use of money, inflation also discourages the supply of labor to be exchanged for money. In this way, inflation may affect aggregate output in addition to the timing of consumption.

More generally, we might say that inflation causes people to economize needlessly on the benefits offered by the use of money to conduct transactions. Therefore, inflation will reduce welfare in any model or real economy where money offers benefits of any sort to those who use it and people face a nontrivial choice of how much money to hold.[5]

3.3 The Golden Rule Monetary Policy in a Growing Economy

Up to this point in the chapter, we have held the population constant. We would like to see how the results of this chapter change if we allow for a growing population. With such a modification of the environment, we can then analyze an economy in which fiat money supply and demand both change over time.

Consider our basic overlapping generations model when the consumption good cannot be stored and the economy is growing so that $N_t = nN_{t-1}$ for every period t, where n is greater than 1. Let $M_t = zM_{t-1}$. Any increases in the fiat money stock will finance a lump-sum gift of a_{t+1} goods to each old person in period $t + 1$. Hence, this setup will be identical to the one just covered, except that we now allow for a growing population. What will be the rate of return on fiat money in this economy?

If we set the supply of money equal to its demand in period t and period $t + 1$, we have the expression for the real return of money like those we found previously in Equations 2.19 and 4.9

$$\frac{v_{t+1}}{v_t} = \frac{\frac{N_{t+1}(y-c_1)}{M_{t+1}}}{\frac{N_t(y-c_1)}{M_t}} = \frac{\frac{N_{t+1}}{M_{t+1}}}{\frac{N_t}{M_t}} = \frac{N_{t+1}}{N_t}\frac{M_t}{M_{t+1}} = \frac{nN_t}{N_t}\frac{M_t}{zM_t} = \frac{n}{z}. \tag{4.13}$$

---

[5] The literature's first formal discussion of the welfare cost of inflation was by Bailey (1956). For a more modern survey, see Abel (1987).

As before, we are making use of the fact that, in a stationary equilibrium, $a_{t+1} = a$ and $c_{1,t} = c_1$ for all t. The other cancellations occur because of the assumptions about how the fiat money stock and the population change over time.

Because we restrict ourselves to stationary equilibria, in which money demand per person is the same in every period, the only source of change in total money demand in our model is the growth in population.

The budget line in this economy is the same one we found in Equation 4.6:

$$c_{1,t} + \left[\frac{v_t}{v_{t+1}}\right] c_{2,t+1} \leq y + \left[\frac{v_t}{v_{t+1}}\right] a_{t+1}, \tag{4.14}$$

but with $v_t/v_{t+1} = z/n$ and stationarity:

$$c_1 + \left[\frac{z}{n}\right] c_2 \leq y + \left[\frac{z}{n}\right] a_t. \tag{4.15}$$

Again, we must compare the budget set with the feasible set. The printing of money does not alter what is feasible, so the feasible set remains

$$N_t c_{1,t} + N_{t-1} c_{2,t} \leq N_t y \tag{4.16}$$

which, in a stationary allocation with a growing population, simplifies to

$$c_1 + \left[\frac{1}{n}\right] c_2 \leq y. \tag{4.17}$$

Again, we note that the expansion of the money stock does nothing to alter what is feasible (neither z nor a appears in Equation 4.17).

To compare the monetary equilibrium with the feasible set, we graph the two together (the feasible set line is the thick line). As before, we take advantage of our knowledge that the point of maximum utility in the budget set (point B in Figure 4.4) must lie on the edge of the feasible set.

In Figure 4.4, we see that there are many feasible points (such as A) that offer greater utility to both future generations and the initial old than does the monetary equilibrium (point B). Point A lies on a higher indifference curve, indicating that the future generations prefer it, and it offers more c_2, indicating that the initial old prefer it.

The expansion of the money stock ($z > 1$) distorts the budget set by changing its slope from n to n/z. In this way, the budget set is no longer the same as the feasible set. This means that the budget set no longer offers a person a choice of all feasible allocations. In Figure 4.4, for example, we can see that, although allocation A is feasible and is preferred to allocation B, it is not available within the person's budget set. People cannot choose allocation A because the expansion of the money stock lowers the rate of return to fiat money below n, taxing people's money balances. People who hold more money in an effort to get to allocation A would find themselves not at A but at a point below A on the budget line. They do not get to A

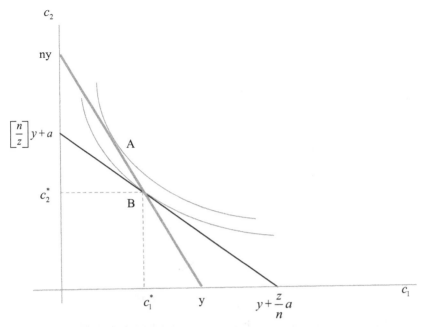

Figure 4.4. Equilibrium in an economy with positive population growth and monetary expansion. The monetary equilibrium when the fiat money stock increases at the rate z and the population grows at rate n is represented by Point B in the diagram. The monetary equilibrium is inefficient because the allocation represented by Point A is not attainable. Point A's allocation is preferred to all the monetary equilibrium with increasing fiat money stock.

because the more money they hold, the more value they lose to the newly printed money.

3.4 A Government Policy to Fix the Price Level

In the case just analyzed, the population grew at the rate n, implying that the total endowment of the economy also grew at this rate. We saw in Chapter 2 that the value of a unit of money rises with time when the economy is growing but the money stock is fixed. Many economists have suggested that if the economy is growing, the money supply should grow at the same rate to keep the value of money constant.[6] Let us examine this policy suggestion in two steps. First, let us ask what rate of fiat money creation will maintain constant prices. Second, let us ask whether such a policy will make people better off.

From Equation 4.13, we see that, to keep the value of money (and thus the price level) constant, the rate of expansion of the fiat money stock z must be set to equal the rate of growth of money demand, which is the rate of growth of the population

---

[6] Notably, Friedman (1960). Friedman (1969) no longer supported this view in "The Optimum Quantity of Money."

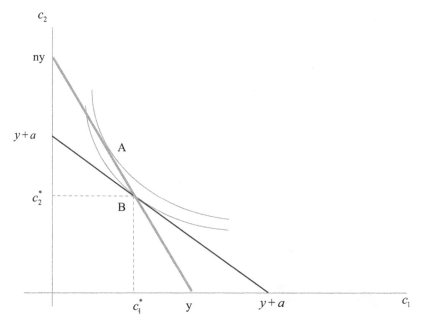

Figure 4.5. A monetary equilibrium when the government fixes the price level. In this diagram, we assume the government sets the money growth rate equal to the growth rate of the economy; that is, $z = n$. The monetary equilibrium is at Point B in the diagram. The monetary equilibrium is inefficient because the allocation represented by Point A is feasible and preferred to the constant-price monetary equilibrium.

n. Speaking more generally, we will maintain a constant value of money when the stock of fiat money expands at the same rate as the demand for fiat money.

The question that remains is whether it is desirable to increase the money stock at the same rate at which money demand is growing. To answer this question, we must compare the monetary equilibrium with $z = n$ to the feasible set when $n > 1$. When z is equal to n, the lifetime budget set in a stationary monetary equilibrium (Equation 4.15) becomes

$$c_1 + c_2 \leq y + a.$$

This budget set, along with the feasible set (which is still given by Equation 4.17), is displayed in Figure 4.5. As we can see from the diagram, there are many points, like point A, that everyone prefers to the monetary equilibrium (represented by point B). Point A is feasible and is preferred to point B by both the future generations and the initial old. Future generations prefer point A because it lies on a higher indifference curve. The initial old prefer point A because it represents more second-period consumption.

What is wrong with this policy of setting z equal to n? When the price level is fixed, a person's budget set has slope equal to -1. This tells the person that, by consuming one less good today, he will receive one more good in the next period. In other words, the budget set tells the person that goods are equally available in every period. However, this is not the true state of the economy. The economy is growing. Therefore, if in each generation young people consume one less good when young, there will be n extra goods available for old people in each generation. In other words, the economy can provide n goods for old people for each single good not consumed by young people. For this reason, the feasible set has the slope $-n$.

The message that the economy can offer n goods to the old for each good not consumed by the young is not conveyed through the budget set if prices are constant over time. Because the rate of return on money is 1, people see instead that giving up one good when young will get them only one good when old. As a result, at the monetary equilibrium B, people consume more when young and less when old than at the best feasible allocation A.

How, then, can we convey to people the message of the extra availability of goods for the old? The budget set faced by individuals must be identical to the feasible set. We saw in Chapter 2 that the feasible and budget sets (Equations 2.15 and 2.20, respectively) are identical when there is no expansion of the fiat money stock. When there is no change in the fiat money stock, fiat money offers the rate of return n, which signals to people the true state of the growing economy; for each good not consumed by a young person, an old person can consume n goods. In this case, the budget set is identical to the feasible set, so that people who choose the highest level of utility afforded by their budget are selecting the point with the highest feasible utility. For this reason, the golden rule monetary policy is to maintain a fixed stock of fiat money, whatever the growth rate of the economy. Although the policy prescription that the growth rate of the money supply should be set equal to the growth rate of the economy (here, $z = n$) keeps the price level constant, this policy does not maximize the utility of future generations.

4 Financing Government Purchases

In the preceding section, we found that the government was able to costlessly print new units of fiat money that were valued by the public. It follows that a government that needs to raise revenue for government purchases of goods may do so by printing new units of fiat money. The use of money creation as a revenue device is called "seigniorage." Let us examine the welfare effects of such a policy.

Again, let $M_t = zM_{t-1}$ for every period t, where z is a constant greater than 1. This implies that

$$M_t - M_{t-1} = (z - 1)M_{t-1} = \left(1 - \frac{1}{z}\right)M_t \tag{4.18}$$

units of new fiat money are created each period. This rate of money creation can finance the government's acquisition of

$$G_t = \left[1 - \frac{1}{z}\right]v_t M_t \tag{4.19}$$

goods per period. Denote (constant) government purchases per old person as $g = G_t/N_{t-1}$. Equation 4.19 is the government's budget constraint when the revenue from printing money is used to finance government purchases of goods (in contrast to the government subsidies already studied).

We assume that the goods the government acquires from its seigniorage revenue are used in such a way as not to affect an individual's consumption bundle choice. We might think of such an expenditure as foreign aid or defense expenditures, which may be necessary or desirable but have no direct effect on the relative desirability of c_1 or c_2. For simplicity, we could even think of the government as merely dumping the acquired goods into the ocean. We make this assumption so that we may study the effects of acquiring revenue for the government in isolation from the benefits of the government purchases.

The problem of the individual is the same as it was in the case with no subsidy in that the budget line is still $c_{1,t} + \left[\frac{v_t}{v_{t+1}}\right]c_{2,t+1} = y$, as in Equation 2.4.

We can again use the equality of supply and demand in the money market $v_t M_t = N_t[y - c_{1,t}]$ (Equation 2.5) and stationarity to get an equation for v_t,

$$v_t = \frac{N_t(y - c_1)}{M_t}. \tag{4.20}$$

Assume, for now, that the population is constant ($N_t = N$ for every period t). Then

$$\frac{v_{t+1}}{v_t} = \frac{\frac{N_{t+1}(y - c_1)}{M_{t+1}}}{\frac{N_t(y - c_1)}{M_t}} = \frac{M_t}{M_{t+1}} = \frac{1}{z}. \tag{4.21}$$

Note that because the money supply increases at the same rate in each period, we again looked at the stationary solution ($c_{1,t} = c_1$ for all t). Through cancellation of terms, we know that the value of money declines when money is created in a nongrowing economy. In other words, money creation causes inflation because an increasing number of dollars bid for the same number of goods.

Given that the rate of return on fiat money is $1/z$, the individual's lifetime budget constraint becomes

$$c_1 + zc_2 \leq y. \tag{4.22}$$

In Figure 4.6, the resulting budget set is graphed with an arbitrarily drawn indifference curve indicating the monetary equilibrium (c_1^*, c_2^*). Note two effects of an increase in z. As before, the slope of the budget line has been made flatter, which implies that an individual must give up more of c_1 to get a unit of c_2 in the presence of inflation because money has a lower rate of return. In addition, we now find that the budget set has shrunk; it lies inside the budget set without inflation. This occurs because the goods acquired by the expansion of the money stock are now being used up by the government instead of being returned to individuals as a subsidy.

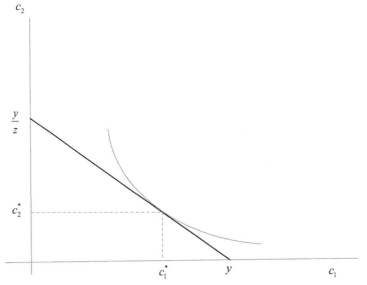

Figure 4.6. A monetary equilibrium in an economy with seigniorage used to finance purchases of government goods. The monetary equilibrium is represented by (c_1^*, c_2^*). The rate of money growth determines the slope of the budget line. Note that the horizontal intercept is now at y because the transfer payment was eliminated.

4.1 Is Inflation an Efficient Tax?

As before, to discuss the optimality of this monetary equilibrium, we need to find the feasible set to see if any feasible allocations are preferred to the monetary equilibrium (c_1^*, c_2^*). To find the feasible set, we look at the total resources available and require that they not be exceeded by the goods used up. However, now we must be sure to include the goods used up by the government so that we compare the utility of individuals given the same level of government purchases G_t. Therefore, the feasible set for stationary allocations is now given by

$$N_t c_1 + N_{t-1} c_2 + G_t \leq N_t y. \tag{4.23}$$

To get the per-capita form, divide through by N_t

$$c_1 + \left[\frac{N_{t-1}}{N_t} \right] c_2 + \frac{G_t}{N_t} \leq y \tag{4.24}$$

$$\Longrightarrow c_1 + \frac{c_2}{n} + g \leq y.$$

For $N_t = N$ (constant population so that $n = 1$),

$$c_1 + c_2 + g \leq y. \tag{4.25}$$

From Equation 4.25, we see that the new feasible set touches the horizontal axis at $c_1 = y - g$. We also know that the monetary equilibrium (c_1^*, c_2^*) lies on the

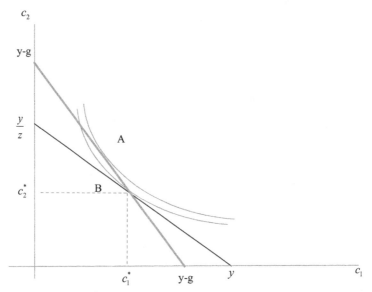

Figure 4.7. The inflation tax creates a distortion. The monetary equilibrium is inefficient when the government uses seigniorage to finance government purchases. As we have seen before, the monetary equilibrium – represented by the bundle (c_1^*, c_2^*) – is not the most preferred bundle. Indeed, there are many bundles, such as Point A, which are feasible, provide the same level of government revenue, and are preferred to $\frac{y}{z}$.

line defining the feasible set because, after the government has taken its share, no consumer will elect to throw goods away.

We can use this information to add the feasible set to Figure 4.6, as we do in Figure 4.7. Note that, because the indifference curve is tangent to the budget line with a slope of $-1/z$, the feasible set line going through (c_1^*, c_2^*) with a slope of -1 must intersect the indifference curve if $z \neq 1$. This implies that the feasible set can reach a higher indifference curve than can the budget set. Therefore, a move from (c_1^*, c_2^*) to A, as shown in Figure 4.7, benefits the current young and future generations. Also, because this move increases second-period consumption c_2, it also benefits the initial old. Therefore, the monetary equilibrium in this case is not optimal because point A, among other allocations, will make everyone better off.

4.2 A Nondistorting Tax

Can we get a budget set of a monetary equilibrium to reflect the feasible set and so make point A attainable? Yes. Consider a fixed tax of τ goods collected from each old person. We refer to such a tax as a *lump-sum tax* because the amount paid to the government is not affected by any actions the individual may undertake. The equations defining this budget when young and old become

$$c_{1,t} + v_t m_t = y \quad \text{and} \quad c_{2,t+1} = v_{t+1} m_t - \tau \tag{4.26}$$

or, combined,

$$c_{1,t} + \left[\frac{v_t}{v_{t+1}}\right] c_{2,t+1} = y - \left[\frac{v_t}{v_{t+1}}\right] \tau. \qquad (4.27)$$

If the entire amount of government purchases is raised through lump-sum taxation ($\tau = g$), the money supply is held constant. As we found before, the rate of return on money (v_{t+1}/v_t) in a stationary equilibrium will equal 1 when both population (i.e., money demand) and the stock of money are fixed over time. (You will be asked to study the case of a growing population in Example 4.1.) The budget set for $\tau = g$ and $z = 1$,

$$c_1 + c_2 + y - g, \qquad (4.28)$$

is identical to the per-capita feasible set. Therefore, the point of the maximum feasible utility for the future generations (point A) also lies within the budget set and is thus attainable by individuals. By using lump-sum taxes, the government raised the desired revenue with no distortion of the budget set – that is, without inducing people to reduce their money balances in an effort to avoid inflation's implicit tax on those money balances. Moreover, with lump-sum taxation, the demand for fiat money is greater than when revenue is raised through inflation, implying a greater real value of the money balances owned by the initial old. This, in turn, implies an improvement in the welfare of the initial old.

We see from the previous work that money creation is inferior to lump-sum taxation as a revenue device. Indeed, any tax on an economic activity (unless activity is socially undesirable) is inferior to a lump-sum tax because it reduces the incentive to undertake that activity. Given that we do not see lump-sum taxes in the real world (perhaps because societies want the rich to pay more than the poor), seigniorage may just be one of the many imperfect taxes in an imperfect world.

An obvious advantage of printing money to raise revenue is the means with which it is executed. It requires no army of accountants or police; the only administrative costs are the costs of printing the notes. It costs pennies to produce a $1,000 bill (or a $1 bill). This may explain the heavy use of money creation in poorer nations that may be lacking the extensive informational infrastructure required to enforce income taxes.

The burden of seigniorage falls on those who hold currency. Although everyone uses currency to make purchases, most U.S. currency is held by nonresidents or by people engaged in illegal activities who do not want their transactions observed.[7] Seigniorage may then be desirable as a way to tax these groups.[8]

---

[7] See Avery, Elliehausen and Kennickell (1987).
[8] The case for seigniorage is made by Aiyagari (1990).

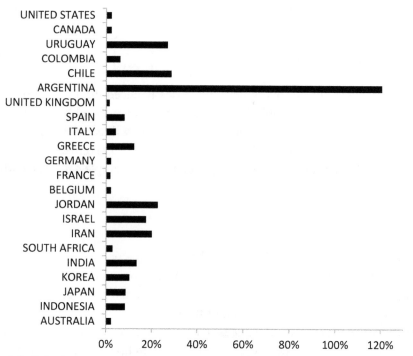

Figure 4.8. Seigniorage revenue as a percentage of government revenues. Reliance on seigniorage as a source of government revenue varies across countries. Although the use of seigniorage varies most substantially across regions of the world, we also see substantial variation within regions. *Source:* International Monetary Funds, *International Financial Statistics*, Tables 14a for base money and 81 for nominal government revenue, respectively.

The use of seigniorage as a source of government revenue varies from country to country.[9] For most developed countries during normal times, seigniorage contributes very little to government revenue. In the United States, during the period from 1948 to 1989, on average, seigniorage accounted for less than 2 percent of total federal government revenues and for about 0.3 percent of gross national product (GNP). Alternatively, Fischer (1982) found significant reliance on seigniorage in high-inflation countries like Argentina, Uruguay, Chile, and Brazil. As an example, seigniorage accounted for approximately 46 percent of Argentinian government revenues (6.2 percent of GNP) for the period from 1960 to 1975. Figure 4.8 presents data on seigniorage revenue as a percentage of total government revenue for several countries.

An extreme case in point is provided by Germany during its hyperinflation of the early 1920s. To help finance subsidies to workers in the French-occupied Ruhr and other government expenditures after World War I, Germany turned to the

---

[9] For an excellent cross-country accounting of revenue from seigniorage, see Fischer (1982). See Barro (1982) for seigniorage estimates for the United States.

printing press. As a result, seigniorage revenue was eventually 10 to 15 percent of GNP.[10]

Example 4.1 Let $N_t = nN_{t-1}$ and $M_t = zM_{t-1}$ for every period t, where z and n are both greater than 1. The money created in each period is used to finance government purchases of g goods per old person. Prove that the monetary equilibrium does not maximize the utility of future generations. *Hint:* Follow the steps of the example just completed. Explain, but do not formally prove, why the feasible set line goes through the monetary equilibrium (c_1^*, c_2^*).

5 The Limits to Seigniorage

Does seigniorage represent an unlimited source of government revenue? Can the government simply print enough money to pay all its bills without the bother of direct taxation? Although the government is able to print any number of dollars, the value of those dollars shrinks as the government prints more fiat money. Therefore, government revenue in terms of real goods is limited by the real value of the fiat money stock.

To see this, recall that real government revenue from seigniorage at t can be written as

$$(M_t - M_{t-1})v_t = \left[1 - \frac{1}{z}\right]v_t M_t \tag{4.29}$$

The term $v_t M_t$ in Equation 4.29 represents the real value of the fiat money stock. Because this is the object being taxed, we may consider this the seigniorage "tax base." The term $1 - 1/z$ represents the fraction of the value of the real fiat money stock that winds up as government revenue; therefore, it may be considered the seigniorage "tax rate."

Assume for the moment that the real value of the fiat money stock $v_t M_t$ remains constant as the rate of money creation, z, is increased. This assumes people desire the same level of real balances of fiat money, whatever the rate of inflation. If this is the case, real seigniorage revenue is always increasing in z. It is nevertheless bounded. As z is driven to infinity, the seigniorage tax rate goes to $1 - (1/\infty) = 1$, and the entire real value of money balances, $v_t M_t$, is acquired by the government. But this quantity is finite, limited to the real value of desired money balances by the equality of supply and demand for money (Equation 2.5):

$$v_t M_t = N_t[y - c_{1,t}]. \tag{4.30}$$

There is in fact a more severe limit on the real value of seigniorage revenue. Suppose that a fixed amount of government expenditure is raised through some combination of lump-sum taxes and seigniorage. As the rate of inflation increases,

---

[10] Barro (1982).

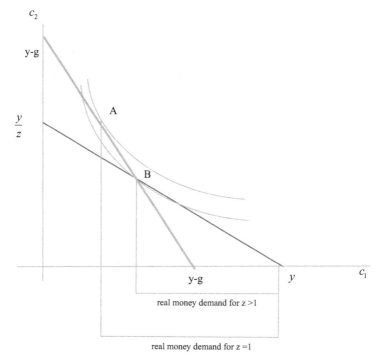

Figure 4.9. Compare seigniorage revenue for two different money growth rates. In the monetary equilibrium represented by Policy B, the government finances purchases of goods by printing fiat money. The monetary equilibrium represented by Policy A there is no seigniorage revenue collected because the money stock is constant. Note that the real demand for money shrinks in under Policy B compared with Policy A. The implication is that the seigniorage tax base shrinks as the money growth rate increases.

each individual will choose to reduce the real balances of money held $(y - c_{1,t})$ in an attempt to reduce the amount of goods lost to the government through inflation.

To see this reduction in the demand for fiat money, let us examine the budget set when a fixed amount of government purchases is raised through some combination of lump-sum taxes and seigniorage. (You are asked to find this budget set in Exercise 4.6.) Figure 4.9 graphs the budget set and the monetary equilibrium for two alternative policies raising the same government revenue: policy A, in which all revenue is raised through lump-sum taxes ($\tau = g$; $z = 1$), and policy B, in which some revenue is raised through an expansion of the fiat money supply ($z > 1$). It illustrates how the seigniorage tax base $N_t(y - c_1^*)$ falls as the rate of money creation z increases. The reduction of the demand for fiat money reduces the real value of fiat money balances and thus the real value of the fiat money the government is printing.

We can see the effect of the rate of fiat money creation on the real demand for fiat money by looking at data from the hyperinflationary episodes after World War I studied by Sargent (1986a).

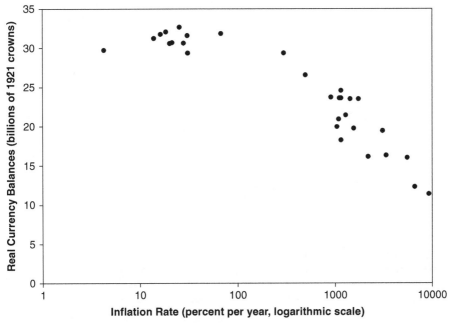

Figure 4.10. Real money balances during the Austrian hyperinflation. During this hyperinflationary episode of the 1920s, real currency balances tended to fall as the rate of inflation increased. *Source:* Authors' calculations using the data from Young (1925) as published in Sargent (1986a, Tables 3.2 and 3.3, pages 49 and 51).

Austria, to illustrate such a case, printed fiat money at extremely high rates during the early 1920s to finance government deficits. For example, Austrian notes in circulation increased by more than 70 percent from July to August 1922. This rapid increase in fiat money creation led to annual inflation rates that approached 10,000 percent per year. As shown in Figure 4.10, data from this episode demonstrate the tendency for real money balances to fall as the inflation rate increases.

We see from Figure 4.11 that, for a given level of government purchases, there is a more severe limit on the real value of seigniorage revenue. An increase in the rate of fiat money expansion discourages people from using money, which reduces the demand for fiat money ($y - c_1$). In this way, an increase in the rate of fiat money expansion reduces the seigniorage tax base as it increases the seigniorage tax rate. It follows that, if the government inflates the stock of fiat money too rapidly, it may raise less revenue in real terms than it could raise with a lower rate of money creation. Although the exact shape of the revenue function depends on the utility function of individuals and anything else that affects the demand for fiat money, the general shape of the revenue function may be something like that in Figure 4.11.[11]

Hyperinflations are dramatic examples of cases in which governments seek to raise revenue from money creation. Though less dramatic, the United States

[11] See Bailey (1956).

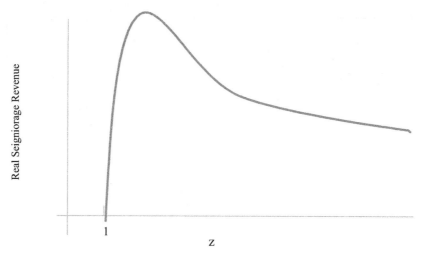

Figure 4.11. Seigniorage revenue plotted with the growth rate of the fiat money supply. As the government increases the rate of monetary expansion, seigniorage revenue is depicted as increasing initially as the seigniorage tax rate increases faster than the decline in the seigniorage tax base. Eventually, the picture shows that the seigniorage tax base falls faster than the seigniorage tax rate increases, resulting in total seigniorage revenue declining. This is a monetary Laffer curve.

has experienced a sizeable increase in the quantity of fiat money creation since the 2007 Financial Crisis. So, one might wonder how this recent United States' experience compares with hyperinflationary episodes. The largest December-to-December increase occurred in 2013 when the Federal Reserve reported a $1.043 trillion increase in the quantity of monetary base. The 2013 fiscal year shows that the Federal Government collected $2.775 trillion in total revenues. Thus, the United States collected 37.6 percent of its revenues from money creation in 2013. Historically, this is a very high percentage of revenues collected by money creation in the United States. Despite this increase in money creation, there has been no corresponding increase in the inflation rate. We need more economics to help us explain why. You will have to wait until Chapter 11 where we will provide a theory that can account for the apparent breakdown in the quantity theory.

Such a relationship between tax rates and tax revenues may sound familiar. The Laffer curve hypothesizes a similar relationship between income tax rates and income tax revenue.[12] The notion that a government might increase tax revenues by cutting income tax rates is analogous to the possibility that the government might increase seigniorage revenue by decreasing the rate of money creation.

In Chapter 7, we see that the introduction of alternative forms of saving will place additional limitations on the amount of seigniorage revenue that can be generated by the government.

---

[12] Economists discussed this relationship between tax rates and tax revenue long before its popularization by Arthur Laffer during the promotion of *supply-side economics* by the Reagan administration.

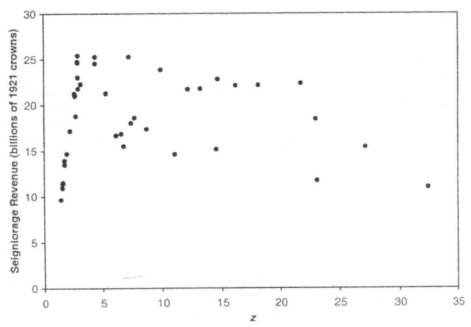

Figure 4.12. Seigniorage revenue during the Austrian hyperinflation. Continual increases in the rate of fiat money creation eventually corresponded to lower levels of real seigniorage revenue. *Source:* Authors' calculations using data from Young (1925) as published by Sargent (1986a, Tables 3.2 and 3.3, pages 49 and 51, respectively).

In Figure 4.12, data from the Austrian hyperinflation show that after a certain point, real seigniorage revenue declines at higher rates of fiat money creation.

6 Summary

Whereas Chapter 1 concentrates on the demand for fiat money, this chapter analyzes the effects of a changing supply of fiat money. We concentrate on increases in the fiat money stock that were used to finance government policies such as lump-sum subsidies and government purchases of goods.

The model of this chapter has one overriding theme. In each of the cases considered, the monetary equilibria with an increasing fiat money stock did not attain the golden rule. An increasing fiat money stock acts as an implicit tax on money holdings, causing individuals to economize on their holdings of fiat money. By economizing on their money holdings, individuals do not fully take advantage of the benefits that fiat money provides. Real money holdings fall below the optimal level. The consumption pattern of individuals is altered, tilting it away from the good (c_2) that requires fiat money for its acquisition and toward the good (c_1) that does not. This results in a lower level of utility than could be attained without monetary expansion.

7 Exercises

4.1. Let $N_t = nN_{t-1}$ and $M_t = zM_{t-1}$ for every period t, where z and n are both greater than 1. The money created each period is used to finance a lump-sum subsidy of a_t^* goods to each *young* person.

a. Find the equation for the budget set of an individual in the monetary equilibrium. Graph it. Show an arbitrary indifference curve tangent to the set and indicate the levels of c_1 and c_2 that would be chosen by an individual in this equilibrium.

b. On the graph you drew in part a, draw the feasible set. Take advantage of the fact that the feasible set line goes through the monetary equilibrium (c_1^*, c_2^*). Label your graph carefully, distinguishing between the budget and feasible sets.

c. Prove that the monetary equilibrium does not maximize the utility of the future generations. Support your assertion with references to the graph you drew of the budget and feasible sets.

4.2. Consider an economy with a shrinking stock of fiat money. Let $N_t = N$, a constant, and $M_t = zM_{t-1}$ for every period t, where z is positive and less than 1. The government taxes each old person τ goods in each period, payable in fiat money. It destroys the money it collects.

a. Find and explain the rate of return in a monetary equilibrium.

b. Prove that the monetary equilibrium does not maximize the utility of the future generations. *Hint:* Follow the steps of the equilibrium with a subsidy, noting that a tax is like a negative subsidy.

c. Do the initial old prefer this policy to the policy that maintains a constant stock of fiat money? Explain.

4.3. Consider an overlapping generations mode with the following characteristics: Each generation is composed of 1,000 individuals. The fiat money supply changes according to $M_t = 2M_{t-1}$. The initial old own a total of 10,000 units of fiat money ($M_0 = \$10,000$). Each period, the newly printed money is given to the old of that period as a lump-sum transfer (subsidy). Each person is endowed with 20 units of the consumption good when born and nothing when old. Preferences are such that individuals wish to save 10 units when young at the equilibrium rate of return on fiat money.

a. What is the gross real rate of return on fiat money in this economy?

b. How many goods does an individual receive as a subsidy?

c. What is the price of the consumption good in period 1, p_1, in dollars?

4.4. Consider the following economy: Individuals are endowed with y units of the consumption good when young and nothing when old. The fiat money stock is constant. The population grows at rate n. In each period, the government taxes each young person τ goods. The total proceeds of the tax are then distributed equally among the old who are alive in that period.

a. Write down the first- and second-period budget constraints facing a typical individual at time t. (*Hint:* Be careful; remember that more young people than old people are alive at time t.) Combine the constraints into a lifetime budget constraint.

b. Find the rate of return on fiat money in a stationary monetary equilibrium.

c. Does the monetary equilibrium maximize the utility of future generations?

d. Does this government policy have any effect on an individual's welfare?

e. Does your answer to part d change if the tax is larger than the real balances people would choose to hold in the absence of the tax?

f. Suppose that tax collection and redistribution are (very) costly, so that, for every unit of tax collected from the young, only 0.5 unit is available to distribute to the old. How does your answer to part d change?

4.5. Describe the essential features of a model economy of rational people for which each of the following statements is true: (These features might include the pattern of population growth, monetary growth, endowments, and government policies. Note that there may be more than one model that yields the given results.)

a. The gross rate of return on fiat money is 1. The monetary equilibrium also maximizes the utility of the future generations.

b. The price level doubles from period to period. The monetary equilibrium also maximizes the utility of the future generations.

c. The gross rate of return on fiat money is 1. The monetary equilibrium does not maximize the utility of future generations.

4.6. Assume that people face a lump-sum tax of τ goods when old and a rate of expansion of the fiat money supply of $z > 1$. The tax and the expansion of the fiat money stock are used to finance government purchases of g goods per young person in every period. There are N people in every generation.

a. Find the individual's budget constraints when young and when old. Combine them to form the individual's lifetime budget constraint and graph this constraint.

b. Find the government's budget constraint.

c. Graph together the feasible set and the stationary monetary equilibrium.

d. Find the stationary monetary equilibrium when $z = 1$ and add it to the graph in part c.

e. Use a ruler on your graph to compare the real balances of fiat money when $z > 1$ to the values when $z = 1$.

4.7. (**advanced, requires calculus**) Assume that the utility function of people in the economy described in Exercise 3.6 is $\log(c_{1,t}) + \log(c_{2,t+1})$.

a. Find the real demand for money ($q = v_t m_t$) as a function of z and τ. *Hint:* See appendix to Chapter 1 for a discussion of solution techniques.

b. Find the government budget constraint in a stationary equilibrium. Solve it for τ as a function of z. (The expression will also involve y and g.)

c. Substitute your expression for τ from the government budget constraint (part b) into the demand for money (part a). Use this to represent seigniorage as a function of z alone. Graph seigniorage as a function of z. For the graph, use the following parameter values: $N = 1,000$, $y = 100$, and $g = 10$.

4.8. (**advanced**) Consider an economy with a constant population of $N = 1,000$. Individuals are endowed with $y = 20$ units of the consumption good when young and nothing when old. All seigniorage revenue is used to finance government expenditures. There are no subsidies and no taxes other than seigniorage. Suppose that preferences are such that each individual wishes to hold real balances of fiat money worth

$$\frac{y}{1 + \frac{v_t}{v_{t+1}}} \text{ goods.}$$

a. Use the equality of supply and demand in the money market to find the total real balances of fiat money in a stationary equilibrium as a function of the rate of fiat money creation z.

b. Use your answer in part a to find total seigniorage revenue as a function of z. Graph this function and explain its shape.

4.9. (**advanced**) Suppose the monetary authority prints fiat money at the rate z but now does not distribute the newly printed money as a lump-sum subsidy. Instead, the government distributes the newly printed money by giving each old person α new dollars for each dollar acquired when young. Assume that there is a constant population of people endowed only when young.

a. Use the government budget constraint to find α as a function of z.

b. Find the individual's budget constraints when young and old. Combine them to form the individual's lifetime budget constraint.

c. What is the inflation rate p_{t+1}/p_t? What is the real rate of return on fiat money? *Hint:* The real rate of return on a unit of fiat money is not simply v_{t+1}/v_t in this case.

d. Compare the individual's lifetime budget constraint with the feasible set. Demonstrate that the monetary equilibrium satisfies the golden rule regardless of the rate of inflation. Explain why inflation does not induce people to reduce their real balances of fiat money in this case.

8 Appendix: Equilibrium Consumption Is at the Edge of the Feasible Set

We wish to prove algebraically that all goods are consumed in equilibrium – that is, that the monetary equilibrium consumption bundle (c_1^*, c_2^*) is on the line defining the feasible set. From the work done previously, we know that the following equations – the lifetime budget constraint, the definition of the subsidy a, and the market clearing condition – describe the stationary monetary equilibrium:

$$c_1^* + \left[\frac{z}{n}\right]c_2^* = y + \left[\frac{z}{n}\right]a, \tag{4.31}$$

$$a = \frac{\left[1 - \frac{1}{z}\right]v_t M_t}{N_{t-1}}, \tag{4.32}$$

$$v_t M_t = N_t(y - c_1^*). \tag{4.33}$$

From Equation 4.32 and 4.33, we have that

$$a = \frac{\left[1 - \frac{1}{z}\right]v_t M_t}{N_{t-1}} = \frac{\left[1 - \frac{1}{z}\right]v_t M_t n}{N_t} = \left(1 - \frac{1}{z}\right)n[y - c_1^*]. \tag{4.34}$$

Substituting Equation 4.34 into the lifetime budget constraint, Equation 4.31, we find that

$$c_1^* + \left[\frac{z}{n}\right]c_2^* = y + \left[\frac{z}{n}\right]\left(1 - \frac{1}{z}\right)n[y - c_1^*]. \tag{4.35}$$

Collecting and cancelling terms, we find that

$$zc_1^* + \left[\frac{z}{n}\right] c_2^* = zy. \tag{4.36}$$

Dividing through by z, we find that

$$c_1^* + \left[\frac{1}{n}\right] c_2^* = y, \tag{4.37}$$

proving that (c_1^*, c_2^*) is on the line defining the feasible set.

Chapter 5

International Monetary Systems

1 Roadmap

We continue on the theme of government and money in this chapter. Instead of having only one government at a time, however, we move on to consider a world in which each government has its own monetary policy. Indeed, the main piece added in this chapter is to examine the question: What happens when each country issues its own fiat money? The organizing principle is that there is a price at which each currency trades for another country's currency. In other words, the exchange rate is the rate at which one country's currency is traded for another country's currency. In this international monetary currency, we consider a basic friction; each country requires its young people to hold its home country's money. From here, we can determine what the exchange rate will be when there is a single consumption good and the Law of One Price holds. In addition, we can see the effects of different monetary policies and different economic growth rates on the equilibrium exchange rate.

In the second part of this chapter, we get rid of the friction and allow young people to hold any kind of currency they want. In doing so, we face a new economic outcome; namely, what happens when the equilibrium exchange rate is indeterminate. Now there is a coordination game between governments that sets the exchange rate. If these agreements are fragile, the exchange rate becomes more volatile. We describe two means of defending a particular exchange rate. In one defense, the two governments work together while in other defense, a country works alone.

One last note to make. This is the first time we look at an economy in which there is at least two stores of value coexisting. Up to this point, we have examined only closed monetary economies; that is, economies that operate entirely in isolation with a single fiat money. Trade and financial links between countries are increasingly important in the modern world, raising the importance of monetary links. Therefore, in this chapter we examine the role of money in economies that encompass more than one country and currency. We examine how exchange rates are determined and seek to explain observed exchange rate changes, especially the dramatic fluctuations of recent decades. We then go on to ask what kind of international monetary system should be in place. In particular, we ask the question addressed by the European Economic Community: Should trading partners agree to fix their exchange rates or, going even further, adopt a single currency?

2 A Model of International Exchange

To address these international issues, we assume that there exist two countries, a and b, each with its own fiat money. As in Chapter 3, people live two-period lives in overlapping generations. They are endowed with goods when young but not when old, yet they want to consume in both periods of life. The endowments in each country consist of the same goods (a good in country a is indistinguishable from a good in country b). People are indifferent to the origin of the goods they purchase. We use superscripts a and b to identify the parameters and variables of each country; for example, countries a and b have population growth rates n^a and n^b and money growth rates z^a and z^b, respectively. Assume that all changes in the fiat money stock are used to purchase goods for the government. We assume there is free international trade in goods.

The monies of the two countries can be traded at the "exchange rate" e_t, which is defined as the units of country b money that can be purchased with one unit of country a money.

For example, suppose country a is the United States and country b is Japan. Then the exchange rate is

$$e_t = \frac{\text{Japanese yen}}{\text{U.S. dollar}},$$

the number of Japanese yen per U.S. dollar or, alternatively, the number of yen that can be bought with a dollar. (There is, of course, a second exchange rate, the number of U.S. dollars that can be bought with a Japanese yen, which is simply the inverse of the first exchange rate. It does not matter which one we study.)

As in our single-country model, old people seek to trade their fiat money for the goods owned by young people. Naturally, the old people wish to purchase the most goods possible with the money they have. By definition, the owner of a unit of country a money at time t can buy v_t^a goods, and the owner of a unit of country b *money at time t can buy* v_t^b goods. If people are free to trade monies at the exchange rate e_t, then the owner of a unit of country a money has the option of purchasing v_t^a goods with country a money or trading a unit of country a money for e_t units of country b money, which will buy $e_t v_t^b$ goods. Similarly, an owner of a unit of country b money has the option of purchasing v_t^b goods with country b money or

Table 5.1. *An old person born in country a (the upper panel) has two options regarding what to do with their money balances. Option A describes an old person using their home-country currency to purchase the consumption good. Option B describes how the old person can exchange the home-country money for the money issued by country b's government and then purchase goods in country b. The bottom panel gives the same two options for an old person born in country b.*

A Person born in Country a	
Option A	**Option B**
Keep the country a money Purchase v_t^a goods	Trade for e_t units of country b's money Purchase $e_t v_t^b$ goods
A Person born in Country b	
Option A	**Option B**
Trade for $1/e_t$ units of country a money Purchase v_t^a/e_t goods	Keep the country b money Purchase v_t^b goods

trading a unit of country b money for $1/e_t$ units of country a money, which will buy v_t^a/e_t goods. These options are depicted in Table 5.1.

If $v_t^a > e_t v_t^b$, everyone prefers country a money (option A). Owners of country b money will want to trade for country a money to make their purchases, but owners of country a money will not want to trade their money for country b money. Because owners of country b money are not content with the form of their money balances, this cannot be an equilibrium in which both fiat monies are valued. The exchange rate e_t must be higher or v_t^a/v_t^b must be lower. Similarly, if $v_t^a < e_t v_t^b$, everyone prefers country b money (option B). Owners of country a money will want to trade for country b money to make their purchases, but owners of country b money will not want to trade their money for country a money. This also is not an equilibrium in which both fiat monies are valued, because the owners of country a money are not content with the form of their money balances.

Only if $v_t^a = e_t v_t^b$ will owners of both countries' monies be indifferent between their two options and thus satisfied with the form of their money balances. Therefore, if both fiat monies are valued, in equilibrium it must be that

$$v_t^a = e_t v_t^b \quad \text{or} \quad e_t = \frac{v_t^a}{v_t^b}. \tag{5.1}$$

We wish to determine the behavior of this exchange rate under alternative international monetary arrangements. In particular, we will examine two arrangements: one in which young people are constrained to hold the money of their home country and one in which young people are permitted to hold any country's currency.

3 Foreign Currency Controls

The first international monetary system we look at is one that completely separates the monetary sectors of the two countries through a policy of "foreign currency controls" and flexible exchange rates. By foreign currency controls, we mean that the citizens of each country are permitted to hold over time only the fiat money of their own country. Foreign currency controls do not rule out the possibility of trade between the two countries. An old citizen who wishes to buy goods from another country may exchange his money for the foreign currency and then make the purchase. However, the young of each country can hold only their country's money from one period to the next.

Remember that there is a single consumption good in the world. Young people hold the money issued by the country into which they were born. They do not migrate. However, when they are old, they can take their money and exchange for any other country's money they desire and travel freely to purchase the consumption good. People do not migrate from one country to another to work, but old people are free to migrate wherever they want to consume. In the absence of any restrictions on where you buy the consumption good and with the ability to travel to any country without bearing any transaction cost, competition results in the price of the good being the same across countries. This is the Law of One Price. As you will see, this does not mean the exchange rate is equal to one, it only means that we need to know the demand for and supply of a country's money supply to determine what the exchange rate will be.

The imposition of foreign currency controls implies that each country has its own money supply and demand that independently determine the value of its fiat money:

$$v_t^a M_t^a = N_t^a \left(y^a - c_{1,t}^a \right) \tag{5.2}$$

$$v_t^b M_t^b = N_t^b \left(y^b - c_{1,t}^b \right). \tag{5.3}$$

The exchange rate $e_t = v_t^a / v_t^b$ is therefore

$$e_t = \frac{v_t^a}{v_t^b} = \frac{\frac{N_t^a (y^a - c_{1,t}^a)}{M_t^a}}{\frac{N_t^b (y^b - c_{1,t}^b)}{M_t^b}} = \frac{N_t^a (y^a - c_{1,t}^a)}{N_t^b (y^b - c_{1,t}^b)} \frac{M_t^b}{M_t^a}. \tag{5.4}$$

Note that the exchange rate, the value of country a money in terms of country b money, depends simply on the relative values of the demand for money and the supply of money in the two countries. The greater the demand for country a money relative to the demand for country b money, the higher the value of country a money (the exchange rate). The greater the supply of country a money relative to the supply of country b money, the lower the value of country a money.

To illustrate how the exchange rate operates to ensure the Law of One Price is satisfied, suppose that the United States is country a and China is country b.

Suppose $v_t^a = 2$ so that a young person in the United States exchanges 2 units of the consumption good for each U.S. dollar. Next, suppose $v_t^b = 0.5$ so that a young person in China exchanges 0.5 units of the consumption good for each Chinese yuan. By Equation 5.4, we know the yuan-dollar exchange rate is 4; that is, $e_t = \frac{v_t^a}{v_t^b} = \frac{2}{0.5} = 4$. In other words, each U.S. dollar is exchanged for 4 Chinese yuan. So, an old person in the United States with one unit of money can purchase two units of the consumption good in the home country. Alternatively, the old U.S. citizen can exchange the dollar for 4 Chinese yuan, go to China, and purchase two units of the consumption good there. The implication is clear: the national origin of the money does not matter. An old person can afford the same quantity of goods no matter what national money is used.

Next, we examine how the exchange rate changes over time. If the value of money is important for determining the exchange rate at a point in time, the rate of return on money will be important for determining how the exchange rate changes over time. Following the steps described in Equation 4.13, we can use Equations 5.2 and 5.3 to find the rates of return of the two monies to be

$$\frac{v_{t+1}^a}{v_t^a} = \frac{n^a}{z^a} \quad \text{and} \quad \frac{v_{t+1}^b}{v_t^b} = \frac{n^b}{z^b}. \tag{5.5}$$

Essentially, everything here is just what we found in the one-country case of Chapter 4 (but with superscripts now attached for each country).

Let us now determine the path of the exchange rate over time. The rate of change of the exchange rate is e_{t+1}/e_t. Using the definition of the exchange rate (Equation 5.1), we can express this in terms of the values of the two countries' monies at t and $t+1$,

$$\frac{e_{t+1}}{e_t} = \frac{\frac{v_{t+1}^a}{v_{t+1}^b}}{\frac{v_t^a}{v_t^b}}, \tag{5.6}$$

at which point we can make use of the expressions for the rates of return of the two monies (Equation 5.5) to find

$$\frac{e_{t+1}}{e_t} = \frac{\frac{v_{t+1}^a}{v_{t+1}^b}}{\frac{v_t^a}{v_t^b}} = \frac{v_{t+1}^a}{v_t^a} \frac{v_t^b}{v_{t+1}^b} = \frac{n^a}{z^a} \frac{z^b}{n^b} = \frac{n^a}{n^b} \frac{z^b}{z^a}. \tag{5.7}$$

From Equation 5.7, we can determine how the exchange rate will change over time: The greater the growth rate of country a's population relative to country b's, the greater the rate of growth of the exchange rate, the relative value of country a money. This happens because the growth of a country's population causes an increase in its demand for fiat money. Indeed, any increase in the demand for money in a country will drive up its relative value. An increase in a country's endowments (in y, the output of young people), for example, will have the same effect. If both countries expand the money stock at the same rate $z^a = z^b$ but country a grows faster (in output or population), the relative value of country a's money will increase over time; country a will experience an "appreciation" of its exchange rate.

We can also see from Equation 5.7 that the greater the growth rate of country a's money supply relative to country b's, the lower the rate of growth of the exchange rate, the relative value of country a money. Suppose, for example, that the two countries have equal rates of growth in the demand for money ($n^a = n^b$): If country a expands its money at a faster rate than does country b, the value of country a's money will fall relative to country b's money; country a will experience a "depreciation" of its exchange rate.

3.1 Fixed Exchange Rates

A fixed exchange rate is defined as an equilibrium in which the exchange is constant over time. Formally, a fixed exchange rate is defined as $e_{t+1} = e_t$. From Equation 5.7, a fixed exchange rate implies

$$z^a = \frac{n^a}{n^b} z^b. \tag{5.8}$$

To fix the exchange rate, therefore, one or both of the countries must choose rates of fiat money creation that satisfy Equation 5.8. Of course, a monetary authority committed to a fixed exchange rate can no longer freely set the rate of money creation in order to raise a chosen level of seigniorage revenue. A country can choose the rate of money creation to fix the exchange rate or to acquire its preferred level of seigniorage revenue, but it cannot meet both objectives.

Suppose, for example, that country a desires to keep a fixed exchange rate with country b. It will then set its growth rate of fiat money creation according to Equation 5.8. If country b now increases its fiat money creation growth rate, country a will be forced to follow suit and increase z^a if it wants to keep the exchange rate fixed.

Note also that Equation 5.8 implies that the fiat monies of both countries will have the same rate of return ($n^a/z^a = n^b/z^b$) under fixed exchange rates. Alternatively stated, they will have the same inflation rates. If country a wishes to maintain a fixed exchange rate and the monetary authority of country b inflates, country a's monetary authority will be forced to inflate, too. Country a loses its independence in monetary policy by following its fixed exchange rate policy.[1]

Example 5.1 Suppose that the United States (country a) and Great Britain (country b) have foreign currency controls in effect. The demand for money is growing at 10.25 percent in the United States and at 2 percent in Great Britain (net rates) each

---

[1] Countries with a history of overusing seigniorage may actually choose to fix their exchange rate with respect to a country that is not likely to inflate. Chapter 17 examines why countries may need to make commitments that limit their ability to print money at will.

period. The fiat money supplies in the United States and Britain are growing at 5 percent and at 6.25 percent net rates in each period, respectively.

a. Defining the exchange rate (e_t) as in the text, what are the units in which the exchange rate is measured, U.S. dollars per British pound or British pounds per U.S. dollar?
b. What is the rate of return on fiat money in the United States? In Great Britain?
c. In a system of flexible exchange rates, what is the time path of the exchange rate between the United States and Great Britain; that is, what will (e_{t+1}/e_t) be?
d. Suppose the United States desires to fix the exchange rate. How can the U.S. government set its gross rate of fiat money creation z^a to accomplish this goal?

Example 5.2 Suppose the (gross) rate of return on fiat money in the United States (country a) is 2.0 and that of Canada (country b) is 1.0. The (gross) growth rate of the Canadian population (n^b) is 1.2. Foreign exchange controls are in effect.

a. What is the time path of the exchange rate (e_{t+1}/e_t)?
b. Suppose Canada wishes to maintain a fixed exchange rate with the United States. To accomplish this goal, Canada must set its gross rate of fiat money creation (z^b) to what value?

3.2 The Costs of Foreign Currency Controls

So far, we assume that people do not care where goods come from. Suppose instead that people want to consume at least some goods from another country. Foreign currency controls require that when an old person of country a buys a good from a young person of country b, the young person of b cannot simply keep the country a money and use it to make a purchase in old age. Because he is allowed to hold only his own country's money, he must either require that the country a person exchange his country a money and pay in country b money or accept the country a money and immediately exchange it himself. In either case, an exchange of monies occurs that would not be necessary in the absence of foreign currency controls.

In the model of an international economy just described, there seems to be little cost to the money changing. It was assumed that people could exchange one money costlessly for another to purchase goods from another country. Anyone who has traveled abroad, however, knows that the exchange of one money for another is not costless. Money changers incur expenses in providing the offices and labor required to conduct the exchanges and charge for this service.[2]

---

[2] There is a second reason for the inefficiency of foreign currency controls. If the monies of the two nations have different rates of return, their citizens differ in their willingness to trade (c_1 for c_2) (have different marginal rates of substitution). This is inefficient because the separation of the two economies prevents citizens from making mutually beneficial trades. See Kareken and Wallace (1977).

4 The Indeterminacy of the Exchange Rate

Because foreign currency controls force people to exchange money to buy the goods of another country, they impose extra costs on international trade in a world of costly money exchange. Therefore, let us consider our two-country model economy with young people free to hold and use the money of any country.[3]

To find the exchange rate in such a world, we turn, as before, to the equality of money supply and demand. Because people are now allowed to hold the money of either country, we can no longer determine the money supply and demand of each country separately but must examine the world's supply of and demand for money. The world supply of fiat money, measured in goods, is $v_t^a M_t^a + v_t^b M_t^b$, and the world demand for fiat money is $N_t^a(y^a - c_{1,t}^a) + N_t^b(y^b - c_{1,t}^b)$. Setting supply equal to demand, we have that

$$v_t^a M_t^a + v_t^b M_t^b = N_t^a \left(y^a - c_{1,t}^a \right) + N_t^b \left(y^b - c_{1,t}^b \right). \tag{5.9}$$

A serious problem now appears in our effort to find the exchange rate. We have the single Equation 5.9 with which to determine two variables, v_t^a and v_t^b. Such an equation has an infinite number of solutions. Because $e_t = v_t^a / v_t^b$, we can find an equilibrium in which world money supply equals world money demand for any positive exchange rate e_t.

This indeterminacy of the exchange rate did not appear when foreign currency controls limited citizens to their own country's money. In that case, the equality of money supply and money demand determined the value of fiat money in each country; the two market-clearing equations, Equations 5.2 and 5.3, determined the two variables v_t^a and v_t^b, which, in turn, determined the exchange rate.

Now, however, we have only a single market-clearing condition with which to try to determine the value of two monies. The right-hand side of Equation 5.9 tells us the total world demand for money, but it cannot tell us whether the dollars of country a are worth more or less than the yen of country b.

Substitute $e_t v_t^b$ for v_t^a in Equation 5.9. We find that

$$e_t v_t^b M_t^a + v_t^b M_t^b = N_t^a \left(y^a - c_{1,t}^a \right) + N_t^b \left(y^b - c_{1,t}^b \right)$$

or

$$v_t^b \left[e_t M_t^a + M_t^b \right] = N_t^a \left(y^a - c_{1,t}^a \right) + N_t^b \left(y^b - c_{1,t}^b \right). \tag{5.10}$$

The term $[e_t M_t^a + M_t^b]$ in Equation 5.10 is the world money supply (measured in units of the consumption good), and $v_t^b[e_t M_t^a + M_t^b]$ is therefore the real value of the world money supply.

---

[3] The ideas expressed in this section are drawn from the work of Kareken and Wallace (1981). The exposition owes much to Wallace's (1979) article "Why Markets in Foreign Exchange Are Different from Other Markets."

Note that, because people are free to hold either country's money, the size of one nation's money demand affects the real value of the world money supply. However, it no longer determines the rate of exchange, because a nation is no longer restricted to using only its own money. Similarly, the supply of money printed by any one country does not determine the exchange rate, because this money can be used in any country.

To better understand this indeterminacy, suppose that a single government issued two types of currency (e.g., green and blue) in a single, unified economy but neglected to put any numbers on the bills, choosing instead to let the free market determine the rate of exchange between the two. What would the exchange rate be? Would people value the green bills more or less than the blue? It is impossible to say. Either bill could be worth more than the other. There is nothing to pin down the rate at which people will exchange two intrinsically useless fiat currencies.

Now suppose that the green bills are printed in New York and the blue bills are printed in Des Moines, Iowa. Does this change our answers? No. If the two bills can be traded freely in all parts of the country, their rate of exchange is still undetermined. Printing the bills in two different locations does not end the indeterminacy as long as they are acceptable in trade everywhere. Note that neither the size of the city nor the number of bills printed in the city affects the exchange rate.

Finally, suppose the blue bills are printed in Toronto, but the United States and Canada allow the holding and use of both colors of money. The political border should not make any difference to our answer. If the two colors of bills are perfect substitutes for each other within North America, nothing pins down their rate of exchange.[4]

4.1 Exchange Rate Fluctuations

In the absence of the government determination of the exchange rate, the exchange rate in a unified world economy can be whatever people believe it to be. It follows that, if these beliefs fluctuate, the exchange rate will also fluctuate because there is nothing to pin it down. These fluctuations need not be tied to changes in real economic conditions. Therefore, the dollar may fall against another currency simply because everyone believes it will fall, regardless of whether U.S. output or some other real factor has changed.

There is one example that is frequently cited as evidence that changes in beliefs can dramatically affect exchange rates. In 1971, President Richard Nixon announced the abandonment of all U.S. efforts to control exchange rates. Figure 5.1 shows exchange rates for six developed countries. The shaded region is the decade

---

[4] On both sides of the U.S.-Canadian border, the currencies of both countries do circulate, but there remain some exchange controls that make the currencies less than perfect substitutes, for example, the restriction that only U.S. dollars can be used as reserves for U.S. bank deposits. (Reserve requirements are studied in Chapter 7.)

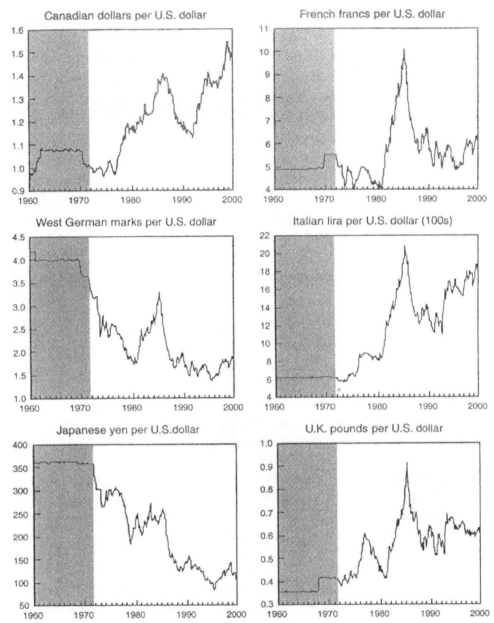

Figure 5.1. The U.S. exchange rate against six major currencies. The United States abandoned efforts to stabilize the exchange rate in 1971. We see a marked change in the volatility in the exchange rates between major currencies. The shaded region is the period in which the United States attempted to stabilize the exchange rates. The evidence indicates that fluctuations in exchange rates between the dollar and the currencies of Canada, France, former West Germany, Italy, Japan, and the United Kingdom increased sharply after 1971 compared with the period from 1960 to 1971.

Table 5.2. *Exchange rate movements. The right-hand column reports percentage changes in exchange rates over two-month periods for five countries. To put these fluctuations into some perspective, imagine if you sold 100 francs at the beginning of December 1973 and bought dollars. If the franc depreciated 9.4 percentage points by the end of January 1974 against the dollar, you could purchase 109.4 francs with the same number of dollars. If we assume the price of the consumption good in France was the same from December 1973 to January 1974, the selling and buying of francs would permit you to buy 9.4 percent more goods.*

Country	Time Period	Exchange Rate Movement
France	Dec 1973–Jan 1974	9.4% depreciation of the franc
Germany	Jun 1973–Jul 1973	9.4% appreciation of the mark
Italy	Sep 1992–Oct 1992	11.3% depreciation of the lira
Japan	Sep 1998–Oct 1998	10% appreciation of the yen
United Kingdom	Sep 1992–Oct 1992	11.7% depreciation of the pound

before President Nixon's announcement and the unshaded region covers the period after the announcement. Exchange rates were certainly not constant during the decade before the Nixon announcement. However, the data show that in each of these countries, the exchange rate was much more volatile after the announcement.

To get a clearer sense of the volatility that over short periods of time, we report changes in the exchange rates for five developed countries over a two-month period. In each case, the percentage change is computed in the exchange rate of the country's currency and the dollar. If beliefs did not matter, then movements in the exchange rate are driven by changes in growth rates and money growth rates for the two countries. The fluctuations in exchange rates cannot be readily traced to changes of similar magnitude in a country's money supply or its demand for money. None of the countries in Table 5.2 printed or destroyed more than 9 percent of its money stock in a single month, nor did it have a one-month change in real economic activity of that magnitude, nor did the combination of one-month changes in money supply and demand across the two countries reach the magnitude of these changes in the exchange rates. A possible explanation for this exchange rate volatility may be the existence of sufficiently large sectors of the world economy that are free to hold multiple currencies. Although you or I may not be part of this group, there exist multinational institutions that certainly are.

4.2 International Currency Traders

Volatility in the exchange rates is part of a bigger story. When you acquire a store of value, the future value can be quite different than what you expected. (We will deal with uncertainty explicitly in Chapter 6.) Indeed, large, random fluctuations in exchange rates can be very costly to someone who holds currencies as part of their portfolio. One way to hedge against exchange rate risk is for a person to hold a perfectly balanced portfolio of different currencies. If such a financial instrument existed, buying the collection of currencies means that a person would not be subject to exchange-rate risk since a depreciation in one currency would be offset by appreciation in another currency. However, it is expensive to buy all the currencies. So, basically only multinational institutions follow this portfolio advice. The nuisance and costs of determining and acquiring a balanced portfolio of monies may be the reason, or it may be that people are subject to government regulations that force them to use the local currency. As a result, fluctuations in the exchange rate put the value of people's money balances at risk.

To make this point more precisely, consider a model economy suggested by King, Wallace, and Weber (1992), in which there are three types of people:

1. citizens of country a, forced by law to hold only country a's money;
2. citizens of country b, forced by law to hold only country b's money;
3. multinational people, free to hold either currency.

Let N_t^a, N_t^b, and N_t^c, respectively, represent the number of people of each type in a generation born in period t. (We use superscripts to indicate a person's type for all variables.)

As always, the value of each country's currency (and thus the exchange rate) is affected by the demand for it. Each country's money is held by its own citizens and perhaps by multinational people as well. Let λ_t represent the fraction of the multinational people's money balances that is held in the form of country a's money. We can now write the two equations that represent the markets for the currencies of countries a and b, respectively:

$$v_t^a M_t^a = N_t^a \left(y^a - c_{1,t}^a \right) + \lambda_t N_t^c \left(y^c - c_{1,t}^c \right), \tag{5.11}$$

$$v_t^b M_t^b = N_t^b \left(y^b - c_{1,t}^b \right) + (1 - \lambda_t) N_t^c \left(y^c - c_{1,t}^c \right). \tag{5.12}$$

It is obvious from Equations 5.11 and 5.12 that the more the multinational people (type c) want to hold country a's money (i.e., the greater the value of λ_t), the greater the value of country a's money will be and the lower the value of country b's money will be. This, in turn, implies that the greater the value of λ_t, the greater the exchange rate e_t will be. However, because the multinational people are free to hold any fraction of their money balances in each country's money, there are many possible equilibrium exchange rates. To see this point, note that from Equations 5.11 and 5.12, the exchange rate in this world economy is

$$e_t = \frac{v_t^a}{v_t^b} = \frac{\frac{N_t^a \left(y^a - c_{1,t}^a \right) + \lambda_t N_t^c \left(y^c - c_{1,t}^c \right)}{M_t^a}}{\frac{N_t^b \left(y^b - c_{1,t}^b \right) + (1 - \lambda_t) N_t^c \left(y^c - c_{1,t}^c \right)}{M_t^b}}. \tag{5.13}$$

As an illustration, consider a simple case in which the total real demand for currency is identical across the different types of people. In other words, suppose that $N_t^a(y^a - c_{1,t}^a) = N_t^b(y^b - c_{1,t}^b) = N_t^c(y^c - c_{1,t}^c)$. We can then factor those terms out of Equation 5.13. We find that the exchange rate is

$$e_t = \frac{v_t^a}{v_t^b} = \frac{\frac{1+\lambda_t}{M_t^a}}{\frac{1+(1-\lambda_t)}{M_t^b}} = \frac{\frac{1+\lambda_t}{M_t^a}}{\frac{2-\lambda_t}{M_t^b}}. \tag{5.14}$$

Equation 5.14 illustrates that, for given stocks of fiat money in countries a and b, changes in λ_t will cause fluctuations in the exchange rate. An increase in λ_t will cause the exchange rate to rise, and a decrease in λ_t will cause the exchange rate to fall. As an example, verify to yourself that, if the two countries issue the same nominal number of notes (i.e., $M_t^a = M_t^b$), the exchange rate can take on any value between $\frac{1}{2}$ and 2. (*Hint:* What is the range of values for λ_t?)

Example 5.3 Suppose there are three types of people in our model of two countries and two currencies. Type a people can hold only the money of country a, type b can hold only the money of country b, and type c can hold the money of either country. Every person wants to hold money worth 10 goods. There are 300 type a people, 200 type b people, and 100 type c people. There are 100 units of country a money and 200 units of country b money.

a. Find the range of stationary equilibrium values for v_t^a, v_t^b, and e_t.
b. Now suppose that 100 type a people and 100 type b people become type c people (able to hold the money of either country). Now find the range of stationary equilibrium values for v_t^a, v_t^b, and e_t. Has the range of equilibrium exchange rates expanded or contracted? Explain this change.

As we saw in the section with exchange-rate indeterminacy, the multiplicity of exchange rates that satisfy the conditions for a stationary equilibrium suggests that exchange rates may fluctuate dramatically as multinationals change the composition of their money balances. These fluctuations make each currency a risky asset.[5] Those who have access to only a single currency, however, will see the real value of their money balances, and thus their consumption, rise or fall with the exchange rate. Multinationals can free themselves from this risk if they hold a balanced portfolio of both monies so that if the exchange rate changes, the decreased value of one currency is offset by the increased value of the other. Although this equalizing of currency balances may free multinationals from risk, it may be bothersome or otherwise costly to hold perfectly diversified stocks of both countries' currency.

---

[5] Fluctuating exchange rates also make risky the real value of any contract denominated in a single country's currency.

Monetary authorities may therefore wish to stabilize the exchange rate to free their citizens from the risk of a decline in the value of their money balances or from the bother of perfectly balancing their money balances.

5 Fixing the Exchange Rate

Here, we describe two ways in which countries operate to fix the exchange rate. In the first case, the two countries work together in what is called cooperative stabilization. In the second case, one country operates alone in what is called unilateral defense.

5.1 Cooperative Stabilization

How can we organize the world to provide a stable exchange rate? We focus on world economies in which there are no foreign currency controls and the exchange rate is indeterminate. To help us think about stabilization policies, we can borrow from policies that are implemented by national central banks. What determines the exchange rate between two different bills in a single national economy? Quite simply, the government tells us the rate of exchange by printing the denomination on each bill and standing ready to exchange the bills at that rate. In the United States, a bill with a picture of Benjamin Franklin – the $100 bill – trades for 100 bills with pictures of George Washington because the monetary authority of the United States, the Federal Reserve, will exchange the bills at a rate of 100 to 1. This exchange rate does not depend on how many pictures of Washington have already been printed.

The exchange rate in a national economy also fails to depend on where the bills are printed. Each piece of U.S. currency carries the name of one of the 12 Federal Reserve banks, but the bills always trade one for one. No merchant in California sells goods for a higher dollar price if the dollars happen to be marked with the name of the Boston Federal Reserve bank. No bank trades two pictures of Washington marked "Federal Reserve Bank of New York" for one picture of Washington marked "Chicago." When the Texas economy is in a slump, the value of bills marked "Dallas" does not fall.[6]

A key part of fixing the exchange rates among different forms of national money is the willingness of the monetary authority to accept any amount of one form of money in exchange for money at a different form at the fixed rate. No matter how many Franklins you wish to trade for Washingtons, the Federal Reserve will exchange them at the rate of 100 Washingtons per Franklin. And no matter how many bills with the stamp of Dallas you wish to trade for bills with the stamp of Boston, they can be had at the rate of one for one. How can the monetary authority

---

[6] Rolnick and Weber (1989) discuss the notion that Federal Reserve notes are distinct currencies trading at fixed exchange rates. See their paper for an excellent comparison of fixed and floating exchange rates.

make such an unbounded promise? What if they run out of Washingtons or bills with the stamp of Boston?

No one worries about a scarcity of Washingtons or bills with the stamp of Boston. If for any reason people want more of any type of bill, the Federal Reserve can simply have more printed. There is no limit to the exchanges the Federal Reserve can make, and if they burn the bills turned in, there is no inflationary consequence. Because people know this, no one ever worries about a shortage of any particular bill or believes that a bill stamped with one city's name will sell at a premium relative to that with another city's name. As a result, there is never any reason to avoid any type of bill. Indeed, most people never even look at the stamp indicating a city's name.

So why might there be any problem with fixing the exchange rates of any two fiat monies, such as those of two different countries? They are just bills with the names of countries instead of cities. If there is a monetary authority that can print any amount of one nation's currency for that of another, there is indeed no problem in maintaining a fixed exchange rate between the currencies of the two countries.

What is true for a single national economy is also true for a world economy unified in its use of currencies. Cooperative stabilization refers to exchange rate policies conducted by two governments that stand ready to exchange currencies at some given rate. If the central banks of all countries stood ready to give $2 whenever presented with a British pound, people would be indifferent between £1 and $2. In this way, the exchange rate would become determined.[7]

The exchange rate would also be fixed over time. In the absence of foreign currency controls, fiat currencies are held voluntarily. However, no currency will be held voluntarily if its value will fall over time relative to the value of other currencies. Such a currency offers a lower rate of return than the others, inducing everyone to switch to other currencies.

This solution seems so easy that one wonders why we rarely see fixed exchange rates. The European Economic Community (EEC), for example, although an advanced and integrated international economy, had tremendous difficulties in maintaining fixed exchange rates despite the pledges of the European governments.[8] During 1992, several countries in the EEC encountered difficulties maintaining fixed exchange rates with one another. For example, after attempts to fix the value of the British pound relative to the German mark, Britain abandoned such measures in September 1992, allowing the pound to fall more than 10 percent

---

[7] A recent example of fixing the exchange rate in this way came during the reunification of Germany, when the German central bank announced that it would accept East German marks at a one-for-one rate of exchange with West German marks, despite the fact that they were trading well below that rate of exchange before the announcement.

[8] Actually, the members of the European Monetary System agreed to keep exchange rates between pairs of member countries within narrow bands ($+/- 2.25$ percent) of a fixed exchange rate. These bands were increased to $+/- 15$ percent after several countries abandoned attempts to maintain the narrow bands during September 1992.

in value relative to the mark. We will now examine two major impediments to the stabilization of exchange rates when facing speculative attacks on currencies and the strong incentive to inflate when exchange rates are fixed.

5.2 *Unilateral Defense of the Exchange Rate*

You can imagine that it is difficult to get all the countries to agree on what the exchange rate should be for every currency. Sovereign nations generally do not practice unlimited commitment. If, for example, every holder of the British pound decided to turn in his pounds for Japanese yen, it is unlikely that the central bank of Japan (the Bank of Japan) will actually print all the yen necessary. The Bank of Japan might be ready to exchange smaller quantities of British pounds, but not the entire British money supply. For one thing, Japan might fear that the United Kingdom will decide at some future date to reimpose foreign currency controls. If so, then British citizens will send all those yen back to Japan, perhaps creating an inflationary tidal wave.[9]

How can the fixed exchange rate be supported without the full cooperation of foreign central banks? In other words, what would it look like if a country unilaterally defended its currency? Basically, how would a government keep its promise to exchange foreign currency for the domestic currency at a fixed exchange rate? One way would require the government to tax its citizens, using the revenue to purchase the foreign currency demanded.[10]

If people believe that a government is committed to maintaining an exchange rate but unwilling to impose foreign currency controls, there will be little incentive for anyone to turn in one form of money for the other. Both currencies can be used and held in either country (because of the absence of foreign currency controls) and neither loses value relative to the other (because of the fixed exchange rate). The two "national" currencies essentially function as two denominations of a single, internationally accepted currency. People will be indifferent between the two types of currencies. Thus, if the commitment is believed, the government may never be obliged to actually tax its citizens or spend its stockpile.

To be believable in all circumstances, the government commitment to tax must be large enough to acquire enough goods to redeem all of its money that might be turned in to it – all of that nation's money in the hands of those who are free to exchange one currency for another. This quantity could be quite large.[11] One must

---

[9] See Exercise 5.2.

[10] Another option is to dedicate a stockpile of storable goods like gold as reserves for the defense of the currency. Government stockpiles, of course, do not materialize out of thin air; they come from an earlier taxation of the people or an earlier decision not to distribute the stocks among the people. Interest-bearing assets may also function as reserves, as we will see in Chapter 10.

[11] Restricting our attention to currency, we find an extreme example in the United States, whose currency is used worldwide in official and unofficial transactions. Porter and Judson (1996) estimate that two-thirds of the stock of U.S. currency is held abroad.

ask if it is believable that the government would actually tax its citizens to defend a fixed exchange rate in the circumstance in which a large number of people are trying to exchange the domestic currency for another.

To illustrate how a unilateral defense would work, consider our two-country model economy with no foreign currency controls and no cooperation between central banks. The government of country a pledges to tax the old in order to defend a fixed exchange rate. (The tax is levied on the old because they are the citizens who will lose if the nation's money loses value.) Because of the absence of foreign currency controls we will assume that some of each country's currency is held by the old of each country. Recall that the world market for currency is given by

$$v_t^a M_t^a + v_t^b M_t^b = N_t^a \left(y^a - c_{1,t}^a \right) + N_t^b \left(y^b - c_{1,t}^b \right)$$

or

$$\bar{e} v_t^b M_t^a + v_t^b M_t^b = N_t^a \left(y^a - c_{1,t}^a \right) + N_t^b \left(y^b - c_{1,t}^b \right), \tag{5.15}$$

where $\bar{e}$ denotes the fixed exchange rate.

Now suppose that the entire world arbitrarily decides to exchange a part of its holdings of country a money for country b money. In contrast to cooperative stabilization in which the holders of country a money exchange the currency for country b money, unilateral defense requires taxes to be collected. In effect, country b says they will not trade one type of money for another. However, country b's central bank will exchange money for goods.

To better understand the differences between cooperative stabilization versus unilateral defense of the exchange rate, let us consider a numerical example. Suppose countries a and b are identical. In each country, the population of every generation is 100 ($N_t^a = N_t^b = 100$), and each young person wants real money balances worth 10 goods. This implies that aggregate really money balances in each country are

$$N_t^a \left(y^a - c_{1,t}^a \right) = N_t^b \left(y^b - c_{1,t}^b \right) = (100)(10) = 1,000.$$

Also assume that the total fiat money stock of country a is \$800 and that of country b is £600. We assume that there are no foreign currency controls in effect and that each money is held in both countries. In particular, we assume that the fiat money stocks are equally dispersed among the initial old of both countries. Because there are 100 people born in each generation, there are 200 initial old people across the two countries. This implies that each member of the initial old holds \$4 ($= \$800/200$) and £3 ($= £600/200$), regardless of citizenship. Finally, assume that the exchange rate is fixed at $\bar{e} = 1/2$; that is, \$1 trades for £0.5.

From the world money market-clearing condition (Equation 5.13), we can find the value of each country's fiat money in a stationary equilibrium.

$$\bar{e}v_t^b M_t^a + v_t^b M_t^b = N_t^a \left(y^a - c_{1,t}^a\right) + N_t^b \left(y^b - c_{1,t}^b\right)$$

$$\frac{1}{2}v_t^b (800) + v_t^b (600) = 1,000 + 1,000$$

$$1,000v_t^b = 2,000$$

$$v_t^b = 2.$$

Because the exchange rate is fixed at $1/2$, we can derive the value of country a money:

$$v_t^a = \bar{e}v_t^b = \frac{1}{2}(2) = 1.$$

The consumption by each old person in both countries is equal to the real value of that person's total money holdings. In other words,

$$c_t^a = c_t^b = v_t^a (4) + v_t^b (3) = (1)(4) + (2)(3) = 10 \text{ goods}.$$

Now suppose that every member of the initial old of both countries decides to cut their real balances of country a money in half. Each member of the initial old therefore turns in \$2 to the monetary authority of country a in order to acquire country b money. Assume that the monetary authority of country b has agreed to cooperate by printing as much of its currency as demanded, sending it to the monetary authority of country a. This is an example of cooperative stabilization. Because the exchange rate is fixed at $1/2$, country b must print £0.5 for every dollar turned in by the old, or £1 per old person. At the end of the currency exchange, the stock of dollars has shrunk by \$400 and the stock of pounds has grown by £200. In this situation, the total fiat money stock of each country has become \$400 and £800, respectively.

As we did earlier, use the world money market-clearing condition to solve for the value of country b money. We find no change in the value of country b's money. Plug the values of the exchange rate, quantity of each country's money, population and saving per young person into the market clearing condition

$$\bar{e}v_t^b M_t^a + v_t^b M_t^b = N_t^a \left(y^a - c_{1,t}^a\right) + N_t^b \left(y^b - c_{1,t}^b\right)$$

to obtain

$$\frac{1}{2}v_t^b(800) + v_t^b(800) = 1,000 + 1,000$$

$$1,000v_t^b = 2,000$$

$$v_t^b = 2.$$

With the exchange rate fixed at $1/2$, we see that v_t^a is still equal to 1. The consumption of each old person is equal to

$$c_t^a = c_t^b = v_t^a(4) + v_t^b(3) = (1)(2) + (2)(4) = 10 \text{ goods.}$$

Thus, there is no change to the consumption by each old person under a policy of cooperative stabilization. Demand for real money balances is unchanged and the supply of world money is unchanged in a cooperative stabilization as people hold fewer dollars and more pounds.

Now let us see how the results differ when country a attempts a unilateral defense of the exchange rate. Suppose country b refuses to print fiat money to accommodate the desires of the old to trade in their dollars for pounds. Assume that the government of country a decides to honor its pledge to exchange currency through an equal tax on every one of its old citizens. To do this, the government of country a must raise tax revenue sufficient to honor its pledge to provide all of the country b money demanded. The monetary authority in country a gives goods collected from taxes to those giving up country a money. The people can then go to the monetary authority in country b to acquire the desired money.

We begin by describing the steps in the unilateral defense. There are 200 old people across the two countries and each is turning in \$2. With $\bar{e} = 1/2$, the process ends when the number of dollars is exchanged for pounds. Thus, country a's monetary authority must acquire $(200)\$2\bar{e} = (200)\$2(1/2) = (200)£1 = £200$. Next, the central bank must give goods to the old equal in value to the currency. Remember that country b's monetary authority is not printing any new currency. So, country a's monetary authority must give up the value of country b's money times the total quantity of money acquired, which is represented by $v_t^b(£200)$ goods. Because country a can tax only its own citizens, each old person of country a will be required to pay a tax equal to the real value of the currency obtained divided by the number of old in country a. The first question, therefore, is how much will country a have to collect its citizens. To get the answer, the numerator is the value of country b's currency divided by the number of old people in country a. Or,

$$\frac{200v_t^b}{100} = 2v_t^b.$$

To determine the quantity of the tax, therefore, we need to know the value of country b's money. With 200 old people each turning in \$2 of initial money holding, the dollars per old person will decline from \$4 to \$2. Or, the total fiat money stock of country a falls to

$$M_t^a = (N_t^a + N_t^b)\$2 = (100 + 100)\$2 = \$400,$$

which is half of its previous level. However, unlike the case of cooperative stabilization, the fiat money stock of country b is unchanged because country b refuses to print additional money. Country b's total fiat money stock remains at £600. Using the world money market-clearing condition, we find that the value of country b money is

$$\bar{e}v_t^b M_t^a + v_t^b M_t^b = N_t^a \left(y^a - c_{1,t}^a\right) + N_t^b \left(y^b - c_{1,t}^b\right)$$

$$\frac{1}{2}v_t^b (400) + v_t^b (600) = 1{,}000 + 1{,}000$$

$$800v_t^b = 2{,}000$$

$$v_t^b = 2.5.$$

Given the fixed exchange rate of $1/2$, the value of country a money increases to 1.25. By decreasing the total world money supply and leaving the demand for money unchanged, we see that the value of all currency will increase under a unilateral defense of the exchange rate. This stands in marked contrast to the cooperative stabilization solution in which we found that the value of each currency remained unchanged.

Now that we know the value of country b money, it is straightforward to compute how much each old person living in country a must be taxed

$$2v_t^b = 2(2.5) = 5 \text{ goods.}$$

Now that the tax has been collected, country a is capable of acquiring new money from country b's monetary authority. Remember, there are 500 goods divided by 200 old people, so that country a purchases 2.5 goods worth of newly printed pounds. At 2.5 goods per pound, each old person will acquire one additional pound. So now after turning in \$400, leaving \$2 per old person, each old person started with £3 and ends up with £4. What effect does this have on the consumption of each old person? For the old of country b, who do not pay any taxes, old-age consumption is equal to

$$c_t^b = v_t^a (2) + v_t^b (4) = (1.25)(2) + (2.5)(4) = 12.5 \text{ goods.}$$

The old of country b benefit from the unilateral defense policy because the real value of their currency holdings increases and they are not subject to a tax.

Because the old of country a must pay a tax to defend their currency, their old-age consumption is equal to the real value of their money holdings less the tax:

$$c_t^a = v_t^a (2) + v_t^b (4) - (tax) = (1.25)(2) + (2.5)(4) - 5 = 7.5 \text{ goods.}$$

Because of the tax, the old of country a are made worse off by this policy of unilateral defense than they were under the cooperative stabilization policy, where their consumption was 10 goods.

In effect, the unilateral defense policy has resulted in a transfer of 2.5 goods from each old person of country a to each old person of country b. Only the citizens of country a pay the tax that increases the value of all money holders, transferring wealth from the taxpayers of the country defending the exchange rate to the money holders of the other country.

5.3 Speculative Attacks on Currencies

A unilateral policy of fixing the exchange rate relies on the government's willingness to take actions (taxation) that make its citizens worse off. People may quite rationally question the government's commitment to follow through with a policy that hurts its own citizens. If the government lacks the will to take any of the actions it promises, people will rationally anticipate the promise of a fixed exchange rate as meaningless, returning the economy to equilibrium of undetermined exchange rates.

Perhaps the government is prepared to take limited action to defend the exchange rate. Suppose, for example, that the government is willing to tax its citizen's a limited amount – for example, F goods, where F is less than the total value of the country's stock of currency. The government is committed to exchanging foreign for domestic currency until the tax bill of this policy has reached F goods, at which point it will abandon its efforts and let the exchange rate fluctuate. If people turn in fewer than F goods worth of domestic currency for exchange, the fixed exchange rate is maintained.

As pointed out by Salant and Henderson (1978) and Krugman (1979),[12] a limited government commitment may encourage speculative attacks in foreign currency markets in a way that does not occur when the government commitment is total. European countries (e.g., Britain and Sweden) in 1992–1993 and East Asian countries (e.g., South Korea and Indonesia) in 1997 experienced recent waves of such speculative attacks.

Suppose you are holding some currency balances of a country with a limited commitment to defend its exchange rate. You decide to exchange that currency for the money of another country. If the commitment of that country is sufficient to meet the entire demand for foreign exchange, the exchange rate does not change and you are no worse off than before. If that country's commitment is too small to meet the entire demand for foreign exchange, its currency will fall in value, and the foreign currency will gain in value. If you are one of the lucky ones who arrive at the foreign exchange window before the government's limit is reached, you will profit by acquiring the currency that is about to gain in value. This is a can't-lose proposition for speculators: They either win or are not hurt.[13] Faced with these possible outcomes, every holder of that country's currency will want to rush to the foreign exchange window.[14]

---

[12] See also Krugman and Rotemberg (1991).
[13] Of course, there is a chance of a loss if the currency they purchase is also subject to a speculative attack.
[14] Your only cost is the cost of making the transaction, which may be small for large traders of foreign currency.

This is also a can't-win policy for taxpayers. If a speculative attack occurs and the commitment proves sufficient, taxpayers have still been taxed to meet the attack. If the commitment proves insufficient, the taxpayers are taxed and the currency depreciates nevertheless. The government must decide which action results in the smallest losses to their people.

5.4 *Inflationary Incentives*

In the absence of foreign currency controls, the exchange rate is independent of national money stocks. Look again at the world money market-clearing condition (Equation 5.13). The value of a unit of money is determined by the total world money supply and not the money supply of the issuing nation. Therefore, an increase in the stock of one money reduces the value of all money and not just the money whose supply is expanded.

Let us examine this implication of the absence of foreign currency controls in the context of a national economy. If the monetary authority prints and distributes a large number of new $1 bills, the real (goods) value of the $1 bills will fall, but the real (goods) value of $10 bills will also fall. Why? The two are perfect substitutes for each other and have a fixed rate of exchange. Therefore, if inflation reduces the real value of $1 bills, it also reduces the real value of $10 bills. Similarly, an increase in the number of Federal Reserve notes marked "Boston" will reduce the value of all Federal Reserve notes in every part of the United States.

For the same reasons, in an international economy of perfectly substitutable currencies trading at a fixed exchange rate, an increase in the stock of one country's money reduces the real value of all monies. This can occur because people, indifferent between currencies in the absence of foreign currency controls, treat the different currencies as simply different denominations of world money free to circulate in all nations. Therefore, it does not matter which denomination (which nations' money) is increased during an expansion of the world stock of money; all currencies will fall in real value.

The expansion of one nation's money stock does not affect the real value of other currencies when foreign currency controls are in effect because the currencies are not perfect substitutes and do not trade at a fixed exchange rate. Citizens hold only their own country's money and thus are not affected by inflation of some other country.

The transmission of inflation across countries in the absence of foreign currency controls raises an important political problem. We learned in Chapter 4 that a nation that expands its money stock acquires revenue by lowering the value of the outstanding money stock, in effect by taxing money holders. In the presence of foreign currency controls, a nation willing to see the value of its money fall by half can raise seigniorage equal to half the value of the nation's money balances. In the absence of foreign currency controls, however, a nation willing to see the value of its money fall by half can raise seigniorage equal to half the value of the world money balances; the seigniorage tax base is greatly expanded, and with it, seigniorage revenue. In this way, seigniorage can be collected from the citizens of other countries.

The political incentives created by a single world demand for currency in the absence of foreign currency controls are obvious. Imagine the inflation that would result if local governments were free to issue nationally accepted money. If any tax is favored by politicians, it is a tax collected in large part from people unable to vote against them in the next election. The same logic applies to the international case. Because every national government will wish to inflate to collect seigniorage from the citizens of other countries, a large inflation of the world's money stock will result.

This inflation can be prevented if governments are willing to agree to limit the rate at which each is allowed to expand its fiat money stock. Such coordination may work if each government wishes to rely on seigniorage to roughly the same degree. If, however, some countries want to rely on seigniorage far more than others, it may be difficult to reach an agreement.

If it is not possible to coordinate monetary policies, a nation can avoid the politically induced inflation only by separating the demand for its currency from that of the others – that is, by imposing foreign currency controls that prevent the currency of other countries from substituting for their own currency. Of course, under foreign currency controls, the citizens incur the costs of exchanging money whenever they trade with the people of another nation.

6 The Optimal International Monetary System

If political coordination were not a problem, what sort of international monetary system would we want? Let us answer this by first asking what monetary system we would want within a nation (a politically coordinated entity). Would we want each city and town to have its own money? If they did, imagine the costs of learning the current exchange rate and changing money as one makes purchases in different towns. The obvious way to eliminate these transaction costs and facilitate trade is to have only a single money for the entire nation. This is the monetary system selected by every nation.

How do these nations prevent their cities from issuing money to tax each other through seigniorage? They simply authorize a single national authority as the only issuer of fiat money. This means that the cities within any nation are not free to pursue distinct seigniorage policies. Nevertheless, cities seem willing to yield their sovereignty over monetary policy in order to reduce the costs of trade among themselves.

The same solution suggests itself to the world economy. The costs of conducting trade between nations would be minimized if a single money were used worldwide.

People would not have to exchange their money to make purchases from other countries, nor would they have to fear that their money would suddenly lose its value because of an exchange rate change. A single world money would require that nations surrender their sovereignty over monetary policy to some trusted nation[15] or international institution, preferably with strict instructions about the rate of money expansion and the disposition of the revenue from seigniorage. This solution, in the form of a single European currency with a single European monetary authority, has been implemented by the EEC. Adoption of the U.S. dollar, long established in Panama, has been considered in Argentina and is commonly discussed in other countries in the Americas.

If world money is too much to ask for, most of the benefits of world money can be acquired if there are multiple currencies trading at fixed exchange rates with no currency controls. In this case, the different currencies function as different denominations of the world money supply, freely traded everywhere. This requires that monetary policies be coordinated to prevent speculative attacks and also to prevent the temptation for each national government to tax the entire world through inflation.

In actuality, political coordination may not be a trivial prerequisite. If countries considering a monetary union differ greatly regarding whether seigniorage is an important source of government revenue or regarding some other aspect of monetary policy, the gains to reducing the costs of international trade may not justify foregoing an independent monetary policy. It follows that monetary union is more likely among countries with similar economies, like the countries of the EEC. Even these, however, differ significantly in their reliance on seigniorage. Seigniorage as a percentage of tax revenue ranged from 1 to 16 percent during the period from 1973 to 1978.[16] Figure 4.8 of Chapter 4 presents data on seigniorage revenue for the countries of the EEC.

7 Summary

The goal of this chapter was to make clear the implications of different international monetary systems. This study is important in today's world, where countries are considering adopting widespread reforms of the systems under which they operate.

We first looked at a system in which currency controls are in effect. We found that the exchange rate between two countries' currencies is determined by the

---

[15] At the close of World War II, the Western nations and others pledged at Bretton Woods, New Hampshire, to conduct their monetary policies in a way that maintained a fixed rate of exchange with the U.S. dollar, which pledged to redeem dollars in gold. Although this era is not strictly an example of world money, its political implications are similar because the fixed exchange rates required that nations maintain rates of money creation compatible with that of the United States. The agreement broke down in the Vietnam War era, when the United States effectively printed dollars to help finance the war. In 1971, President Nixon announced that the United States would no longer maintain a fixed exchange rate or its commitment to redeem dollars for gold.

[16] See Fischer (1982). See Canzoneri and Rogers (1990) for a discussion of the trade-off faced by the EEC.

factors affecting the relative supply and demand of those currencies. With floating exchange rates and currency controls, the value of each country's money is unaffected by the other country's money supply or demand.

Currency controls require a potentially costly exchange of money to make a purchase in another country. These costs of the exchange of currencies can be avoided if people are free to hold and use any country's money. In this case, however, the exchange rate becomes indeterminate. This indeterminacy may give rise to erratic fluctuations in exchange rates, which expose money holders to the risk of a sudden drop in the value of the money they hold.

The indeterminacy problem can be solved if countries agree to fix the exchange rate. When all monies are perfect substitutes, however, there exists the temptation to tax the citizens of other countries through seigniorage. This implies that countries fixing their exchange rate must also coordinate their monetary policies.

8 Exercises

5.1. Suppose that Japan (country a) and China (country b) do not have foreign currency controls in effect. The total demand for money is always 2,000 goods in Japan and 1,000 goods in China. The fiat money supplies are 100 yen in Japan and 300 yuan in China.

    a. Find the value of each country's money if the exchange rate e_t (as defined in the text) is 3. Do the same if $e_t = 1$. Is one exchange rate likelier than the other? Explain.

    b. Suppose the exchange rate is 3 and China triples its fiat money stock, whereas Japan prints no new money. How many goods will China gain in seigniorage? What fraction of this seigniorage comes from Japanese citizens?

5.2. Consider two identical countries in our standard overlapping generations model. In each country, the population of every generation is 100 and each young person wants money balances worth 10 goods. There are $400 of country a money and £100 of country b money. The exchange rate is fixed at 1. There are no foreign currency controls, and the monetary authorities do not cooperate. Each country is willing to raise up to 500 goods in taxes on their old citizens in order to defend the exchange rate.

    a. What is the value in goods of a dollar? Of a pound?

    b. Find the value of a dollar if people abandon use of the pound and the value of a pound if people abandon use of a dollar.

    c. To be free from a speculative attack, a country's commitment to defend the exchange rate must be sufficient to purchase all of its currency if it is offered for foreign exchange. Which of these two countries is subject to a speculative attack? (*Hint:* In answering, you will need to use your answers to part b, not to part a.)

5.3. Consider two identical countries, a and b, in our standard overlapping generations model. In each country the population of every generation is 200 and each young person wants money balances worth 50 goods. Assume that the money of country a is the only currency that currently circulates in the two countries. There are $800 of country a money split equally among the initial old of both countries.

a. Find the value of a country *a* dollar and the consumption of the initial old.

b. Suppose country *b* issues its own money, giving £10 to each of the initial old of country *b*. To ensure a demand for this currency, country *b* imposes foreign exchange controls. Find the value of a pound and the value of a dollar. Find the consumption of the initial old in country *a* and in country *b*. Who has been made better off by this policy switch?

5.4. Consider a two-country economy with no currency restrictions.

a. Write down the money market-clearing condition.

b. Discuss the exchange rate in this economy. In particular, discuss why the exchange rate may exhibit greater volatility in this economy.

5.5. Consider two identical countries in our standard overlapping generations model. In each country, the population of every generation is 100 and each young person wants money balances worth 18 goods. Each member of the initial old starts with $3 of country *a* money and £3 of country *b* money, regardless of citizenship. The exchange rate is fixed at 2: $1 is worth £2. There are no foreign currency controls.

a. Find the value (measured in goods) of a unit of each country's money in a stationary equilibrium with unchanging money stocks. (Use the world money market-clearing condition [Equation 5.13].) What is the consumption of each old person? (Remember that each old person owns currency from both countries.)

b. Suppose each member of the initial old of both countries decides to cut his real balances of country *a* money by one-third (to 8 goods). He turns in $1 to the monetary authority of country *a* in order to acquire more country *b* money. Assume that the monetary authority of country *b* has agreed to cooperate by printing as much of its currency as is demanded. What will the total nominal stock of each country's money be? What will the value of a unit of each country's money be?

c. Suppose each member of the initial old turns in $1 to the monetary authority of country *a* in order to acquire more country *b* money at the fixed exchange rate, but the monetary authority of country *b* refuses to cooperate. Assume that the government of country *a* decides to honor its pledge through an equal tax on every old citizen. What is the value of a unit of each country's money? How many goods must each old citizen of *a* be taxed? Who prefers this policy to the policy in part b? Who does not?

d. Suppose each member of the initial old decides to cut his real balances of country *a* money by one-third (to 8 goods), and the government decides not to intervene to fix the exchange rate. What is the new exchange rate? What is the consumption of each old person? Why doesn't the exchange rate change hurt anyone? Who prefers this policy to the policy in part c? Who does not?

5.6. Consider a standard overlapping generations economy in which Euroland is the name given to area over which the euro is the regional currency. Suppose the population of Euroland is 1,000 people born each period. Each young person wants money balances worth 50 goods. There are 2,000 euros circulating.

a. Assume there is nothing outside Euroland. Compute the value of the euro using money market-clearing condition for a single country.

b. One part of Euroland, Greece, attempts to create its own currency, called the drachma. There are 50 young Greeks born each period, each wanting to hold money balances worth 50 goods. Greece prints 100 drachmas to circulate. Suppose both the euro and drachma are each accepted across Euroland, what will the exchange rate be between the euro and the drachma?

c. Assume the exchange rate is fixed at 5 drachmas per euro. Compute the value of the euro. Compute the value of the drachma.

Chapter 6

Price Surprises

1 Roadmap

In this chapter, there are two new things to include our analysis. First, we analyze random, unforecastable changes in monetary policy. In Chapter 4, we studied how a permanent, anticipated changes to the fiat money stock growth rate would affect the return and welfare. Now we can talk about monetary surprises and their effects.

Second, we analyze a model economy in which production of goods and services take center stage. Together, we use these two features so that we can explain (i) how does monetary policy affect prices and output across countries; and (ii) what is the relationship between money supply changes and output over the business cycle.

To make things really interesting, we are trying to see if unpredictable movements in the money supply can cause production to change. The idea goes back to Milton Friedman and Anna Schwartz (1963) who carefully documented movements in the money supply and movements in output over business cycles. They observed that changes in the money supply frequently occurred before movements in output. Robert Lucas developed a model that would explain why movements money supply could explain future movements in output and the monetary theory of the business cycle was made formal.

As we do so, we also study the more general question of how data correlations resulting from policy surprises may mislead naïve policy makers about the effects of the sustained implementation of their policies.

2 The Data

One of the first things that should strike you is that observation will play a key role in this chapter. Armed with the observations, the student is motivated to discover

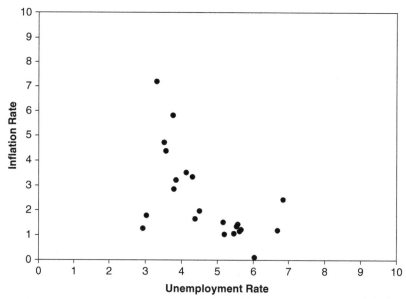

Figure 6.1. The Phillips Curve. Here, we plot combinations of the unemployment rate and inflation rate for the period 1948 through 1969. Before the 1970s, it appears that there is a stable inverse relationship between the inflation rate and the unemployment rate, often referred to as the Phillips curve. *Source:* The Federal Reserve Bank of St. Louis FRED database (http://www.stls.frb.org/fred/index.html).

economic theory that can account for what is observed. We start with the plot of the unemployment rate and the inflation rate.[1]

2.1 The Phillips Curve

In 1958, A. W. Phillips discovered a significant statistical link between inflation and unemployment for the United Kingdom over a century.[2] Subsequent work uncovered the same correlation for many other economies. Although it was not understood why such a correlation existed, this discovery excited many in the economics profession. The excitement was stirred by the formulation of economic theory that suggested there is an exploitable trade-off between inflation and unemployment; through the monetary authority's actions aimed at increasing inflation, the government might achieve lower unemployment and greater output. The apparent inverse relationship between inflation and unemployment rates that existed in the United States data between 1948 and 1969 is illustrated in Figure 6.1.

---

[1] In 1998, V. V. Chari wrote, "A central question in macroeconomics is whether monetary policy can and should be used to moderate business cycle fluctuations. It is this kind of question that the data alone cannot answer. Models are needed."

[2] Actually, Phillips investigated a relationship between *wages* and the unemployment rate. Although the statistical correlation between the inflation rate and the unemployment rate bears Phillips' name, Fisher (1926) originally pointed out such a relationship.

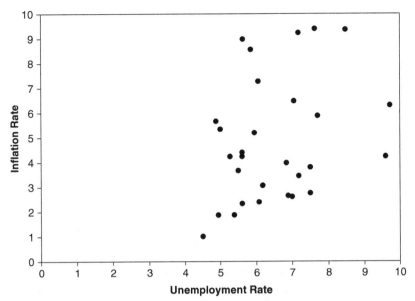

Figure 6.2. The Phillips Curve. Here, we plot combinations of the unemployment rate and inflation rate for the period 1970 through 2000. After the 1960s, it appears that there is a slight positive relationship between the inflation rate and the unemployment rate. *Source:* The Federal Reserve Bank of St. Louis FRED database (http://www.stls.frb.org/fred/index .html).

In the following decades, many governments tried to use monetary policy to stimulate the economy. Suddenly, the Phillips curve, a stable relation for more than a century, disappeared. Inflation occurred with no gains in output or employment. The disappearance of the stable relationship between the inflation rate and the unemployment rate becomes obvious when we look at U.S. data on these variables for the period from 1970 to 2000, as shown in Figure 6.2.

What happened? Did some malevolent god, to frustrate the progress of humanity, suddenly alter the "laws" of economics at the very moment we discovered the way to end recessions?

2.2 Cross-Country Comparisons

Comparisons across countries add to the puzzle. Lucas (1973), for example, found that, if anything, inflation rates are on average higher in countries with lower average real growth rates, as shown in Figure 6.3. How can these seemingly contradictory correlations come from a single world?

3 Expectations and the Neutrality of Money

In "Expectations and the Neutrality of Money," Lucas (1972) addressed this puzzle, proposing a model economy consistent with

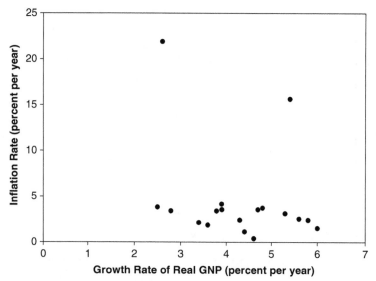

Figure 6.3. Lucas cross-country observations. Here, we plot combinations of the inflation rate and output growth across countries. These observations suggest a weak tendency for countries with high average inflation rates to have low average output growth rates. *Source:* Lucas (1973).

- a positive short-run correlation between inflation and output;
- the disappearance of that correlation when policy makers attempt to exploit it; and
- a negative correlation between long-run inflation and output across countries.

   With this model as an illustration, Lucas revolutionized the methods of modern macroeconomic theory and practice.

3.1 The Lucas Model

For his model, Lucas adopted the standard overlapping generations model of money, adding the assumption that people live on two spatially separated islands. The total population across the two islands is constant over time. Half of the old people in any period live on each of the islands. The old are randomly distributed across the two islands, independently of where they lived when young. The young, however, are distributed unequally across the islands, with two-thirds of the young living on one island (and one-third on the other), in our simplified version of the original model.[3] The random assignment of people across the two islands is depicted in Figure 6.4. In any single period, each island has an equal chance of having the large population of young. The outcome of this random assignment of population in any period has no effect on the outcome in any other period.

---

[3] We draw some of our exposition from a similarly simplified version of the Lucas model presented by Wallace (1980).

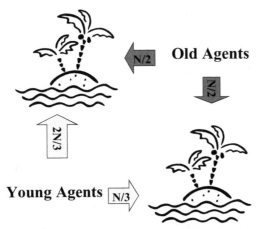

Figure 6.4. The Lucas islands model. In this picture, we see that the old people are evenly distributed across the two islands. For young people, 2/3 are located in the northeast island while 1.3 are located on the southwest island.

The stock of fiat money grows according to the rule $M_t = zM_{t-1}$. As seen in Chapter 4, increases in the fiat money stock are effected through lump-sum subsidies to each old person in every period t worth $a_t = [1 - (1/z_t)](v_t M_t/N)$ units of the consumption good.[4]

The next thing is to describe what people know. We will see that informational assumptions are critical to individual behavior in this model. In any period, the young cannot directly observe how many young people are on their island. We further assume that young people do not know the size of the subsidies to the old. The nominal stock of fiat money balances is known with a delay of one period. The price of goods on an island is observed, but only by the people on that island. No communication between islands is possible within a period.

Although people are assumed to be unable to directly observe the realization of a variable of importance, the population of young people on their island, we do not assume that these people are stupid or irrational. They are assumed to know the possible outcomes they face and the probability of each outcome. They are free to infer whatever they can from the price they observe. We assume that they make the most correct inference possible given the pieces of information available to them. The assumption that people understand the probabilities of outcomes important to their welfare was introduced by Muth (1961) as "rational expectations."

While working with the overlapping generations model in this chapter, we reinterpret a person's problem to better reflect the difference between market and nonmarket goods. People are endowed when young with y units of time, which can be used in leisure, c_1, or as labor. The young work (give up leisure) to produce goods to sell to the old. We let $l_t^i = l(p_t^i)$ to represent that the choice of labor

---

[4] Lucas (1972) assumes subsidies proportional to an individual's balances of fiat money.

by a person born in period t depends on the given price of goods, p_t^i, on island i. Each unit of labor produces one unit of goods, implying that $l(p_t^i)$ also represents the person's production of goods. In other words, the amount of labor supplied by a person depends on the price the person receives on the goods produced. The person's budget constraint when young in period t on island i can now be written as

$$c_{1,t}^i + l_t^i = c_{1,t}^i + v_t^i m_t^i = y. \tag{6.1}$$

The notation is that used in previous chapters, but with i superscripts to denote the island on which the person was born. A young person's holdings of fiat money (in units of the consumption good $v_t^i m_t^i$) is equal to the amount of goods that person produces and sells on the market l_t^i. This represents the person's real demand for fiat money. These holdings of fiat money, along with the lump-sum government transfer, will serve to finance consumption when old. In terms of notation, the budget constraint of an old person in period $t + 1$ may be represented by

$$c_{2,t+1}^{i,j} = v_{t+1}^j m_t^i + a_{t+1} = \left[\frac{v_{t+1}^j}{v_t^i} \right] l_t^i + a_{t+1} = \left[\frac{p_t^i}{p_{t+1}^j} \right] l_t^i + a_{t+1}. \tag{6.2}$$

Note that second-period consumption depends on the island i, where the person is born, and on the island j, where the person is randomly assigned when old. People choose their work effort l_t^i to maximize their expected utility for a given local price, p_t^i. Preferences are restricted to the case in which the young will choose to work more the greater the rate of return to their work. For a given future price of goods, the greater the current price of goods, the greater the rate of return to labor p_t^i/p_{t+1}^j. Therefore, we are assuming that an increase in the current price of goods, *other things being equal*, will induce the young to work more.[5] In the words of standard microeconomic theory, the substitution effect of an increase in price (a high relative price of goods encourages output) is assumed to dominate the wealth, or income, effect (a high relative price of goods makes people wealthier and thus more desirous of reducing work in order to consume more leisure).

3.2 Nonrandom Inflation

Let us start by examining a simple version in which the money stock grows at a fixed rate $z_t = z$ in all periods. In this case, rational people can easily determine the current money stock by multiplying last period's money stock, which they are assumed to know, by z.

The money market-clearing condition will tell us the value of money on an island with N^i young people. In period t, each young person sells the output of their labor

---

[5] See Lucas (1972) for the exact restrictions assumed on preferences.

so that the demand for fiat money is $l_t^i = l(p_t^i) = v_t^i m_t^i$ goods. Because there are N^i young people on island i, the total demand for fiat money is $N^i l(p_t^i)$. Because the old people are equally distributed across islands regardless of their island of birth, half of the fiat money stock is brought to each island. Equating the total real supply of fiat money in period t, $v_t^i(M_t/2)$, we obtain the following condition clearing the market of fiat money for goods

$$N^i l\left(p_t^i\right) = v_t^i \frac{M_t}{2}. \tag{6.3}$$

Because the value of fiat money v_t^i is equal to the inverse of the price level p_t^i, we can rewrite Equation 6.3 as

$$N^i l\left(p_t^i\right) = \frac{M_t/2}{p_t^i}. \tag{6.4}$$

N^i is either $(1/3)N$ or $(2/3)N$, respectively depending on whether island i has a small or large number of young people. Rearranging Equation 6.4, we find that

$$p_t^i = \frac{M_t/2}{N^i l\left(p_t^i\right)}. \tag{6.5}$$

Because the population of the young on each island is the only random variable, the market-clearing condition implicitly expresses the price level as a function of the population of the young (N^i). Therefore, observing the price of goods p_t^i allows all of the young to infer the number of the young on their island. It is as if the random number of young people is revealed by the equilibrium price. Let p_t^A and p_t^B denote the price of goods when the population is small $[N^A = (1/3)N]$ and large $[N^B = (2/3)N]$, respectively. From Equation 6.5 we find the equilibrium price on island A is

$$p_t^A = \frac{M_t/2}{N^A l\left(p_t^A\right)} = \frac{M_t/2}{\frac{1}{3} N l\left(p_t^A\right)}, \tag{6.6}$$

and on island B is

$$p_t^B = \frac{M_t/2}{N^B l\left(p_t^B\right)} = \frac{M_t/2}{\frac{2}{3} N l\left(p_t^B\right)}. \tag{6.7}$$

By comparing Equations 6.6 and 6.7, we can see that $p_t^A > p_t^B$. So, the price of goods is high when the population is low. For a given supply of money on an island, the demand for money is lower when the number of young people is lower. In other words, the price of goods is driven up by the scarcity of young people producing goods. (We present a proof that $p_t^A > p_t^B$ in the appendix of this chapter.) Because the price of goods in the next period is independent of the price of goods in this period, the greater the price in this period, the greater the rate of return to producing goods, p_t^i/p_{t+1}^j. In sum, when the population on an island is low, people want to work more because the price of their goods and thus the rate of return on their labor is great.

Put another way, those young people on an island with plenty of young people face a relatively low demand for their product; there are many young people available to produce for the old. A low price of goods results. Those young people on an island with few young people face a relatively high demand for their product; there are few young people available to produce for the old. A high price of goods results.

Our assumption that the substitution effect dominates the wealth effect ensures that the young respond to favorable rates of return by working more. This means that when there are few young people to produce for the old, each young person produces more; where there are many young people, each produces less. Of course, because there is always one island with $(2/3)N$ people and another with $(1/3)N$ young people, aggregate output does not depend on which of the islands has the larger number of young.

Prices here do the job we expect of them in market economies. They signal the true state of the world so that people can choose the quantity of their output that maximizes their well-being, given their true situation.

Will the young react to high prices in the same way if they know that the high prices are caused by a once-and-for-all higher level of fiat money stock? No. Look at the rate of return to work when the money stock is higher in both this period and the next:

$$\frac{v_{t+1}^j}{v_t^i} = \frac{p_t^i}{p_{t+1}^j} = \frac{\frac{M_t/2}{N^i l(p_t^i)}}{\frac{M_{t+1}/2}{N^j l(p_{t+1}^j)}} = \frac{N^j l(p_{t+1}^j)}{N^i l(p_t^i)} \frac{M_t}{M_{t+1}}. \tag{6.8}$$

A permanent increase in the money stock raises both M_t and M_{t+1} by the same portion and so fails to affect the relative price of goods in this period and the next. Therefore, a high current price caused by a permanent increase in the money stock does not affect at all the rate of return to labor and thus the desire to work. As we saw in Chapters 2 and 4, money is neutral in this economy.

What is the effect of anticipated inflation on work? Is money superneutral? No. Look again at Equation 6.8, this time with $M_{t+1} = zM_t$. As z increases, $M_t/M_{t+1} = M_t/zM_t = 1/z$ decreases, and the rate of return to work falls, discouraging work because the money balances earned from labor are taxed by the expansion of the money stock.[6] The decline in work effort as z increases translates into lower output.

Let us now construct a graph plotting output as a function of the (steady) rate of expansion of z of the fiat money stock.

---

[6] Lucas (1972) assumed subsidies to an individual's money balances. In this case, output is unaffected by rate of expansion z of the fiat money stock.

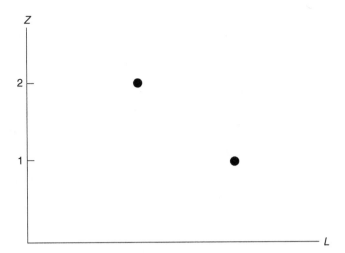

Figure 6.5. Inflation and output across islands in the Lucas model. The figure plots the output and inflation rate predicted by the Lucas for island economies. This picture plots two different monetary growth rates. With a high money growth rate, the rate of return on money is low and output is lower compared with the economy with a lower money growth rate.

Figure 6.5 reports data generated by the model economy. We see a negative correlation between inflation and output, the opposite of the Phillips curve correlation. (Not exactly having unemployment rates in this model, we use the total labor supplied [denoted L in the diagram], or equivalently aggregate output, which we expect to be negatively correlated with the unemployment rate.) It is important to keep in mind that Figure 6.5 represents a *cross section* – that is, a comparison of two distinct economies – each with a different fixed inflation rate. In this way, Figure 6.5 is better compared with Lucas (1973) study of the correlation of average inflation and output across countries, which, like Figure 6.5, shows a negative correlation between inflation and output.

In contrast, the Phillips curve is a *time-series* comparison of inflation and unemployment in different periods of the same economy. Therefore, to judge whether our model is also consistent with the Phillips curve, we must introduce variations in the inflation rate over time.

3.3 Random Monetary Policy

Now let us consider a single two-island economy with the following random monetary policy:

$$
\begin{aligned}
M_t &= M_{t-1} &&\text{with probability } \theta \quad (z_t = 1) \\
&= 2M_{t-1} &&\text{with probability } 1 - \theta \quad (z_t = 2). \quad (6.9)
\end{aligned}
$$

The realization of monetary policy (the realized value of z_t) is kept secret from the young until all purchases have occurred – that is, people do not learn M_t until period t is over.

As before, in order to determine their preferred work effort, the young wish to know whether they live with many or few other young people. Prices are the only thing directly observable by the young. Can they still deduce the population of young on the island by observing prices, as they were able to do in the case in which z was nonrandom? Look again at the market-clearing condition (Equation 6.3):

$$N^i l \left(p_t^i \right) = v_t^i \left(M_t / 2 \right), \tag{6.10}$$

or

$$p_t^i = \frac{M_t/2}{N^i l \left(p_t^i \right)} = \frac{z_t \left(M_{t-1}/2 \right)}{N^i l \left(p_t^i \right)}. \tag{6.11}$$

Because both the island population N^i and the money stock are unknown to people, it is no longer always possible to infer the number of young by looking at the price of goods. A high price, for example, may result from either a low population of young workers or a high fiat money stock. The distinction is important to the young. If the high price comes from a small number of young people, all of the young will want to work hard because they anticipate a good average return to their labor. Alternatively, if the high price comes from an increase in the fiat money stock, there is no reason to work especially hard. A high current money stock does not affect the anticipated rates of return to money and labor because it does not affect expectations of the future rate of money printing M_{t+1}/M_t; the monetary shocks are independent over time ("serially uncorrelated").

Is there anything about N^i that the young can learn from the price of goods? In our simplified version of the model with two possible population sizes and two possible rates of money printing, there are four possible states of the world represented by the various combinations of young people on the island and the realized value of z. Making use of Equation 6.11, let us look at what happens to the price level in each of those four cases.

Note from Table 6.1 that $p_t^a < p_t^b = p_t^c < p_t^d$. Therefore, two of the possible prices are unique: each can have occurred in only one particular combination of events. The price p_t^a can occur only when the money stock is small and the population is large, and the price p_t^d can occur only when the money stock is large and the population is small.

Therefore, if the young observe the price p_t^d, they can infer that the population on their island must be small. This implies that, on average, they can expect a good return to work, which encourages them to work hard, supplying l_t^d units of labor. Note that the price p_t^d is observed only when the fiat money stock is large ($z_t = 2$).

Table 6.1. *With a random money stock and random population, there are now four possible values for the price level. Only two of these four are unique. The low price P_t^a can occur only when the growth rate of money is low and the population is large. The high price P_t^d can occur only when the money growth rate is high and the population is small. However, the intermediate price $P_t^b = P_t^c$ is observed and young people cannot infer what values the money growth rate and the population take.*

	Number of Young People	
	$\frac{2}{3}N$	$\frac{1}{3}N$
Growth Rate of Fiat Money Stock		
$z_t = 1$	$P_t^a = \dfrac{M_{t-1}/2}{\frac{2}{3}Nl\left(P_t^a\right)}$	$P_t^b = \dfrac{M_{t-1}/2}{\frac{1}{3}Nl\left(P_t^b\right)}$
$z_t = 2$	$P_t^c = \dfrac{2M_{t-1}/2}{\frac{2}{3}Nl\left(P_t^c\right)}$	$P_t^d = \dfrac{2M_{t-1}/2}{\frac{1}{3}Nl\left(P_t^d\right)}$

Similarly, if the young observe the price p_t^a, they can infer that the population on their island must be large. This implies that, on average, they can expect a poor return to work, which encourages them to work little, supplying l_t^a units of labor. Note that the price p_t^a is observed only when the fiat money stock is small ($z_t = 1$).

What happens in cases b and c? In these two cases, the young are unable to infer the number of young on their island. We call this a signal extraction problem because a person cannot extract the accurate signal of the random variable by observing the price and output. There is one piece of information, the price, and two random variables affecting that variable. In the setting with nonrandom money, the price was the single piece of information that completely unveiled the one random variable, population. Here, people cannot tell if they are on an island with a small number of young people and a small money stock (case b) or on an island with a large number of young people but also a large money stock (case c). Unable to infer anything about the number of young on their island, each young worker in this situation will produce l^*, less than he would if he knew the population to be small and more than if he knew the population to be large. This will result in an intermediate price level, p^*, which is higher than p^a and lower than p^d.

Note that this randomized monetary policy does not always increase output. Although in case c people produce more than they would have if they knew their actual situation, in case b they produce less, imagining that the price they see may signal an increase in the money stock instead of an increase in the demand for their product. This output behavior is summarized in Figure 6.6.

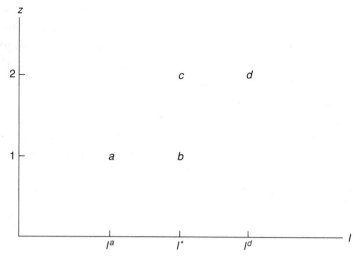

Figure 6.6. Inflation and output across islands. This figures plots the output and inflation combination predicted by the Lucas model for islands in a single economy in which the money growth rate is randomly set high or low.

In an economy, there is always one island with a large population of young and another with a small population of young. Therefore, in periods when the money stock is large ($z_t = 2$), one island will be in case c and another will be in case d, and total output will be a weighted average of l^c and l^d. Similarly, in periods when the money stock is small ($z_t = 1$), one island will be in case a and another will be in case b, and total output will be a weighted average of l^a and l^b. A graph of total output L will look something like Figure 6.7. This results in a relationship similar to the Phillips curve. Output is high (unemployment is low), when the inflation rate is high (a high value of z).

4 The Lucas Critique of Econometric Policy Evaluation

Suppose that economists look at the time series plotted in Figure 6.7. The economist sees this pattern is the economy's experience during, say, 100 years, but has no understanding of the model economy that generated it. The historical record clearly demonstrates that output is higher in the periods when fiat money stock is expanded. What might the economist be tempted to infer? The natural answer is to believe that money printing causes increased output.

The government controls the fiat money stock. Does this historical correlation suggest that the government can control aggregate output through its control of the money stock? If economists believe their government to be always more concerned with achieving high output than low rates of inflation, what policy might they then be tempted to propose? Print money to stimulate output in every period!

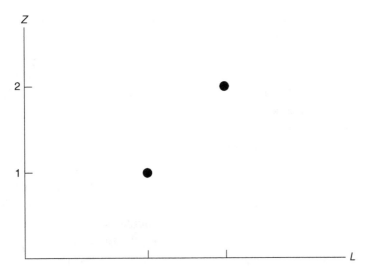

Figure 6.7. Inflation and aggregate output. This figure plots the combination of total output predicted by the Lucas model in a single economy in which the money growth rate is randomly set high or low.

Will this policy work? What happens to output in this economy if the money stock is expanded in every period? We have already worked out the answer in Figure 6.5. Output is reduced, not increased. When the government inflates the fiat money stock in every period, people will no longer be confused about the state of the world. They know that cases a and b will no longer occur. Therefore, if they see price p^c, they will know that there is a large number of people on their island, leading them to work less and create less output. Because they observe that the government always inflates, they will no longer imagine that they might be in case b, with a small number of young people and a small money stock. Inflation's boost to output under a random monetary policy no longer works because people are no longer fooled about the state of the world. (Inflating almost rarely does the trick, either. Suppose the government inflates in 99 of 100 periods. It is possible that people may find themselves in case a and b under this policy. Suppose that someone observes an intermediate price, call it p^*, knowing that there is a 99 percent chance that this is caused by a high money stock and only a 1 percent chance that it is caused by a low number of young people. Although they may shade their labor decision a tiny bit to reflect the 1 percent chance of being in case b, young people observing p^* will base their labor reaction to the far likelier possibility that the price is almost surely the result of case c, a large population and a large stock of money.)

Thus, the atheoretical economists will have egg on their faces. They went to the monetary authorities with a well-intentioned policy designed to permanently stimulate output and ended up reducing it instead. A correlation stable for 100 years changed the very moment the government tried to exploit it. What went wrong? Why did the inflation/output curve change the sign of its slope?

The correlation of money and output, or indeed any set of variables, results from the reaction of decision makers to the environment they face. An important feature of this environment is government policies. In particular, the relation between money and output depends on the monetary policy being followed. When the policy changed in this economy from one of random inflation to one of steady inflation, the reactions of producers also changed.

A correlation between variables that is the result of equilibrium interactions of an economy can be called a reduced-form correlation. In our example, this would be represented by the slope of a line connecting the points in Figure 6.7. The Lucas critique points out that these reduced-form correlations are subject to change when the government changes its policies and thus the rules under which decision makers operate. The example we have studied is particularly startling in that when the government changes from a policy of random inflation to one of steady inflation, the correlation (slope) not only changes, but it also changes sign – from positive to negative.

How, then, can we evaluate policies? We need some understanding about how people will react to the new policy: We need a theory. If we understand people's motives (preferences) and constraints (physical limitations, informational restrictions, and government policies), we can predict how people will react to changes in a policy. Lucas's point is not that econometric policy evaluation is impossible but that it cannot be done without theory, an understanding of how the economy works. It is not sufficient just to look at the data. The correlations found in the data are subject to change when the government policy changes.

5 Optimal Policy

What is the best policy? Should the government play dice with the economy? Let us look at the welfare consequences of a randomized monetary policy.

By randomizing the rate of expansion of the fiat money stock, the government creates confusion about the meaning of prices. In essence, the government is withholding information about the true state of the world. People are not always sure whether a price increase signals an increase in demand for their product, in which case they benefit by producing more, or an increase in the money stock, in which case they will not make themselves better off by increasing production. The more often the government expands the money stock, the more people believe that any observed price increase is just the government playing with the money stock. It follows that a major cause of randomizing the money stock is that people fail to take advantage of *actual* increases in the demand for their output.

Even if the government is able to fool people, should it? Why should the government want to fool people into producing more than they would choose to produce if they knew their actual situation? A baseball pitcher or a soccer player will randomize the location of the ball to fool the batter or goalie, but these players are on opposing teams. Isn't the government on the same team as the public it represents? Is the proper goal of a government manipulation of output or the welfare of its citizens?

An optimal policy would first specify the objective. For a benevolent government, a strategy aimed at manipulating the money supply does not maximize its citizens' lifetime welfare. The critical feature in our model economies is that people form expectations about the future – they are forward looking – and have incentives to learn money supply rules aimed at fooling them. As people learn how these rules work, or a close approximation, the policy surprise results in higher prices, no gains in output, and lower welfare.

6 Summary

We began this chapter by noting the observed relationship between the unemployment rate and the inflation rate and the subsequent breakdown of that relationship. This chapter presented a model consistent with these observations – a simplified version of Lucas's 1972 model.

In this model, young people cannot directly observe a real variable important to their output decision, the number of other young people producing on the island where they were born. We first considered a case of nonrandom inflation, where the monetary authority adheres to a fixed growth rate of the fiat money stock. In this case, agents could infer the number of young people producing on their island by observing the price of goods. An increase in inflation, which in this case is always known, lowers the rate of return on labor, discouraging work effort and lowering output. This is consistent with Lucas's observation that average inflation rates and output are negatively correlated across countries.

When we examined random inflation in our model, the relation of inflation to output changed dramatically, generating a Phillips curve. Random inflation complicated a person's work-effort decision because there is no way to infer the number of young people on their island by observing the price of the good. On the other hand, if a high price is caused by a small number of young people on the island, the young would want to work hard because they expect a high average return to their labor. On the other hand, if a high price is caused by an increase in the fiat money stock, there is no incentive to work hard. Because of the randomness of the money stock, prices are less informative about the true state of the world. This inability of people to determine the true state of the world causes them, at times, to work harder and produce more output than they would choose to do if they were able to determine their true situation. At other times, they mistakenly work less than they would choose to do if they were able to determine their true situation. When we observe this economy over time, we find that high inflation rates are associated with high levels of output (low unemployment rates) – the Phillips curve.

This relation between output and inflation depends crucially on the assumption of random inflation. A government attempting to exploit this relation by inflating in any systematic way will find that the positive correlation between inflation and output disappears.

The importance of the Lucas model lies not primarily in its explanation of the money/output correlation, as interesting as it may be. There are certainly other explanations, some of which we will study in later chapters, that may or may not do a better job of explaining that correlation.

Lucas's paper changed macroeconomics by demonstrating that the correlations among macroeconomic aggregates are subject to change when economic policy changes. This showed macroeconomists the pitfalls of evaluating policy by looking simply at correlations in the data, without a working theory of how people may react to policy changes. Those macroeconomists who open their eyes to Lucas's critique are thereafter compelled to fully specify the environment in which the economic agents studied make their decisions. It is with the Lucas critique in mind that this book endeavors to present only explicit models, specifying all our assumptions about people's preferences and constraints.

7 Exercises

6.1. Suppose there are two islands. The total population on the two islands is 500 people. The initial stock of fiat money is $500. The money stock increases according to $M_t = 1.1M_{t-1}$. The probability that a person is on Island 1 is 1/4 and the probability that a person is on Island 2 is 3/4. Let $l(p_t^i) = 4$ (so that labor supply does not depend on price).

a. Write down the money market-clearing condition for each island.

b. Solve for the equilibrium price level in date 1.

c. Write down the per-person transfer that the government gives to each old person.

d. Compute the value of the transfer.

6.2. Consider the following version of the model of this chapter. The number of young people born on island i in period t, N_t^i, is random according to the following specification:

$$N_t^i = \frac{4}{5}N \qquad \text{with probability .5}$$

$$= \frac{1}{5}N \qquad \text{with probability .5}$$

Assume that the fiat money stock grows at the fixed rate $z_t = z$ in all periods.

a. Set up the budget constraints that a person faces when young and when old in terms of l_t^i. Also set up the government budget constraint and money market-clearing condition. Find the lifetime budget constraint (combine the budget constraints of the young and old by substituting for l_t^i).

b. On which island would you prefer to be born? Explain with reference to the rate of return to labor.

c. Show how the rate of return to labor and the person's labor supply depend on the value of z.

For the following parts, assume that the growth rate of the fiat money stock z_t is random according to

$$z_t = 1 \quad \text{with probability } \theta$$
$$= 4 \quad \text{with probability } 1 - \theta.$$

The realization of z_t is kept secret from the young until all purchases of goods have occurred (people do not learn M_t until period t is over). Given these changes in assumption, answer the following questions.

d. How many states of the world would agents be able to observe if information about every variable were perfectly available? Describe those possible states.

e. How many states of the world are the agents able to distinguish when there is limited information (they do not know the value of z_t)?

f. Draw a graph of labor supply and the growth rate of the fiat money stock in each possible state of the world when there is limited information. What is the correlation observed between money creation and output?

g. Suppose the government wanted to take advantage of the relation between money creation and output. If it always inflates ($\theta = 1$), will the graph you derived in part f remain the same? Explain fully.

6.3. **(advanced)** Suppose a version of the model economy in which the money growth rate is a random variable. Let the probability be $4/5$ that $z_t = 1$ and the probability be $1/5$ that $z_t = 2$. The realization of monetary policy (the realized value of z_t) is kept secret from the young until all purchases have occurred – that is, people do not learn M_t until period t is over. Prices are the only thing directly observable by the young. Let $l(p_t^i) = 5 + 0.2p_t^i$.

a. Use Equation 6.11 to solve for the equilibrium price level on Island 1 and Island 2.

b. What does the price level tell the worker about the money supply change?

8 Appendix: A Proof by Contradiction

After presentation of Equations 6.6 and 6.7, we claimed that $p_t^A > p_t^B$. This appendix offers a proof of that claim. We utilize a common technique in mathematics whereby a proof is established by assuming the opposite conclusion and by then showing that this assumption leads to a contradiction.

We assume the opposite of our conclusion: $p_t^A \leq p_t^B$. From the assumption that people supply a greater amount of labor the larger the price they obtain for their output, this implies that

$$l\left(p_t^A\right) \leq l\left(p_t^B\right). \tag{6.12}$$

Multiplying both sides of Equation 6.1 by $(1/3)N$, we obtain

$$\frac{1}{3}Nl\left(p_t^A\right) \leq \frac{1}{3}Nl\left(p_t^B\right), \tag{6.13}$$

which in turn implies

$$\frac{1}{3}Nl\left(p_t^A\right) \le \frac{1}{3}Nl\left(p_t^B\right) < \frac{2}{3}Nl\left(p_t^B\right). \tag{6.14}$$

Rearranging Equation 6.14 yields

$$\frac{1}{\frac{1}{3}Nl\left(p_t^A\right)} > \frac{1}{\frac{2}{3}Nl\left(p_t^B\right)}. \tag{6.15}$$

By multiplying both sides of Equation 6.15 by $M_t/2$, we find that

$$\frac{M_t/2}{\frac{1}{3}Nl\left(p_t^A\right)} > \frac{M_t/2}{\frac{2}{3}Nl\left(p_t^B\right)}. \tag{6.16}$$

Comparing Equation 6.16 with our expression for p_t^A and p_t^B in Equations 6.6 and 6.7, we see that the left-hand side of Equation 6.16 is p_t^A and the right-hand side is p_t^B. This implies that $p_t^A > p_t^B$. This contradicts our original assumption that $p_t^A \le p_t^B$. The original assumption must be wrong, proving that, in fact, $p_t^A > p_t^B$.

Part II

Banking

Chapter 7

Capital

1 Roadmap

So far, people in our model economy have had only one way to acquire consumption at a later time – by holding fiat money. In the real world, however, there are many other assets. In this chapter, we concentrate on one particular alternative asset, capital. Capital is different from fiat money in that when people acquire capital this period, the capital produces goods next period and thus affects an economy's output. In contrast, fiat money allows a person to purchase some of the existing output next period but does not increase the quantity of output. We will see how the presence of an alternative asset affects people's willingness to hold fiat money. At a basic level, we see that different stores of value compete against each other. In this chapter, we start with the simplifying assumption that different stores of value are perfect substitutes. It is easy to see how changes in monetary policy could affect the stock of capital and thus the level of output.

Before taking all the challenges on at once, we begin by looking at the simplest model in which capital is the only store of value.

2 Capital

Consider the following production technology: If k_t units of the consumption good are converted into capital goods at time t, at time $t + 1$ you will receive xk_t consumption goods, where x is some positive constant. This implies that the gross real return on capital is x. In this book, we assume that date-t capital goods disintegrate in date $t + 1$. In other words, capital goods mature, producing consumption goods but are useless themselves. This is the same as saying that the capital depreciates at a 100 percent rate in the production period and therefore has no salvage value.[1]

---

[1] The linear capital production technology was introduced into the overlapping generations model by Cass and Yaari (1966). See also Wallace (1980). A production technology that used capital and labor together is described by Diamond (1965).

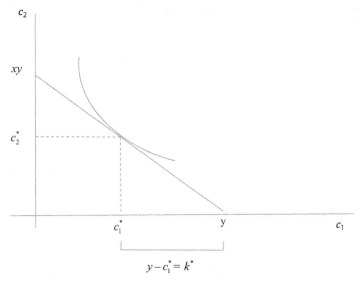

Figure 7.1. The person's choice of capital. This figure depicts the budget line when capital pays the gross return x. Each person maximizes utility by choosing the consumption pattern (c_1^*, c_2^*). Each person's capital holdings will be ($k^* = y - c_1^*$).

As in previous models, people in the single-country economy are endowed with y units of the consumption good when young and zero units when old. Population grows at the gross rate n. Each member of the initial old begins with a stock of capital that produces xk_0 goods in the first period.

Let us first analyze an equilibrium without fiat money. The capital technology enables the young to use some of today's consumption good to produce the consumption good at a later date. When young, people can convert part of their endowment into capital and consume the rest. This implies that in the first period of life, the budget constraint facing a person born in period t is

$$c_{1,t} + k_t \le y. \tag{7.1}$$

When old, the person will consume the goods produced by capital xk_t. The second-period constraint is then

$$c_{2,t+1} \le xk_t. \tag{7.2}$$

We can combine Equations 7.1 and 7.2 into a lifetime budget constraint. Equation 7.2 tells use that $k_t \ge c_{2,t+1}/x$. Substituting this into Equation 7.1, we obtain the lifetime budget constraint

$$c_{1,t} + \frac{c_{2,t+1}}{x} \le y. \tag{7.3}$$

We can see that x determines the slope of the budget line. If, for example, $x > 1$, then the vertical intercept of the budget line will lie farther from the origin than the horizontal intercept. How much capital will a person desire? As before, the answer is derived by superimposing the person's indifference map on the budget set. This is done in Figure 7.1.

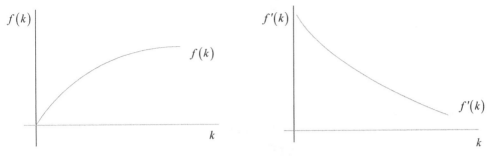

Figure 7.2. The total and marginal product of capital. These two drawings depict the return on capital when we relax the assumption that is constant. On the left-hand-side, we plot combinations of the capital stock and the total (future) product of capital under the assumption of diminishing marginal returns. The curvature in the left-hand-side drawing shows that as capital increases, total product increases, but a decreasing rate. We then transcribe the rate at which total product increases for each small increase in the capital stock on the right-hand-side drawing; that is, the marginal product of capital is decreasing as the capital stock increases. The marginal product of capital is simply the slope of the total product curve. The return on capital is the marginal product of capital.

This simple model of capital assumes that the output from each unit of capital is simply assumed to be some number unaffected by any economic forces. Although the assumption of a fixed rate of return of capital makes the model very easy for us to use, we sometimes need a more general model, especially to answer questions about how economic forces of government policies may affect the rate of return on capital.

Consider then the alternative assumption that capital exhibits a "diminishing marginal product"; as capital is increased, the added output from an extra unit of capital gets smaller (total output will still rise as long as the marginal product of capital is positive). We write output from capital as a function, $f(k)$, of capital per person k. Then the "marginal product of capital," the added output resulting from the addition of one extra unit of capital, can be written as $f'(k)$. The case of a diminishing marginal product of capital is graphed in the right frame of Figure 7.2.

Figure 7.2 also plots $f(k)$ (the upward-sloping curve, left frame), which represents the amount of output (or total product) generated in period $t + 1$ from the purchase of k units of capital in period t. Diminishing marginal product of capital is portrayed by the fact that the slope of the $f(k)$ curve decreases as k increases. In fact, the marginal product curve $f'(k)$ is merely the slope of the $f(k)$ curve.[2] So the marginal product could be downward sloping as it is in Figure 7.2 or a horizontal line as depicted in Equation 7.2 with the marginal product of capital $f'(k)$ equal to a constant, x.

---

[2] For those students familiar with calculus, the marginal product function $f'(k)$ is the derivative of the function $f(k)$.

3 Rate-of-Return Equality

Capital is not the only alternative to fiat money. People can store value over time in many other ways. They might purchase land and sell it when they want to consume. They might make loans to people who want to borrow against future income.[3]

What are the implications of the presence of alternative assets? Consider, for example, an economy with both capital and private debt (loans) that offers the rate of return r. Is there a relationship that must hold between the rates of return on capital and private debt?

Suppose the rate of return on private debt r is less than the rate of return on capital x. Would people be willing to make loans to other people who wish to borrow? No. To do so would imply accepting a lower rate of return which can be obtained by creating capital. In this case, people would prefer to put all of their savings into the creation of capital and would make no loans.

But what if borrowers must obtain loans? Consider, for example, someone with an endowment of goods when old but nothing when young. (Recall that we have assumed that people in our models will go to great lengths to avoid situations in which their consumption is zero in any period.) This implies that borrowers are placed in a position in which they must entice people to make them loans. How can they do so? By offering at least as good a rate of return on loans as a person could obtain by creating capital.

Suppose, on the other hand, that r exceeds x – that the rate of return on private loans exceeds that on capital. Would anyone choose to save in the form of capital? Again, the answer is no. In such a circumstance, people would choose to save solely in the form of loans to borrowers.

From our discussion here, it is clear that, for people to be willing to hold both capital and loans as assets, the rates of return on these two assets must be identical ($r = x$). Any imbalance between the two rates of return will imply that people will gravitate to the asset, loans or capital, that pays the highest rate of return.

However, it is important to realize that we have been implicitly assuming that private debt and capital are perfect substitutes from the viewpoint of people willing to save. Either asset can provide for second-period consumption just as well as the other. In such a circumstance, to observe both assets being held, their rates of return must be identical.

Consider more general versions of the preceding model in which there are many assets available to people. Furthermore, suppose there is no uncertainty about returns and no government restrictions that interfere with people's holdings of assets. If people are willing to hold all available assets simultaneously, the rates of return on these assets must be identical. We refer to this as the principle of "rate-of-return equality."

---

[3] We present a detailed model economy in which private loans exist in the appendix of this chapter.

4 Can Fiat Money Coexist with Another Asset?

Now suppose that we introduce fiat money into our economy with capital and private loans, so that we now have three potential ways for lenders to save. People who want to save will view capital, loans, and fiat money as perfect substitutes. Extending our previous discussion, it should be obvious that, for lenders to be willing to hold all three assets as a form of saving, their rates of return must be equal. We know that the rate of return on fiat money is n/z when the population and the stock of fiat money are growing at gross rates n and z, respectively. Therefore, if all three assets are held, rate-of-return equality requires that $n/z = r = x$.

If the rate of return on fiat money is less than that on loans or capital, then lenders will not choose to use fiat money as a form of saving. So for fiat money to be valued, its rate of return must be at least as large as those of the alternative assets, capital and loans.

Example 7.1 Consider an overlapping generations economy with two assets – capital and money. Suppose the number of young people born in period t is determined by $N_t = 1.5N_{t-1}$. Capital pays the gross rate of return $x = 1.25$. For what values of z will fiat money be valued?

4.1 The Tobin Effect

We have seen that, in a model economy where capital and fiat money coexist as perfect substitutes, we will observe rate-of-return equality between these two assets. Let us further explore the implications of this result in a situation in which capital displays diminishing marginal product.

When capital and fiat money are both valued, the desired capital stock is determined by the condition that the rate of return on fiat money n/z. What is the rate of return on capital in the case of a diminishing marginal product? This is given by capital's marginal product, $f'(k)$, which tells us how much additional output is produced when the capital stock increases by 1 unit. Hence, rate-of-return equality implies that $f'(k)$ must be equal to n/z. From this condition, we can determine a person's desired capital stock. When the rate of return on fiat money equals n/z, the capital stock is k^*, as shown in Figure 7.3.

Let us now consider a permanent increase in the anticipated rate of fiat money creation from z to z'. This increase in z generates inflation and lowers the anticipated rate of return on fiat money from n/z to n/z'. The lower rate of return on fiat money induces people to hold capital instead of fiat money. This switch to capital increases the capital stock, which lowers the marginal product of capital. People will stop switching from fiat money to capital either when fiat money balances have fallen to zero or when the rate of return to capital falls to the new lower rate of return on fiat money (when capital reaches k'^* in Figure 7.3). The substitution of private capital

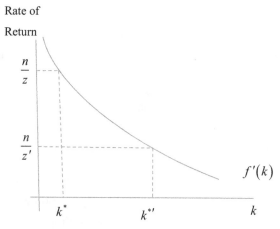

Figure 7.3. A person's capital choice with fiat money available. When fiat money and capital coexist as perfect substitutes, a person invests in capital up to the point where the marginal product of capital $f'(k)$ is equal to the rate of return on fiat money n/z. A permanent increase in the anticipated rate of fiat money growth lowers the return on fiat money from n/z to n/z' for $z' > z$. As we see in the diagram, people will choose to hold a larger quantity of capital.

for fiat money in reaction to an increase in anticipated inflation described by Tobin (1965), is called the "Tobin effect."

We conclude that, when capital and fiat money are substitutes, an increase in the rate of fiat money creation leads to an increase in the capital stock. Given that capital generates output in the following period, the larger capital stock implies a subsequent increase in output. In period t, total real output ("gross domestic product," or "GDP") in this economy equals the total endowment ($N_t y$) plus output generated by capital that was created in the previous period. Because in period $t-1$ each person created k_{t-1} units of capital and there were N_{t-1} born at date $t-1$, real GDP in period t equals

$$GDP_t = N_t y + N_{t-1} f(k_{t-1}). \tag{7.4}$$

If we live in a world where capital and money are perfect substitutes, should we use anticipated inflation brought about by an increase in z as a tool to increase output? The answer may be no – for two distinct reasons.

First, we must remember not to confuse output with welfare. The goal of a benevolent government is to increase the welfare (utility) of its citizens and not solely the output. The increase in z caused people to increase their holdings of capital, with the result being a decline in the rate of return on capital. As a consequence, the economy's capital stock may not be at its optimal level. As we show in Appendix B of this chapter, an economy's capital is optimal when the marginal product of capital is equal to n, the growth rate of the economy. A government policy of inflation would lead to capital formation above the optimal level.

Second, it is important to note that this effect is not large in the real world. Relative to the capital stock, the size of the fiat money stock in an economy is miniscule. At the end of 2013, the total net private capital stock in the United States was $38,054 billion. At the same time, the total fiat money stock was $3,716 billion.[4] Even if the entire fiat money stock were replaced by capital, the capital stock would increase by less than 10 percent.

5 When Fiat Money and Other Assets Are Not Substitutes

Let us now take a closer look at the effects of anticipated inflation on interest rates, capital, and output when fiat money and other assets are not substitutes. In particular we will examine the case in which the rate of return of capital and other assets exceeds that of fiat money. This certainly seems to be the case in most economies, where most debt pays (nominal) interest and fiat money pays none. This raises an obvious question: Why would fiat money still be valued? We postpone this important question for later chapters. For now, let us simply assume that each young person is required by law to acquire real balances of fiat money worth a fixed number of goods, q^*. This requirement is a simple way to ensure that fiat money is valued even if another asset has a better rate of return. This lets us take a first look at the effects of anticipated inflation when the rate of return of fiat money is dominated by that of other assets.[5]

5.1 Nominal Interest Rates

The interest rates cited by financial intermediaries and the press in the real world are nominal rates, describing the number of dollars paid in interest for each dollar lent. In times of inflation, these nominal rates do not reflect the real rate of return, the number of goods paid in interest for each good lent. Because utility depends on real consumption, it is important to learn the connection between real and nominal rates.

Let us use R_t to denote the nominal interest rate in period t. The nominal interest rate measures the return in units of money. Let r_t be real interest rate, which measures the return in goods. As always, we refer to gross rates of return. Remember that to find net rates of return, just subtract 1 from the gross rate. Let p_t denote the price of a good in fiat money and the inverse of the value of a unit of fiat money. The gross nominal rate on a one-period loan made at t (R_t) is the dollars received at $t + 1$ divided by the dollars lent at t. Therefore, to find the real rate from the given

---

[4] The capital stock data are taken from the *Survey of Current Business*. (See the Bureau of Economic Analysis Web site at http://www.bea.gov/national/ Table 2.1.) It is the amount of fixed private capital (nonresidential and residential). The value of the fiat money stock is series BOGUMBNS from the Federal Reserve Bank of St. Louis FRED database (http:www.stls.frb.org/fred/).

[5] We take a more serious look at required holding of money in Chapter 8.

nominal rate, we must divide each dollar value by the price level at that time (or multiply by the value of a dollar at that time). This is done in Equation 7.5 for a loan of d dollars.

$$r_t = \frac{\frac{R_t d}{p_{t+1}}}{\frac{d}{p_t}} = \frac{R_t p_t}{p_{t+1}}. \tag{7.5}$$

By the definition of these terms, Equation 7.5 relates the gross rates of nominal interest, real interest, and inflation. Rearranging terms, we can express this relation in the following way:

$$R_t = r_r \left(\frac{p_{t+1}}{p_t} \right). \tag{7.6}$$

If we subtract 1 from each side of Equation 7.6, we can express this relationship in terms of net rates:

$$R_t - 1 = r_r \left(\frac{p_{t+1}}{p_t} \right) - 1$$

$$= [(r_t - 1) + 1] \left[\left(\frac{p_{t+1}}{p_t} \right) - 1 + 1 \right] - 1$$

$$= (r_t - 1) + \left(\frac{p_{t+1}}{p_t} - 1 \right) + (r_t - 1) \left(\frac{p_{t+1}}{p_t} - 1 \right). \tag{7.7}$$

Equation 7.7 states that the "net nominal interest rate" $(R_t - 1)$ equals the "net real rate" $(r_t - 1)$ plus the "net inflation rate" $[(\frac{p_{t+1}}{p_t} - 1)]$ plus the product of the two. For low values of the real interest rate and the inflation rate, this last term is small and is often ignored.

What is the net inflation rate, according to the results of our model? In Chapter 4, we learned that the gross rate of return on fiat money (v_{t+1}/v_t) in the case of a growing economy and an expanding fiat money stock is n/z. We also learned that the price level in every period t is related to the value of fiat money in the same period by

$$p_t = \frac{1}{v_t}. \tag{7.8}$$

From the relationship $(v_{t+1}/v_t) = n/z$ and Equation 7.8, we find that the net inflation rate is

$$\frac{p_{t+1}}{p_t} - 1 = \frac{v_t}{v_{t+1}} - 1 = \frac{z}{n} - 1. \tag{7.9}$$

Example 7.2 Suppose that fiat money stock changes according to the rule $M_t = 1.5 M_{t-1}$, and the number of young people born in each generation evolves according to $N_t = 1.25 N_{t-1}$. Let the gross real interest rate be 1.1.

a. Calculate the gross and net inflation rates.
b. Calculate the gross and net real rates of return on fiat money.

c. Calculate the gross and net nominal interest rates.
d. Calculate the net nominal interest rate using the approximation $R - 1 = (r - 1) + (p_{t+1}/p_t - 1)$. Compare your answer here with the one in part c.

5.2 Anticipated Inflation and the Nominal Interest Rate

If we return to Equation 7.7, we can examine the effect of inflation on real and nominal rates of interest. In particular, we want to ask if the nominal rate fully adjusts to an anticipated change in the inflation rate so that the real interest rate remains unchanged. The predicted full adjustment of the nominal interest rate to anticipated inflation is called the "Fisher effect," after Irving Fisher, an American economist of the early part of this century.

Assume that capital pays a constant gross rate of return, x. By the rate-of-return equality, the real interest rate in this economy must equal the real rate of return on capital, a parameter given by the physical environment. No one would make a loan unless it paid at least this real return. A loan must therefore offer a nominal rate of return, R, so that

$$x = \frac{\frac{R}{p_{t+1}}}{\frac{1}{p_t}} = \frac{Rv_{t+1}}{v_t} = \frac{Rn}{z}, \tag{7.10}$$

or

$$R = x\left(\frac{z}{n}\right). \tag{7.11}$$

Therefore, the nominal interest rate rises with anticipated inflation to keep the real interest rate constant at x.

As shown in Figure 7.4, there is a tendency for nominal interest rates and inflation rates to move together in accordance with the Fisher Effect. However, because of changes in the real interest rate, the gap between the nominal interest rate and the inflation rate is not constant. It is not possible to tell from this graph whether real interest rate changes are influenced by the rate of inflation or by some other factor. The following section suggests one way that inflation may affect real interest rates.

5.3 Anticipated Inflation and the Real Interest Rate

An exception to the Fisher effect may occur if two conditions are met. If fiat money and capital are substitutes, a rise in the anticipated inflation rate will encourage people to reduce their holdings of fiat money and increase their holdings of capital.[6] This is the Tobin effect.

If we also assume that capital has a diminishing marginal product, the increase in capital described by the Tobin effect can occur only with a reduction in the marginal

---

[6] Freeman (1985) shows that a fixed fiat money stock is optimal in this economy, just as it was in the economy without capital.

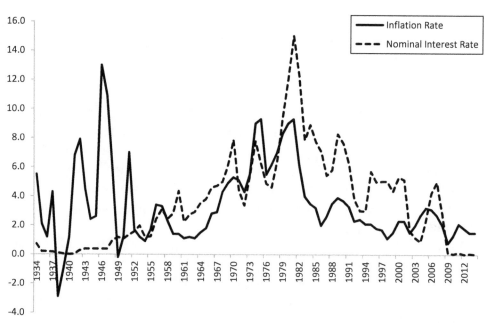

Figure 7.4. The nominal interest rate and the inflation rate. Periods of high inflation rates are typically associated with high nominal interest rates. *Source:* The inflation rate is the annual inflation according to the GDP deflator. The interest rate is the 90-day Treasury bill rate. Both series are obtained from the Federal Reserve Bank of St. Louis FRED database (http://www.stls.frb.org/fred/index.html).

product of capital. This represents a reduction in the real return on capital and thus, by rate-of-return equality, a reduction in the real rate of interest. In this case, the increase in anticipated inflation will still lead to a rise in the nominal interest rate; however, because of the simultaneous decrease in the real interest rate, the nominal rate will not rise by the full amount of the rise in anticipated inflation.

6 Risk

There is another way to get two stores of value to coexist in equilibrium. The idea is to include risk in the form of uncertain returns on capital. So far, we have assumed that all assets pay a rate of return that is known with complete certainty. Then all we need to do is compare returns on the two assets and people will choose the one with the highest return. Often, the future unfolds differently than what people expect. We do not possess perfect foresight as we have been assuming for most of this book. Now one asset can offer a higher average return than another. People are willing to hold both assets – the average high-return one and the low-return one – as part of a diversified portfolio.

To make this more concrete, what would happen to rate-of-return equality if instead we assumed that one asset had a random rate of return? There are limitless ways to introduce random future events into the model economy. For example, what happens if we assume that not every borrower repays their loan? Suppose there is some positive probability that a loan will not be repaid by the borrower – the borrower may "default" on a loan. This means that there is an element of risk in making a loan. As before, suppose the capital always pays the rate of return x. Now capital and loans are not viewed as perfect substitutes; one of the assets (loans) pays an uncertain return, and the other (capital) pays a certain, or guaranteed, return.

We refer to people as being "risk neutral" if they do not care about uncertain events. Risk-neutral people would concentrate solely on the expected return. With risk-neutral people, we would expect rate-of-return equality to hold on average. For lenders to be willing to make a loan, they would have to receive on average a rate of return on loans that equaled the rate of return on capital. By an asset's average or expected rate of return, we mean the expected value of its rate of return. If there are a finite number of possible rates of return, the expected rate of return can be calculated as the sum of each rate of return multiplied by the probability that it will occur. Suppose an asset pays return $r_1, r_2, \ldots, r_n$. The probabilities of paying each rate of return $r_1, r_2, \ldots, r_n$ are $\pi_1, \pi_2, \ldots, \pi_n$, respectively. The "expected rate of return" on this asset is measured by the expected value of its rate of return, which we denoted as $E(r)$. We calculate this expected value by

$$E(r) = \pi_1 r_1 + \pi_2 r_2 + \cdots + \pi_n r_n. \tag{7.12}$$

Consider, for example, a loan paying either a 15 percent net interest rate (a gross rate of return of 1.15), or there is a 10 percent chance of default returning only half the principal. This loan offers two possible rates of return. With a probability of .9, the loan pays a gross rate of return of 1.15. When there is a default, the loan pays a gross rate of return of 0.5, with a probability of .1. To calculate the expected gross rate of return of this loan, we add the possible rates of return multiplied by their respective probabilities,

$$E(r) = (0.9)1.15 + (0.1)(0.5) = 1.085,$$

or an expected net rate of return equal to $1.085 - 1 = 0.085 = 8.5$ percent.

Example 7.3 Find the expected rate of return of farm machinery that costs 10 goods but produces 18 goods in normal weather, 8 goods in rainy weather, and 5 goods in a drought. There is a one-fourth chance of rainy weather occurring and a 10 percent chance of drought. Find the expected rate of return. Note that the gross rate of return is the total return divided by the amount invested.

Are people risk neutral? Suppose you were offered this bet: A fair coin will be tossed. If it lands on heads, you will lose all of your possessions; if it lands on tails, your possessions will be doubled. Will you take this bet? If not, you are "risk averse." Most people are likely to refuse this bet because the drop in utility from losing the bet exceeds the gain in utility from winning the bet, even though the potential loss and potential gain are equal when measured in goods.

If people are risk averse, it does not mean that they will never accept a risky asset. As a risk-averse person, you may not wager $1,000 on the toss of a fair coin if you stand to win only another $1,000. You may, however, take the chance of losing $1,000 if you will gain $100,000 by winning the toss. If people dislike risk (are risk averse), they will not hold a risky asset if its expected rate of return equals that of the risk-free asset. They will hold a risky asset only if its expected rate of return exceeds that of the risk-free asset, compensating for the risk. The extra average rate of return that is necessary to entice people to hold a risky asset is called a risk premium. The greater the potential loss and the greater the probability of the loss, the larger the risk premium must be.

Suppose a risky asset pays an expected rate of return equal to $E(r_{risky})$ and that a risk-free asset always pays the rate of return r_{safe}. Then the risk premium on the risky asset is defined by

$$\text{risk premium} = E(r_{risky}) - r_{safe}. \tag{7.13}$$

7 Summary

In earlier chapters, money was the only asset available to the people in our model economies. However, in the real world, many alternative assets to fiat money exist. The goal of this chapter was to demonstrate the effects that the presence of these alternative assets might create.

To begin, we introduced a simple model of capital, an important alternative asset to money because capital produces goods. At first, we considered capital in isolation in a model without fiat money.

We then asked what might happen if we introduced other assets into the model so that these alternative assets competed with capital. It is here that we encountered the important principle of rate-of-return equality. This principle states that, if assets are viewed as perfect substitutes, then for people to be willing to hold all the assets simultaneously, their rate of return must be equal.

However, we must keep in mind the strong assumptions behind the principle of rate-of-return equality. It is important that all of the assets be viewed as perfect substitutes for one another. If, for example, one of the assets is risky and the others are not, we would not expect rate-of-return equality to hold. Because it is easily observed that, in the real world, fiat money does not pay the same rate of return as capital and many other assets, we must look for reasons that fiat money is not a perfect substitute for other assets. We study this topic in the next chapter.

8 Exercises

7.1. Suppose people in our overlapping generations model have the opportunity either to hold fiat money with complete safety or to lend to someone who may never repay the loan. The chance of such a default is 10 percent. Assume a stationary monetary equilibrium in which the population grows at a net rate of 8 percent and the fiat money stock is fixed. What real interest rate will be charged to the borrower if people are risk neutral? What can you say about the level of the real interest rate if people instead are risk averse?

7.2. Suppose capital is risky and pays gross real rates of return of 1.2, 1.1, and 0.9 with probabilities .1, .7, and .2, respectively. A risk-free asset pays a safe gross real rate of return of 1.04. What is the expected rate of return on capital? What is the risk premium of capital?

7.3. Consider an economy in which the money growth rate permanently increases from 3 percent to 10 percent. What is the effect of this policy change on the capital stock?

9 Appendix A: A Model of Private Debt

In Chapter 7, we introduce a model in which people hold capital. We also discuss the implications of introducing private loans into that model. In this part of the appendix, we develop a formal model of private debt, IOUs issued by people.

9.1 Private Debt

To introduce IOUs into our simple model of two-period lives, let there be two types of people – borrowers, endowed with nothing when young and y when old, and lenders, endowed with y when young and nothing when old.[7] For simplicity, there is no fiat money or capital in the economy (we introduce capital later in the appendix).

9.2 The Lender Problem

A lender in the first period of life divides her endowment between consumption ($c_{1,L}$) and loans to borrowers (l). When old, her consumption ($c_{2,L}$) is limited by the amount received by loans repaid with interest (rl). (To reduce the notational burden, we drop the time subscripts and consider only stationary equilibria.) Note that r is the gross real rate of interest on private loans. This is the return from both principal and interest, which is 1 plus the net rate of interest. If, for example, the net rate of interest is 9 percent, the gross rate of interest is 1.09. We write a lender's constraints at equality as

$$c_{1,L} + l = y, \tag{7.14}$$

$$c_{2,L} = rl. \tag{7.15}$$

Combining these constraints, we obtain the lifetime budget constraint for a lender:

$$c_{1,L} + \frac{c_{2,L}}{r} = y. \tag{7.16}$$

---

[7] For a more formal undergraduate-level treatment of the interaction of fiat money with loans, see Wallace (1984).

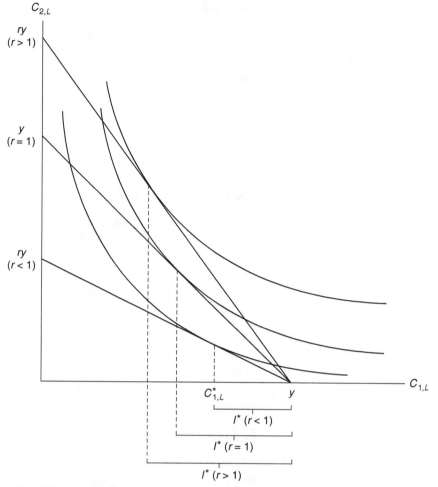

Figure 7.5. The Lender Problem. Here, we consider different values of the real interest rate and how these changes will affect what a lender's chooses in terms of consumption and loan bundles. With preferences represented by an indifference map in the diagram, the lender chooses to increase loans as r, the real interest rate increases.

In Figure 7.5, we graph this budget line for various levels of the real interest rate r. If we knew the person's exact preferences, we could learn the number of goods lent by a person for each value of r. One such function is graphed in Figure 7.6. Note that this relationship does not have to be positively sloped everywhere, although a typical assumption is that higher interest rates lead to a greater supply of loans.

9.3 The Borrower Problem

A borrower, when young, can consume ($c_{1,B}$) only what he borrows (b). When old, he may consume ($c_{2,B}$) what is left of his endowment after he repays his loan. These

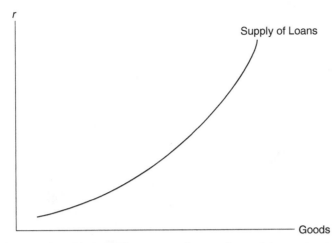

Figure 7.6. The supply of loans. We assume that as the real interest rate increases, the amount of loans made by the typical lender also increases. When we aggregate across all people in the economy, the total supply of loans will vary directly with the real interest rate.

constraints can be written as

$$c_{1,B} = b, \tag{7.17}$$

$$c_{2,B} = y - rb. \tag{7.18}$$

These constraints can be combined to get the borrower's lifetime budget line:

$$c_{1,B} + \frac{c_{2,B}}{r} \leq \frac{y}{r}. \tag{7.19}$$

This budget line is graphed in Figure 7.7 for $r > 1$, $r = 1$, and $r < 1$.

Note that, for a typical indifference curve, as r decreases, $c_{1,B}$ increases. Because $c_{1,B} = b$, the amount borrowed also increases as r decreases. This gives us an individual demand curve for loans that is negatively sloped. Aggregating across all borrowers in the economy, we obtain a total demand for loans curve that is also negatively sloped. We can combine this demand curve with the supply curve for loans to find the equilibrium quantity of loans L^* and the equilibrium interest rate r^*, as shown in Figure 7.8.

9.4 Private Debt and Capital

Now suppose that we introduce capital into our model of borrowing and lending. For simplicity, we assume that capital pays the constant gross rate of return x. Now lenders have two assets from which to choose – capital and loans. Let us also assume that there is no risk inherent in either of the two assets. Our discussion of the principle of rate of return equality will help us to discover which asset the borrowers will choose.

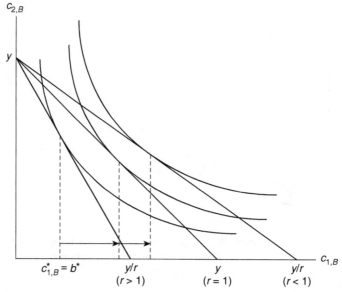

Figure 7.7. The borrower's problem. As the real interest rate fall, for example, a typical borrower will want to increase consumption when young. Because consumption when young is financed by borrowing, the borrower's demand for loans will increase, for example, as the real interest rate decreases.

Suppose the rate of return on capital x is less than r^*. Lenders will choose the asset that pays the greater rate of return, so if $x < r^*$, lenders will make only loans; there holdings of capital will be zero. People will choose to hold capital only if $x \geq r^*$.

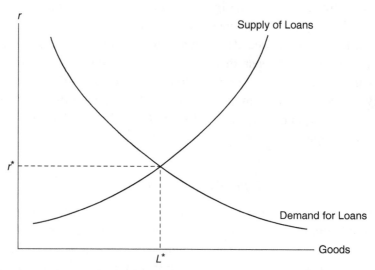

Figure 7.8. The equilibrium real interest rate. If we plot the total demand for loans and the total supply of loans on the same graph, we can determine the equilibrium quantity of loans (L^*) and the equilibrium real interest rate (r^*).

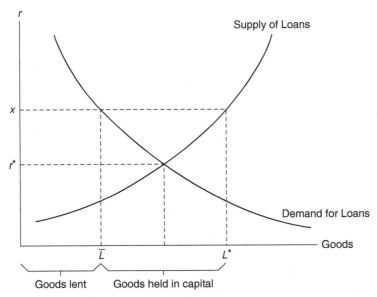

Figure 7.9. Holdings of capital and loans when $x > r^*$. When the rate of return on capital exceeds r^*, lenders will hold a mixed portfolio of capital and loans. The total amount of loans made is equal to $\bar{L}$ and the total amount of capital is equal to $L^* - \bar{L}$.

Now suppose that $x > r^*$. We know that lenders can be enticed to make loans to borrowers only if the real interest rate on loans is equal to x. This means that the real interest rate will exceed r^*. Such a case is illustrated in Figure 7.9.

Note from Figure 7.9 that at the rate of return x, borrowers want to borrow only $\bar{L}$, but lenders want to save L^*. The difference is held in the form of capital.

9.5 Appendix Exercises

7.4. Use the graph in Figure 7.9 to answer the following questions:

    a. Suppose the government restricts total borrowing to an amount less than $\bar{L}$. What would the effect be on capital holdings?

    b. Find the effect of an increase in the supply of loans on capital and the interest rate. What would the effect be on the interest rate if there were no capital?

    c. Find the effect of a decrease in capital's rate of return on the amount borrowed and the stock of capital.

7.5. Consider an economy of three-period-lived people in overlapping generations. Each person is endowed with y goods when young and old and nothing when middle-aged. The population of each generation born in period t is N_t, where $N_t = nN_{t-1}$. There are no assets other than loans. Explain how credit can be used to provide for consumption when middle-aged. Point out who lends to whom and write the condition for the equality of supply and demand for loans in period t. Write the budget constraints for the young, the middle-aged, and the old. Be sure to define any notation you introduce.

7.6. Consider an overlapping generations model with 200 lenders and 100 borrowers born in every period. Everyone lives for only two periods. Each lender is endowed with 20 goods when young and nothing when old. Each borrower is endowed with nothing when young and 40 goods when old. The lenders want to save 10 goods each, regardless of the rate of return on their savings. Each borrower wants to borrow $10/r$ goods each, where r is the gross real interest rate on private IOUs. The lending market is free and competitive.

    a. In a nonmonetary equilibrium, what will the market-clearing value of r be?

    b. Now turn to a monetary equilibrium. Suppose $z = 0.5$. What will the real fiat money holdings of a typical lender be?

10 Appendix B: The Golden Rule Capital Stock

Is more capital always desirable? At first glance, it may appear that more capital is always desirable, because it leads to higher output in the future. However, we must realize that, to create capital, a person must give up consumption today. With this realization, we may also wish to ask the following questions: What is the optimal level of capital? Will a free market necessarily induce the optimal level of capital?

We answer these questions in the context of a model in which capital is created at t and pays the return $f(k_t)$ at $t + 1$, with the diminishing marginal product $f'(k_t)$.[8] To determine the optimal capital stock, we must first learn what combinations of consumption and capital are feasible in an economy with capital; that is, we must find the feasible set for economies with capital. With the addition of capital to our model, we now have a source of goods in addition to endowments. The goods available for use in period t now include the output from capital created in the previous period $N_{t-1}f(k_{t-1})$ as well as endowments of the current young $N_t y$. There is also a new use for goods: investment. The total use of the consumption good in period t is for consumption by the young ($N_t c_{1,t}$), consumption by the old ($N_{t-1}c_{2,t}$), and investment in capital ($N_t k_t$). Hence, the feasible set can be written as

$$N_t c_{1,t} + N_{t-1} c_{2,t} + N_t k_t \leq N_t y + N_{t-1} f(k_{t-1}). \tag{7.20}$$

As before, we divide through by N_t to find the feasible set in per-young-person terms. If we also restrict ourselves to stationary solutions, we can eliminate the time subscripts. These simplifications result in

$$c_1 + \frac{c_2}{n} + k \leq y + \left[\frac{f(k)}{n} \right] \tag{7.21}$$

or

$$c_1 + \frac{c_2}{n} \leq y + \left[\frac{f(k)}{n} - k \right]. \tag{7.22}$$

Equation 7.22 reveals the conditions under which capital is desirable in a stationary allocation. The right-hand side of this equation represents output net of

---

[8] This is a slightly simplified version of Diamond's (1965) original analysis.

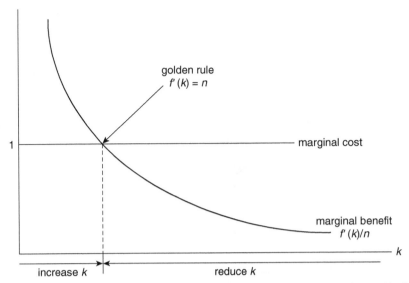

Figure 7.10. The golden rule for capital accumulation. In determining the optimal capital stock, we compare the marginal benefits of creating capital with the marginal cost. As long as the marginal benefit exceeds the marginal cost, the capital stock should be increased. On the other hand, too much capital is being created if the marginal benefit is less than or equal to the marginal cost. The optimal capital stock is where the marginal product of capital is equal to the growth rate of the economy.

costs of investment, or "net domestic product," per young person. These are the goods available for consumption. The optimal stationary capital stock maximizes the goods available for consumption in a stationary allocation.

Consider first the case for a constant population ($n = 1$). A one-unit increase in capital per young person in each generation, k, has two effects on output net of investment. It increases output from capital [$f(k)$] by its marginal product $f'(k)$ but increases the cost of investment by one. As long as the unit of capital produces more than it costs, it will increase the goods available for consumption in stationary allocations.

The case of a growing population ($n > 1$) is only slightly different. The marginal benefit per young person of an increase in k is the marginal product of capital divided by n because the output from capital comes from a smaller number of people; there are only $1/n$ old people for each young person. Therefore, a one-unit increase in capital per old person increases the goods available for consumption by $f'(k)/n$. It follows that extra capital is desirable in a stationary allocation as long as its benefits, $f'(k)/n$, exceed its costs, one. The golden rule for capital accumulation is therefore to increase capital until its marginal product just equals the rate of population growth, as depicted in Figure 7.10.

Recall that the principle of rate-of-return equality requires that interest rates must equal the marginal product of capital. It is simple, therefore, to learn whether a stationary economy is at the golden rule: simply compare its interest rate with its growth rate. If its growth rate exceeds its interest rate, an economy has too much

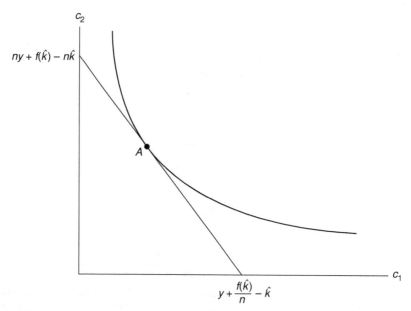

Figure 7.11. The golden rule allocation of consumption. If capital creation is at its golden rule level, the feasible set is as illustrated in this diagram. The golden rule consumption allocation, point A, can be found at the tangency of the feasible set line and the highest attainable indifference curve.

capital, or "capital overaccumulation"; if the interest rate exceeds the growth rate, an economy has too little capital relative to the golden rule, or "capital underaccumulation."

As soon as capital is at the level $(\hat{k})$ that maximizes net output, it remains to find the golden rule allocation of consumption between c_1 and c_2. Graphing the feasible set at $\hat{k}$, we find a line of slope $-n$, as graphed in Figure 7.11. As before, we find the golden rule allocation of consumption at the unique tangency between the feasible set and an indifference curve (point A in Figure 7.11).

Nothing guarantees that a free market will lead to an interest rate that equals the economy's growth rate. The stock of capital is determined by the amount that people wish to save for later in life. If this amount is smaller than the golden rule capital stock (capital underaccumulation), the marginal product of capital will be higher than n. If this amount is larger than the golden rule capital stock (capital overaccumulation), the marginal product of capital will be lower than n.

When the interest rate is n, both conditions for the golden rule are met:

1. Capital is at the level that maximizes output (its marginal product equals the interest rate n).
2. Consumption is distributed among young and old in the way that maximizes stationary utility.

When capital is overaccumulated, one way to get to the golden rule is to issue a constant stock of fiat money, with the golden rule rate of return n. With this asset as an alternative, no one will choose to invest in any capital whose marginal product is less than n. Moreover, at the golden rule rate of return, people will also choose the combination of c_1 and c_2 that maximizes steady-state utility.

Another way to alter the accumulation of capital in equilibrium is through intergenerational transfers, like social security in the United States and social insurance in Canada. Taxing young people to pay old people reduces the amount that people will save on their own to provide for retirement, reducing the need for capital as a form of saving. This can help an economy out of an overaccumulation of capital. If the economy faces instead an underaccumulation of capital, the transfer must go in the opposite direction, with old people taxed to fund subsidies to young people. This will increase private saving through capital, as young people have more available for savings and a greater need for savings because of the taxes they will face when old. The effects on capital, consumption, and savings of taxes and subsidies involving the young and old are more carefully studied in Chapter 16.

10.1 Appendix Exercise

7.7. (advanced) Consider an economy of two-period-lived people in overlapping generations. Each person produces from labor y goods when young but nothing when old. The number of people born doubles in every period. There is the following capital technology: If k_t goods per young person are turned into capital at t, the capital produces $f(k_t)$ goods at $t + 1$. The diminishing marginal product of capital is $f'(k_t)$. After production takes place, δ units of capital are lost to depreciation. However, the remaining units of capital can be consumed.

    a. Find an equation that represents the set of feasible stationary allocations and explain it in words.

    b. Find the equation that describes the golden rule capital stock for this economy. You may use either calculus or a marginal cost and marginal benefit analysis.

Chapter 8

Liquidity and Financial Intermediation

1 Roadmap

In Chapter 7, started with new stores of value that were perfect substitutes for fiat money. In these economies, we learned that if the rate of return on other assets is greater than that of fiat money, fiat money will not be valued. Yet, when you look around, you see that fiat money is valued in many real economies even though other assets, like capital, have a greater return than fiat money. One way to get money and capital to coexist is to assume the return on capital is riskier than the return on money. Here, we consider the additional possibility that fiat money is valued because it is more liquid than alternative assets.

To incorporate liquidity into the basic framework, we add an extra period to a person's life. With three-period-lived people, liquidity is easy to characterize: a store of value is more liquid if it can be turned into the consumption good at any time in a person's life at the lowest cost. After presenting a model economy in which liquidity differences exist, we talk about banks as a means of overcoming liquidity problems. A bank, or any financial intermediary, is a private company that can arrange to offer people a liquid substitute for fiat money. Why might it wish to do so? The difference in the rate of return of liquid and illiquid assets opens up an opportunity for profits through arbitrage – by borrowing at the low rate of return of money while investing at the high rate of return of the illiquid asset.

As we develop these topics, there is an important friction that keeps people from doing a bank's jobs on their own. Specifically, we do not allow people to create their own paper claims that would allow them to effectively sell part of their capital. The information problem arises because it is assumed to be too costly for anyone to verify that such a claim is valid or not.

2 Money as a Liquid Asset

As we saw in Chapter 7, if fiat money and other assets were perfect substitutes, people would value only the asset with the greater rate of return. To explain why fiat money is valued despite offering a lower rate of return than other assets, it may help to note evidence that fiat money and capital are held for different motives. Fiat money changes hands much more frequently than other assets (is held for shorter periods of time) and (with other money-like assets) is used in the bulk of all transactions. Money's acceptance, despite its low rate of return, may therefore be linked to its usefulness in exchange.

Whenever an exchange takes place, there may be "transaction costs" incurred that would not have been incurred if the owners had held simply onto the items exchanged. It is generally accepted that money is less costly to exchange than other assets. A person can exchange $10 worth of currency for $10 worth of the consumption good in the blink of an eye. There is virtually no transaction cost associated with exchanging dollars, for example, for goods. In contrast, suppose you wanted to exchange a house for consumption goods today. The cost incurred when a house changes hands is compared with the negligible cost of exchanging fiat money. It costs thousands of dollars to verify the quality of the house and that ownership is legal. To make a house sell quickly, a person will need to drop the price so that the house's price and its value – what it would sell for in a reasonable amount of time – can be substantially different. We call the drop in price relative to value and the other selling costs a transaction cost. For a house, the transaction cost can be much greater if you have to sell a house in 24 hours compared with allowing a house to be sold over a normal course of time.

It is true that if held for more than 20 years, a house pays a much better return (including both its resale value and the value of the shelter it provides) than fiat money does. Is this true for a shorter period? Approximate the rate of return, net of transaction costs, on a house owned for a week. Which asset now offers the greater rate of return? Note that the notion that people value an asset for its rate of return is not violated by the example of liquid assets so long as we note that an asset's rate of return may depend on transaction costs and the holding period of the asset.

We say that an asset is "liquid" if it is exchanged easily, quickly, and at little cost. Fiat money is obviously a more liquid asset than a house, but why? What properties of houses make them so costly to exchange? Houses are useful as an extreme example of transaction costs because just about everything about them makes them difficult to exchange. For one, they cannot be transported, and they come in units far too large for most transactions. One might get around these difficulties by issuing portable paper titles to a fraction of a house (entitling the owner to a fraction of the rent), but even these house-backed assets are unlikely to circulate.

There remains the problem of ascertaining the value of the title. A store manager will not accept a fractional house title in exchange for goods because it is not possible to verify that it is worth what the seller claims without checking for termites and the quality of the local schools. Such costs are transaction costs because they are incurred only if the house changes ownership. Other assets, such as personal IOUs or stocks, without land's problems of portability or divisibility, still have values that are costly for buyers to learn. In contrast, the value of fiat money is easy to learn. If counterfeiting is not a major problem, the value of fiat money is learned instantly or after a few seconds of counting.

2.1 A Model of Illiquidity

Let us now try to capture the essential distinctions between liquid and illiquid assets in an expanded version of our model.[1] In particular, we seek to describe a model economy consistent with the following observations about real economies:

1. Fiat money and capital are both valued.
2. The rate of return of capital exceeds that of fiat money.
3. Fiat money is exchanged more often than capital (fiat money is held for the short term, and capital is held for the long term).

Consider an economy of overlapping generations in which people live for three periods. People are endowed with y units of the consumption good when young and with nothing in the other two periods of life. We will extend our usual assumptions about preferences to a three-period case. As before, let N_t represent the number of people in the generation born at t, with $N_t = nN_{t-1}$. We also assume that there is a constant supply of fiat money M in the economy. The initial old possess this stock of money in the first period. Extending our previous notation, $c_{1,t}$, $c_{2,t+1}$, $c_{3,t+2}$ will denote a member of generation t's consumption in the first, second, and third periods of life, respectively.

There is a single *physical* asset, capital, in this economy.[2] A unit of capital, k_t, may be created from a unit of the consumption good in any period t. Capital may be created in any amount. Two periods after it is created, a unit of capital produces X units of the consumption good and then disintegrates. Let $X > n^2$.

Two assumptions about information will be key to the liquidity of capital in this economy. First, assume that it is expensive to observe the capital created by others; indeed, to avoid any ambiguity, let us assume that it is impossible for others to observe it. Second, let us assume (for now) that it is impossible to enforce the repayment of IOUs because people can costlessly hide from anyone looking for them and in this way avoid repaying their IOUs. As a result, no one is willing to lend. Later in the chapter we examine this economy when the repayment of IOUs can be enforced.

We can easily characterize the individual's holdings of capital and money. Given the pattern of endowments, individuals must find a means of providing for consumption in the second and third periods of their lives. To provide for consumption

---

[1] The model is taken from Freeman (1985).

[2] As we saw in Chapter 6, alternatives to capital will offer the same rate of return, adjusted for risk. For this reason, we lose little by looking only at a single asset. We chose capital to be that asset for most of this book because its rate of return is easy to describe. More importantly, the capital stock affects output.

for the third period of life, a person can create capital in the first period of life. Capital, however, produces nothing in the second period of life. Moreover, a person cannot trade the capital for second-period consumption because it is impossible for others to observe the holdings of capital and ascertain its value.

So how does a person provide for second-period consumption? A person born in period t can sell some of the endowment in the first period of life for fiat money. These holdings of fiat money will then be used in the second period of life to buy some of the consumption good from the young born in that period.

Individuals can also provide for third-period consumption by holding fiat money, but they will not choose to do so. To see this, we need to compare the rate of return on capital and the rate of return on fiat money. Given our assumption of a changing population and a constant fiat money supply, the one-period rate of return on fiat money in a stationary equilibrium is n. However, in providing for third-period consumption (two periods in the future for a young person), it is the two-period rate of return on fiat money that is relevant (v_{t+2}/v_t).

Following our earlier derivations, it is easy to show that the rate of return on fiat money over two periods is n^2. To see this, recall that the one-period rate of return on fiat money, given a constant money stock, is n. This implies that the two-period rate of return on fiat money is

$$\frac{v_{t+2}}{v_t} = \frac{v_{t+2}}{v_{t+1}} \frac{v_{t+1}}{v_t} = nn = n^2. \tag{8.1}$$

Given our assumption that $X > n^2$, the rate of return on capital exceeds the rate of return on fiat money over a two-period horizon. Hence, individuals will choose to provide for third-period consumption by holding capital.

We can summarize these observations by writing down the budget constraints faced by a person born in period t:

$$c_{1,t} + v_t m_t + k_t \leq y, \tag{8.2}$$

$$c_{2,t+1} \leq v_{t+1} m_t, \tag{8.3}$$

$$c_{3,t+2} \leq X k_t. \tag{8.4}$$

If we combine these three equations, we can write the lifetime budget constraint for a person born in period t as

$$c_{1,t} + \left[\frac{v_{t+1}}{v_t}\right] c_{2,t+1} + \left[\frac{1}{X}\right] c_{3,t+2} \leq y. \tag{8.5}$$

This is a linear equation in $c_{1,t}$, $c_{2,t+1}$, and $c_{3,t+2}$. Unfortunately, our usual method of graphing budget constraints becomes cumbersome in this three-dimensional problem: the frontier of the budget set would be a plane in three-dimensional space. The optimal ($c_{1,t}^*, c_{2,t+1}^*, c_{3,t+2}^*$) combination would be located where an indifference curve is tangent to this plane.

Let us make some observations about our results. The two-period rate of return on capital is X, whereas on fiat money it is n^2. Because $X > n^2$, we see that the two-period rate of return on capital exceeds that of fiat money. Furthermore, the one-period rate of return on capital is zero and that on fiat money is n, establishing that the one-period rate of return on fiat money exceeds that of capital. A casual interpretation of our analysis in Chapter 7 suggests that, if individuals are willing to hold two types of assets simultaneously, their rates of return must be equal. However, that clearly is not the case here. It appears that the general rule of rate-of-return equality is violated in this economy. Why?

To understand this, it is important to reiterate some of our earlier observations. For the rule of rate-of-return equality to hold, the assets involved must be perceived as perfect substitutes. In this model, fiat money and capital are not perfect substitutes. In particular, the assumption that individuals cannot observe another individual's holdings of capital means that it is impossible for this economy to develop a market in which a middle-aged individual's holding of capital is traded. In other words, capital is illiquid. A person can never sell capital for a medium of exchange in the second period of life, nor can capital itself be used as a medium of exchange.

Given these fundamental differences between fiat money and capital, it should seem reasonable that the two do not pay the same rate of return. The principle of rate-of-return equality still applies to this economy, although in modified form. Individuals hold capital over two periods because it offers the best two-period rate of return; they hold money over one period because it offers the best one-period rate of return.

Also note the frequency of trade of the two assets in this model. The **velocity** of an asset may be defined as the amount of the asset that is exchanged in a given period of time divided by the total stock of that asset. In any period t, the total stock of fiat money exchanges hands. This implies that the velocity of fiat money is 1. What is the velocity of capital?

Suppose we view a young person's creation of capital as an exchange. In each period t, the current young create a total of $N_t k_t$ units of capital. What is the total capital stock in period t? It consists of the capital held by the current young ($N_t k_t$) and by the middle-aged who purchased capital in period $t - 1$. The latter amount is $N_{t-1} k_{t-1}$. Hence, the total capital stock in period t is $N_t k_t + N_{t-1} k_{t-1}$. Viewing the young people's creation of capital as capital being exchanged, we then have that

$$\text{(velocity of capital)}_t = \frac{N_t k_t}{N_t k_t + N_{t-1} k_{t-1}} < 1. \tag{8.6}$$

For example, in the simple case in which the total capital stock does not change in size over time, the velocity of capital is 1/2. More generally, we see from Equation 8.6 that the velocity of capital is less than the velocity of fiat money (which is 1).[3]

---

[3] If we do not view a young individual's original creation of capital as an exchange, then the velocity of capital is 0.

3 The Business of Banking

Let us return to the economy of three-period-lived people, with one change. Assume now that at least some people cannot hide from their creditors, so that enforcement of their IOUs is possible. This allows for the emergence of banking and a new form of liquid asset – "inside money" – which is money issued by private intermediaries.

Suppose there is a single person – the banker – in this economy who can issue IOUs. How might the banker use that ability to borrow to make large profits? Recall the difference in the rate of return on long- and short-term assets (capital and money, respectively) in the previous economy. Making profits through rate-of-return differences is called "arbitrage." Is there a way to borrow at the low rate and invest at the high rate?

3.1 A Simple Arbitrage Plan

Given that the bank has a monopoly on issuing private IOUs, it is easy to conceive of such an arbitrage plan. In period t, the bank borrows one good and invests it in the creation of capital. This good could be borrowed from a young person who was born in that period. This young person, in the previous case in which there were no IOUs, would use fiat money to finance second-period consumption. We know that fiat money pays a one-period rate of return of n. So, if the bank offered to pay at least the rate of return on fiat money (n), this person would be willing to make a one-period deposit to the bank.

At $t + 2$, the bank owes the rate of return n on the n goods you borrowed at time $t + 1$, for a total of n^2 goods. For the banker, the return from the unit of capital created is X, which exceeds n^2. This leaves the banker with a clear profit of $X - n^2 > 0$.

Figure 8.1 offers a sketch of what happens each period. Given that the bank borrowed 1 unit of the consumption good in period t, then it owes n goods to middle-aged lenders in period $t + 1$. Unfortunately, the bank does not yet have the payoff from capital. To pay off your lender, you then borrow n goods from the next generation of young people.

This act of arbitrage represents financial intermediation, the job of banking. The intermediary issues a string of one-period IOUs (accepts deposits) and uses the proceeds to invest in capital with a two-period maturity. In other words, the bank addresses a liquidity mismatch by transforming illiquid assets into liquid bank liabilities. There is a clear incentive to perform this maturity transformation; the bank has an opportunity to make arbitrage profits.

3.2 The Effect of Arbitrage on Equilibrium

Let us now assume that the bank is not the only one able to issue IOUs. In the previous example, the incentive was clear; because there was a barrier to entry, the

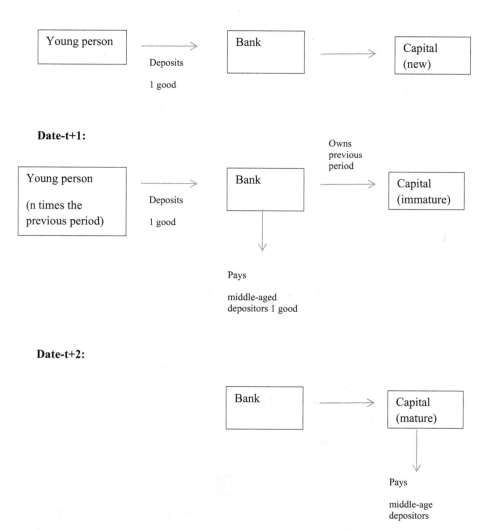

Figure 8.1. Basic bank operation. The bank accepts deposits from young people. In order to meet it schedule of payments, the bank accepts deposits from young people in date-$t+1$ to pay for withdrawals made by middle-aged people when they were young. At date $t+2$, the capital acquired at date t is now mature and the proceeds can be used to pay middle-age people.

single bank could earn a profit. If we eliminate the barriers to entry, would a bank emerge? Put another way, if a large number of competitive people can costlessly issue IOUs and invest in capital, what will the one-period rate of return (call it r^*) paid on these IOUs in a competitive equilibrium be?

To answer this question, let us consider a numerical example in which we compute the profits for a monopoly bank. Suppose the two-period rate of return on capital X is 1.21 and the rate of population growth n is 1.05. Let's suppose that the banker agrees to pay a one-period rate of return of 1.05 on deposits. Call this rate of return on deposits r. According to the previous argument, this is the minimum rate of return that the banker must offer to attract depositors. Suppose a banker accepts 100 units of the consumption as deposits, transforming the goods into capital. In period $t + 1$, the banker must repay 105 units of the good to depositors. To do so, the banker accepts deposits of 105 units of the good from the young born in that period, again offering the same 1.05 rate of return. The intermediary will owe 110.25 $[= (100)(1.05)(1.05) = 100r^2]$ goods in period $t + 2$ to these date-$t + 1$ depositors. In period $t + 2$, the banker's capital matures, yielding a gross amount of 121 $[= (100)(1.21) = 100X]$ goods. The intermediary makes a profit of 10.75 $(= 121 - 110.25)$ goods. Note that the profit made is equal to $100(X - r^2)$.

However, according to similar reasoning, a bank down the street could also make profits and attract all of the depositors of the previous bank by offering a rate of return of $r = 1.06$ on deposits. This bank will make profits equal to $100(1.21 - 1.06^2) = 8.64$ goods.

If we continue this analysis, we see that for $r < 1.1$, a bank or intermediary makes profits.[4] As long as $r < 1.1$, new intermediaries will enter the industry and offer higher rates of return on deposits. To stay in business, the existing intermediaries will have to follow suit. We see that a competitive intermediation industry will force the rate of return on deposits to be equal to $r^* = 1.1$. Note that 1.1 is equal to $1.21^{0.5} = X^{0.5}$. When $r^* = X^{0.5}$, the intermediary's profits are equal to $100(X - X^{0.5}X^{0.5}) = 0$. There will be no incentive to offer higher interest rates on deposits; doing so would lead to negative profits. This argument should sound familiar. It is much the same as the argument that perfectly competitive firms will force the price of their output down to marginal costs so that zero profits are displayed.

Intermediation will also affect capital and output in this economy. In the absence of intermediation, capital was held only to acquire consumption in the third period of life; fiat money was held to acquire consumption in the second period of life. With intermediation, inside money replaces fiat money in the acquisition of consumption in the second period of life. People not only invest in capital directly to acquire consumption in the third period of life but also do so indirectly through intermediaries to acquire consumption in the second period of life. In this way, intermediation serves to mobilize all the saving of the economy for investment in capital, including saving in the form of liquid assets, money balances. The greater investment in capital due to intermediation implies greater output.

The welfare effects of replacing fiat money with inside money are mixed. On the one hand, future generations will benefit from inside money's greater rate of

---

[4] Here, r is the one-period return on deposits. So it is equivalent to state that bank profits are equal to $D(X - r^2)$ or $D(X^{0.5} - r)$, D is the quantity of goods deposited.

return. On the other hand, those holding fiat money balances in the initial period (the initial middle-aged) lose the value of those money balances if fiat money is abandoned.

4 Banks as Monitors

In this section, we consider other possible services banks could provide to people. In the previous model, financial intermediation emerged to reconcile a mismatch of asset maturities; capital produced a return only in the long run, but individuals needed an asset that paid a return in the short run.[5] Banks could increase total consumption in an economy. What if we introduce risks into the basic model? Now, can banks increase returns by reducing costs?

Consider an economy in which each borrower is a risky investment. Moreover, there is the ability to hide the outcome of investment project and costly for the lender to verify the actual outcome. One thing banks can do is monitor loan repayment. Banks also offer depositors a (nearly) risk-free way to invest in risky assets. Therefore, let us examine ways in which banks can reduce the costs of monitoring the repayment of loans and the risks to which depositors are exposed.[6] The model we build will display four features of banks we observe in actual modern economies:

1. Each bank deals with large numbers of both depositors and entrepreneurs.
2. Loans that must be monitored are made by banks (or other financial intermediaries) rather than individuals.
3. Banks offer depositors a risk-free return while holding risky assets.
4. Depositors do not monitor the banks' performance.

Consider an economy with a large number of potential restaurateurs (males) who lack the funds to start their restaurants and an equal number of potential investors (females) who have funds to invest but have no desire to run a restaurant. For simplicity, assume that it takes no effort to run a restaurant. Each investor has k goods to invest, and each restaurant requires an investment of μk (μ is an integer greater than 1). (Note that there are not enough goods to fund all potential restaurants. There must be μ investors for each funded restaurant.)

Restaurants are a risky business. We will assume that each restaurant has a two-thirds chance of being successful, with a return equal to $x\mu$, and a one-third chance of failure, with a return equal to zero. Only after investment has occurred does the

---

[5] It may also be the case that through financial intermediation, people can insure each other (Diamond and Dybvig, 1983), reduce the cost of evaluating loans (Boyd and Prescott, 1986), or enjoy other economies of scale (Greenwood and Jovanovic, 1990). Recent work on financial intermediation is surveyed by Bhattacharya and Thakor (1993). We study additional models of intermediation in Exercise 7.3 and Chapters 12 and 13.

[6] The model of banks as monitors that we present is adapted from that of Diamond (1984). The initial study of optimal contracts with monitoring is Townsend's (1979). The simplified version here owes much to Williamson (1987), who also presents some simple extensions.

restaurateur learn whether he is successful. The success or failure of a restaurant is not costlessly observable to others. Only by an investigation costing θ goods can someone other than the restaurateur learn of the success or failure of a restaurant. (Assume also that the consumption by the restaurateur and his payments to others are unobservable, so that an investor cannot infer success or failure indirectly.)

Note that when a restaurant fails, the restaurateur has no resources with which to pay anything to his investors. Therefore, any contract written between the restaurateur and his investors cannot require the restaurateur to make payments when his restaurant fails.

Can there be a contract without monitoring? In the absence of monitoring, a successful restaurateur has an incentive to declare his restaurant a failure and therefore that he is unable to repay what he owes. Knowing that the restaurateur otherwise will want to lie, investors will want to investigate claims of failure by the restaurateur. We assume that they will investigate every claim of failure.[7]

4.1 Unintermediated Investment

Because there are more potential restaurants than can be funded, and because it takes no effort to run a restaurant, competition among potential restaurants will ensure that investors receive the entire output of the restaurants, x goods for each good invested.[8]

Suppose each investor splits k goods she invests among J restaurants (i.e., she invests k/J goods with each of J restaurants). Then the average return to an investor from each restaurant is

$$\frac{2}{3}x\frac{k}{J} + \frac{1}{3}(-\theta). \tag{8.7}$$

Note that the cost of investigating does not depend on the size of an investor's investment. The total return to J such investments is therefore

$$\frac{2}{3}xk + \frac{1}{3}(-\theta)J. \tag{8.8}$$

The costs of monitoring hurt investors without intermediaries in two ways. First, because it costs an investor θ goods to investigate each failure, regardless of the size of her investment, an investor who splits her goods among many different restaurants will spend more on average for investigations. To minimize investigations, she must therefore minimize the number of restaurants in which she invests by investing in only one. This lack of diversification, however, puts all of her eggs in one basket, exposing her to the risk that this single restaurant will fail, lowering the expected utility of risk-averse investors.

---

[7] In general, it is optimal to engage in random monitoring, but to keep things simple we ignore that strategy here.
[8] If it takes effort to run a restaurant (as it surely does), competition will ensure that investors receive all the output that remains after the restaurateurs are compensated for their effort.

Second, without intermediation, there is a great deal of duplication in monitoring restaurants. Each investor who monitors a restaurant spends resources to learn what others are also learning. Might there not be some way to conduct only a single investigation of each restaurant?

Suppose a single investor is designated to be the sole monitor of a restaurant. A successful restaurateur could then lie and announce a failure, offering to split with the monitor the amount owed to others if she will back up his lie. In other words, who monitors the monitor?

4.2 Intermediated Investment

There is, however, a way to avoid both the costly duplication of monitoring and the risk from not diversifying. Consider an intermediary that promises a fixed return, r^*, on all goods entrusted to it. It invests these goods with a large number of restaurateurs but guarantees depositors r^* whatever happens to its investments. The intermediary monitors restaurateurs who claim to have failed.

How can the intermediary guarantee a fixed return when restaurants are risky investments? The answer is that, although each individual restaurant is a risky enterprise, diversifying investments among a large number of restaurants is not very risky, because two-thirds of them will succeed. An intermediary investing in a large number of restaurants will take in approximately the average rate of return for each restaurant in which it invests

$$\frac{2}{3}x\mu + \frac{1}{3}(-\theta).$$
(8.9)

Because there are μ depositors (of k goods each), it can offer a depositor of k goods the return

$$\frac{2}{3}x + \frac{1}{3}\left(\frac{-\theta}{\mu}\right).$$
(8.10)

If there is free entry into the business of intermediation, this is the return that will be offered in (a competitive) equilibrium. Note that, because of its lowering monitoring costs, this return exceeds the return that could be earned without intermediation (from Equation 8.8, $[2/3]x + [1/3][-\theta]J$).[9]

This financial arrangement achieves this greater return by minimizing monitoring without inducing anyone to lie. Each restaurant that declares itself a failure is monitored only once. Moreover, depositors do not have to monitor the intermediary because their return is not contingent on anything. The arrangement also reduces risk. Through the intermediary, each depositor diversifies her investment over a large number of projects, which is why the intermediary can offer depositors a risk-free return.

---

[9] Recall that the minimum for J is 1 and that $\mu > 1$.

5 Summary

Chapter 7 concluded that if money and other assets are considered to be perfect substitutes for one another, then money will be valued only if its rate of return is at least as large as those of the other assets. However, we can point to many real-world assets whose rates of return are greater than that of money while at the same time money is valued. Why does the principle of rate-of-return equality appear to be violated? To answer this question, this chapter focused on the possibility that money and other assets are not perfect substitutes. In particular, the first model of this chapter concentrated on the observation that money may be more liquid than other assets. By looking at a model with illiquid capital and money, we found that capital can indeed pay a higher rate of return than valued fiat money.

We have also discovered that rate-of-return differences provide a natural incentive for the development of financial intermediaries. These intermediaries provide a service by correcting the mismatch of maturities between liquid money and illiquid capital. By funneling saving to investment in capital, the presence of intermediaries leads to higher output in an economy.

We consider another role for banks. Banks may serve as monitors of risky ventures. Banks offer lower risk through diversification and lower monitoring costs than people could find by lending on their own.

6 Exercises

8.1. Consider our model of three-period-lived individuals of this chapter. Suppose the two-period real rate of return on capital is $X = 1.44$, the rate of population growth is $n = 1.1$, and the rate of fiat money creation is $z = 1.2$. Find the following net rate for both one and two periods:
   a. nominal rate of interest,
   b. real rate of interest,
   c. rate of inflation, and
   d. real rate of return on money.
8.2. Suppose the intermediation of capital goods costs ϕ units of the consumption good for each unit of capital intermediated ($\phi < X^{0.5}$). Assume that transaction costs occur when agents withdraw from banks (when they are middle-aged). What will the equilibrium rate of return offered by intermediaries be if they are the ones who bear the transaction costs? For what value of ϕ, X, z, and n will fiat money be valued in this economy?
8.3. Consider an economy in which people live two-period lives in overlapping generations but are endowed only in the first period of life. Capital has a minimum size, k^*, which is greater than the endowment of any single individual but less than the total endowment of a single generation. Capital pays a one-period gross real rate of return equal to x. The population grows 10 percent in each period. There exists a constant nominal stock of fiat money owned by the initial old.

a. In what sense is capital illiquid in this economy? Is fiat money subject to this same liquidity problem?

b. Describe an intermediary that might overcome the illiquidity of capital so that inter-mediated capital may be used to acquire consumption in the second period of life.

c. Suppose there is only one person in each generation who is able to run an intermediary. What is the minimum rate of return that person must offer to attract depositors? For what values of x can this person make a profit?

d. What rate of return will be offered on deposits if there are many people in each generation able to run an intermediary?

8.4. Consider an economy with a large number of potential online game providers. The provider lacks the funds to start their projects. There is an equal number of investors who have the funds but no desire to create online games. Each investor has 10 goods to invest. Each online game requires 20 goods to create. Suppose each investor can choose up to 10 online games. Assume that 25 percent of the online game projects fail and return zero goods to the investor. The monitoring cost is 1 good per failed project.

a. Compute the expected total return for each investor when the investor chooses 10 projects and divides the goods evenly amongst all 10 projects.

b. Compute the expected total return for each investor when the investor chooses one project.

c. Explain why the expected total return is greater when only one project is funded by the investor.

8.5. Consider an economy with a large number of potential online game providers. The provider lacks the funds to start their projects. There is an equal number of investors who have the funds but no desire to create online games. Each investor has 50 goods to invest. Each online game requires 200 goods to create. Assume that 25 percent of the online game projects fail and return zero goods to the investor. The monitoring cost is two goods per failed project. Assume that a bank operates costlessly in this economy. Also assume there are no barriers to entry in the banking industry.

a. Compute the expected return for each game project for the bank.

b. What return will the bank offer a depositor?

Chapter 9

Central Banking and the Money Supply

1 Roadmap

From Chapter 8, we have explained how banks can improve welfare by transforming illiquid capital into liquid deposits. An important by-product of this explanation is that there are two types of money: fiat money and deposits. One distinctive characteristic is that fiat, or outside, money is a liability of the monetary authority and a bank deposit, or inside money, is a liability of a commercial bank.

In this chapter, we want to extend the basic illiquid capital version of the model economy in which a bank offers liquid deposits. In order to have both inside and outside money valued in equilibrium, we introduce a legal restriction that forces fiat money to be valued; that is the reserve requirement. Here, the monetary authority may wish to regulate institutions creating inside money in order to control the total stock of money or to enhance revenue from seigniorage. To meet these ends, the monetary authority, which now may also be called a central bank, generally has two tools at its disposal – reserve requirements and loans to banks – in addition to its ability to print fiat money. At the end of this chapter, we show that loans to commercial banks, also known as discount window loans, are really just temporary ways to reduce reserve requirements.

We begin by offering a complete set of analyses studying the effects that changes in reserve requirements have on key economic outcomes. Note that people do not hold currency in this model economy. Instead, banks hold fiat money in the form of reserves. The most important takeaway is that we develop an approach in this chapter that serves as the first step toward a model that can account for why both fiat money and deposits coexist.

2 Legal Restrictions on Financial Intermediation

Financial intermediation allows privately created assets to serve as money. One consequence of permitting unfettered intermediation is that, if intermediation is not too costly to use and operate, people may choose to use inside money instead of fiat money. This will occur if the rate of return of inside money, net of transaction costs, exceeds that of government-created fiat money.

If people prefer inside money to fiat money for every use of money, fiat money will lose its value. This would have two effects: first, prices would have to be expressed in some other unit of account, second, the government would be unable to raise any revenue from seigniorage. If the government still wishes to maintain fiat money as a unit of account or a means of revenue, it must force people to hold fiat money.

There are many ways for the government to shore up the demand for fiat money. Most directly, it can simply require people to hold a certain amount of fiat money. An example is a "reserve requirement" – a requirement that a bank must hold fiat money balances equal to a legally prescribed fraction of its deposits. Less directly, the government may simply outlaw certain forms of intermediation or certain alternatives to fiat money. For example, banks are often prohibited from issuing their own currency (notes payable to the bearer, or bank notes).

Because of the prevalence of these interventions into the monetary system, in this chapter we examine the effects and desirability of these interventions and related government policies.[1]

3 Reserve Requirements

Let us start by introducing into our model of intermediation a common form of legal restriction on financial intermediaries, a reserve requirement. A "reserve requirement" obliges financial intermediaries to hold in the form of fiat money a legally specified fraction of their deposits. Before introducing reserve requirements into our model, let us briefly discuss their implementation under U.S. and Canadian law. Depository institutions in both countries are required by law to hold reserves in relation to their levels of deposits.

In the United States, these reserves must be held in the form of vault cash or deposits with the Federal Reserve Banks.[2] Reserve requirements are imposed on what the Federal Reserve (the Fed) calls net transactions accounts – basically checkable deposits. As of January 2015, these accounts were subject to the following reserve requirements: no required reserves on the first $14.5 million of reservable deposits, the reserve requirement is three percent on reservable deposits less than $103.6 million, and is ten percent on reservable deposits exceeding $103.6 million.

Reserve requirements on Canadian chartered banks were completely phased out as of the summer of 1994. We will return to the implications of this policy change later in the chapter.

---

[1] See Fama (1980) for a discussion of banking with and without interventions.

[2] Institutions that are not members of the Federal Reserve System may hold reserve balances with institutions approved by the Federal Reserve.

Assets		Liabilities	
Reserves	γH	Deposits	H
Interest-bearing Assets	$(1+\gamma)H$	Net Worth	0
Total Assets	H	Total Liabilities	H

Figure 9.1. A bank's balance sheet. A balance sheet shows the relationship between assets and liabilities. For a bank, its deposits represent a liability. Deposits (H) are subject to a reserve requirement, γ, so that the bank must hold total reserves not less than γH. Because capital offers a higher return, the bank will satisfy the reserve requirements, using the remainder of the funds raised from deposits to purchase interest-bearing assets equal in amount to $H - \gamma H = (1 - \gamma)H$.

3.1 Banks with Reserve Requirements

Let us continue our analysis using the model of people with three-period lives and illiquid capital from Chapter 8.[3] Capital pays a rate of return of X two periods after its creation. Let $X > (n/z)^2$. Let $M_t = zM_{t-1}$ with $z \geq 1$. Because money will be used to consume in the second period of life, we assume that the initial middle-aged begin with the stock of fiat money.

As we saw in Chapter 8, the difference in the rate of return of capital and fiat money will induce people to try to make arbitrage profits through intermediation. We assume that the intermediation of capital is costless and competitive. A bank will accept deposits, offering the one-period return equal to $X^{0.5}$. Recall that in this model economy, people would not hold fiat money; bank deposits were just as liquid as fiat money and offered a higher return.

The following reserve requirement is imposed on banks or anyone else intermediating capital. For each good deposited at a bank, the bank is required to hold a reserve of fiat money worth a fraction, γ, of that good. The rest, $1 - \gamma$, can be invested in capital.

The operation of a bank may be summarized in its balance sheet. A balance sheet lists side by side a bank's asset and its liabilities. The assets of a bank may be divided into two parts – reserves and interest-bearing assets. The liabilities of a bank are the deposits at the bank (what is owed to depositors at the bank) and the bank's net worth (what is owed to the shareholders of the bank). The total assets of a solvent bank equal its liabilities (the lists of assets and liabilities must balance). For simplicity, we have assumed that the banks of our model have zero net worth. The balance sheet of such a bank with aggregate deposits equal to H is presented in Figure 9.1. For our purposes, the key feature is that the balance sheet shows bank deposits and fiat money are both held in positive quantities.

Let us now examine the determinants of key variables in the model.

---

[3] This analysis builds on the work of Romer (1985) and Freeman (1987).

3.2 Prices

The price level, which we call p_t, is the value of a good in dollars, the inverse of the value of a unit of fiat money, v_t. Define h_t as the goods deposited in banks by an individual. As always, v_t is determined by the equality of the supply and demand for fiat money

$$v_t M_t = \gamma N_t h_t. \tag{9.1}$$

Equation 9.1 requires some explanation. In period t, each person makes h_t deposits in banks (in real terms). In the aggregate, $N_t h_t$ deposits are placed in banks. Against these deposits, banks are required to hold the fraction γ in fiat currency as reserves. This implies that the total amount of required reserves in real terms is $\gamma N_t h_t$. Given that individuals in this model do not hold currency, the banks' demand for fiat money as reserves represents the total demand for fiat money. Note that increases in the reserve requirement increase the value of fiat money by increasing the demand for fiat money. From Equation 9.1 we can find the price level, the inverse of v_t:

$$p_t = \frac{M_t}{\gamma N_t h_t}. \tag{9.2}$$

At this point, a note is in order about the zero reserve requirement policy in effect in Canada. Equation 9.2 tells us that if $\gamma = 0$, the price level is infinite ($v_t = 0$). The intuition is that in this model, if $\gamma = 0$, there is no demand for fiat money, making it valueless. So why don't we observe an infinite price level in Canada? The answer must be that our model is missing an important source of demand for fiat money. There must be another source of demand for fiat money other than by banks as reserves. In Chapter 10, we present a model in which fiat money is held in the form of currency. In Chapter 13, we present a model in which banks would demand fiat money even in the absence of a legal restriction.

3.3 Seigniorage

Another variable that might be of interest is seigniorage, the revenue from fiat money creation. Recall from Equations 4.16 and 4.17 that seigniorage equals

$$(\text{seigniorage})_t = v_t [M_t - M_{t-1}] = v_t M_t \left[1 - \frac{1}{z} \right] \tag{9.3}$$

when $M_t = z M_{t-1}$. Using the expression for $v_t M_t$ that we found in Equation 9.1, we can write seigniorage as

$$(\text{seigniorage})_t = \gamma N_t h_t \left[1 - \frac{1}{z} \right]. \tag{9.4}$$

From this equation, we can determine the factors that can increase seigniorage:

- an increase in the reserve requirement γ;
- an increase in $N_t h_t$, the real stock of bank deposits; and
- an increase in z, the rate of fiat money creation.

3.4 Capital and Output

Output is the sum of the production of labor (the endowment) and of capital. In this economy, capital comes from both direct investment k_t and investment through intermediaries $(1 - \gamma) h_t$. Recall that capital produces output with a lag of two periods. Hence, output in period t will be affected by capital created in period $t - 2$, whether from direct investment or through intermediaries. Therefore,

$$GDP_t = N_t y + N_{t-2} X k_{t-2} + N_{t-2} X (1 - \gamma) h_{t-2}. \tag{9.5}$$

Note that an increase in the reserve requirement γ reduces GDP because, for any given level of deposits (h_{t-2}), less capital is intermediated through banks. An increase in the monetary base M_t has no such direct effect on real output.

Equation 9.5 tells us that a reduction in reserve requirements would lead to an increase in real GDP caused by an increase in intermediated capital. How large might this effect be? At the end of 2008, the total net private capital stock in the United States was \$34,261 billion. At this time, total required reserves held by U.S. commercial banks amounted to \$53 billion.[4] If reserve requirements were completely eliminated and commercial banks chose to replace all loans with new capital, the capital stock would rise by less than 0.2 percent.

3.5 Deposits

In examining the effects of reserve requirements and the monetary base on prices, seigniorage, and output, we took the amount deposited at banks, $N_t h_t$, as given. The willingness of people to make deposits at banks, however, is likely to depend on the rate of return offered on deposits. Let's find this rate of return.

Given that the two-period rate of return on capital is X, the one-period rate of return on intermediated capital is $X^{0.5}$, which we call x. If the intermediation of capital is costless, competition will force banks to offer depositors the rate of return they earn on the assets held by the banks. Therefore, the total one-period rate of return from the deposit of one good, the gross real rate of return on deposits, must

---

[4] The capital stock data are taken from the *Survey of Current Business*. See the Bureau of Economic Analysis Web site at http://www.bea.gov/national Table 2.1. The capital stock is measured as the amount of fixed private capital (nonresidential and residential). The measure of reserves is total reserves held by commercial banks, not adjusted for changes in reserve requirements (from the Federal Reserve Bank of St. Louis FRED database, http://research.stlouisfed.org/fred).

equal the amount held in reserves of fiat money times the rate of return on fiat money plus the amount held in capital times the rate of return on capital:

$$r^* = \gamma \left(\frac{n}{z}\right) + (1 - \gamma)x \tag{9.6}$$

$$= x - \gamma \left[x - \left(\frac{n}{z}\right)\right]. \tag{9.7}$$

We assume that fiat money pays a lower rate of return than capital ($x > n/z$), implying from Equation 9.7 that r^* is a diminishing function of γ. Therefore, an increase in the reserve requirement lowers the rate of return on deposits. Although the current monetary base M_t has no direct effect on the rate of return of deposits, the expected rate of money creation z reduces the rate of return on fiat money reserves and thus on deposits partially backed by fiat money reserves.

On the one hand, the effect of a lower rate of return may discourage people from using deposits. On the other hand, the low return on deposits reduces c_2 for any given level of deposits. Therefore, individuals may increase their deposits to reduce the drop in c_2.[5]

3.6 Welfare

Finally, and most importantly, let us ask about the effects of the reserve requirement on the welfare of the members of this economy. As always, we wish to distinguish between initial generations and future generations.

The initial money holders (the middle-aged) begin with the initial stock of fiat money. What effect would a larger reserve requirement have on the real value of this stock? Setting t equal to 1 in Equation 9.1, we see that an increase in γ will cause an increase in the value of money in period 1. Because this will increase the total amount of goods that can be purchased with a given holding of fiat money, the initial money holders can attain a higher level of utility with an increase in the reserve requirement.

An increase in the fiat money stock will reduce the value of each initial unit of fiat money. Therefore, the initial money holders are made worse off if the initial fiat money stock is increased unless the increase in the fiat money stock is given to them. The initial money holders will also be made worse off by anything that reduces the demand for deposits and thus the demand for fiat money.

An increase in the reserve requirement or the rate of money creation would affect the utility of future generations through its effect on the rate of return paid on deposits. We have already found that an increase in either γ or z lowers the

---

[5] If the revenue from seigniorage were not spent by the government but were returned to people as a lump-sum subsidy to the middle-aged, c_2 for any given level of deposits would not be reduced. In this case, therefore, only the first effect would occur and the lower rate of return on deposits would discourage deposits.

rate of return to deposits, thus reducing the utility of future generations. The higher reserve requirement lowers the utility of future generations by forcing them to hold more of the asset (fiat money) with the lower rate of return. The greater seigniorage revenue taxes members of the future generations, reducing what they can consume over their lifetimes. However, if the seigniorage revenue is returned to future generations, the lower rate of return on deposits artificially discourages the use of deposits (consumption in the second period of life). The utility of future generations is reduced in much the same way that lower return on fiat money reduces the welfare of future generations when it discourages the hold of fiat money, as we learned in Chapter 4.

4 Central Bank Definitions of Money

Economists have created multiple measures of money. In economies with no alternative to fiat money, this measurement is easy; the total nominal money stock is simply the stock of fiat money. In economies with outside and inside money, there are distinctions about the various "moneyness" qualities associated with different types of deposits. Checking accounts are widely accepted as a means of payment. Savings accounts are not used in transactions but are very liquid because there are small costs associated with transferring balances from a person's savings account into their checking account. So you can see that as the degree of moneyness, or liquidity, differs across different kinds of bank deposits, alternative measures of money are put forward.

Central banks are naturally the authoritative definers of alternative measures of money, which are often called "monetary aggregates." There is no universally accepted method of defining monetary aggregates. Indeed, bank deposit contracts vary from country to country leading to different definitions of monetary aggregates across countries. Moreover, banks create new types of deposits over time, resulting in measures in a particular country being redefined. It would be naive to believe that they will not change in the future.

We will present the monetary aggregates as defined by the central banks of the United States and Canada. These central banks are called the Federal Reserve and the Bank of Canada, respectively. There are some common features in the measures of the two countries. The narrowest measure of money in both countries is called "M1" and includes only highly liquid assets that typically can be used to make transactions. Other measures of money build on one another with each successive monetary aggregate, including assets that are somewhat less liquid than the previous measure. For example, "M2" includes all the components of M1 plus assets that can be easily converted into a medium of exchange.

Table 9.1 details the components of the various monetary aggregates as defined by the Federal Reserve and the Bank of Canada, along with their magnitudes. In viewing this table, be sure to note that, although there are some similarities between

Table 9.1. *Monetary aggregates as defined by the Federal Reserve Board and the Bank of Canada.*

United States	Canada
M1 equals	M1 equals
Currency in hands of nonbank public	Currency in the hands of the nonbank public
+ Demand Deposits[a]	+ Demand Deposits less Float
+ Other Checkable Deposits	+ Adjustments[b]
+ Traveler's checks	
	M2 equals
M2 equals	M1
M1	+ Personal Notice Deposits[c]
+ Savings Deposits, including Money Market Deposit Accounts[d]	+ Personal Term Deposits
+ Small Time Deposits	+ Nonpersonal Notice Deposits
+ Retail Money Market Mutual Funds	+ Adjustments

Notes: [a] Demand deposits are non-interest-bearing checking accounts less cash items in process of collection and Federal Reserve Float Cash items in process of collection are checks and other cash items that have been deposited with the Reserve banks for collection on behalf of an institution having an account. Float is checkbook money that appears on the books of both the check writer (the payor) and the check receiver (the payee) while a check is being processed. Federal Reserve float is float present during the Federal Reserve's check collection process.
[b] Adjustments or "continuity adjustments" are the statistical process that adjusts the time series when there are structural breaks such as new definitions or new types of accounts created.
[c] Includes checkable and noncheckable personal notice deposits.
[d] Also includes small denomination repurchase agreements. A repurchase agreement is the sale of a security which stipulates that the seller will buy the security back over a pre-specified, often short, period of time.
[e] Includes checkable and noncheckable nonpersonal notice deposits.

the two countries' definitions, there are many important differences. The components of these measures are discussed in more detail later.

The monetary aggregates in both countries include only amounts held by the nonbank public. Quantities of the above assets held by banks, the governments, and the central banks are not included in these measures.

Some of the components of the monetary aggregates may deserve some discussion to clarify exactly what they include. Let's begin with the narrowest measure of money, M1.

- **M1** – In the United States, M1 includes currency, travelers checks of nonbank issuers, demand deposits at commercial banks, and other checkable deposits in the hands of the nonbank public. Currency, of course, is composed of paper currency and coins. The quantity of demand deposits at commercial banks is adjusted for checks in the process of being collected and for the effect of float. Other checkable deposits included negotiable orders of withdrawal (NOW accounts) and automatic transfer services (ATS) at depository institutions, credit union share draft accounts, and demand deposits at thrift institutions.

The Canadian definition of M1 is narrower than its U.S. counterpart. Only demand deposits created by Canadian chartered banks are included in M1. Checkable deposits created by other depository institutions (trust and mortgage loan companies, credit unions, and *caisses populaires*) are not counted in M1.[6] This is an illustration of the arbitrary nature of these measures.

In general, M1 in both countries consists of currency and various types of checkable deposits – those on which checks can be drawn. As mentioned previously, the components are typically accepted in making transactions.

• **M2** – M2 builds on M1 by also including certain assets that are readily converted into a medium of exchange. For the most part, the assets that are added to M1 to obtain M2 are savings and time deposits at depository institutions (commercial banks and thrift institutions).

More precisely, M2 in the United States includes the components of M1 as well as savings deposits, money market deposit accounts, small-denomination (less than $100,000) time deposits, small-denomination retail repurchase agreements,[7] and balances in retail money market mutual funds.

In Canada, M2 adds to M1 personal notice and term deposits[8] as well as non-personal notice deposits. As in the United States, these types of deposits are essentially various types of savings deposits. However, a portion of the notice deposits included in Canadian M2 are checkable, whereas in the United States all checkable deposits are included in its measure of M1. This points out another discrepancy between the U.S. and Canadian measures.

4.1 The Total Money Supply in Our Model

In our model economy, there is only one type of deposit account offered by the bank. With this in mind, define $(M1)_t$ as a measure of what is often called the "money supply." To correspond to the model economy, $M1$ is the total nominal stock of deposits at banks in period t. (Note that, because at this point in our analysis there is no money held outside banks [no money held as currency], deposits are the only form of money in this economy. We change this assumption in Chapter 10. Hence, for now, our definition of $[M1]_t$ roughly corresponds to the Federal Reserve's and Bank of Canada's M1 measures in the absence of currency.) Recall that a fraction γ of $(M1)_t$ must be held in fiat money. The stock of fiat money M_t in

---

[6] Those other checkable deposits, among other items, are included in a Canadian measure called M2+. This measure is not presented in Table 9.1.

[7] A repurchase agreement is a short-term loan (often overnight) by an institution with temporarily idle funds to another institution. The borrower puts up collateral in the form of U.S. government securities and agrees to "repurchase" the securities on the agreed date.

[8] Notice deposits are deposits that technically (although not in practice) require that the holder give "notice" to the bank before withdrawal. Term deposits, analogous to U.S. time deposits, have a specific maturity date.

a reserve requirement economy is called the "monetary base." We can express the relation between the money supply and the monetary base in a reserve requirement economy through either of the following equations:

$$M_t = \gamma\,(M1)_t \tag{9.8}$$

$$\Rightarrow (M1)_t = \frac{M_t}{\gamma}. \tag{9.9}$$

Equation 9.9 tells us how we can find the total money supply from two things known by the central bank: the reserve requirement and the monetary base. Because $\gamma < 1$, we know that $(1/\gamma) > 1$. An increase in the monetary base will result in an increase in the total money stock of $1/\gamma$ times the increase in the monetary base. The total money stock is $1/\gamma$ times the monetary base. For this reason, the ratio of $(M1)_t$ to M_t, which in this economy equals $1/\gamma$, is often called the "money multiplier," and the monetary base is often called the stock of "high-powered money."[9]

Example 9.1

a. Suppose the requirement is 20 percent. By how much would $(M1)_t$ change if the monetary base were increased by 100?
b. What would happen to the total money supply $(M1)_t$ if the reserve requirement were doubled?

Is the total money stock a useful measure? If so, it should help us to predict important economic variables. Let us look first at the relation between the total money stock and the price level:

$$p_t = \frac{M_t}{\gamma N_t h_t}. \tag{9.10}$$

Recalling that $M_t/\gamma = (M1)_t$, we can rewrite our expression for the price level as

$$p_t = \frac{(M1)_t}{N_t h_t}. \tag{9.11}$$

As in previous chapters, the behavior of prices in this economy is consistent with the quantity theory of money; any increase in the total nominal money supply causes a proportionate increase in the price level (assuming a constant demand for money, $N_t h_t$). In this economy, the total nominal stock of money $(M1)$ is more useful than the monetary base alone in predicting the behavior of prices. Prices change in proportion to $M1$, regardless of whether the change in $M1$ is caused by a change in γ or in the stock of fiat money. The stock of fiat money is not as tightly linked to prices because prices change with no change in the fiat money stock if there is a change in the reserve requirement.

If, however, the demand for deposits, $N_t h_t$, is affected by the rate of return on deposits, the change in the price level will depend on the tool used to change $M1$.

---

[9] As we learn in Chapter 9, the money multiplier will not always equal $1/\gamma$.

The relationship between M1 and the return on deposits depends on the underlying force that changes $M1$. If, for example, $M1$ increases because the reserve requirement is lowered, we know from Equation 9.7 that the return on deposits will increase. In contrast, if $M1$ increases because there is an increase in the monetary base, then the return on deposits either decreases because the rate of fiat money expansion, z, is permanently higher or the return on deposits is unchanged because the increase comes from a one-time increase in the monetary base. Because the tool through which the money stock is changed affects the rate of return on deposits, the demand for deposits and thus the price level will depend on the tool used.

We will now check whether $M1$ is a useful measure for predicting the behavior of other economic variables. That is, do the relations between $M1$ and other variables depend only on $M1$, or do they depend on the way in which $M1$ is changed?

We have already found that the two ways of increasing the total money stock, an increase in the monetary base M_t (i.e., $z > 1$) increases seigniorage, but a decrease in the reserve requirement γ lowers seigniorage. We have found similar differences in their effects on output. An increase in the total money stock resulting from a decrease in the reserve requirement would increase capital and real output. In contrast, an increase in the monetary base M_t has no such direct effect on real output. In this economy, the effects on seigniorage and output of a change in $M1$ depend on the means by which $M1$ is changed. For these reasons, we may wish not to look only at $M1$ when we ask about monetary policy.

Example 9.2

a. Suppose that each of the economy's 600 young agents has deposits worth 100 goods with a bank no matter what the rate of return. Assume that the reserve requirement is 10 percent and the monetary base is \$3,000. Let $x > n$.

  i. What is the total nominal money stock?
  ii. What is the value of a unit of fiat money?
  iii. What is the price of a good in units of fiat money?
  iv. How many goods would the government acquire if it increased the monetary base by 50 percent?
  v. What is the real value of investment by banks?

b. How would your answer to each question in part a change if the reserve requirement doubled to 20 percent? Explain each of these changes in your own words.
c. Suppose the reserve requirement stays at 10 percent but banks voluntarily hold an extra 10 percent of deposits as fiat money reserves. Would your answers to part b change?

5 Central Bank Lending

Banks are required to demonstrate regularly that they meet the level of reserves required for their level of deposits.[10] If they fall short, they are faced with one

---

[10] For example, biweekly in the United States.

of three options: (1) they can sell interest-bearing assets for fiat money; (2) they may borrow from other banks;[11] or (3) they may borrow from the monetary authority.[12]

The generally stated purpose of central bank lending is to permit banks to meet their reserve requirements when they find themselves unexpectedly short without being forced to precipitously sell off their interest-bearing assets. If the central bank approves, banks with reserves below the level required may borrow from the central bank to make up the difference. The reserves borrowed must be paid back with interest. In Chapter 12, we build a model economy in which there are temporary reserve shortages and secondary markets where assets can be traded. Indeed, one of the most interesting features of the 2007 banking crisis involves the development of special lending facilities and the necessary collateralized trades to deal with such shortages. We discuss how the Federal Reserve introduced these emergency lending facilities in our detailed discussion of the 2007 banking crisis, also in Chapter 12.

Central bank lending may also be used to affect capital, output, the price level, and seigniorage even in stationary equilibria. While the discount window is considered a separate tool, we present the loans by the central bank as a means to alter the effective reserve requirement faced by banks. In this section, we examine this role of central bank lending.

With its control over the stock of fiat money, a central bank has no trouble lending to a private bank: It simply prints whatever amount it wishes to lend and gives it to the private bank in return for the bank's promise to repay the loan, possibly with interest, at a later date. As long as the rate of interest owed to the central bank does not exceed the rate of return that can be earned on the bank's interest-bearing assets, the private bank will want to borrow from the central bank.

5.1 Limited Central Bank Lending

Let's now carefully work through the effects of central bank lending. A central bank's lending policy consists of the amount it is willing to lend and the rate of return it charges. Let δ represent the fraction of a bank's reserves financed by loans from the central bank. A bank with deposits of H and reserves of δH. In the case of limited central bank lending, let the limit be captured by borrowings that do not exceed $\delta \gamma H$ from the central bank, where $0 \leq \delta \leq 1$. Let Γ_t^B represent the total nominal amount of borrowed reserves. We continue to let M_t denote the stock of fiat money that has not been borrowed from the central bank (*nonborrowed reserves*).[13]

---

[11] In the United States, the market for loans between banks is called the "federal funds market."

[12] Banks in the United States borrow at the Federal Reserve's "discount window."

[13] Because deposits are the only form of money, fiat money is held only as reserves. This changes in Chapter 10, when fiat money is also used as currency.

Assets		Liabilities	
Reserves	γH	Deposits	H
Interest-bearing Assets	$\delta\gamma H + (1 - \gamma)H$	Loans from Central Bank	$\delta\gamma H$
		Net Worth	0
Total Assets	$\delta\gamma H + H$	Total Liabilities	$\delta\gamma H + H$

Figure 9.2. A bank's balance sheet with central bank loans. The bank has two types of liabilities in this setting. The bank can borrow some fraction of their reserves, $0 < \delta < 1$. The bank can use the resources from the central bank to add to the quantity of interest-bearing assets.

It follows that borrowed reserves as a fraction of all reserves is given by

$$\delta = \frac{\Gamma_t^B}{\Gamma_t^B + M_t},\qquad(9.12)$$

implying that, as Γ_t^B goes to infinity, δ goes to 1.

A profit-maximizing bank will use central bank loans to acquire additional interest-bearing assets. As a result of a central bank loan, the balance sheet of a private bank is altered, as shown in Figure 9.2.

We can find the effects of central bank lending on key variables by following the same steps we used to find the effects of reserve requirements.

The value of a unit of fiat money is found, as always, from the equality of fiat money's supply and demand. The demand for fiat money comes from the reserve requirement, which now may be satisfied with a combination of borrowed ($\delta\gamma H = \delta\gamma N_t h_t$) and nonborrowed ($v_t M_t$) reserves:

$$\delta\gamma N_t h_t + v_t M_t = \gamma N_t h_t.\qquad(9.13)$$

From Equation 9.13 we can find the price level, the inverse of v_t:

$$v_t M_t = \gamma N_t h_t - \delta\gamma N_t h_t$$

$$v_t M_t = \gamma (1 - \delta) N_t h_t$$

$$v_t = \frac{\gamma (1 - \delta) N_t h_t}{M_t}$$

$$p_t = \frac{1}{v_t} = \frac{M_t}{\gamma (1 - \delta) N_t h_t}.\qquad(9.14)$$

Note from Equation 9.14 that the presence of central bank lending ($\delta > 0$) results in a higher price level than when it is absent ($\delta = 0$). Note from Equation 9.14 that, if all reserves are provided by the central bank ($\delta = 1$), the effect is the same as having no reserve requirement – fiat money will have no value (the price level will be infinite).

Lending by the central bank functions as a reduction in the reserve requirement. By supplying some of the reserves needed to meet the reserve requirement, central bank lending essentially lowers the reserve requirement from γ to $\gamma(1 - \delta)$. By lowering the demand for nonborrowed reserves in public hands (M_t), it lowers the value of fiat money, increasing the price level.

Central bank lending also expands intermediated investment. Note from the bank's balance sheet in Figure 9.2 that central bank lending allows private banks to increase their holdings of interest-bearing assets to

$$(1 - \gamma) N_t h_t + \delta \gamma N_t h_t = [1 - \gamma(1 - \delta)] N_t h_t. \tag{9.15}$$

Central bank lending has the same effect on intermediated investment as a reserve requirement lowered to $\gamma(1 - \delta)$. Note that the size of the change in intermediated investment depends on the size of the central bank loan (δ) but not on the rate of interest charged by the central bank. Although the nominal amount of central bank lending is unlimited, in real terms, the most that the central bank lending can add to intermediated investment is $\gamma N_t h_t$, the real value of reserves.

Central bank lending also affects the total nominal money stock. Required reserves must now equal the sum of borrowed and nonborrowed reserves,

$$\gamma (M1)_t = \delta \gamma (M1)_t + M_t, \tag{9.16}$$

which yields a new form for the equation defining the money multiplier:

$$(M1)_t = \frac{M_t}{\gamma(1 - \delta)}. \tag{9.17}$$

Central bank lending expands the total nominal stock of money by allowing greater nominal deposits for each dollar of nonborrowed reserves. Once again, central bank lending works exactly like lowering the reserve requirement to $\gamma(1 - \delta)$.

The effects of central bank lending on government revenue and the rate of return to depositors depend on the rate of return that must be paid to the central bank for its loans. Let ψ denote the real gross rate of return that must be paid on central bank loans.

Let us now derive the rate of return paid by banks on deposits. Against each unit of deposits, the fraction γ is held as reserves, which pay the real rate of return n/z. When the central bank lends a fraction δ of the required reserves, the fraction $[1 - \gamma(1 - \delta)]$ of deposits is held in capital, which pays the real rate of return x. Hence, the total real rate of return that the bank receives on its assets is equal to $\gamma(n/z) + [1 - \gamma(1 - \delta)]x$. To find the real rate of return on deposits, we must subtract from this amount the return that must be paid to the central bank for the loan of $\delta \gamma$:

$$r^* = \gamma \left(\frac{n}{z}\right) + [1 - \gamma(1 - \delta)]x - \psi \delta \gamma. \tag{9.18}$$

Note that, in the absence of central bank lending ($\delta = 0$), Equation 9.18 is equivalent to our earlier expression for r^*, Equation 9.6.

Suppose the real interest rate of central bank loans ψ is equal to the market interest rate x. In this special case, Equation 9.18 simplifies to

$$r^* = \gamma \left(\frac{n}{z}\right) + [1 - \gamma (1 - \delta)] x - x\delta\gamma$$

$$= \gamma \left(\frac{n}{z}\right) + x - \gamma x + \gamma \delta x - \gamma \delta x$$

$$= \gamma \left(\frac{n}{z}\right) + (1 - \gamma) x \quad \text{(given } \psi = x\text{).} \tag{9.19}$$

In this case, the rate of return on deposits is unaffected by central bank lending (δ does not appear in the expression determining r^* [Equation 9.19]). Although central bank loans enable banks to invest more in capital, the return from these investments is paid back to the central bank, leaving depositors no better off. If the central bank offers loans at an interest rate below the market return (i.e., if $\psi < x$), the rate of return on deposits will increase as a result of central bank lending.

As another special case, suppose the central bank charges no nominal interest rate on its loans ($\psi = n/z$). Then we see from Equation 9.18 that

$$r^* = \gamma \left(\frac{n}{z}\right) + [1 - \gamma (1 - \delta)] x - \left(\frac{n}{z}\right) \delta\gamma$$

$$= [1 - \gamma (1 - \delta)] x + \gamma (1 - \delta) \left(\frac{n}{z}\right) \quad \text{(given } \psi = n/z\text{).} \tag{9.20}$$

What Equation 9.20 tells us is that a given increase in the return on deposits, for instance, can be implemented through a decrease in the reserve requirement or through an increase in the rate of central bank lending.

5.2 Unlimited Central Bank Lending

We have assumed until now that the central bank sets a limit, δ, on the fraction of required reserves that may be borrowed. An alternative policy is for the central bank to set only the interest it will charge, ψ, and permit banks to borrow as much as they desire.

When the market rate of return is determined by a fixed rate of return to capital, x, a policy of unlimited central bank lending results, the set of possible equilibria could be very large. This simply means that if the central bank sets the interest rate on its loans *above* the return on capital – that is, $\psi > x$ – no bank will borrow from the central bank. In contrast, if $\psi < x$, bank will borrow unlimited amounts and the equilibrium price level is infinity. If $\psi = x$, any amount of borrowed reserves between zero and infinity is possible and the equilibrium price level is indeterminate.

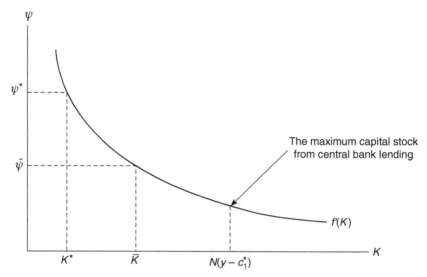

Figure 9.3. The effect of lowering the central bank's interest rate on loans to banks. If a central bank lowers its interest rate on loans to banks from ψ^* to $\overline{\psi}$, the total capital stock rises from K^* to $\overline{K}$. The total capital stock is limited by the total endowment of people that is not consumed when young. In other words, $K < N(y - c_1)$.

One way to avoid such varied equilibria is to assume that the marginal product of capital is diminishing. With $f'(K)$ a diminishing function of the total capital stock, banks will not continue to borrow limitlessly from the central bank. For quantities of capital in which $f'(K)$, exceeds the rate of return they must pay, ψ, borrowing from the central bank occurs. With each additional unit of capital financed by the bank, capital also expands, lowering the marginal product of capital and thus the market rate of return. Borrowing from the central bank and capital continues to expand until the marginal product of capital just equals the rate of return charged by the central bank. By lowering the rate of return it charges, in this way the central bank can expand lending by private banks and thus the capital stock. Figure 9.3 shows the effect on capital of lowering the central bank's interest rate from ψ^* to $\tilde{\psi}$.

Before advocating ever lower interest rates on central bank loans as a way to greatly expand the economy, we must remember to consider other factors. First, expanding central bank lending raises the price level (which hurts the current holders of fiat money). Second, the real effect on capital of lowering the rate charged by the central bank is limited to the real value of reserves $\gamma N_t h_t$. This is but a small fraction of the total capital stock.

Example 9.3 Assume the demand for deposits equals 100,000 goods and the non-borrowed part of the monetary base is \$20,000. Let the reserve requirement be 12 percent.

a. Find the price level, the total money stock, and the real value of investment by banks in the absence of central bank lending.
b. Now assume that the central bank allows banks to meet one-third of their reserve requirement by borrowing from the central bank and that banks take full advantage of this privilege. Answer part a given this new assumption.

5.3 Central Bank Lending Policies in the United States and Canada

The extent of borrowing from the central bank depends on the difference between the rate charged by the central bank (the "discount rate" in the United States, the "bank rate" in Canada) and the rate private banks charge each other (called the "federal funds rate" in the United States). The rate banks charge each other is determined by the market and therefore is tied to the rate of returns banks can get through loans or the purchase of securities. If the central bank rate is below the market interbank rate, banks have an arbitrage incentive to borrow as much as possible from the central bank in order to lend at the higher market interest rate.

To prevent banks from exploiting their borrowing privileges at the central bank, the central bank may choose to limit bank borrowing to cases of special need. Alternatively, it could choose to set the central bank rate equal to or greater than the market rate to eliminate the arbitrage incentive to borrow from the central bank.

As examples of the actual implementation of central bank lending practices, it is interesting to compare and contrast those of the Bank of Canada and the Federal Reserve. From 1980 through 1995, the Bank of Canada pursued a policy whereby its Bank rate was set equal to the Government of Canada's 91-day Treasury bill rate plus one-quarter of 1 percent. Such a policy could be called a floating penalty rate, because the rate adjusts to market conditions and is above market rates. In this way, the incentive for banks to take out loans from the central bank for profit motives is reduced. During this period, the Bank of Canada could affect the Bank rate only indirectly by policies that impacted the Treasury bill rate. Because the arbitrage incentive is reduced with such a policy, the Bank of Canada did not discourage loans to the chartered banks during this period.

In contrast, the discount rate in the United States is an administered rate. It is set by the Federal Reserve and changes infrequently. Consequently, there are times when the discount rate is lower than market interest rates. When this occurs, banks have an incentive to borrow from the Federal Reserve. Since 1995, the Bank of Canada also has followed a policy of an administered rate.

We conclude our discussion of how the discount rate is administered by plotting the quantity of discount window loans over time. Figure 9.4 plots the aggregate value of loans made by the Federal Reserve to commercial banks for the period January 1959 through May 2015. The data show there is a huge bump in the quantity that occurs between 2008 and 2011. Indeed, for most of the period, discount window loans are between zero and $400 million. We will talk in greater detail

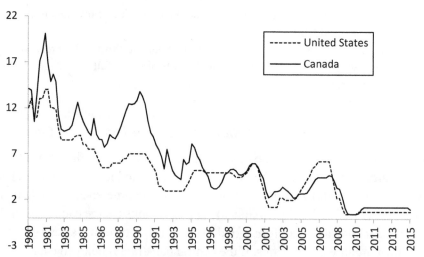

Figure 9.4. The Bank of Canada's Bank rate and the Federal Reserve's discount rate. Before 1996, the Bank of Canada followed a policy whereby its lending rate to chartered banks (the Bank rate) was set slightly above the interest rate on Government of Canada Treasury bills. By contrast, the Federal Reserve's discount rate is an administered rate that remains constant for periods of time. *Source:* The Bank rate is from various issues of the Bank of Canada *Review*. The discount rate is from the *Federal Reserve Bulletin* (various issues). Both series consist of monthly observations.

about the financial crisis in Chapter 12, but here we can see the effects. In March 2008, the Federal Reserve reported total loans jumped to $19 billion, peaking at $403 billion in October 2008. Federal Reserve loans exceeded $10 billion until November 2011. The Federal Reserve has not loaned more than $1 billion through the discount window since November 2012. More concretely, data indicate that loan balances have been less $10 *million* to banks each month in 2015.

5.4 Central Bank Lending since the 2007 Financial Crisis

By itself, the quantity of loans does not indicate the extent which loans have reduced the effective reserve requirement. To put this into perspective, Figure 9.5 plots the level of required reserves for the period 1984 through 2015. Using the recent data, required reserves have risen steadily to $92 billion in 2015. Thus, $10 million in discount loans have had a negligible effect on the effective required reserves for commercial banks. Suppose we pick another date. In July 1999, for example, required reserves were $6.5 billion. The Federal Reserve was loaning about $350 million to commercial banks through the discount window in July 1999. Using Equation 9.12, values are $\delta = \frac{0.35}{0.35+6.5} = 0.072$; in other words, the Federal Reserve was loaning out about 7.2 percent of reserves in July 1999. To help illustrate how the effective reserve requirement as lowered, suppose reservable deposits were equal to $65 billion in July 1999 with a reserve requirement equal to 10 percent. Banks were

Required Reserves, 1984-2015

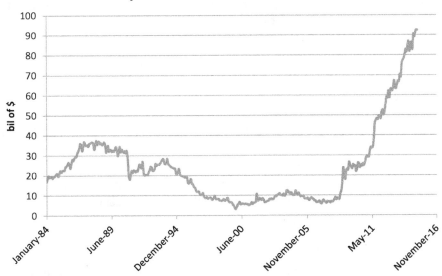

Figure 9.5. Required Reserves. We see that the most recent data indicate a sharp upturn in required reserves since 2008. Here, the values of required reserves provide some context for the size of discount window loans.

holding $6.15 billion = $6.5 billion less $0.35 billion of reserves and borrowing the remainder. As such, effective reserve requirement was $\frac{6.15}{65} = 0.0946$. Thus, the effective reserve requirement in July 1999 was 9.46 percent, not 10 percent.

In extreme cases such as the 2007 Financial Crisis, banks are borrowing from the Federal Reserve to meet liquidity needs. The most extreme version of this occurred in October 2008. At that time, the Federal Reserve loans were $403 billion while required reserves at roughly $10 billion. Clearly, the Federal Reserve was lending multiple times the required reserves. From Equation 9.12, we find that the October 2008 value was $\delta = 0.974$; so in October 2008 the Federal Reserve loaned out 97.4 percent of reserves and approximately *40 times* required reserves.

6 Summary

This chapter has focused on two tools typically used by central banks – reserve requirements and loans to banks.

Reserve requirements give rise to a simple money multiplier whereby the total money supply is a multiple of the monetary base. This money multiplier is inversely related to the size of the reserve requirement. Reserve requirements increase the value of fiat money by increasing the demand for it. However, they also allow less intermediation of capital by banks, which in turn causes lower output. Higher reserve requirements also induce a lower level of utility for future generations by lowering the rate of return that banks can pay on deposits.

Banks that find themselves short of the amount of reserves required by law may turn to the central bank as a source of loans. In its effect, central bank lending is generally equivalent to a decrease in the reserve requirement.

7 Exercises

9.1. Consider an economy with a constant population in which people wish to hold bank checking deposits worth a total of 5,000 goods in every period. The economy has a total endowment of 10,000 goods in each period. There is a total stock of unintermediated capital of 1,000 goods in each period. Bank deposits are the only form of money in the economy. Deposits at banks are subject to a reserve requirement of 20 percent. The net real rate of return on capital is 10 percent per period. After meeting the reserve requirement, banks invest the remainder of all deposits into capital. Individuals do not hold capital. The fiat money stock (monetary base) is $2,000 in every period. Calculate values for the following variables:

   a. The price of a good (in dollars).

   b. The gross real rate of return on deposits that will be offered by banks in a competitive economy.

   c. The total nominal money stock $M1$.

   d. The money multiplier.

   e. The total capital stock.

   f. Real GDP.

9.2. Answer each part of Exercise 9.1 assuming that the central bank allows banks to borrow up to one-half of required reserves at a net interest rate of 8 percent.

9.3. Consider an economy in which the reserve requirement is increased from 10 percent to 20 percent.

   a. Explain why the increase in the reserve requirement ratio causes welfare to decline.

   b. Construct a graph in $c_1 - c_2$ space (the axes) showing how the increase in the reserve requirement ratio will affect a person's lifetime budget constraint.

9.4. Suppose the central bank sets the reserve requirement ratio at 5 percent. The maximum the central bank is willing to lend is 25 percent of required reserves, charging the gross real return of 1 on discount window loans. We assume the gross real return on fiat money is 1.02 and the gross real return on capital is 1.08.

   a. What is the gross real return on deposits?

   b. If the supply of fiat money is $10,000, what is the quantity of M1 in this economy?

9.5. Consider an economy in which the central bank is willing to loan any quantity of reserves to banks. Let the gross real return on capital be x.

   a. What amount would a bank choose to borrow if the central bank rate of discount window loans is less than x?

   b. Reconsider your answer to part a but with capital exhibiting diminishing marginal product.

Chapter 10

Money Stock Fluctuations

1 Roadmap

In this chapter, we develop a model economy in which people hold currency and deposits. When we look at data, we observe lots of movements in our measures of the monetary aggregates. Why is this so? By definition, the total money stock is the product of the monetary base and the money multiplier. Observable changes in the monetary aggregates that do not come from changes in the monetary base must result from changes in the money multiplier. If the money multiplier is random, a central bank cannot exactly predict the impact its policies will have on the monetary aggregates even though it knows how much money has been printed (the monetary base). In Chapter 9, the money multiplier was found to be simply the inverse of the reserve requirement. Because reserve requirements rarely change (and would be well known to the central bank), they cannot be the source of the observed fluctuations in the money multiplier. Something else must be responsible.

We propose a way to explain the observed fluctuations in the money multiplier by studying a model economy in which currency is valued. One key to this model economy is that people differ in terms of their income when young. Some have high incomes and some have low incomes. The other key is a friction that exists; specifically, banks are subject to a flat fee in order to verify a depositor's identity. This friction combined with differences across people result in two groups: those who use currency as the store of value and those who use deposits as stores of value.

Lastly, we revisit the relationship between money and output that we studied in Chapter 6. If you remember, the monetary aggregates are positively related to output. Our goal is to be able to explain why this correlation exists. In addition, we can use the model economy to explain observations with respect to movements in the money multiplier. In this model economy, we have a larger set of facts that we can attempt to explain; in addition to the money-output correlation, we can explain why the money multiplier fluctuates.

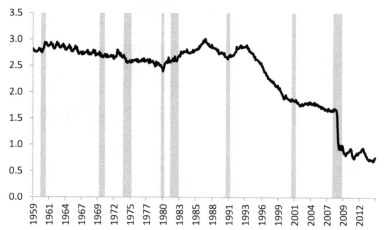

Figure 10.1. The money multiplier for the U.S. economy. In the graph, shaded regions correspond to period in which the U.S. economy was in a recession as dated by the Business Cycle Dating Committee from the National Bureau of Economic Research. The money multiplier tends to decline in recession years of 1961, 1974, 1979, 1980, 1991, 2000, and 2008. *Source:* The money multiplier is calculated as the ratio of M1 to the monetary base.

2 The Correlation between Money and Output

One of the most puzzling phenomena in monetary economics is an observed positive correlation between the nominal money aggregates and output. It is easy to understand a link between the number of dollars and nominal output (the dollar value of production), but why should there be any link between the number of dollars and output (the goods value of production)? Can these nearly fictitious units of account have any influence on the productivity of workers and machines?

This is potentially the most important question in monetary economics. The monetary authority has the power to change the fiat money stock at will. Therefore, if the fiat money stock influences output, the monetary authority can influence output. At a minimum, this implies that reducing fluctuations in the fiat money stock will reduce fluctuations in output; at best, this implies that the monetary authority can stimulate output at will.

When people talk about the money-output correlation, however, they are referring to the positive relationship between the monetary aggregates and output. Of course, movements in the fiat money stock and in money multiplier are both candidates for explaining the co-movements between the monetary aggregate and output. Figure 10.1 plots quarterly money multiplier data for the U.S. economy. Note the patterns in the money multiplier in relation to recession years (shaded regions of the graph).

Fluctuations in the money multiplier are of special interest because they appear to be linked with output. Researchers have focused on the relationship between innovations in output and innovations in the monetary aggregates. Innovations are measured as the unpredictable movements in an economic variable. Researchers use past behavior to compute what is predictable and then compute the innovation as the difference between the actual value and predicted value. The evidence indicates that innovations in the money multiplier are positively correlated with innovations in output. If we can find a source of fluctuations in the money multiplier, we may also be able to explain one of the most puzzling monetary phenomena: the observed correlation between the nominal money aggregates and output. That is the goal of this chapter.

Before we get carried away with visions of ending the business cycle through the creative manipulation of the money aggregates, we should acknowledge some other possibilities. Perhaps the changes in output cause the changes in the money stock. It is also possible that an observed correlation between two variables does not imply that one of the variables causes the other to change. Instead, it may be that changes in some third, unobserved variable cause the changes in both observed variables, generating the observed correlation.

Let us be more explicit about the patterns observed in the data concerning money and output. An "innovation" in some variable may be defined as the difference between a variable's actual value and the value predicted by the variable's recent behavior; loosely speaking, an innovation represents the unpredicted change, or surprise, in a variable. The following patterns in the data have been observed:

1. Innovations in output are positively correlated with innovations in the total nominal money stock.[1]
2. The innovations in the total nominal money stock occur before the innovations in output.[2] An innovation in money thus helps predict a subsequent innovation in output.
3. When observations of the interest rate are studied together with observations of money and output, innovations in the interest rate help predict innovations in money and output, and innovations in the money stock do not provide additional help in predicting innovation in output.[3]
4. The money innovations linked to output innovations primarily take the form of changes in the deposit-to-currency ratio (and the money multiplier).[4]

The observed precedence of money innovations to output innovations (pattern 2) led many to suspect that the innovations in the money stock cause the innovations in output. The loose reasoning was that if the output innovations had the money innovations, the output innovations would have occurred first.[5]

The other evidence, however, casts doubts on the idea that the monetary authority can use its control of the money stock to effect changes in output. An economist who looks only at money and output, omitting interest rates, will observe only the

---

[1] See Friedman and Schwartz (1963b).

[2] See Sims (1972, 1980).

[3] See Sims (1980) and Litterman and Weiss (1985).

[4] See Cagan (1965) and King and Plosser (1984).

[5] Output innovations still may be the cause of money innovations if the monetary authority anticipates output changes and acts even before the output innovations occur. This was suggested by Tobin (1970).

correlation between money and output. Pattern 3 suggests that this correlation may be spurious. Both money and output may be reacting to interest rates or some other variable related to interest rates.

Pattern 4 links output to the deposit-to-currency ratio, which is precisely that part of the money stock that the government does not control. Given that we observe a correlation between monetary aggregates and output, the open question is whether the correlation owes to parts of the money stock that are under the control of the monetary authority – for example, the monetary base, or to parts that endogenous, like the currency-to-deposit ratio.

We need an explanation consistent with all of the observed patterns. Because one of these observations is that the money multiplier fluctuates with output (pattern 4), let us start by building a model of the money multiplier.

3 A Model of Currency and Deposits

In the model of Chapter 9, the money supply was exactly determined by the fiat money stock and reserve requirements. The special assumptions in that model – that bank deposits are the only form of money and that these deposits are subject to a binding reserve requirements – lead to the model's simple prediction of a fixed money multiplier equal to the inverse of the reserve ratio.

In the model of Chapter 9, we discovered that changes in reserve requirements could lead to changes in the total money stock and output. However, because reserve requirements rarely change, they cannot be important determinants of the observed fluctuations in money and output. Because the link between money and output appears to be primarily a link between the money multiplier and output,[6] we adapt our model to permit a money multiplier that can fluctuate even when the reserve requirement is fixed. We do so by allowing the people in our model to choose between currency (made up of fiat money) and bank deposits (inside money backed by bank assets invested in capital). For simplicity, we assume that there are no reserve requirements. (The appendix presents a version of this chapter's model with reserve requirements imposed.)

3.1 A Model of Inside and Outside Money

Consider an economy of overlapping generations of two-period-lived people.[7] There exists a constant stock of fiat money. In each generation, there are three types of people – workers, entrepreneurs, and bankers. All three types are risk neutral. A constant number of people of each type are born each period.

---

[6] See, for example, the evidence cited by Cagan (1965) or by King and Plosser (1984).

[7] This model is adapted from Freeman and Huffman (1991), who draw on Sargent and Wallace (1982) and Prescott (1987). See also Lacker (1988) and Schreft (1992).

We begin with a description of each type of person living in the economy, starting with workers. Here, we assume that workers are endowed with labor production time when young but not when old. With this labor, workers produce an amount of the nonstorable consumption good. In order to consume when they are old, workers will use money either in the form of currency or in the form of deposits. The decision depends on which offers a higher return. We further assume that each worker produces a different quantity of the consumption good when young. Old-age consumption is a normal good which means that saving is positively related to the quantity produced. We have to keep track of different workers and use the notation that worker i desires money balances worth s_i units of the consumption good. Note that all workers look alike. Workers, however, may choose to identify themselves. Self-identification is part of withdrawing deposits from a bank. In order to identify oneself – that is, to verify that worker i is actually worker i – is costly. In other words, there is a transaction cost associated with verifying a worker's identity. We assume it costs ϕ units of the consumption good to verify each person's identity.

Entrepreneurs are distinguished from workers by having one extra ability. Just like workers, entrepreneurs have one unit of productive time when young and nothing when old. In addition, entrepreneurs have the ability to transform units of the consumption good into units of capital. Here, each unit of the consumption good converted in capital at date t will yield x units of the consumption good at date $t + 1$. We assume $x > 1$. Entrepreneurs can create capital goods from their own production or from others. The greater the rate of return on capital, the more entrepreneurs will invest from their own endowments. We assume that entrepreneurs cannot be located by workers.

Bankers are the third type and their key role is to serve as match maker for workers and entrepreneurs. Bankers have no endowment when young nor when they are old. By themselves, bankers cannot create capital. However, bankers have two advantages over the other two types. First, bankers are able to locate entrepreneurs. Second, bankers are costlessly known to workers and to entrepreneurs. Bankers do expend resources whenever a worker/depositor withdraws goods from the bank. This withdrawal operates the same way as if the worker uses a check to pay for old-age consumption: the check means the old worker gets units of the consumption good and the young person receives units of the consumption good from the bank.

Now that we know who lives in this economy, it is possible to describe why the two forms of money can coexist. One option is for workers to acquire fiat money, or currency. Because the quantity of fiat money is constant and the population is constant, the return to fiat money is 1. Everyone recognizes currency as the generally accepted medium of exchange. With this property, young people will accept it from old people without needing to verify the person's identity so the transaction cost associated with using currency as a means of payment is lower than that associated with using deposits. However, if you want to use deposits, the bank must verify that worker i is a depositor. To make this more concrete, the bank uses up ϕ goods to verify the depositor's identity. So, for example, suppose a young person deposits 1 good into a bank and the bank promises r goods next period. Next period, the old person shows up at the bank and receives $r - \phi$ goods.

What determines the return that the bank offers to workers? The steps to determine the return are as follows: (i) with the goods obtained from depositors, bankers make loans to entrepreneurs, (ii) entrepreneurs transform each unit of the consumption good into a unit of capital, (iii) each unit of capital in date t yields x units of the consumption good at date $t + 1$, (iv) bankers know the return on capital and are paid x units of next period's consumption for each unit loaned to entrepreneurs this period.[8] If $x > r$, the difference in returns should encourage enterprising bankers to seek to profit through arbitrage. Basically, bankers can profit by borrowing from workers at a low rate of return and lending to entrepreneurs at a higher rate of return. Now, to pin down the return on deposits, let us describe an intermediation arrangement that may spring up as a result of $x - r > 0$. The arguments for the development of such an arrangement are similar to the arbitrage ones developed in Chapter 7. In a competitive market, bankers will be able to receive the rate of return x on anything lent to entrepreneurs. Any lower rate of return implies excess profits to the entrepreneurs. In this case, any banker can demand a higher rate of return, r, knowing that some entrepreneur will accept the loan because he can still make profits of $x - r$ on each good he accepts from the banker. In this way, the interest rate paid to bankers will rise until $r = x$, where entrepreneurs are no longer interested in accepting any more loans. In the same way competition among bankers will also increase the rate of return on workers' deposits to x.

The story does not end here because the transaction cost ϕ exists. We think of the costs as time and effort that it takes when a person withdraws deposits from a bank. For example, ϕ could represent the costs of going to the bank, waiting in line, and identifying oneself in order to make a withdrawal. Alternatively, it could be the cost associated with identifying oneself when writing a check or the fee the bank charges to cover the cost of clearing the check. Note that if the bankers were allowed to issue private bank notes (tradable notes payable to the bearer but issued by private banks), then no identification cost would be incurred when these notes were exchanged (ϕ would be zero). We are assuming that bankers are not allowed to issue private currency. The prohibition on private bank notes is a nearly universal restriction in modern economies, perhaps to enable the collection of seigniorage. The critical thing is that the transaction cost does not depend on the size of the withdrawal. The cost associated with processing a depositor's withdrawal is the same whether the amount withdrawn is \$10 or \$1,000.

---

[8] You might think, why would an entrepreneur agree to a loan in which the bankers take the entire proceeds? The point is that entrepreneurs are indifferent between this activity and doing nothing; in both settings they get zero goods. We assume that they accept the loan, produce next-period goods and return all the goods to the bankers. In contrast to the withdrawal, entrepreneurs can go to the bank and borrow goods at zero transaction costs.

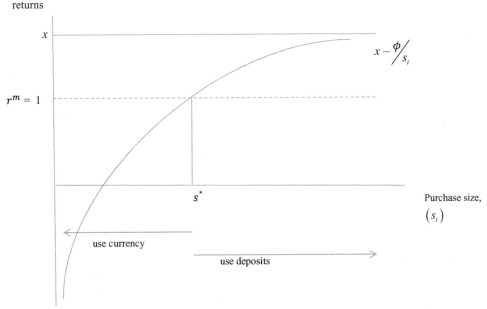

returns

x

$r^m = 1$

$x - \phi/s_i$

s^*

Purchase size, (s_i)

use currency

use deposits

Figure 10.2. The choice between using currency versus using deposits. In determining whether to use currency or deposits for making purchases, people compare the returns on the two alternative assets. For purchasing small quantities of old-age consumption (less than S^*), the return on currency exceeds that on deposits. So, these people will use currency. In contrast, for purchasing larger quantities of old-age consumption, the return on deposits dominates, and these people will use deposits.

For any asset, the gross return is the total amount received from the asset divided by the amount paid for the asset. From the earlier discussion, we know that banks will pay a rate of return of x on deposits (before transaction costs).[9] If we now include transaction costs, the return from depositing s_i with a banker is $xs_i - \phi$. Then the average return per good deposited is, after transaction costs, $(xs_i - \phi)/s_i = x - (\phi/s_i)$. This average rate of return is negatively related to the size of the transaction cost and positively related to the size of the deposit (s_i). With a small deposit, the transaction cost will be large relative to the size of the deposit and therefore will have a large adverse effect on the average rate of return.

Currency does not have a transaction cost (because there is no need to identify oneself when using fiat money). Its rate of return is the same as (v_{t+1}/v_t), whatever the size of the person's currency balances. If the stock of fiat money and the demand for currency do not change from time t to time $t + 1$, the rate of return on currency is simply 1.

In Figure 10.2 we graph the rates of return of deposits and currency as functions of the size of the transaction. Note from the graph that fiat money provides a

---

[9] As we found in Chapter 8, banks subject to a requirement to hold fraction γ of deposits in reserves of fiat money would pay the rate of return $(1 - \gamma)x + \gamma n/z$. To keep things simple, we assume here that banks are not subject to a reserve requirement.

better rate of return than deposits for small transactions but not for large ones. Ask yourself if you behave in the same way when making purchases.

Let's define H_t as the real value of total inside money balances in any period t and Q_t as the real value of total fiat money balances at t. The "deposit-to-currency ratio" in this economy can therefore be written as H_t/Q_t. Ask yourself what happens to the deposit-to-currency ratio as s^* increases or decreases.

Let us now take a closer look at three key macroeconomic aggregates in this economy in any period t – the price level, p_t (the price of a good in units of fiat money, e.g., dollars); the total nominal money stock, $(M1)_t$; and total output, GDP_t. Note first that, if the price of a good in dollars is p_t, then

$$p_t Q_t = M_t \quad or \quad p_t = \frac{M_t}{Q_t}. \tag{10.1}$$

Now recall that the total nominal money stock $(M1)_t$ is the sum of currency and bank deposits, measured in dollars. The nominal stock of currency equals M_t because fiat money is used entirely for currency, given that banks in this version of the model hold no reserves. The nominal stock of deposits can be written as real deposits multiplied by the price of goods, or $p_t H_t$. Therefore, we have that

$$(M1)_t = M_t + p_t H_t. \tag{10.2}$$

Because $p_t = M_t/Q_t$, from Equation 10.1, we can also write

$$(M1)_t = M_t + \left[\frac{M_t}{Q_t}\right] H_t \tag{10.3}$$

$$= \left[1 + \frac{H_t}{Q_t}\right] M_t. \tag{10.4}$$

We see that $[1 + H_t/Q_t]$ is the "money multiplier" – the number by which we multiply the monetary base to find the total money stock. Unlike economies in which deposits (subject to a reserve requirement) are the only form of money, this economy has a money multiplier that depends on the public's relative preference for deposits and currency (the deposit-to-currency ratio, H_t/Q_t). As a result, the money multiplier can no longer be reduced to the simple $1/\gamma$.

To see the mechanics of the money multiplier, suppose that, in period t, people want to hold more deposits at banks and less currency. In such a circumstance, H_t rises and Q_t falls. From Equation 10.4, we see that the money multiplier increases. For a fixed fiat money stock, the money supply as measured by $(M1)_t$ rises.

What might cause fluctuations in the money multiplier? We see from Figure 10.2 that anything affecting the rates of return of currency or deposits will change s^*, altering the deposit-to-currency ratio and thus the money multiplier. We suggest one possible source of fluctuations in the next section, a source that also accounts for the observed correlation between the money multiplier and output.

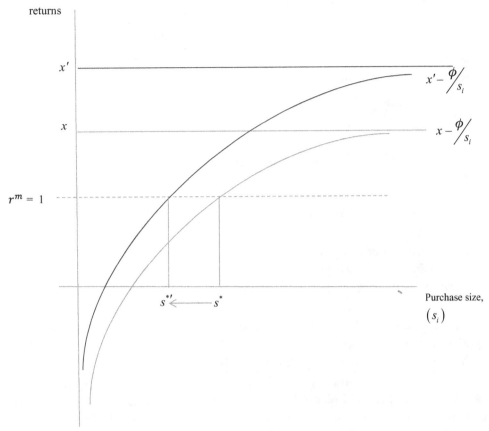

Figure 10.3. An unanticipated increase in the productivity of capital. If the return on capital unexpectedly increases from x to x', bankers can increase the return paid on deposits. The curve representing the returns shifts up from the blue line to the green line in the diagram. This causes a decrease in the breakeven level of old-age purchases. As the breakeven level decreases, more old-age people will use deposits. Hence, fewer people will use currency to make old-age purchases. In terms of the model, H increases and Q decreases.

4 Linking Output and the Money Multiplier

Suppose that, in period t, there is an unanticipated, permanent increase in the productivity of capital as represented by x. More precisely, suppose that x increases to x'. Such a change is captured by an upward shift in the rate of return on deposits, as shown in Figure 10.3.

As the diagram clearly shows, the increase in x causes a decrease in s^* to $s^{*\prime}$. This implies that there is a decrease in the minimum purchase size for which deposits offer a higher rate of return than fiat money. In the aggregate, more people will use deposits (H_t, inside money, increases) as a form of money and fewer will use fiat money (Q_t, outside money, decreases). Hence, the deposit-to-currency ratio H_t/Q_t will increase. This, in turn, implies an increase in the money multiplier

The Real Sector	The Monetary Sector
Capital rises	Money multiplier rises, $\left(1 + \frac{H_t}{Q_t}\right)$ ↑
Direct Investment, K_t ↑	Deposits rise, H_t ↑
Intermediated investment rises, H_t ↑ (bank loans rise)	Currency demand falls, Q_t ↓
Output rises, GDP_{t+1} ↑	The price level rises, p_t ↑
	The total money stock rises, $(M1_t)$ ↑

Figure 10.4. The effect of a productivity change on real and monetary sectors. Consider an unanticipated increase in productivity, x.

$[1 + (H_t/Q_t)]$. For a given monetary base (M_t), the increase in the money multiplier will cause an increase in $(M1)_t$.

The decreased demand for currency (fiat money) causes a decrease in its value – that is, an increase in the price level p_t (see Equation 10.1). Note that the price level moves in the same direction as the total money stock even if there has been no change in the monetary base. Because the shock is permanent, it decreases the demand for currency in both periods t and $t + 1$, leaving currency's rate of return unaffected.[10]

What are the effects of the productivity change on the real sector of the economy? The rise in the productivity of capital means that, for any given stock of capital, more output will be produced. In addition, capital's greater rate of return will encourage more investment in capital from entrepreneurs, who invest directly, and from workers, who invest indirectly, when they make deposits at banks. Capital produces in the period after it is created, so output in period $t + 1$ will be

$$GDP_{t+1} = Y_{t+1} + x'H_t + x'K_t, \tag{10.5}$$

where Y_{t+1} is the sum of the endowments of the young workers and entrepreneurs born in period $t + 1$, $x'H_t$ is the output created in period $t + 1$ by capital that was created by intermediaries in period t, and $x'K_t$ is the output from capital created through direct investment. The increase in output in period $t + 1$ is caused by the combined effect of increases in x, H_t, and K_t.

The effects of the productivity change on the real and monetary sectors of the economy are summarized in Figure 10.4.

Note that our model displays the features described at the beginning of this chapter. First, the total money stock $(M1)_t$ is positively correlated with output (here, they both increase). Second, the increase in the money stock precedes the increase in output by one period. Finally, changes take place in the form of changes in the deposit-to-currency ratio and the money multiplier.

---

[10] If the shock is temporary, the rate of return of currency is affected but the model's implications are not. See Freeman and Huffman (1991).

4.1 Correlation or Causality?

A casual observer looking at monetary aggregates and measures of output may come to the conclusion that because the increase in $(M1)_t$ preceded the change in output, it caused the change in output. This is an unwarranted conclusion. The original source of the change in output was the increase in the productivity of capital as measured by x. This change in x also induced an increase in the rate of return on deposits, which, in turn, caused an increase in deposits and thus in the total money stock. However, the initial cause of the increase in output was the change in x, not the change in $(M1)_t$. The changes in the money stock preceded the output changes because people were able to adjust the composition of their money balances more rapidly than they could adjust production.

This is an important lesson to remember. We have noted that the total money stock is positively correlated with output. This merely states that, as the money stock increases, so does output. It is not a statement of causality. Even though the change in the total money preceded the change in output, we cannot infer that it caused the change. The example demonstrates that correlation, or even precedence, does not imply causality.[11]

4.2 A Once-and-for-All Change in the Fiat Money Stock

Now let us consider another experiment. Suppose there is a once-and-for-all increase in the stock of fiat money owned by the initial old (M_0 increases). For example, suppose we double the stock of fiat money owned by the initial old. However, as before, the fiat money stock will remain fixed at this new, higher level in subsequent periods ($M_t = M_0$ for all t). What will be the effect of such a change in our model?

Clearly, because the fiat money stock remains fixed over time, the rate of return on fiat money is still equal to 1 (recall that the population is fixed). Figure 10.2 indicates that nothing has been altered by this change. Only changes in the rate of return on fiat money or the rate of return on deposits affect s^*. Because s^* is unaltered, there is no effect on H_t or Q_t. Given that there is no change in the deposit-to-currency ratio, the money multiplier will remain fixed. Furthermore, the absence of any change in H_t or x implies that output (as measured in Equation 10.5) will remain the same.

Are there any effects from this change? Yes. According to Equation 10.1, the price level in all periods increases because of the increase in M_t. In the case of a doubling of M_t, the price level is twice as high in every period. Furthermore, Equation 10.4 indicates that the total money stock $(M1)_t$ increases (doubles). Here we note an increase in the total money stock with no increase in output.

---

[11] See Leamer (1985) and Cooley and LeRoy (1985).

Suppose now that an economy experiences shocks to both the productivity of capital (x) and the monetary base (M_t).[12] Both shocks affect the total money stock. Output, however, changes only in response to changes in the productivity of capital. An economist who looks only at the total money stock [$(M1)_t$] and output will still find a correlation between the two because both are affected by changes in the productivity of capital. An economist who looks at the real interest rate (x) along with money and output, however, will find that it is the real interest rate, not money, that is correlated with output. In this economy, output changes if and only if the real interest rate changes but only some of the time that money changes. Therefore, money has no remaining correlation with output as soon as interest rate changes have been accounted for. This is consistent with pattern 3 in the data. It is also a good illustration of how the omission of important variables can mislead empirical work. Two variables (here, money and output) that are directly unrelated but are affected by a third variable (the productivity of capital) can appear to linked to one another. An economist who looked at only money and output would be overlooking the variable that is the true source of all of the changes.

5 A Monetary Stabilization Policy?

Many economists argue that active monetary policies can help alleviate fluctuations in output. Our model can help to provide some insights into this claim. By an active monetary policy, we mean one that changes in response to the state of the economy. The nature of such an active policy will become clear in the following example.

Suppose economists have been studying an economy in which shocks to x have occurred over a long period of time. They note and statistically verify that the total nominal money stock is positively correlated with output. They are convinced that, because the shocks to money occur before the shocks to output, the money shocks must cause the output shocks. They go on to argue that, if the stock of fiat money is increased enough to offset a decline in the stock of inside money, the fluctuations in output will not occur because the total money stock will no longer fluctuate.

Let us examine these arguments in the context of our model. Suppose there is a decline in the productivity of capital as measured by x. This is the opposite of the case studied previously. It is represented by a downward shift in the curve depicting the rate of return on deposits that appeared in Figure 10.2. By reasoning similar to that pursued earlier, such a development would cause an increase in outside money (Q_t), a decrease in inside money (H_t), a decline in the deposit-to-currency ratio (H_t/Q_t), and a decline in the money multiplier [$1 + (H_t/Q_t)$]. In the absence of any offsetting monetary policy, it would also cause a decline in the total money stock ($M1)_t$. We also know that it would cause a decline in intermediated capital,

---

[12] Repeated shocks make currency a risky asset and thus less desirable to risk-averse people. This does not affect the behavior of risk-neutral people we have chosen to study here.

resulting in a decline in output in the following period. Can we void the decline in output by printing more fiat money, as suggested by the economists?

An unchanged total money stock can be maintained by offsetting the decline in inside money with an increase in the fiat money stock. To see how this might be accomplished, recall Equation 10.4:

$$(M1)_t = \left[1 + \frac{H_t}{Q_t}\right] M_t.$$

The decline in $[1 + (H_t/Q_t)]$ could be perfectly offset by increasing M_t by an appropriate amount. For example, if the money multiplier fell by half, the total money stock $(M1)_t$ could be held constant by doubling the monetary base.

Would such a policy succeed in its goal of avoiding the decline in output in the following period? The answer is no. The decline in productivity and stock of capital would still cause a decline in output in the following period. The total money stock is statistically linked to output only because the stock of inside money is linked to output. If we offset the decline in inside money with an increase in outside money, there will still be a decline in total output in the following period. In this model economy, the monetary authority can stabilize the monetary aggregate $(M1)$ by adjusting the quantity of monetary base in response to movements in the money multiplier. However, the monetary authority's aggregate-stabilizing actions do not stabilize output and would result in no observable correlation between the monetary aggregate and output.

Example 10.1 Suppose there is an unanticipated, permanent decrease in transaction costs, as represented by ϕ. Find its effect on s^*, the price level, the deposit-to-currency ratio, the money multiplier, the total nominal money stock, capital, and output. Explain each of these effects. Verify that the model economy displays a correlation between the nominal money stock and output. Will a one-time increase in the monetary base cause an increase in output?

5.1 Another Look at Monetary Aggregates

Much attention is paid to monetary aggregates, measures of the total quantity of money that include both inside and outside money. Because these aggregates do not distinguish between inside and outside money, we should pay attention to them only if the total stock of money is important but its composition is not.

In the model economy we have just studied, the total money stock is a good indicator of the price level. We see that, whenever there is an increase in the money stock, whether from an increase in the monetary base or an increase in the money multiplier, there is also an increase in the price level.

The total money stock is not a useful measure when we look at output in the model. Inside and outside money have very different statistical links to output. It is not surprising that inside money has links to output, and outside money does not. Inside money is deposits invested through banks in productive capital. In contrast, outside money is merely unbacked pieces of paper with no direct links to production.

If we look only at aggregates of the total money stock and ignore the composition of those aggregates, we can easily be misled. A correlation of inside money with output appears to be a correlation of total money with output when economists do not distinguish between changes in inside or outside money. This tempts the observer to believe, incorrectly, that changes in outside money, which is controlled by the central bank, may exhibit the same correlation. This error can be avoided if economists distinguish between changes in inside and outside money in their observations.

6 Anticipated Inflation and Output Revisited

Although current increases in the monetary base are not linked to current or future output, in this economy, anticipated future increases in the monetary base will affect the money multiplier and thus capital and output. If the fiat money stock grows at the rate z, then the rate of return on fiat money with a constant population is $1/z$. Suppose there is an increase in the (anticipated) rate of money creation. An increase in z lowers the rate of return on fiat money, causing s^* to fall, as shown in Figure 10.5. The lower rate of return on fiat money makes currency less desirable relative to bank deposits. As people add bank deposits, there is an increase in intermediated capital and subsequent output. This is the Tobin effect that we discussed in Chapter 7.

Does this mean that inflation is desirable in this economy? No. The shift away from currency implies that a larger fraction of people are bearing the transaction costs associated with depositing goods in banks. It should be reiterated that the total stock of currency is a small fraction of the size of the nation's capital stock, so that even if deposits replaced the entire stock of currency, the effect on output might be rather small. (See the section on "The Tobin Effect" in Chapter 7.)

7 Summary

In this chapter, we introduced a model of both currency and deposits. The model explains possible sources of observed fluctuations in the money stock that cannot be accounted for by changes in reserve requirements or the monetary base. We found that the money multiplier is determined by the deposit-to-currency ratio, which is outside the central bank's control. Factors that change the public's desired mix of currency relative to deposits lead to changes in the money multiplier and, hence, in the total money supply. These factors consist of anything that might cause the rates of return of deposits or currency to change.

returns

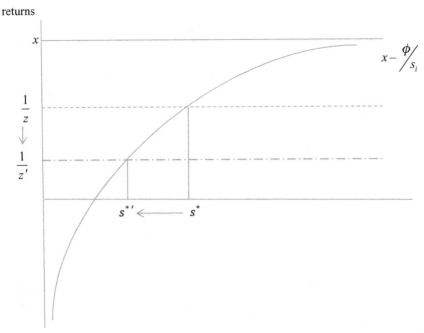

Figure 10.5. The effect of an increase in the rate of fiat money creation from z to z'. With an unanticipated permanent increase in the rate of fiat money growth, the return on fiat money decreases. As the figure shows, this results in a decline in the breakeven level of old-age purchases. As the breakeven level decreases, more old-age people will use deposits. Hence, fewer people will use currency to make old-age purchases. In terms of the model, H increases and Q decreases.

Because deposits – inside money – are used by banks to invest in capital, deposits and the money multiplier are linked to events in the real economy. Such events, like an anticipated increase in the productivity of capital, may therefore affect both output and the money stock, through the money multiplier, and output. Therefore, the observation of a money/output correlation does not imply that changes in the money supply cause the changes in output.

8 Exercises

10.1. Consider an economy in which there are 100 workers. One-half of the workers are endowed with 200 units of the consumption good when young and nothing when old. The remaining workers are endowed with 20 units of the consumption good when young and nothing when old. Each worker saves 30 percent of their endowment when young. Let the gross real return on capital be 1.25. Money supply grows according to following rule: $M_t = 1.1 M_{t-1}$. Assume that each worker uses 10 goods to identify themself and make a withdrawal from a bank.

a. For the high-income worker, compute the return on deposits.

b. For the high-income worker, compute the return on money.

　　c. For the low-income worker, compute the return on deposits.

　　d. For the low-income worker, compute the return on money.

　　e. Based on the answers to part a through d, what store of value should a high-income worker choose? A low-income worker?

10.2. Consider an economy in which there are 1,000 workers. One-half of the workers are endowed with 50 units of the consumption good when young and nothing when old. The remaining workers are endowed with 10 units of the consumption good when young and nothing when old. Each worker saves 30 percent of their endowment when young. Let the gross real return on capital be 1.1. Let the stock of money be constant over time with $M_0 = 10,000$. Assume that each worker uses 10 goods to identify themself and make a withdrawal from a bank.

　　a. What is the aggregate level of deposits in the economy?

　　b. Write down the money market-clearing condition. Compute the equilibrium price level.

　　c. What is the aggregate level of real money balances in the economy?

　　d. Compute the money multiplier.

10.3. In each of the following instances, an exogenous change is described. Use a graph to show how the particular exogenous change can result in an increase in the equilibrium return on deposits.

　　a. A permanent increase in the money growth rate.

　　b. A permanent increase in the productivity of capital

　　c. A permanent decrease in the cost of identification to a bank.

10.4. Consider an economy in which there are 200 workers. Three-fourths of the workers are endowed with 100 units of the consumption good when young and nothing when old. The remaining workers are endowed with 20 units of the consumption good when young and nothing when old. Each worker saves 50 percent of their endowment when young. Let the gross real return on capital be 1.25. There are 50 entrepreneurs in the economy. Each entrepreneur is endowed with 50 units of the consumption good when young and nothing when old. Entrepreneurs only want to consume when they are old. Let the stock of money be constant over time. Assume that each worker uses 20 goods to identify themself and make a withdrawal from a bank. At date t, there a permanent increase in the return on capital to 1.3.

　　a. Compute GDP in period t.

　　b. Compute GDP in period $t + 1$.

　　c. What are aggregate deposits in dates t and $t + 1$?

　　d. For this model economy, what is the correlation, if any, between aggregate deposits and GDP over the two time periods?

9 Appendix: The Money Supply with Reserves and Currency

In Example 10.1 we determined the money supply assuming there were bank deposits with reserve requirements but no currency. In the actual U.S. economy, there are both currency and bank deposits with reserve requirements. To study this case and for further practice in distinguishing between inside and outside money, do Appendix Exercise 10.1.

To do the exercise, you may want to remind yourself of the following definitions: the total nominal money stock $(M1)_t$ is defined as the sum of currency and bank deposits held by the nonbank public, measured in dollars.

$$(M1)_t = \text{nominal currency held by the nonbank public at } t$$

$$+ \text{ nominal bank deposits at } t. \tag{10.6}$$

Part of the fiat money stock is held as currency by the nonbank public, and part is held by banks as reserves:

$$M_t = \text{nominal currency at } t \text{ + nominal reserves at } t. \tag{10.7}$$

This implies that

$$(M1)_t = M_t + \text{nominal bank deposits at } t - \text{nominal reserves at } t$$

$$= M_t + p_t H_t - \gamma p_t H_t$$

$$= M_t + p_t(1 - \gamma)H_t$$

$$= M_t + \text{nominal intermediated capital at } t. \tag{10.8}$$

Note that real inside money $(1 - \gamma)H_t$, which represented all deposits when there was no reserve requirement $(\gamma = 0)$, now represents only that part of deposits backed by capital. The total real demand for fiat (outside) money includes currency held by the nonbank public (Q_t) and bank holdings of reserves, which are a fraction of the demand for deposits (γH_t).

By following the steps taken in Equations 10.1 to 10.4, we can derive the money multiplier in the presence of a reserve requirement. The money market-clearing condition becomes

$$M_t = p_t Q_t + \gamma p_t H_t \Rightarrow p_t = \frac{M_t}{Q_t + \gamma H_t}. \tag{10.9}$$

From Equation 10.8, the total nominal money stock is

$$(M1)_t = M_t + \left[\frac{M_t}{Q_t + \gamma H_t} \right](1 - \gamma)H_t$$

$$= \left[1 + \frac{H_t(1 - \gamma)}{Q_t + \gamma H_t} \right] M_t. \tag{10.10}$$

The term in brackets is the money multiplier in the presence of both currency and deposits subject to reserve requirements. As we found in Chapter 9, a decrease in the reserve requirement causes an increase in the total money stock $(M1)_t$.

Note that the expression for the money multiplier in Equation 10.10 includes the two special cases we have already studied. When no currency balances are held ($Q_t = 0$), the money multiplier from Equation 10.10 reduces to $1/\gamma$. When no reserves are held ($\gamma = 0$), it reduces to $[1 + (H_t/Q_t)]$.

10 Appendix Exercises

10.5. Consider an economy in which people wish to hold bank checking deposits worth a total of 5 million goods and currency worth 2 million goods in every period. In addition, there is a stock of unintermediated capital worth 10 million goods. Fiat money is the only asset used as currency. Deposits at banks are subject to a reserve requirement of 20 percent. After meeting the reserve requirement, banks invest the remainder of all deposits into capital. The monetary base is $1 million. *Hint*: The key to this exercise is understanding the difference between inside and outside money.

   a. Find the value (in goods) of a dollar.

   b. Find the total nominal money stock as measured by the Federal Reserve's definition of $M1$.

   c. Find the money multiplier.

   d. Find the total capital stock.

   e. Find the revenue (in goods) from seigniorage if the monetary base triples every period.

   f. Suppose people want to keep more their money balances in the form of cash, although their total demand for money does not change. What will happen to each of your answers to parts a to e?

Chapter 11

Fully Backed Central Bank Money

1 Roadmap

Perhaps you are seeing a recurring message appearing in Part II of this book. Specifically, when productive capital (i.e., when $x > n$) is available as a competing store of value, fiat money can be inefficient in two possible ways. First, fiat money offers a lower rate of return, which discourages people from holding and using this liquid form of money. Second, as people hold more real balances of fiat money, they hold less of productive capital, which reduces real output. In Chapter 10, for example, we saw that people chose between fiat money – with no transaction costs but unbacked by capital – and deposits – backed by capital but costlier to use.

In this chapter, we ask if there is a way to have both minimal transaction costs and money backed by capital? We have speculated that, if we freed private intermediation from all restrictions, inside money might replace fiat money entirely, giving us a money fully backed by capital and paying the same rate of return as capital. Doing so excludes the government from collecting seigniorage. In addition, there are potential information hurdles that arise when a private bank tries to provide a single money acceptable to all. So we modify the private-bank/backed money view to one in which the central bank backs its money.

There are advantages to specifying a model economy in which the central bank has assets and its liability is fiat money. For one thing, we can talk about open market operations. This model economy also allows us to examine recent policies like paying interest on reserves. More concretely, we develop a model economy in which the central bank backs fiat money with productive capital. We find that the effects of monetary policy differ greatly when the central bank pays interest on the money it issues. We see that, by paying interest on money, the central bank acts as a zero-profit financial intermediary rather than as a revenue agent for the

Assets	Liabilities
Interest-bearing assets (Including loans to banks)	Notes of the central bank (to be held as currency or reserves)

Figure 11.1. A central bank's balance sheet.

government.[1] This setup is offered as a description of how we might want our monetary institutions to operate and as a way to study some particularly timely current events.[2]

2 Paying Interest on Money

An obvious way to increase the rate of return on government money is to pay interest to those who hold that money. How can this interest be paid? What level is feasible? And how does this policy affect economic activity?

To this point, we have studied only economies in which the government in the initial and subsequent periods issues unbacked money, which it can give away or use to purchase goods. An alternative monetary arrangement would back government-issued money with productive assets. A monetary arrangement with backed money requires that any issuance of government money, including the initial stock of money, must be used to purchase a real asset paying interest at the prevailing market rate. A purchase (or sale) of an interest-paying asset by the monetary authority is called an "open market operation."[3] In this way, the monetary authority itself becomes an intermediary with assets and liabilities, just like a privately owned financial intermediary. Its liabilities are the notes it issues as money, whether held as currency or deposited with the central bank as bank reserves. The balance sheet of a central bank may be represented as shown in Figure 11.1.

From the return on the assets it owns, the central bank can pay interest on the money it issues.[4] The monetary authority now is no longer a revenue agent for the government but truly a central *bank*. The Federal Reserve began paying interest on reserves in October 2008.

The model of three-period-lived people in which capital pays a return after two periods will prove a bit cumbersome at this point. The reason people turn to financial intermediaries is not essential to the point we wish to study – the backing of money. Therefore, let us return to the simpler model of intermediation. In this model economy, people live for two periods. Capital pays a one-period gross real

---

[1] For an empirical look at these issues, see Smith (1988).

[2] The payment of interest on reserves has been advocated by Tolley (1957), Friedman (1960), and the U.S. Federal Reserve itself (see Feinman [1993]). This particular model of paying interest on government money is adapted from the work of Smith (1991) and Freeman and Haslag (1995).

[3] The distinction between open market operations and monetary expansions to fund subsidies or government spending is proposed by Metzler (1951).

[4] If the central bank receives interest from its assets but does not pay interest on its liabilities (money), the central bank earns profits, which can be turned over to the government. We take up this case in Chapter 14.

rate of return equal to $x > 1$. We assume that capital has a minimum size, k^*, which is greater than the endowment of most people.

Capital is illiquid in this economy because of its lack of divisibility into small units. It is easy to see how an intermediary can overcome this illiquidity. Simply pool the savings of many people to an amount greater than k^*. Assuming that the intermediation is costless and competitive, private intermediaries will offer the rate of return x on deposits. (If it were costly, the competitive return would be x minus the cost.) There may be some people who have an endowment large enough to invest in capital without the aid of an intermediary, but we focus our attention on those who must use intermediaries. For the rest of the model, let us return to the simplest overlapping generations model, with a constant population of two-period-lived people endowed with y when young and nothing when old.

To illustrate how money is backed by capital, we consider a specific policy that occurs in the first period of the economy. Instead of the usual helicopter drop of money created by printing, suppose the central bank conducts the following open market operation: the central bank exchanges money for capital. To make this more complete, suppose the central bank exchanges money for units of the consumption good. The consumption is costlessly transformed into units of capital at a one-for-one rate and the central bank then possesses capital goods.[5] Thereafter, the nominal stock of money will be held constant at M dollars, and the stock of central bank capital will be held constant at K^g goods. In equation form, the real value of money outstanding is equal to the quantity of capital goods, represented as

$$v_1 M = K^g. \tag{11.1}$$

The capital held by the central bank yields consumption goods next period. We assume that the proceeds from the central bank's holdings of capital will be used to pay net interest of ρ dollars in every period for each dollar held by the public. We assume that the central bank will pay the same interest in every period and will use all of its net earnings from capital to pay this interest. To compute the return on fiat money, therefore, there are now two components. In addition to the return on money measured as the change in value over time, we have an explicitly interest payment. What will be the real rate of return on this backed central bank money for a given interest rate ρ? The cost of a dollar at t is v_t, and at $t + 1$ the dollar returns $1 + \rho$ dollars at its value, v_{t+1}. Thus, the dollar's real (gross) rate of return is

$$\frac{v_{t+1}(1 + \rho)}{v_t}. \tag{11.2}$$

We use our old friend, the money market-clearing condition, to compute the part of money's return associated with changes in the value of money over time. Let the

[5] If the bank does not want to actually operate the capital, it may lend to the operators of capital by buying bonds they issue. In either arrangement, the bank owns an interest-bearing asset backed, directly or indirectly, by capital.

value of a unit of central bank money be determined by its supply and demand,

$$v_t M = N(y - c_{1,t} - h_t),\tag{11.3}$$

where h_t is the person's holdings of deposits at banks, so that $y - c_{1,t} - h_t$ represents the person's demand for real balances of central bank money.

To keep things simple, we focus on $\frac{v_{t+1}}{v_t}$ in a stationary equilibrium. With values of $c_{1,t}$ and h_t that are constant over time, Equation 11.3 tells us that the value of a unit of central bank money is also constant over time ($v_1 = v_t = v$). Thus, in a stationary equilibrium, Equation 11.2 simplifies to

$$\frac{v_{t+1}(1 + \rho)}{v_t} = 1 + \rho.\tag{11.4}$$

We still need to figure out what the return on money will be. In the absence of legal restrictions on private banking, the central bank must compete with private intermediaries; that is, the return on fiat money cannot be less than the return on deposits offered by private banks. In a competitive economy, banks acquire capital offering the return x. So the return on deposits will also equal x; formally, the condition is written as

$$1 + \rho \geq x \quad \text{or} \quad \rho \geq x - 1.\tag{11.5}$$

Next, we need to determine whether satisfying Equation 11.5 is feasible. Or, how can the central bank afford to pay this rate of return? The total return from the central bank's investment is xK^g. To maintain a fixed stock of capital, K^g of this return must be used to replenish the bank's stock of capital (recall that capital is assumed to last only a single period). What remains is the net return

$$xK^g - K^g = (x - 1)K^g.\tag{11.6}$$

In each period of a stationary equilibrium, the real money stock is Mv. The central bank promises to pay net nominal interest of ρ dollars on each dollar held, implying that total real interest payments by the central bank are ρMv. Note that because the stock of money is held constant, the interest on money will be paid with dollars earned from the production of the bank's stock of capital and not from freshly printed dollars. This can written as the central bank's budget constraint:

$$(x - 1)K^g = \rho Mv.\tag{11.7}$$

Because ρ must equal $x - 1$ if the rate of return on central bank money is to meet the competition from private bank money, the central bank's budget constraint is met only when

$$K^g = vM.\tag{11.8}$$

In summary, if the central bank uses all the net return from its assets to pay interest on its money, it must be that $K^g = vM$. This constraint is met when all

Assets		Liabilities	
Capital	K^g	Money in circulation	vM

Figure 11.2. The central bank's balance sheet when paying interest on money.

money issued is used to purchase real capital. Essentially, the central bank has become a zero-profit, zero-cost intermediary offering the same rate of return on its liabilities (money) that it receives from its assets.[6] The central bank's balance sheet in real terms is displayed in Figure 11.2.

3 Another Look at the Quantity Theory

Let's try a simple experiment in this model economy. What happens to the price level if the central bank increases the nominal stock of its money? Will the price level rise as it did when money was unbacked (e.g., as in Chapter 4), or will it be unchanged? The answer depends on what is done with the increased stock of money.

First, suppose the central bank uses the increase in the stock of money to purchase an even larger stock of capital. Suppose, in particular, that we double the central bank nominal money stock and use it to double the stock of capital. Is there still an equilibrium at the same price level as before? To answer, recall that to pay the market rate of return ($\rho = x - 1$), the central bank's budget constraint requires that the stock of central bank's capital K^g equals the real value of the central bank's liabilities (the money it issues) vM or

$$v = \frac{K^g}{M} \Rightarrow p = \frac{1}{v} = \frac{M}{K^g}. \tag{11.9}$$

Obviously, if we double both the nominal stock of central bank money and the stock of central bank capital, this equality still holds. When the central bank doubles its real capital, it doubles the amount it can pay in real interest. It can then afford to pay the market rate of interest on twice as much central bank money with no change in the value of that money (no change in the price level). How can the economy absorb twice as much central bank money without lowering its value? Look again at the supply and demand for central bank money in a stationary equilibrium (where real money holding and real balances of deposits are constant over time):

$$vM = N(y - c_1 - h). \tag{11.10}$$

To determine what happens to c_1 and h when $K^g = vM$, let us examine the budget constraints of our usual two-period-lived person (endowed when young but not when old) who must choose their real balances of central bank money ($v_t m_t = vm$)

---

[6] If there are costs to private intermediation, the same costs can be expected to apply to intermediation by the central bank.

and their real balances of deposits ($h_t = h$). The first-period budget constraint is

$$c_1 + vm + h = y. \tag{11.11}$$

Second-period consumption is financed by the returns from a person's holdings of money and deposits at banks. With the central bank paying the net interest rate ρ for each dollar held, the real return from a person's fiat money holdings when old are $(1 + \rho)vm$. Adding to that the real return from holding deposits (xh), we obtain the person's second-period budget constraint:

$$c_2 = (1 + \rho)vm + xh. \tag{11.12}$$

Because both assets offer the same rate of return ($1 + \rho = x$), Equation 11.12 can be written as

$$c_2 = xvm + xh = x(vm + h). \tag{11.13}$$

The sum $vm + h$ represents a person's total real money balances (real balances of central bank money plus real balances of money in the form of deposits at private banks). Note that, because both forms of money offer the same return, a person is indifferent between them. If we solve Equation 11.13 for this sum and substitute the result into the first-period budget constraint (Equation 11.11), we find the lifetime budget constraint:

$$c_1 + \frac{c_2}{x} = y. \tag{11.14}$$

People will pick the c_1^* and c_2^* that maximize their utility subject to this budget constraint (Equation 11.14). Note from Equation 11.14 that a person's budget constraint does not depend on the relative size of his balances of private bank and central bank money (h and vm). Therefore, he will choose the same c_1^* and c_2^*, whatever his balances of central bank money. If he holds more central bank money, by choice or by government requirement, he simply will hold that much less private bank money so that c_1^* and c_2^* remain at the levels that maximize his utility. In this way, the size of the open market operation in the initial period is irrelevant to the welfare of people and the total capital stock.[7]

Suppose, for example, that $y = 10$ and $x = 1.1$ and that facing this budget constraint, a person chooses $c_1^* = 4$ and $c_2^* = 6.6$. (Check that this choice satisfies the lifetime budget constraint [Equation 11.14].) By plugging the values in his budget equations – specifically, Equations 11.11 and 11.13 – one can see that he can achieve his consumption choice with any combination of h and vm so that $h + vm = y - c_1^* = 6$. The person is indifferent between $h = 4$ and $vm = 2$ and $h = 1$ and $vm = 5$, for example, because in both cases his real money balances total 6. Moreover, because both types of money are now backed by capital, the

---

[7] For a related case and fuller exposition of the irrelevance of open market operations, see Wallace (1981).

capital stock of a young person is the same (6 in this example), whatever the real value of central bank money.

Let us now return to the question of how the economy adjusts to an increase in central bank money that is fully backed ($K^g = vM$). We have just learned that the consumption choice of the person does not depend on the amount of central bank money. We can therefore write the equality of supply and demand for central bank money (Equation 11.10) as

$$vM = N(y - c_1^* - h), \tag{11.15}$$

or

$$Nh + K^g = N(y - c_1^*). \tag{11.16}$$

If the real stock of central bank money $vM = K^g$ increases and consumption stays the same, private bank money Nh must decrease by the same amount as the increase in central bank money. Note that the total real money stock, the total stock of intermediated capital, is $K^g + Nh$, which must equal $N(y - c_1^*)$, which is unaffected by the size of the central bank money stock. In earlier chapters, we saw that an increase in real balances of fiat money may lead to a reduction in the economy's capital stock. This is no longer the case when the central bank backs its money with capital. An increase in real balances of unbacked, fiat money (e.g., through an increase in the reserve requirement) implied that people held larger balances consisting of unproductive pieces of paper and smaller balances of deposits backed by capital at private banks. However, when the money of both the central bank and private banks is backed by capital, a switch from private bank money to central bank money does not change the total holding of capital.[8]

The only limit to the expansion of central bank money is that it cannot exceed $N(y - c_1^*)$ if we assume that private banks cannot have negative deposits ($Nh \geq 0$). Up to this limit, however, one can increase the stock of backed central bank money without affecting the value of a unit of that money. An increase in the quantity of central bank money does not rate the price level – it lowers the quantity of private bank money. The equality of money supply and demand ensures that quantity equation is satisfied (nominal total money equal the price level times a constant),

$$M + pNh = pN(y - c_1^*), \tag{11.17}$$

but it is satisfied by the adjustment of nominal private bank money and not by the adjustment of the price level.

Why doesn't an expansion of unbacked central bank money have the same effect on the price level as an expansion of fiat money, as studied in Chapter 4? The key is the difference in the backing of the two types of money. To see this, suppose that

---

[8] Whether we want private or public intermediation of capital therefore depends on which is more likely to choose the wisest investments and operate at the lowest costs, two factors we have omitted from our simple model.

our central bank decides to double the initial stock of its money but, instead of using the increase to purchase capital, it uses it to purchase consumption goods for the pleasure of government officials. As before, the central bank commits to using its entire net revenue from capital to pay interest (the central bank's budget constraint [Equation 11.7]). The real value of the interest payment ρv must therefore equal net revenue $[(x-1)K^g]$ divided by the number of dollars (M) on which it must pay interest:

$$\rho v = \frac{(x-1)K^g}{M}. \tag{11.18}$$

Recall that to meet the competition from private banks, the central bank must offer a rate of interest, $\rho = x - 1$, which implies that

$$v = \frac{K^g}{M} \Rightarrow p = \frac{1}{v} = \frac{M}{K^g}. \tag{11.19}$$

In this case, the nominal stock of money M has doubled but not the capital stock backing it, K^g. The central bank has twice as many dollars on which to pay interest but the same real capital stock from which to pay this interest. For this reason, the central bank's budget constraint (Equation 11.19) reveals that the value of a unit of the central bank's money must fall by 50 percent (the price level doubles). However, the ability of the bank to pay interest is limited by the stock of capital in its portfolio. It cannot increase the real value of its interest payments without increasing its real stock of capital. Therefore, the real value of the stock of central bank money vM must always equal the real value of its stock of capital K^g.

We can explain the difference in price level effects of these two types of expansion of central bank money if we think of a unit of central bank money as a share in the assets of a firm called the central bank.[9] If a firm doubles the number of its shares without doubling its investment in capital, each new share is worth half the value of an old share. If, instead, a firm doubles the number of shares while doubling its capital stock and resulting profits, there is no change in the value of the firm's shares. The same must hold for a central bank that pays interest on money out of its return from capital. The analysis does not change when we change the labels from "firm" to "central bank" and from "shares" to "money."

3.1 Money and Prices: 2007–2015

At the time this chapter goes to press, the interest rate on reserves is the same as the return on risk-free, short-term government securities. It has been this way since the 2007 Financial Crisis. In practice, this period's events are in line with the economic environment described in this model economy. Therefore, current conditions are a

---

[9] A further exposition of this analogy is offered by Smith (1985).

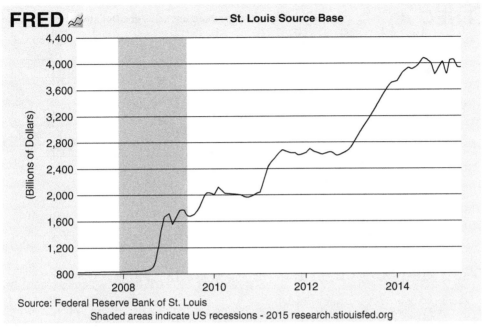

Figure 11.3. Fiat money supply for period 2007 through 2015.

test of the implications of this model economy. Figure 11.3 is a plot of the monetary base from 2007 through 2015. The graph shows that in 2008, the monetary base expanded from $800 million to $4 trillion in 2014.

According to the Quantity Theory of Money associated with unbacked fiat money, the price level would have begun to increase sometime after money supply increase occurred. Yet Figure 11.4 shows that the price level has increased approximately 13 percent compared with the 400 percent increase in the monetary base. However, when we amend the model economy to consider backed fiat currency, the relationship between the money supply and the price level over the eight-year period is easier to explain. With an increase in the supply of backed fiat money that pays interest, there is no upward pressure on the price level. From the perspective of the central bank, Equation 11.9 tells us that numerator and the denominator changed by the same proportion. From the perspective of people, the open market purchase is an exchange on one interest-bearing asset (fiat money) for another one (government bonds).

So the Federal Reserve began backing fiat money in 2008 by offering interest on reserves. With this policy change, the model economy predicts that changes in the fiat money supply do not result in proportional changes in the price level. Based on the evidence since 2008, the model economy can account for why the percentage increase in the price level has been negligible compared with the percentage change in the fiat money supply.

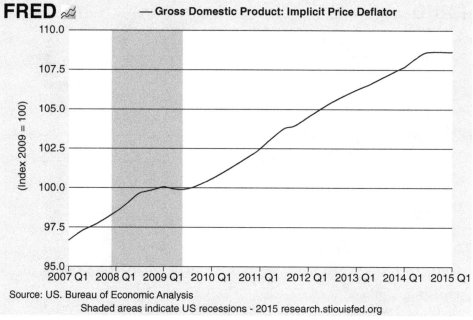

Figure 11.4. GDP Implicit Price Deflator 2007 through 2015.

4 Deflation

It is not much of a problem to pay interest on reserves deposited at the central bank. But how can one pay interest on currency in circulation? The advantage of currency in transactions is that one can exchange it for goods without the costly record keeping involved in registering the transaction at a bank. This advantage would be lost if one had to take one's currency to the central bank from time to time to receive interest. Isn't there some way to increase the rate of return on currency without directly paying interest?

Suppose the central bank uses the return from its assets not to pay interest but to purchase and destroy a fraction of the stock of central bank money in public hands. In particular, let the stock of central bank money, M_t, shrink over time according to the rule $M_t = zM_{t-1}$ with $z < 1$. The number of goods spent to reduce the stock of central bank money each period equals

$$v(M_{t-1} - M_t) \quad \text{or} \quad v_t M_t \left[\frac{1}{z} - 1 \right]. \tag{11.20}$$

We have already found that the net return from central bank assets (after renewing the capital stock) is $(x - 1)K^g$. If the net return is used only to purchase central bank money, the central bank's budget constraint is

$$v_t M_t \left[\frac{1}{z} - 1 \right] = (x - 1)K^g. \tag{11.21}$$

If the value of central bank money is equal to the stock of capital behind it $(v_t M_t = K^g)$, the central bank's budget constraint (Equation 11.21) becomes

$$K^g\left[\frac{1}{z} - 1\right] = (x-1)K^g, \qquad (11.22)$$

which reveals that the central bank can afford to deflate at the rate z so that

$$\frac{1}{z} = x \quad \text{or} \quad z = \frac{1}{x}. \qquad (11.23)$$

To find the rate of return of fiat money, we proceed as always from the equality of money supply and demand. The demand for central bank money is again $y - c_{1,t} - h_t$ per young person. Therefore, the equality of supply and demand in a stationary equilibrium with a constant population requires that

$$v_t M_t = N(y - c_1 - h), \qquad (11.24)$$

implying that

$$\frac{v_{t+1}}{v_t} = \frac{\frac{N(y-c_1-h)}{M_{t+1}}}{\frac{N(y-c_1-h)}{M_t}} = \frac{1}{z}. \qquad (11.25)$$

Therefore, if the central bank deflates setting $z = 1/x$, it can give central bank money the rate of return on capital x. At this rate of return, people can receive the same rate of return from central bank money that they receive from private intermediaries. Therefore, they do not care how much of the money stock is intermediated through the central bank.

Our analogy to shares in the firm continues to apply. A firm is not limited to dividends if it wishes to distribute business profits to its shareholders. Shareholders are also paid if the firm buys up a fraction of its own shares. The reduction in the number of shares increases the value of the remaining shares, distributing the business profits to the shareholders. A central bank with backed money that reduces the number of its outstanding dollars (shares) similarly makes the remaining dollars more valuable.

5 Currency Boards

Backing the stock of central bank money with interest-bearing assets can also be used to ward off speculative attacks that occur in international currency markets.[10] When we studied speculative attacks in Chapter 5, we noted that a country can prevent a speculative attack if it has enough funds to buy up all its currency in the hands of speculators at the announced exchange rate. We assumed in Chapter 6 that these funds came from a government's ability to tax its citizens. This raised

---

[10] This section presumes a familiarity with the material in Chapter 5.

the question of whether a government would actually go through with a plan to tax its own citizens to pay off foreign exchange speculators.

A country that fully backs its money with interest-bearing assets has made a commitment that it can use to ward off speculative attacks against its currency. With a fully backed currency, a central bank has the resources to redeem any amount of its money that is turned in, whether by its own citizens or by foreign speculators. For example, suppose a central bank has a nominal money stock of M^*, a value of that money of v^*, and a capital stock of K^{g*}. If the money is fully backed, it must be that these three satisfy the central bank's budget constraint (Equation 11.1), written here as

$$v^*M^* = K^{g*}. \tag{11.26}$$

If redemptions cause the nominal stock of central bank money to fall by half, from M^* to $M^*/2$, the central bank can simply sell off half of its capital stock to buy up the money turned in, reducing it from K^{g*} to $K^{g*}/2$. The central bank's budget constraint after these redemptions,

$$v^*\frac{M^*}{2} = \frac{K^{g*}}{2}, \tag{11.27}$$

is met without affecting the value v^* of the money. A currency board works in almost exactly the same way. Consider a currency board along the rough lines of that introduced by Argentina in 1991. Argentina wants to fix the exchange rate of its currency, the peso, relative to the currency of a major trading partner, the U.S. dollar. Suppose the target exchange rate is e^*. To this end, Argentina issues M units of currency (pesos), using it to buy interest-bearing bonds, giving Argentina's currency board A of assets, worth e^*M:

$$e^*M = A. \tag{11.28}$$

The currency board's budget constraint (Equation 11.28) is the same as the central bank's budget constraint (Equation 11.1), with e^* replacing v and A replacing K^g. The response of a backed currency to redemptions is unchanged by these changes in units from goods to dollars. Or, put another way, suppose country A can back its own currency with the currency of country B. If country B backs its currency with an interest-bearing asset, it would be as if country A backed its currency with the interest-bearing asset. For example, if the current holders of Argentina's money come to the currency board to exchange one of their holdings for $e^*M/3$ dollars, the currency board can sell one-third of its dollar assets to meet this demand without triggering a devaluation of its currency. In this way, a country with the will to fully back its currency can unilaterally fix its exchange rate.

Suppose that Country B does not back its currency with interest-bearing assets. Should Country A's currency board back its money with the currency of the other country or with assets denominated in that currency? Obviously, holding assets that pay interest earns a superior return for the currency board, which can be passed

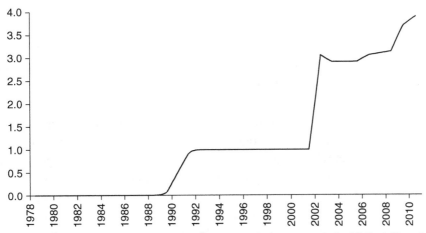

Figure 11.5. The exchange rate between the Argentine peso and the U.S. dollar. After a substantial depreciation in the Argentine peso during the 1980s and early 1990s, a currency board was adopted in Argentina in April 1991. The currency board led to a dramatic stabilization of the exchange rate between the Argentine peso and the U.S. dollar. Argentine ended its currency board in January 2002. *Source:* Federal Reserve Bank of St. Louis.

along to money holders. A currency board that simply purchases the (non-interest-bearing) currency of the other country increases the seigniorage base of that currency, which enriches the other government.

There are two caveats, however. If the currency board earns interest but does not pay interest to its money holders, it earns a profit. If this profit is important to government revenue, people may believe there is a limit to the government's willingness to allow people to trade their currency for the reserve currency. In this case, a speculative attack (see Chapter 5) again becomes possible. To avoid this, the government must convince the public that revenue from the currency board is not essential. One obvious way to do so is to pay interest on money balances wherever possible (e.g., on reserves).

As shown in Figure 11.5, the Argentine peso depreciated dramatically throughout the 1980s and into the early 1990s, with the exchange rate reaching nearly 10,000 pesos per U.S. dollar and with the Argentine inflation rate approaching 1,000 percent per year. In April 1991, Argentina adopted a currency board. Under this plan, the Argentine central bank agrees to exchange pesos for the U.S. dollar at a fixed ratio, in this case a one-for-one rate. Such a policy disciplines the central bank in that the Argentine monetary base can expand only if dollars are exchanged for pesos at the central bank. After this plan was adopted by the currency board, Argentina's inflation rate dropped to single-digit levels.

6 Summary

In this chapter, we considered a plan in which money issued by a central bank is backed by productive capital. Under a system of fully backed money, the central bank issues money only by purchasing interest-bearing real assets. All interest the central bank receives from its holdings of real assets is used to pay interest on the money it issues. This backing of money effectively turns the central bank into a zero-profit financial intermediary, unlike the arrangements studied in earlier chapters, in which a central bank issuing unbacked money was a revenue-generating device for the government.

This policy of backing government-issued money has dramatic implications on how the economy responds to increases in the quantity of central bank money. In previous chapters, in which money was unbacked, increasing the supply of central bank money led to commensurate increases in the price level, transferring wealth from money holders to the government. However, if the central bank increases the stock of central bank money by purchasing productive assets and by paying interest from the returns on those assets, the increase in central bank money merely displaces individual holdings of private bank money. This displacement of private bank money leaves government revenue and the price level unchanged. Wealth is not transferred from money holders to the government.

From a practical point of view, paying interest on currency in circulation would be cumbersome. To avoid this difficulty, the central bank could implicitly pay a rate of return on its money by following a deflationary policy.

Another possible role for fully backed central bank money comes in the form of currency boards. With currency fully backed with interest-bearing assets, a central bank can ward off speculative attacks against its currency.

7 Exercises

11.1. Consider an economy in which people wish to hold money balances worth a total of 5,000,000 goods. They are indifferent between money issued by the central bank and money issued by private banks (so long as both offer the same rate of return). In the initial period, the central bank issues \$1,000,000 and uses the proceeds to purchase capital. The central bank owns a stock of capital equal to its stock of money and uses the return to pay interest on its money. Assume that $x = 1.2$ and a dollar always buys two goods. Intermediation, including the payment of interest on money, is costless.

  a. What rate of interest ρ must the central bank offer to induce people to accept its money? Does this satisfy the central bank's budget constraint?

  b. What is the real value of the total amount of money issued by private banks?

  c. Is there an equilibrium in which a dollar always purchases three goods? In this case, what is the real value of money issued by private banks?

  d. Argue that the people are indifferent between the equilibrium in which a dollar is worth three goods and the equilibrium in which a dollar is worth two goods.

  e. Suppose the central bank pays no interest on its money but maintains a constant stock of capital, using the net return from the capital it owns to buy up and burn a fraction of its money. Find z, the rate of change of the nominal central bank money stock. Check that the government budget constraint is met. (You should no longer assume that $v_t = 2$ in all periods.)

11.2. Consider an economy in which people wish to hold money balances worth a total of 4,000 goods. They are indifferent between money issued by the central bank and money issued by private banks (so long as both offer the same rate of return). The central bank owns a constant stock of capital equal to its stock of money and uses the net return to pay interest on its money. Assume that $x = 1.15$ and a dollar always buys two goods. Intermediation, including the payment of interest on money, is costless.

    a. What net rate of interest must the central bank offer to induce people to accept its money? What is the total net return from assets owned by the central bank? Prove that this satisfies the central bank's budget constraint.

    b. What is the range of dollars that may be issued by the central bank so that a dollar always buys two goods? If the central bank issues $500, what is the total nominal value of money that will be issued by private banks?

    c. Assume again that the central bank has issued $500. If the central bank doubles the nominal stock of central bank money, for what central bank policy will a dollar still buy two goods? For what central bank policy will the value of a dollar fall to one good? Explain why your answer depends on what the central bank does with the new money.

11.3. People in an economy want to hold money balances worth 500 goods. If both central bank, or fiat, money and deposits at a bank pay the same return, people are indifferent between it and bank deposits. The central bank owns a stock of capital equal to the stock of fiat money. Assume the gross real return on physical capital is 1.10. The value of fiat money is two goods per dollar.

    a. Suppose the central bank uses the net return to pay interest on money. What is the net return on money?

    b. Suppose the central bank uses the net return to pay interest on money. What is the aggregate value of fiat money in this economy?

11.4. Consider an economy in which each person is endowed with 1,000 goods when young and nothing when old. When young, each person wants to consume 600 goods. The central bank pays interest on reserves equal to the net return on its capital holdings.

    a. If each person divides savings between fiat money and bank deposits, use the budget constraint when young to compute the holdings of real fiat money balances.

    b. Use the answer derived from part a and the fact that each young person holds $100 to compute the value of fiat money.

    c. If $x = 1.25$, compute old-age consumption by each person in this economy.

11.5. Suppose Canada backs Canadian dollars with U.S. dollars. Canada issues 10 million Canadian dollars to purchase $5 million worth U.S. Treasury bonds. Use Equation 10.28 to compute the implied exchange rate between the Canadian dollar and the U.S. dollar.

8 Appendix: Price Level Indeterminacy

A consequence of the public's indifference between the money of private banks and of the central bank is that the price level may be undetermined – a wide range of price levels may be an equilibrium. Look again at the market-clearing conditions for money balances (from Equation 11.15):

$$Nh + vM = N(y - c_1^*). \tag{11.29}$$

This equation can be satisfied by a range of possible combinations of v and h. If people should decide to hold exclusively central bank money, we find an equilibrium in which $h = 0$ and $v = N(y - c_1^*)/M$. If instead they decide to accept none of the central bank's money, we find an equilibrium in which $h = (y - c_1^*)$ and $v = 0$. Any values of h and v that satisfy Equation 11.29 and lie between these two extremes can also be an equilibrium.

Because people are indifferent between the two forms of money, given that each offers the same rate of return, it is impossible to guess which of the many equilibria will occur.

The central bank has a number of options to pin down the value of a unit of its money. It could set v equal to any number between 0 and $N(y - c_1^*)/M$. With the public indifferent among the various possible equilibria, there would be no difficulty in enforcing any particular value of v within this range. It would be straightforward for the central bank to pick the real value of central bank investments K^g. Because $K^g = vM$ when money is fully backed, by picking K^g and M, the government can determine v.

Another way to determine the value of central bank money involves setting reserve requirements, as we studied in Chapter 10. The central bank can require that each private bank hold reserves of central bank money equal to a fraction (γ) of the value of the private bank's deposits and bank notes. To ensure that banks or the public will not hold central bank money in excess of the required reserves, the central bank can promise to pay interest only on required reserves. Under this monetary regime, the market-clearing condition for money balances becomes

$$Nh = N(y - c_1^*), \tag{11.30}$$

with the reserve requirement specified as

$$\gamma Nh = vM. \tag{11.31}$$

Combining Equations 11.30 and 11.31, we obtain the result

$$vM = \gamma N(y - c_1^*)$$

$$\Rightarrow v = \frac{\gamma N(y - c_1^*)}{M}. \tag{11.32}$$

It is easy to see from Equation 11.32 that, by choosing γ, the central bank may fix the price level.

Chapter 12

The Payments System

1 Roadmap

For the past several chapters, we have been studying model economies in which fiat money and deposits coexist as stores of value. Now we turn our attention to model economies in which fiat money and private debt are both used as means of payment. Here, spatial separation – that is, physically separating debtors and creditors – serves to describe a friction that affects debt clearing. By separating creditors and debtors, there is an information problem that keeps private debt from being used as means of payment. For debt to settle, we specify that there exists central meeting place where the physical separation for debtors and creditors meet and thus, where private debt is settled. With the central meeting place, settlement risk is introduced as a mismatch in terms of when debtors arrive and when creditors leave. Since settlement can only occur at the central meeting place, such mismatches could result in a liquidity problem. There is a secondary debt market in which creditors can sell any unsettled debt they hold. But with insufficient liquidity, the debt will sell at less than par and the creditors bear the cost in the form of reduced old-age consumption.

In this chapter, we examine the role of banks in clearing private debt and the ways central bank policy may help or hinder banks in their role as clearinghouses. We have seen in earlier chapters how fiat money may be used to help people purchase goods. In practice, goods are not only purchased via a cash payment at the time of the transaction but also with a promise to pay at a more convenient time in the future. A purchase by check is an example. A merchant accepting a check receives final payment only when the buyer's bank clears the check by sending fiat money in the form of reserves to the seller's bank, which then credits the merchant's account. Alternatively, if the shopper's bank also possesses a positive balance of checks from accounts at the merchant's bank, it may simply subtract the amount of the check from this balance.

One of the key things we learn from this chapter is the role of settlement, or timing, risk. In this model economy, creditors can need liquidity at specific times. If the clearinghouse has not processed the settlement payment in time for the creditor, the creditor may suffer losses in the form of reduced consumption. The model economy, therefore, offers a glimpse into the role that liquidity plays in an economy. Liquidity problems were very important during the 2007 Financial Crisis. In addition, the liquidity overhang has potentially important implications for monetary policy.

2 Clearinghouses

A clearinghouse is defined as an establishment that is used by financial institutions to settle mutual claims and accounts.[1] In the United States, there are two main clearinghouses: Fedwire and the Clearinghouse for Interbank Payment System, or CHIPS. Fedwire is operated by the Federal Reserve System while CHIPS is bank-owned, privately operated electronic payments system. Both Fedwire and CHIPS serve members by receiving messages to enact a transfer of bank reserves from a debtor to a creditor. As a clearinghouse, neither Fedwire nor CHIPS holds any debt or any reserves. The messages are processed and transfers of bank reserves are implemented.

The volume of payments handled by the two clearinghouses is huge on a typical day. Tables 12.1, 12.2 and 12.3 report the number of transactions and the average daily value of transfers for Fedwire's two services – Funds and Securities – and CHIPS, respectively. A quick comparison shows that the Fedwire Securities Service and CHIPS are both smaller in terms of number of transactions and average daily volume than the Fedwire Funds Service. Over time, we also see that the pattern is different for the three clearinghouses; in both the Fedwire Funds Service and CHIPS, the average daily volume is on an upward trend during the 2000 through 2014 period. Fedwire reports that the number of transfers originated in its Fund Service has increased by about one-third since 2000 while CHIPS reports the number of transfers originated has nearly doubled since 2000. In contrast, the Fedwire Security Service peaked in 2007 and 2008. By 2014, the average daily volume fell to about two-thirds the average daily volume in its peak years. Together, Fedwire and CHIPS reported nearly 250 million transfers originated in 2014. The average daily volume in 2014 is also impressive as a combined $6 trillion were processed by Fedwire and CHIPS on a typical day in 2014. To put this into perspective,

---

[1] For our purposes, we use the terms settlement and clearing interchangeably. The idea is that when a promise to pay is completed and the IOU is retired, then settlement is accomplished. Often, clearing is identified with the process of checks. In this broadened terminology, check clearing occurs when fiat money is transferred. In the sense that clearing ends the process of receiving fiat money from the issuer, then there is a similarity between check clearing and debt settlement.

Table 12.1. *Transfers originated and average daily volume by Fedwire Funds Service.*

Year	Transfers originated (number)	Average daily value of transfers ($ millions)
2000	108,313,521	1,506,970
2001	112,455,615	1,687,675
2002	114,979,176	1,616,581
2003	123,280,721	1,782,238
2004	125,103,104	1,893,071
2005	132,437,838	2,065,923
2006	133,605,267	2,281,457
2007	134,688,381	2,671,974
2008	131,362,107	2,995,931
2009	124,731,244	2,504,473
2010	125,130,561	2,413,991
2011	127,022,420	2,644,771
2012	131,637,349	2,387,253
2013	134,244,177	2,841,874
2014	135,022,749	3,524,111

nominal GDP in the United States was $17.7 trillion in 2014, so that nearly one-third of GDP is flowing through the clearinghouses on a typical day.

If the exchange of fiat money for the clearing of debts always worked seamlessly, there would be little interest in studying it. There are impediments, however, that keep debt from always clearing smoothly. The settlers of British North America complained constantly that, although they had sufficient wealth, they lacked the currency to pay their debts and taxes.[2] In other words, settlers claimed they lacked the liquidity. It is not only in the distant past that economists have stressed the importance of supplying sufficient nominal money stocks in times of particular need. Ben Bernanke (1990) suggests that the Federal Reserve's rapid temporary increase in fiat money was the action needed to handle the enormous volume of transactions without financial disruption during the stock market crash of 1987.

Can a lack of nominal quantities of outside money actually cause financial disruptions? Why won't the price level simply adjust to the nominal stock of money in a way that ensures adequate real money balances? What factors are important signals telling us that current money balances are inadequate at a particular time? Can open market purchases or other central bank policies 'relieve the stringency" of financial disruptions? If so, what is the proper central bank response to a financial disruption? Must this response be one by a government authority?

---

[2] See Hammond (1957, chapter 1).

Table 12.2. *Transfers originated and average daily volume by Fedwire Securities Service.*

Year	Transfers originated (number)	Average daily value of transfers ($ millions)
2000	13,595,988	746,560
2001	15,013,873	845,988
2002	17,436,524	911,981
2003	20,371,395	1,066,312
2004	20,164,811	1,238,835
2005	22,359,335	1,469,708
2006	22,288,805	1,503,022
2007	24,216,823	1,735,369
2008	25,007,806	1,664,076
2009	21,081,242	1,173,578
2010	19,779,423	1,270,333
2011	18,613,058	1,162,645
2012	18,231,152	1,133,074
2013	19,037,148	1,176,041
2014	17,040,141	1,143,841

Table 12.3. *Transfers originated and average daily volume from Clearinghouse for Interbank Payments Systems (CHIPS).*

Year	Transfers originated (number)	Avg daily value of transfers ($ millions)
2000	59,760,495	$1,159,314
2001	60,377,979	$1,241,859
2002	63,297,834	$1,257,803
2003	64,513,387	$1,301,038
2004	68,541,866	$1,366,772
2005	71,481,639	$1,393,907
2006	77,876,444	$1,571,981
2007	87,346,025	$1,934,757
2008	91,992,829	$2,018,884
2009	84,844,034	$1,445,854
2010	90,922,939	$1,448,795
2011	95,057,407	$1,606,968
2012	97,130,016	$1,453,461
2013	103,052,600	$1,513,884
2014	109,409,700	$1,556,555

We address these questions in this chapter. We find a role for institutions, public or private, that aid in clearing debt. We also find that the efficiency of the clearing of debt greatly depends on the policies of the central bank. We find in particular a need for short-run flexibility in the size of the nominal money stock. We consider the roles that settlement and monetary policy have played during the financial crisis that began in 2007.

3 A Model of the Clearing of Debt

To illuminate a bank's role as a clearinghouse of private debts, our model must feature demands for both currency and private nonbank debt. There must also be an impediment to the bilateral settlement of debt to explain why debt is cleared through third parties. Our model displays these features in a model of spatially separated people who trade using credit and currency. Debt is redeemed as each person travels through a common area in which clearinghouses emerge in response to the needs of trading parties. Moreover, in equilibrium, people choose to use currency both as a medium of exchange (to make purchases of goods) and as a means for the repayment of debts.

The model is essentially our standard overlapping generations model with two new features: a market for debt and the spatial separation of people, which impedes the repayment of that debt.[3]

Here, spatial separation is a physical feature of the economy. We assume there exists I (a large number) pairs of outer islands arranged around a central island. Each pair of islands consists of one creditor island and one debtor island. On each island, N two-period-lived people are born in each period. In the first period, each island also has N people (the initial old) who live only in the first period.

Each person born on a debtor island (each debtor) is endowed at birth with y units of a nonstorable good specific to his island and with nothing when old. He wishes to consume the goods of neighboring creditor islands when young and nothing when old.

Each person born on a creditor island (each creditor) is endowed at birth with y units of a nonstorable good specific to her island and with nothing when old. She wishes to consume the good of debtor islands when old and nothing when young. The initial old creditors own a fixed stock of fiat money, totaling M dollars per creditor island.

Over a creditor's lifetime, pairings are opportunities to conduct some kind of exchange. When young, each creditor is paired with a young debtor. When old,

---

[3] The model is based on writings by Freeman (1996a, 1996b) that are extensions of a model of nominal debt by Freeman and Tabellini (1998).

  In the case of creditors the primary risk is to their old-age consumption. As you will see, we simplify preferences so that creditors only care about old-age consumption so that this risk is highlighted. More general preferences would not materially change our conclusions.

a creditor is paired with a young debtor. All the old people – both debtors and creditors – travel to the central island. It is after the old creditor leaves the central island that they are paired with a young debtor. The old creditors arrive at their final destination after all trades among the young have been completed.

The central island is where the government is located. In this setup, the government is endowed with a technology that is capable of costlessly enforcing all contracts and keeping record of all settlements. An institution with the authority to print fiat money also exists on the central island.

3.1 Trading

There are two sets of trades in this model economy. There is trade within a generation as young debtors want to trade with young creditors. In addition, there is trade between generations as old creditors want to trade with young debtors. In both cases, the trade requires a means of payment for mutually beneficial trade to occur. For a better understanding of the sequence of trades that occurs in this economy, see Figure 12.1.

Consider the pairing between young debtors and young creditors. Debtors want goods but creditors do not. In other words, young debtors wish to consume goods from creditor islands but own no goods valued by the young creditors that can be offered in immediate direct exchange. (Recall that the creditors desire to consume the debtor good only when they are old.) Nor do the debtors have any money at the time of this visit. They will be able to sell some of their endowment later for the money of the old, but this money is not yet in the hands of a young debtor when he visits his neighbor. The only thing a debtor can offer creditors is a promise to pay a sum of money in the next period on the central island. So for trades to occur between young debtors and young creditors, IOUs must be the means of payment.

Next, old creditors want to trade with young debtors. To consume when old, creditors must bring something of value to the young debtors. Here, trade between young and old can occur if the old people have fiat money. Where will creditors acquire fiat money? Now that young debtors have fiat money, they can use it to

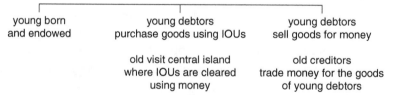

Figure 12.1. The sequence of trades within a period. At the beginning of each period, young people are born and endowed with goods specific to their type of island. In the middle of each period, young debtors travel to neighboring creditor islands and purchase goods using IOUs, which will be repaid next period. Simultaneous to young debtor-creditor trade, old people visit the central island where IOUs are cleared suing fiat money. At the end of each period, young debtors sell their goods to old creditors for fiat money.

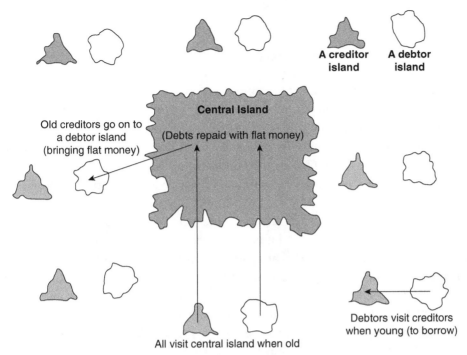

Figure 12.2. The creditor-debtor island economy. The island economy consists of pairs of creditors and debtor islands. Also present is a central island where IOUs carried over from the previous period are settled.

settle the IOUs. The young debtor will acquire this money by selling some of his endowment to old creditors or to others who bring money to the island. When old, the debtor takes the money to the central island and redeems the IOU. Thus, fiat money serves two primary purposes: it is the means of exchange between young and old and the means of settling debt. We describe the physical structure of the island economy and its trading patterns in Figure 12.2.

In this monetary equilibrium, both fiat money and privately issued debt are valued. Money serves both to purchase goods and to repay debts. Money is essential in this model for clearing debts and for the existence of a credit market: without valued money, there is no debt. As we will see, there may be another form of money in addition to fiat money.

The price level is determined, as always, by the money market-clearing condition. In this case, the demand for currency must equal the stock of money arriving at each debtor island. Valuing only the consumption of the neighboring credit island goods, each debtor will choose to sell his entire endowment (y) for currency. In the following period, the debtor uses currency to repay the IOUs incurred when young from the acquisition of goods at the neighboring credit island. The market-clearing condition for currency therefore is

$$Ny = Mv_t = \frac{M}{p_t} \text{ or } p_t = \frac{M}{Ny}. \tag{12.1}$$

4 Institutions for the Clearing of Debt

The description of the equilibrium is not yet complete. It takes as given some not-yet-specified arrangement for the clearing of debt, a *payments system*. If debt markets operate, creditors arrive at the central island with the IOUs of the debtors, and debtors arrive with currency to repay the IOUs. The nature of the transactions at the central island depends on the timing of the visits to the central island. Direct repayment of debt, repayment through a clearinghouse, and the issuance of clearinghouse debt each can represent the equilibrium institutional structure through which debts can be settled. Let us now examine some possible arrival patterns and payments systems.

In the first, and simplest, case, all old people arrive simultaneously at the central island. There are two options and it is easy to demonstrate they are equivalent. In the direct settlement case, debtors bring their fiat money to the clearinghouse. Creditors are also at the clearinghouse so that debtors find their particular creditor such that currency is exchanged for the IOU and settlement is complete. In the indirect settlement case, debtors bring their currency to the clearinghouse but never meet their creditor. Instead, the clearinghouse accepts the creditor's IOUs and exchanges them for the currency given to them by the debtors. Thus, settlement is completed when the clearinghouse gives currency to the creditor and tears up the IOU. The clearinghouse accommodates both direct and indirect meetings and settlement is complete.

Note that the indirect settlement does not result in the clearinghouse possessing the debt or becoming a debtor. The clearinghouse, therefore, looks like Fedwire and CHIPs. At the clearinghouse, both debtors and creditors arrive; creditors present the IOUs they possess in exchange for currency, and debtors present enough currency to clear their debts. At the conclusion of all transactions, the clearinghouses possess neither IOUs nor fiat money. The clearinghouse is an intermediary in this case, offering a check-clearing service (perhaps because of some cost advantage) but never actually purchasing private debt because all debts are cleared simultaneously before anyone leaves the central island.

In the second case, suppose old creditors and old debtors arrive in pairs at the central island. Except in the happy coincidence where the debtor arrives at the central island with their own creditor, the direct repayment of IOUs is ruled out. Here, the clearinghouse plays a much more useful role. To be more concrete, suppose that people visit the central island two at a time – one creditor and one debtor – but the two are drawn from nonadjacent islands. Remember that debtors borrow the same amount and creditors lend the same amount across the island pairs, debtors and creditors drawn from two nonadjacent islands will have the same currency holdings and same IOU value. In other words, the net debt sums to zero. However, because they come from nonadjacent islands, the debtor never holds the personal debt of the creditor with which they are matched. In this case, the clearinghouse can purchase the IOUs brought to it with the fiat money carried by the old debtor. Thus, the debtor has settled the debt and the creditor has accepted payment for the IOU issued. The clearinghouse records these transactions and uses the fiat money payment of the debtor to pay the creditor what is owed. At any given point in this sequence, the clearinghouse holds positive balances of IOUs payable and receivable but has no net position in debt.[4]

The third case involves creditor arrivals that are not synchronized with debtor arrivals. Here, the clearinghouse's role becomes even more important. Suppose there is no overlap in the visits of debtors and creditors to the central island; one group arrives and departs before the other arrives. If the first to arrive are debtors, they will hand over fiat money to the clearinghouse, thus repaying what they owe. As a result, the clearinghouse will at first accumulate positive balances of fiat money. Then, when creditors arrive, the IOUs are brought to the clearinghouse, currency is handed over to the creditors, and all IOUs are settled.

What if creditors arrive first? Now there is a liquidity problem. Creditors bring their IOUs the clearinghouse, wanting currency to settle the debt and using the currency to purchase the consumption good. In the other cases we have studied, creditors could be paid their due with the currency balances brought by the debtors. Suppose that delivering their IOUs to the clearinghouse, old creditors depart the central island. Because debtors arrive too late for the currency to be used in payments to creditors, there is a currency shortage to which private banks or the central bank may wish to respond. Note that the old creditors who depart the central island will not have currency and thus not be able to purchase consumption goods from young debtors.

How creditors can be paid when they arrive first is the central topic of this chapter and an important component of central bank policy. We examine several institutional monetary arrangements for the functioning of a clearinghouse when creditors desire payment from the clearinghouse before debtors arrive.

5 Providing Liquidity

Fiat money is liquidity in this model economy. As you can imagine, creditors are the only ones subject to any risk. For old creditors, consumption depends entirely on the amount of fiat money they receive for their IOUs. They only get the necessary liquidity by settling their IOUs, directly or indirectly, with old debtors or by selling the IOUs in a secondary market. (See the Appendix.) Even with nonsynchronized arrivals by old debtors and creditors, there may be enough liquidity on the central island so that no creditors suffer loss. Here, we study two alternative policies implemented by the central bank.

---

[4] Kahn and Roberds (1999) take a closer look at some of the institutional features and problems of clearing offsetting debts.

The Clearinghouse's Balance Sheet

after the Exchanges with Creditors and the Discount Window

Assets	Liabilities
IOUs issued by debtors	Discount window loans

Figure 12.3. The clearinghouse's balance sheet with discount window loans. Creditors arrive at the clearinghouse before debtors, carrying the IOUs. The monetary authority makes discount window loans in the form of currency to the clearinghouse. This currency is exchanged by the clearinghouse for the creditor's IOUs. When the debtors arrive later at the clearinghouse, they settle their debt with currency holdings. The clearinghouse then pays off its discount window loans with the currency.

5.1 Equilibrium with an Inelastic Money Supply

Suppose fiat money is restricted to be the only monetary asset – the only asset that may be carried by the old from the central island to their destinations around the circle of islands – and that the stock of fiat money is fixed.

Under this strict monetary regime, the clearinghouse has no means of paying creditors if they arrive before debtors. Any agent arriving at the clearinghouse as a creditor receives nothing in exchange for any debt she presents to the clearinghouse. Anticipating that she won't be repaid, a young creditor will refuse to make a loan. In such an autarkic equilibrium, consumption and utility are low for both creditors and debtors, because neither has the means to acquire the goods they desire. Monetary arrangements that remove this constraint will be welfare improving.

To remove the constraint, the clearinghouse must have some means of paying creditors if they arrive before debtors. Additions to the fiat money stock or bank notes issued by the clearinghouse could be used for this purpose. Let us examine these in turn.

5.2 An Elastic Fiat Money Supply

Suppose the monetary authority agrees to temporarily print enough new fiat money to allow creditors to be paid. One institutional arrangement affecting such a policy is a "discount window" (Figure 12.3). At a discount window, the monetary authority (central bank) stands ready to lend at some announced interest rate (discount rate) to clearinghouse bankers who can demonstrate that they are using the loan to purchase "real bills," in this model the debt of late-arriving borrowers.[5] Later, as soon as the debtors have arrived at the clearinghouse to redeem their debts with fiat money balances, the clearinghouse bankers in turn use these fiat money balances

---

[5] Real bills refers to the issuance of money in exchange for IOUs of equal value.

The Clearinghouse's Balance Sheet

after the Exchanges with Creditors

Assets	Liabilities
IOUs issued by debtors	Bank notes

Figure 12.4. The clearinghouse balance sheet with note issued permitted. In this case, the clearinghouse is permitted to issue its own notes. Creditors arrive at the clearinghouse carrying IOUs of the debtors. The clearinghouse pays off the creditors with its own notes. Later, when debtors arrive, the debtors pay off their IOUs with currency.

to redeem the IOUs left with the central bank. The central bank keeps this money out of circulation.

Equivalently, the central bank may print extra money and use it simply to buy the debt held by creditors, an open market operation. Later, the debtors bring money to the central bank to pay off their debt, which the central bank keeps out of circulation. With this temporary printing of fiat money, the liquidity problem has been circumvented.[6]

This increase in the supply of fiat money is not inflationary if it is only temporary – that is, if the fiat money brought by debtors to pay off their debts is removed from circulation as soon as it reaches the central bank. Recall that the price level is determined by the equality of the demand for currency with the stock of money arriving at each debtor island: $Ny = M/p_t$, implying that $p_t = M/NY$. Because the stock of newly printed money is no larger than last period's stock of fiat money (it is now out of circulation in the vaults or furnaces of the central bank), the price level does not rise as a result of this printing of money.

5.3 An Elastic Supply of Inside Money

Consider now an alternative monetary regime, in which clearinghouses are permitted to print their own bank notes entitling the bearer of the note to $1, payable on the demand of the bearer. A clearinghouse may now pay off old creditors with its own money, which they may exchange for the endowment of the young debtors. The young debtors will accept clearinghouse notes as perfect substitutes for fiat money because they know they will travel to the central island in the next period, where they may redeem the notes for fiat money if they choose. Figure 12.4 presents the balance sheet of the clearinghouse after the creditors arrive and again after the debtors arrive.

---

[6] In a variant of this model economy, Gu and Haslag (2014) consider a case in which debtors use goods to produce capital. The autarkic equilibrium, therefore, has welfare and output implications. In other words, the inelastic monetary regime results in less output compared with the elastic monetary regime.

It is clear that the use of private bank notes overcomes the liquidity problem as simply as a discount window with an elastic fiat money supply. The remaining question is its effect on inflation. Will the issuance of private bank notes cause inflation?

To answer this question, we must examine the link between the total money stock and the price level. The quantity theory defines the total money stock as the sum of all assets in public hands that may readily be used to make purchases. In this economy, the total money stock on each debtor island at t is the sum of publicly held balances of fiat money (denote this as M_t^P) and privately issued bank notes (M_t^B). Publicly held fiat money balances do not include the amounts held by the clearinghouse.

As we found earlier, prices will be determined by the clearing of the currency market on each island:

$$p_t = \frac{M_t^P + M_t^B}{Ny}. \tag{12.2}$$

Note that, in accordance with the quantity theory, the price level is strictly proportional to the total money stock, including privately issued bank notes, in public hands.

5.4 Fully Backed Bank Notes

The effects of this regime depend on the backing of the clearinghouse notes. If the notes are always redeemed for fiat money in the period after their issue, the clearinghouse must hold as reserves all of the fiat money it receives from debtors in order to meet the anticipated redemptions. What does this imply for the total stock of currency used on each island? Publicly held currency is made up of publicly held fiat money plus bank notes. By definition, public balances of fiat money $\left(M_t^P\right)$ equal the total fiat money stock minus bank reserves Γ_t:

$$M_t^P = M - \Gamma_t. \tag{12.3}$$

Bank reserves must be equal to the stock of bank notes in anticipation of their redemption:

$$\Gamma_t = M_t^B. \tag{12.4}$$

Therefore, public currency holdings,

$$M_t^P + M_t^B = (M - \Gamma_t) + M_t^B = M, \tag{12.5}$$

are equal in size to the fiat money stock. Total currency in public hands has not been changed by the issuance of bank notes, because the bank notes in public hands simply replace an equal stock of fiat money now held out of circulation in the vault of the clearinghouse. Because the currency stock is unaffected by the extent of private bank note issue, the price level is also unaffected:

$$p_t = \frac{M_t^P + M_t^B}{Ny} = \frac{M}{Ny}. \tag{12.6}$$

Therefore, the equilibrium under this regime is identical to that of the discount window regime – a full provision of liquidity with no inflationary consequence.[7]

6 A Potential for an Inflationary Overissue of Bank Notes

If the bank notes of the clearinghouse have no expiration date and are perceived as perfect substitutes for fiat money, there is no reason for people to redeem them for fiat money. If bank notes are never redeemed, however, the reserves of the clearinghouse are never needed to meet the obligations of the clearinghouse. There is an opportunity for profit taking here; a clearinghouse could use its fiat money reserves to purchase goods for its own consumption without ever going into default.[8] In this case, an issue of bank notes represents an expansion of the total stock of unbacked money: the privately created money is added to the total stock of currency in public hands without an offsetting subtraction of fiat money from circulation. In essence, clearinghouses are given (limited) permission to print fiat money and thus enjoy the profits from creating valued money at no cost. This, of course, is inflationary. To see this, note that when banks hold no reserves of fiat money, Γ_t equals zero and public holdings of fiat money M_t^P are equal to M. The market-clearing condition for money in this case is

$$p_t = \frac{M_t^P + M_t^B}{Ny} = \frac{M + M_t^B}{Ny} > \frac{M}{Ny}. \tag{12.7}$$

Prices rise with the increase in bank notes because an offsetting amount of fiat money has not been withdrawn from circulation, leaving the total money supply larger than before.

We see here that the mere option of exchanging bank notes for fiat money on demand is not sufficient to prevent an inflationary bank note issue, for nothing induces or forces people to turn in their bank notes if people view them as perfect substitutes for fiat money. The absence of bank note redemption is plausible. Because bank notes are a perfect substitute for fiat currency, even a small cost or bother associated with redemption may discourage all redemption. Even if such a cost did not exist for natural reasons, banks, whose seigniorage profits depend

---

[7] For an interesting study of the Suffolk system, a privately run clearing arrangement for privately issued bank notes in 19th Century New England, see Rolnick, Smith, and Weber (1998).

[8] If an interest-bearing investment opportunity were available on the central island, a clearinghouse could also lend its reserves and take the interest as profit.

on less than full redemption, can be expected to actively discourage bank note redemption.[9]

Even though the clearinghouses are restricted to issuing notes only when presented with evidence of private debt that needs to be redeemed, we see the possibility for inflationary bank note creation.[10]

Example 12.1 Graph the path of the total currency supply and prices over time

a. if bank notes are never redeemed,
b. if half of the outstanding stock of bank notes are redeemed in each period.

To prevent the overissue of bank notes, one must ensure that they are fully backed by reserves of fiat money by the end of every period. An obvious way to do this is to require that clearinghouses hold reserves of fiat money equal to 100 percent of the notes issued. In this way, any increase in the issuing of private currency is matched dollar-for-dollar by a decrease in the public holding of fiat money, just as it was when notes were always redeemed after a single period (Equation 12.6). Then the total stock of currency in public hands remains the same, leaving prices unaffected by the amount of privately issued bank notes.

7 The Short-Term Interest Rate

Until now, for simplicity, we have considered an extreme version of the model: The private banking sector has complete credibility when it issues notes and initially has absolutely no fiat money available for creditors. Suppose instead that the initial old bankers living on the central island cannot credibly issue their own bank notes but own a stock of M^* units of fiat money. When young, bankers receive an endowment of nonstorable central island goods. The old bankers use their stock of money to purchase and consume goods from the young of the central island or any debtor island.

In this case, the old bankers own something, fiat money, of value to the creditors who arrive at the central island holding the debt of debtors arriving later. If there is a secondary market, old bankers could use the fiat money to purchase any unsettled debt from the creditors. In doing so, the creditors take this money to make purchases at their final destinations and the bankers take the debt, wait for it to be settled, which is a payment in the form of fiat money by the arriving debtors, and then use the fiat money to make their purchases.

Although the fiat money balances of the bankers offer a way for creditors to exchange their debt holdings for the fiat money they need, the liquidity problem of

---

[9] Although the overissue of bank notes and the inflationary pressures this implies did receive much attention, there is evidence suggesting that overissue need not be a feature of privately issued bank notes. For example, it appears that bank notes issued by Canadian banks during the late 1800s and early 1900s were promptly presented for redemption. See Johnson (1910, p. 23).
[10] See Laidler (1984).

the creditors is not completely overcome if the fiat money balances of the bankers M^* are less than the nominal value of the debt brought in for redemption. According to the model's construction, all money balances in the hands of debtors are used to redeem debt. Because there are I islands, each of which has a stock of fiat money equal to M, the total money balances in the hands of debtors is IM. Therefore, if $M^* < IM$, the bankers cannot possibly redeem the entire debt at par (its full promised value). Creditors instead are forced to sell their debt to bankers at a discount. Let ε represent the discounted value of a debt promising to pay \$1. If $M^* < IM$, because there are only M^* dollars of fiat money available to purchase IM dollars of debt, the discount in a competitive banking market must be the ratio of the two:

$$\varepsilon = \frac{M^*}{IM} < 1. \tag{12.8}$$

The sale of debt below par hurts creditors by lowering the rate of return actually received by them – for each dollar of debt, they now receive only ε dollars (with $\varepsilon < 1$). (Even if there were only a chance that they must sell their debt below par, the average return to lending would still fall.) Clearinghouse bankers obviously benefit from the chance to buy up debt for less than the value at which it will be repaid.[11] If lower rates of return induce lenders to lend less, borrowers will also be made worse off. (Lenders receive a lower rate of return because the owners of reserves pay less than par value for debt and not because the rate of return paid by borrowers has been reduced.)

Example 12.2 Suppose the old bankers on the central island own \$1,000,000 of fiat money and creditors are owed \$1,200,000. At what price will creditors be able to sell the debt they own? How much interest will a banker be willing to pay after the debtors have arrived in order to have one more dollar of fiat money?

7.1 Policy Options

What can be done to lower the short-term interest rate? Suppose the central bank is authorized to issue and lend fiat money equal to the nominal amount of debt presented by any of the bankers.[12] This central bank loan is required to be repaid with fiat money upon the arrival on the central island of the late-arriving borrowers. Let Ψ denote the gross nominal interest rate charged on this central bank loan. The fiat money with which the central bank loan is repaid is removed from circulation.

To determine the effects of this policy, we must first examine the return earned by bankers buying up debt. Each unit of debt costs a banker ε_t and pays him \$1 for

---

[11] This was the experience in the panic of 1907, when the profits of New York reserve banks rose (returning later to their prepanic level). See Tallman and Moen (1990).

[12] An obvious requirement for the workability of this policy is that the central bank is able to identify the bankers, or the debt they present, as creditworthy.

a gross rate of return of $\$1/\$\varepsilon_t$ or $1/\varepsilon_t$. Therefore, bankers can make a nonnegative profit by borrowing from the central bank as long as the rate of interest charged by the central bank does not exceed $1/\varepsilon_t$. Recall that the price of debt ε_t is determined by the ratio of currency owned by bankers to the size of the debt (Equation 12.8). As bankers borrow and supply more currency to creditors, the price at which creditors can sell their debt ε_t rises. In this way, arbitrage induces bankers to borrow from the central bank until $1/\varepsilon_t = \Psi_t$. By choosing Ψ_t, the central bank can determine ε_t, the extent to which bankers temporarily lack the fiat money balances needed to purchase the debt of others. The lower the rate of interest at the discount window ($\Psi \geq 1$), the more currency clearinghouse bankers will borrow and supply to the creditors. The simple discount window policy of setting $\Psi = 1$ allows bankers as much fiat money as they need to purchase the debt of the early-leaving creditors at par ($\varepsilon = 1$).

There is a limit to the power of the central bank to affect the short-term interest rate. Because the price of debt ε_t cannot rise above par, the short-term interest rate Ψ cannot be pushed below 1. It is important to remember that Ψ is the interest rate *within* a period as buyers of unsettled debt are guaranteed to receive payment before the period has ended. So $\Psi \geq 1$ can be thought of as saying that the net intraday rate cannot go below zero. Note also that the central bank intervention directly affects only the short-term (within-period) interest rate. It has no direct effect on the long-run (period-to-period) interest rate paid by the debtors.

The temporary issue of fiat money is not inflationary, because the total stock of fiat money is the same at the end of the period as it was at the beginning. In this way, there is no conflict between the provision of liquidity by the central bank and any price level or inflation targets it may have.

Example 12.3 Suppose the old bankers on the central island own $16,000,000 of fiat money and creditors are owed $20,000,000. What is the short-term rate of interest if the central bank does not intervene? How much will the bankers borrow if the central bank offers loans with a gross short-term interest rate of 1? How much will the bankers borrow if the central bank offers loans with a gross short-term interest rate of 1.1?

Can central bank policies actually affect the pattern of nominal interest rate fluctuations? Look at Figure 12.5. There appears to be an immediate reduction in the variability of the short-term interest rates upon the establishment of the Federal Reserve System at the end of 1913. Because establishment of the Federal Reserve involved a number of major changes in the financial system, a look at a time-series graph cannot establish which reform actually led to the reduced volatility of the short-term interest rate.[13] However, given that the variability of the money stock

---

[13] The pattern of interest rates before and after the founding of the Federal Reserve is investigated by Miron (1986). Alternative models of the inelastic stock of money in the years preceding the Federal Reserve System are offered by Champ, Smith, and Williamson (1996) and Champ, Freeman, and Weber (1999).

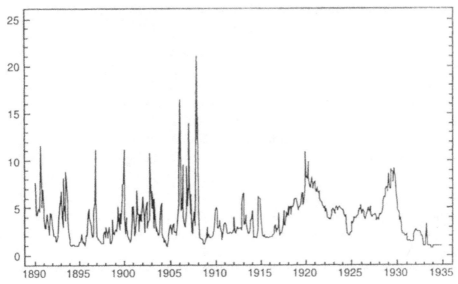

Figure 12.5. Short-term loan rates. Before the founding of the Federal Reserve in 1913, short-term interest rates in the United States were characterized by strong seasonal movements, with peaks in these interest rates often occurring during the fall crop-moving season. Note that after the founder of the Federal Reserve, these short-term loan-rate fluctuations appear to diminish. *Source:* Federal Reserve *Banking and Monetary Statistics.*

also rose with the creation of the Federal Reserve System, the time series is at least consistent with the goal of furnishing an elastic currency, as announced in the title of the act creating the Federal Reserve.

This act was created to provide for the establishment of Federal Reserve Banks, to furnish an elastic currency, to afford a means of rediscounting commercial paper, to establish a more effective supervision of banking in the United States, and for other purposes.

8 Liquidity and the 2007 Financial Crisis

This section is motivated by the unprecedented economic outcomes that emerged beginning in the summer of 2007.[14] Perhaps the absence of turmoil in terms of collapsing financial institutions hid the underlying fragility in the industry for more than a year, but when the United States' economy showed signs of slowing in 2008, those weakened financial firms began to fail. In particular, problems emerged as markets for mortgage-backed securities suffered significant trading problems, due, in part, to information frictions in mortgage performance. By October 2008, trading of mortgage-backed securities came to almost a complete stop. References to the

---

[14] Widespread failures did not occur until 2008. So, why is it the 2007 Financial Crisis? Sengupta and Tam (2008) cite the sharp increase in the spread between London Interbank Offer Rate (LIBOR) and the Overnight Indexed Swap (OIS) rate. Sengupta and Tam present evidence showing that the spread went from 10 basis points to 100 basis points during August 2007, thus indicating perceived risks associated with the financial crisis.

Great Depression abounded in the financial press. This is not to say that liquidity issues were the only problem present in the 2007 Financial Crisis. Our aim is to consider how the model economy explains the role that settlement and liquidity played during this event. In this setup, we can see how monetary policy played an important role during the 2007 Financial Crisis.

Together, the Great Depression and the 2007 Financial Crisis were the most significant financial crises in the United States since the creation of the Federal Reserve. There are important differences when one compares the two; in particular, the business cycle downturn was more severe during the Great Depression. During the 1930s, the unemployment rate reached 25 percent as a national average and there were pockets where the unemployment rate reached much higher. For example, the unemployment rate in Toledo, Ohio, reached 80 percent. At its peak, the so-called Great Recession reported the United States civilian unemployment rate peaked at 10 percent in October 2009. In Canada, the official unemployment rate peaked at 9.1 percent in August 2009. Did differences in monetary policy help explain why the Great Depression was more severe than the Great Recession?

One of the biggest problems emerged in the housing market. Mortgage-backed securities are bundles of mortgages that are traded in financial markets. For this chapter, we ignore anything beyond settlement risk. It is likely that credit risk – the risk that the debtors would not completely repay the IOU – was present during this period. For the purposes of this illustration, suppose that mortgage-backed securities would have settled, but the timing of the settlements was affected. (We save the credit risk features that mattered during the Great Recession for Chapter 14.)

Repurchase agreements are an important way to acquire liquidity. A firm offers a security, like a mortgage-backed security, with a promise to repurchase the security at a future date. In this way, the seller of the security obtains liquidity and the purchaser gets a return because the security is repurchased at a slightly higher price. For our purposes, mortgage-backed securities were not being accepted as part of a repurchase agreement; unable to sell mortgage-backed securities, financial intermediaries found it challenging to obtain the liquidity necessary to settle other debt obligations. As the 34th largest financial firm (by revenues), Bear Stearns was notable, failing in March 2008. In this case, JP Morgan purchased Bear Stearns, applying the marriage model to deal with a failing financial firm; that is, marrying weak, or failing, firms with healthier ones.

As the United States economy weakened and oil prices doubled between August 2007 and June 2008, more financial firms were stressed. As Lehman Brothers, the fourth largest financial firm, and AIG both were in very difficult financial conditions, the marriage approached was not implemented. What followed is the implementation of policy in which the central bank increased the amount of fiat money, measured by monetary based, increased from $800 billion to nearly $4 trillion.

How does the model economy developed in this chapter shed light on the monetary policy being implemented beginning in 2008? In terms of the model economy developed in this chapter, we see that the clearinghouses functioned as they were designed. Unfortunately, there was a significant liquidity shortage. Settlement risk became an acute problem. In the secondary markets, like the repurchase agreements, mortgage-backed securities were sold at much lower prices, if at all, in order to acquire liquidity. So the Federal Reserve increased the amount of liquidity in the economy.

8.1 Unconventional Monetary Policy

As we discussed previously when referring to the Federal Reserve's goals, an elastic currency of private money could have been used to solve the liquidity problems. However, the two major clearinghouses in the United States – Fedwire and CHIPS – are not permitted to create their own banknotes. Alternatively, the central bank can adopt an elastic fiat money policy. In this particular case, extraordinary mechanisms were developed by the Federal Reserve to provide liquidity.

There is a phenomenon that economists refer to as the "zero lower bound problem." According to basic arbitrage rules, nominal interest rates cannot go below zero because people always have the option of holding currency. Put another way, why would any forward-looking person ever make a loan in which the future dollar payment is less than the current dollar value of the loan? As you remember from Chapter 4, fiat money pays a nominal interest of zero. Hence, it would be in a lender's interest to simply hold money as opposed to lending money to others at a negative nominal interest rate.

How would the Federal Reserve deal with the liquidity shortage? It created massive amounts of liquidity. Between July 2007 and November 2008, the federal funds rate – that is, the rate at which banks lend reserves to one another overnight – declined from 5.25 percent to effectively zero. Excess reserves were plentiful and the cost of overnight interbank loans fell. (In the United States, this is the federal funds rate; in Canada, this is the Bank Rate.) In other words, the federal funds rate approached the zero lower bound.

One of the interesting parts of the 2007 Financial Crisis is how the Federal Reserve provided liquidity. During this period, the Federal Reserve implemented unconventional monetary policy.[15] In the United States, conventional monetary policy consisted of asset exchanges involving fiat money for Treasury securities. However, the Federal Reserve created a number of lending facilities so that it could exchange fiat money for private debt. One such facility is the Term Auction Facility (TAF), which was permitted to conduct its last auction in January 2010. In 2009, auctions were conducted in January, February, and March. Under TAF, the Fed

---

[15] In separate studies, Curdia and Woodford (2010) and Gertler and Karadi (2011) have analyzed the effects of unconventional monetary policy in terms of the effects on the interest rate. Williamson (2012) and Gu and Haslag have studied the explicit role that unconventional open market operations could have on liquidity.

would set the amount that would be auctioned and the date on which auctioned funds were to be repaid. Banks would submit bids through the local reserve bank's discount window telephone hotline. According to the terms of the auction, successful bids required that funds be fully backed by other bank assets. The bottom line is that TAF represented a new mechanism for getting liquidity to the banks.

Why did the Federal Reserve create these new mechanisms to provide liquidity? At a basic level, unconventional monetary policy refers to central bank actions in which open market operations involve private-issued securities. Before the 2007 Financial Crisis, mortgage-backed securities were treated as good forms of collateral in repurchase arrangements. In other words, if you had liquidity and wanted to earn interest, a financial institution could acquire a mortgage-backed security with the promise to sell it back at a higher price in the near future.[16] Secondary market prices for mortgage-backed securities declined, in part, to liquidity shortages.[17] Therein lies opportunity; by purchasing mortgage-backed securities the Federal Reserve could engage in a type of elastic money policy. In our model economy, the TAF was a means of implementing a policy of elastic outside currency. Settlements were in jeopardy. By purchasing the mortgage-backed securities, the central bank was offering liquidity. In Chapter 14 we will examine credit risk in the form of economies in which the mortgage-backed securities were less valued. In real time, however, if we suppose the mortgage-backed securities were going to be settled by debtors, then the central bank was purchasing the IOUs at par.

Were the new institutions necessary? In Chapter 9 we learned about the discount window. What kept banks from using the discount window? Discount window borrowing became associated with financial weakness. In other words, banks that had small amounts of equity were primarily the ones that went to the discount window. Thus, borrowing from the discount window was treated as a signal of banks that were susceptible to insolvency. Signals of insolvency could cause the Fed to more closely scrutinize the bank's balance sheet and could trigger an audit. By using sealed bid auctions, others would not know which banks had received funds through TAF. By eliminating the signal, the Federal Reserve hoped that the TAF mechanism would eliminate the "stigma effect."

Compared with the Great Depression, the Federal Reserve increased liquidity during the Great Recession. By dealing with liquidity shortages in this way, consumption by debtors and creditors was not affected to the same extent as it was during the Great Depression. Thus, the unconventional monetary policy can help explain why the decline in economic activity was less severe during the Great Recession than it was during the Great Depression.

---

[16] The temporary holder of the security is viewed as being in a reverse repurchase agreement whereas the temporary liquidity is being held by a party who is engaged in a repurchase agreement.

[17] Gorton (2009) cites the run on shadow banks that occurred as financial institutions became more concerned with quality of the collateral. We will discuss bank runs in much greater detail in Chapter 13.

9 Summary

We have now seen two ways that a central bank can provide the liquidity needed for redemption of debt. It may permit private banks to issue their own currency substitutes, or it may itself run a discount window where banks are permitted to borrow currency at a low interest rate that may be paid to creditors until debtors arrive to redeem their debts. In both cases, the central bank allows an elastic stock of currency to satisfy temporary changes in the need for currency. As long as the stock of currency does not expand from period to period, the provision of an elastic money stock within a period is not inflationary.

The model economy developed in this chapter was particularly helpful for policymakers as they dealt with the 2007 Financial Crisis. Clearinghouses settle more than $7 trillion worth of trades on an average day. Disruptions to the settlement process could have huge ramifications for an advanced economy, as failure of the institutions would disrupt the ways people trade with each other.

10 Exercises

12.1. Suppose the old bankers on the central island own $5,000,000 of fiat money and creditors are owed $7,500,000.

   a. Compute the price at which creditors be able to sell the debt they own.

   b. How much interest will a banker be willing to pay after the debtors have arrived in order to have one more dollar of fiat money?

   c. Suppose the central bank is willing to purchase $2,000,000 worth of debt, what will the price of the debt be in this case?

12.2. Consider a version of the model economy presented in this chapter with fiat and private money. Assume that population is constant with 400 people born each period. Each young person is endowed with 10 units of consumption good when young and nothing when old. Let the central bank issue $10,000. A bank can issue up to $1,000 but has to hold reserves backing every dollar of private money.

   a. Solve for the equilibrium price level in this model economy.

   b. Suppose the backing rule is modified so that the bank can issue $2,000 backed by only $1,000 of reserves. Compute the price level in this new setting. Explain the difference between the two price levels.

12.3. Consider an economy in which there is a morning period and an afternoon period. There are 100 debtors and 100 creditors born each period. When old, one of the debtors arrives in the morning. Before the afternoon starts, 75 percent of the creditors must leave. Each creditor loans 100 units of the consumption good to debtors when young. There is a fixed amount of fiat money equal to $20,000.

   a. How much money did the morning-arriving debtors bring to the island?

   b. At what price would the IOUs held by morning-leaving creditors sell?

   c. How much did the morning-leaving creditors consume? How much did the afternoon-leaving creditors consume?

11 Appendix: A Secondary Market

There is an intermediate case that was initially proposed by Freeman (1996). Let each period be divided into two parts, call the first part morning and the second part the afternoon. Suppose some fraction of debtors arrive at the clearinghouse in the morning and the remainder arrive in the afternoon. Suppose that all old creditors arrive at the clearinghouse in the morning and some fraction depart before the afternoon begins.

Let ω be the fraction of old debtors arriving in the morning. The liquidity, L, available in the morning is

$$\omega Ny = L. \tag{12.9}$$

Let α be the fraction of creditors that need to leave the clearinghouse before the afternoon. So the quantity of IOUs that are morning-leaving creditors have

$$\alpha Ny = S. \tag{12.10}$$

Together, Equations 12.9 and 12.10 describe the supply of liquidity associated with morning-arriving debtors and the demand for liquidity associated with morning-leaving creditors.

What Freeman proposed was a secondary market in which the IOUs could be sold. Morning-leaving creditors want liquidity but some of their debtors have not arrived. So these unsettled IOUs are offered for sale in the secondary market. To illustrate how this works, morning-arriving debtors settle their debt with the creditors. The creditors who did match with the morning-arriving debtors will have fiat money but some of the creditors did not meet their debtors and have to leave before the afternoon. So creditors who do not have to leave until the afternoon will offer a price for the unsettled IOUs offered by morning-leaving creditors.

As with any market, the price of the IOUs depends on the demand for and supply of liquidity. The market-clearing condition is represented as

$$\rho \alpha Ny \leq \omega Ny, \tag{12.11}$$

where ρ is the price of the IOU in the secondary market. It follows that $\rho \leq 1$, since no one will pay more than the face value of the IOU. When the remaining $1 - \omega$ fraction of debtors arrive in the afternoon they will settle the IOUs.

After dividing both sides of Equation 12.11 by Ny, the market-clearing condition simplifies to

$$\rho \alpha \leq \omega. \tag{12.12}$$

From Equation 12.12, the price of IOUs in the secondary market depends on the fraction of morning-leaving creditors relative to the fraction of morning-arriving debtors. Suppose, for example that $\alpha < \omega$, implying that the fraction of morning-leaving creditors is small relative to the fraction of morning-arriving debtors. With a large fraction of morning-arriving debtors, there is a large quantity of liquidity available in the secondary market. With a small number of morning-leaving creditors, there are not many creditors offering IOUs for sale. Consequently, the fraction of creditors leaving in the afternoon willingly pay full price for the IOU because liquidity is sufficiently available.

In contrast, if $\alpha > \omega$, a liquidity shortage emerges. In this case, the fraction of morning-leaving creditors is large relative to the fraction of morning-arriving debtors. In other words, there are many people offering IOUs but only a few people offering to buy. Thus, in the secondary market, the market-clearing price is less than face value.

Chapter 13

Bank Risk

1 Roadmap

Thus far, the banks we have studied have been very simple. A bank accepts deposits and makes loans. The bank does not face any risk and is always solvent. Yet banks are subject to risk as asset values change over time. One particular risk associated with a bank is that its primary job is to transform liquid deposits into illiquid assets. This transformation alone subjects the bank to risks.

In this chapter, we approach this risk from two sides. First, for a given portfolio of assets, we ask how unexpected withdrawals affect bank solvency. In an extreme version, we study equilibria in which unexpected withdrawals are categorized as a bank run. Second, we turn our attention to risks associated with hidden actions by borrowers. Moral hazard arises because banks cannot constantly monitor what borrowers are doing with resources acquired with loans. Of course, borrowers affect the likelihood that a loan will be redeemed.

Thus, when banks, or similar financial intermediaries, fail, they cannot meet their obligations to depositors. Why should the government care more about bank failures than about much more common business failures of restaurants? During the 2007 Financial Crisis, we see that bank failures attract more attention. Banks are seen by many as fragile institutions that depend for their survival on the public trust, a trust that may require support from government guarantees.

As the U.S. public discovered during the 2007 Financial Crisis, bailouts to financial firms can be costly to taxpayers, leading the government to regulate the behavior of the financial institutions guaranteed. Ironically, some forms of government regulation may be blamed for the failures they seek to prevent. These questions are addressed in this chapter.

2 Demand Deposit Banking

Actual banks are different from the banks we have modeled thus far in an important way. They have liabilities that are payable on demand but assets that are not.

The point is that there is a liquidity transformation that occurs from the time that banks accept deposits to the bank's asset choices. More succinctly, bank deposits are more liquid than that portion of the bank's assets transformed into loans. The liquidity mismatch raises the possibility of a "bank panic" or "run." What happens, for example, if depositors all withdraw at once. The bank is charged with transforming the illiquid assets into something liquid that depositors will accept at withdrawal. Usually, depositors want currency so a bank must borrow or sell its assets to pay them off. If the bank is unable to borrow or sell quickly without losses, it may not have enough resources to meet its promises. Even though the bank has the resources to pay off depositors if they withdraw gradually, it cannot meet all the withdrawals made at once. Moreover, there could be a psychology at work; if all depositors fear that the rush of others to withdraw will leave them with nothing, they will rationally join the rush. An equilibrium in which all depositors act in their own best interest and withdraw is called a "bank run."

To understand bank runs, we first must understand why banks might offer demand deposits even though the assets the bank holds cannot be liquidated quickly and costlessly. In this process, we illustrate another way banks offer liquidity unavailable to individuals holding assets on their own.

2.1 A Model of Demand Deposit Banking

Assume that N (a constant) three-period-lived people are born each period (in overlapping generations), each endowed with y goods, only when young.[1]

No one consumes when young. Everyone wants to consume in one of the next two periods of life, depending on their type. They learn their types when they turn middle-aged. Each young person has an equal chance of being either of the following types:

- The "Early" Type consumes in the first period after birth.
- The "Late" Type consumes in the second period after birth.

No one person knows his type when young. So, when middle-aged, a person learns his type; that is, he then knows when he wants to consume. A person's need for liquidity is thus represented by his uncertainty about when he will want to consume.

A person's type is never directly observable by anyone else (it is impossible to tell by looking at a person when he wants to consume). Exactly half of each generation belongs to each type.

People have access to two assets, storage and capital. Storage, the act of hiding goods in the basement, pays the gross rate of return 1 over one period. Storage can

---

[1] The model is taken from Freeman (1988), which builds on the ideas and framework of Bryant (1980) and Diamond and Dybvig (1983).

Table 13.1. *Rates of return for storage and capital.*

Effective rates of return on:	One period	Two periods
Storage	1	1
Capital	$v^k - \theta$	X

Note: In the model economy, storage always pays a gross return equal to 1, regardless of how long goods are stored. Capital produces after two periods and, if held for that period of time, pays the gross return X. If a unit of capital is sold after only one period, the seller receive the price v^k. Furthermore, a verification cost equal to θ is incurred at the point of sale, making the effective one-period gross return on capital equal to $v^k - \theta$.

be done secretly. Capital produces X goods for each good invested ($X > 1$) but only after two periods have elapsed. Capital that has not yet produced can be sold within or between generations. Let v^k denote the price of capital in the period before it produces. It is possible to issue fake capital or fake titles to capital, which are distinguishable from real capital only through costly effort. Verifying that capital is not a fake costs θ goods per unit of capital. Assume that $\theta > X - 1$.

IOUs and other contracts promising future payments are possible among members of the same generation but not between generations. (People know the members of their own generation better than members of other generations.)

The preceding assumptions about assets lead us to find the rate of return for storage and capital presented in Table 13.1. Notice that, because of the transaction cost θ, the rate of return on capital sold before it produces, $v^k - \theta$, is different from its rate of return when held until it produces, X.

What will people pay for capital producing X goods one period later? They should be willing to pay the present value of X. The present value of X is X divided by the one-period gross rate of return. Because storage offers the one-period rate of return 1, the one-period gross rate of return must be at least 1. Therefore, people will pay at most $X/1 = X$ goods today for capital worth X goods tomorrow. Therefore, $v^k \leq X$. Because $\theta > X - 1$ by assumption, we now know that $\theta > v^k - 1$ or $1 > v^k - \theta$. This ensures that the one-period rate of return on storage exceeds the rate of return on capital sold after a single period.

Like the people we have studied in earlier models, these people wish to save goods so that they may consume later. In this model economy, however, no person knows when he will want to consume. This need for liquidity makes a person's selection of assets difficult. If he holds capital but it turns out that he wants to consume after only one period, he will receive the low rate of return $v^k - \theta$ instead of the better one-period rate of return offered by storage. Alternatively, if he holds storage but it turns out that he doesn't want to consume until two periods have passed, he receives only the rate of return 1 instead of the greater two-period rate of return X offered by capital. Because a person does not know his type at the time he must choose his assets, he cannot be sure of getting the best rate of return by holding his own portfolio of assets.[2]

There is, however, a way for people to join together so that each person receives the best rate of return, whatever his type. Note that, although no single young person knows his type, each generation knows that half of its people will be of each type. Imagine therefore an intermediary that offers each person the rate of return 1 after only one period if it turns out that he is the Early type and the rate of return X after two periods if it turns out that the person is the Late type. If each person in a generation deposits his entire endowment, the intermediary can finance these returns by investing half of its deposits ($[Ny/2]$ goods) in storage and half in capital. Because it will turn out that half of the depositors will be of each type, the intermediary can pay off the Early-type people with the returns from its storage ($[Ny/2]$ goods) and the Late-type people with the returns from its capital ($[XNy/2]$ goods).[3]

One of the assumptions of our model is that no one can observe when another person wants to consume. How, then, can the intermediary determine who receives the Early-type person's return and who receives the Late-type person's return? The intermediary must rely on the word of the depositor and make the returns available to any depositor who asks for them after only one period. Deposits that are returned to the depositor whenever requested are called "demand deposits."

Reliance on the truthfulness of depositors works only if depositors are better off when they tell the truth than when they lie. Is this the case? No Early-type person will pretend to be a Late-type person, because to do so means consuming in the second period after birth instead of in the first, when he wants to consume. If a single Late-type person claimed to be an Early-type person, he could withdraw his deposit after only one period and secretly store it until he was ready to consume. This behavior, however, would make him worse off. It would get him only one good in the second period after birth for each good deposited, whereas he could have received X goods if he had not withdrawn early from the intermediary.

In this model we see another way in which intermediaries, in particular banks, provide liquidity. Banks create liquid liabilities (demand deposits) from illiquid assets. They allow people flexibility in the timing of their spending even when assets are not flexible in their returns. The point is that while each person is subject

---

[2] If it were not true that $1 > v^k - \theta$, capital would offer the better rate of return in both the long and short runs, leaving the individual a trivial choice of a portfolio and no role for intermediation. This explains the importance of our assumption that $\theta > X - 1$.

[3] If one type has a lower level of utility than another, the bank may arrange to insure people against that risk by offering that type more than the return from deposits of y goods. We ignore here this form of insurance, which is studied by Diamond and Dybvig (1983).

to random preferences, the law of large numbers means that there is no uncertainty when we look across all the people. A person does not know when he wants to consume and thus cannot select the asset with the best return for his situation. By pooling the resources of many people, however, a bank can be confident that it knows the fraction of its depositors who will withdraw after one period, and thus it can hold the correct fraction of good long-run assets (here, capital) and good short-run assets (storage).[4]

3 Bank Runs

Suppose you are a Late-type who hears a rumor that every other Late-type person is going to pretend to be an Early-type person in order to withdraw his deposits from the bank. (Recall that people are free to retrieve their deposits from the bank at any time because banks cannot tell a lying Late-type person, who is withdrawing earlier than necessary, from an honest Early-type person, who needs to withdraw early.) Should you rush to the bank and also try to withdraw early, or should you wait another period until you truly want to consume?

To answer this question, let us examine the solvency of the bank when a large number of Late-type people withdraw early. The bank has enough in storage to pay the promised return of y goods to only $N/2$ people, the number of truly Early-type people. If, however, Late-type people are also withdrawing early, the bank must sell some of its capital to meet its promise to pay the rate of return 1 to anyone who asks after one period. When the bank sells a unit of capital, it receives only $v^k - \theta$ goods, which is less than 1. Therefore, for each lying Late-type person withdrawing y goods, the bank must sell more than y units of capital to meet its promise to pay y goods on demand. This implies that the bank is selling the capital that normally would finance the return to the honest Late-type people who wait. After the bank has made its payments to the Early-type people and the lying Late-type people, there may be no capital left to pay anything to the Late-type people who wait.

An honest Late-type person may get nothing at all if everyone else withdraws early and he does not. If, therefore, each Late-type person believes that all others will rush to the bank and withdraw early, he will also rush to the bank to get what he can before the assets of the bank are exhausted. All are worse off if such a panic occurs, because by withdrawing early, each gets at best a rate of return of 1 instead of X. Nevertheless, each person is rational in withdrawing early, given that the others are also withdrawing early. In this way, a bank that would have met all of its obligations if the Late-type people had not withdrawn early is unable to meet its obligations during a panic.

---

[4] For a formal model of bank runs in which fiat money serves as the short-run asset, see Loewy (1991).

Example 13.1 Consider the model of demand deposits just described. Suppose $N = 900$, $y = 10$, $v^k - \theta = 0.9$, and $X = 1.2$. Let each person have a two-thirds chance of being an Early type and a one-third chance of being a Late type.

a. What bank portfolio can guarantee the rate of return 1 to all Early-type people and the rate of return 1.2 to all Late-type people? How many goods are placed in storage? In capital?

b. Now suppose the Late-type people pretend to be Early-type people and withdraw early. How many people can be paid before the bank runs out of assets?

c. Suppose that in the period after you made your deposit at the bank, you turn out to be a Late-type person and you learn that all of the other Late-type people are about to pretend to be Early-type people so that they can withdraw early. Is it in your self-interest to also try to withdraw early?

d. Are Late-type people better off than they would be if no Late-type person tried to withdraw early? Reconcile your answer with your answer to part c.

4 Preventing Panics

The possibility of runs in this model resulted from a few key assumptions. Among these are the assumptions that banks cannot borrow from others and that no one can learn a person's type. If these assumptions are altered, banks may not be subject to runs.

4.1 Interbank Lending

A run on a bank makes that bank insolvent by forcing it to sell off its assets at a loss to meet the rush of depositors. If a bank faced with a run can borrow enough to meet all withdrawals, it can avoid those losses that would result from the sale of its capital. These loans could then be repaid in the following period when the bank's capital matures. In this way, the bank would maintain enough capital to meet its obligation to every Late-type person who does not withdraw early. With the capital backing his deposits protected from loss, no Late-type person would have any incentive to misrepresent himself in order to withdraw early.[5]

From whom might a bank borrow? If a bank is threatened by a run, it must borrow from banks or from people who are not experiencing runs. In our model, the young of the next generation would be willing to lend for one period goods they would otherwise store for a period. If these intergenerational loans are possible, panics may not occur. Indeed, if intergenerational loans were costless, banks would never need to hold reserves of the liquid but low-return storage. As we saw in Chapter 8, a bank could afford to place all its assets in high-return capital, despite

---

[5] Interbank lending in the United States takes place in the federal funds market.

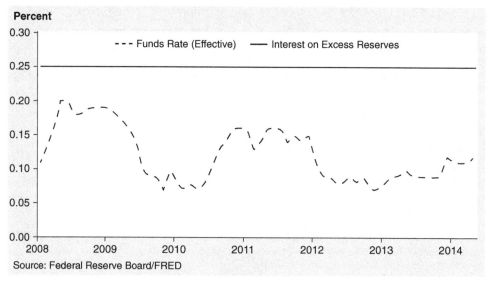

Figure 13.1. Federal funds rate and interest rate on reserves, 2008–2013.

its two-period maturity, and borrow (accept deposits) from the next generation in order to meet withdrawals that occur after one period.

Interbank loans are called federal funds in the United States. How did the Federal Reserve's decision to pay interest on reserves (remember from Chapter 12) affect the federal funds market? First, banks with excess reserves can either loan the funds to commercial banks or retain the reserves and receive the interest. Suppose federal funds and bank reserves are equally safe. The Federal Reserve sets the interest rate on reserves. It seems that the federal funds rate would be at *or above* the interest rate on reserves. If the federal funds rate were below the interest paid on reserves, an arbitrage opportunity would be present. Banks would borrow federal funds from other banks and hold the reserves, earning a profit from the difference between the interest rate on reserves and the federal funds rate. So if federal funds are substitutes for reserves, banks would bid up the federal funds rate until it reached the interest rate on reserves. Yet Figure 13.1 shows that the federal funds rate has been below the interest rate on reserves for an extended period of time.[6] The evidence, therefore, suggests that federal funds are not perfect substitutes for bank reserves.

We see a useful case study on the role of the current state of the economy and legal frictions that could account for the recent relationship between the federal funds rate and the interest rate on reserves. To understand the interest rate differential, it is important to describe the environment and any frictions that pertain to the current events. For one thing, the period of time depicted in Figure 13.1

---

[6] The authors would like to thank Chris Waller for bringing this point to our attention.

is unusual. Interest rates are quite low. The interest rate on reserves is approximately the same return on short-term Treasury securities and close to the zero lower bound. Further, excess reserves are abundant in the banking system, meaning there is less pressure for banks to participate in the federal funds market. Against this backdrop, there are important legal frictions at work. Other financial firms, especially foreign-owned banks in the United States and government sponsored enterprises – such as Fannie Mae and Freddie Mac – are prohibited from earning interest on reserves. So one explanation is that the federal funds market is operating with fewer, specialized participants. And these specialized participants cannot borrow funds in the federal funds market and then earn interest on those reserves. The legal friction imposed on government sponsored enterprises and on foreign-owned banks means that attempts to arbitrage away the interest rate differential fail.

4.2 Identifying Unnecessary Withdrawals

If banks could learn a person's type, they would be able to stop runs by simply refusing to allow Late-type people to withdraw early. In times of runs, banks often have refused to allow large withdrawals without verifying that the withdrawal genuinely was needed. Bank officers would release funds only to those who showed them a bill or payroll that had to be paid.

Even if banks cannot borrow or determine a person's true need to withdraw, there are several ways they can structure themselves to prevent panics. In each case, the key is for the bank to ensure that people who panic and withdraw early are worse off than those who do not panic, no matter how many others withdraw early.

4.3 Suspensions of Withdrawals

One way a bank might structure itself to prevent panics is by temporarily closing its doors when its reserves of the liquid short-term asset (storage) have been used up. The bank then can reopen in the next period when its long-term capital pays its return. If a bank follows such a policy, it will never be required to sell its capital hastily and at a loss. In this way, a Late-type depositor will know that if he wants to withdraw, the bank will still be able to pay him his promised return. Because this return, X, is greater than the return he could get by withdrawing early, 1, the depositor will not rush to the bank.

Note that if a bank has the right to suspend withdrawals, it may never actually need to do so, because depositors will no longer panic. Ironically, bank charters and laws have often forced banks to remain open and pay all depositors who want to be paid. Such a restriction may make panics possible by taking away a means by which a bank can protect its assets from the losses that would result from a hasty sale. The suspension of withdrawals by banks has historical precedence. During the banking panics of 1893 and 1907, banks in the United States restricted the convertibility of deposits into currency.[7]

The suspension of withdrawals will not work perfectly if the number of Early-type people, who truly need to withdraw early, is random. Suspending the rights of depositors to make withdrawals may then stop a truly Early-type person late in the line at the bank from consuming. In this case, a bank would better serve its depositors by reducing the payments to early withdrawers when there are a large number of them. In this way, the bank can protect the capital behind the deposits of the Late-type people without leaving an unlucky Early-type person with nothing to consume.

4.4 Government Deposit Insurance

The government can also help prevent bank runs by guaranteeing Late-type people that they will receive their promised return even if the bank becomes insolvent. If credible, such a guarantee would leave Late-type people with no reason to panic.

How can the government back up its guarantee? It can promise to tax the endowment of the currently young generation if it needs revenue to pay off the depositors of a failed bank. Note that this power of taxation is available only to the government; a private bank cannot tax people. Nor can the bank arrange this guarantee privately. The current young were not born when the bank was formed.

If the government guarantee is believable and believed, no Late-type person will want to withdraw early from a bank, so there will be no panics. If no runs occur, the government will never have to use its power of taxation to bail out a bank that fails because of a run. In this way, the government guarantee prevents panics costlessly. The power to bail out depositors effectively eliminates the need to bail them out.

The costless nature of government deposit insurance disappears, however, when the number of type 1 depositors is random. In this case, a government that has guaranteed the returns promised by the banks will actually have to make some payments to depositors when banks have been forced to sell capital because the number of Early-type people is unusually large.

The government may also have to bail out insured banks if bank assets are risky. When bank assets pay an annually low rate of return, the banks are unable to make their promised payments. In this case, the government is forced to collect taxes to pay depositors their promised return. U.S. taxpayers have been painfully reminded of this fact. The Federal Deposit Insurance Corporation (FDIC) gives the resolution costs of the FDIC and Resolution Trust Corporation as $197.68 billion for

---

[7] For excellent discussions of bank panics in the United States during the late 1800s and early 1900s, see Sprague (1910) and Friedman and Schwartz (1963b).

   Note that in the 1893 and 1907 panics, another option was available. Depositors convert their deposit account, withdrawing gold specie instead of currency.

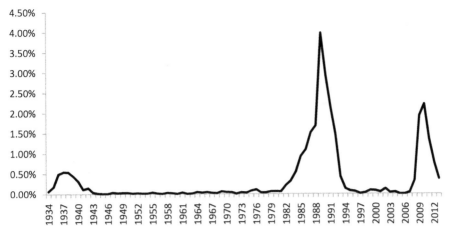

Figure 13.2. Failure rate of FDIC-insured commercial banks and trusts. The figure shows the percentage of beginning-of-year institutions that failed during each year from 1934 through 2013. Failure rates during the 1980s rose to more than 10 times the levels experienced in the period from 1941 to 1979. Similarly, failure rats during the 2007–2009 period rose sharply compared with the levels from 1996 to 2006. *Source:* The FDIC Web site: http://www.fdic.gov/bank.index.html.

all resolutions during the period from 1980 to 1994 (Federal Deposit Insurance Corporation [1998], Chart C.18).

This case of bank failures resulting from the riskiness of bank assets is the subject of the next section.

5 Bank Failures

The United States has a troubled history of bank failures. The worst experience occurred during the period from 1930 to 1933, when bank failures averaged more than 2,000 per year.[8] After the tumultuous 1930s, the number of bank failures dropped significantly. From 1941 to 1981, the number of bank failures averaged five per year. However, beginning in 1982, bank failures rose dramatically, peaking at more than 200 failures in 1988. This significant increase in bank failures during the 1980s is shown in Figure 13.2, which plots total failures expressed as a percentage of the number of banks in operation. We also see that bank failure rates dramatically increased beginning in 2007. Figure 13.3 plots the number of commercial banks operating in the United States for the years 1988 through 2015. After starting at more than 13,000 in the late 1980s, the number of banks has declined to less than 6,000 in 2015.

---

[8] See Friedman and Schwartz (1963b, chap. 7) for a detailed account of problems in the banking system during the Great Depression.

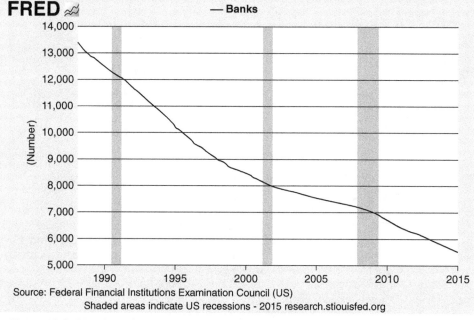

Figure 13.3. Number of commercial banks operating in the United States, 1988–2015.

In the preceding sections, we looked at the way the structure of bank liabilities may make banks insolvent. Now let us look at how bank assets may contribute to bank insolvency.

All investments contain an element of risk. Assets pay off in the future, which is never known with total certainty. Banks, like any other investment opportunity, therefore may suffer low returns on the assets they hold. Relative to other investments, however, banks are seen as fairly safe repositories of wealth.

There are several plausible explanations that can account for why banks were relatively safe. Because bank deposits are used to make payments, it is helpful if people know the exact value of their deposits. If the value of deposits fluctuated greatly, a depositor would have to verify constantly that there was enough in his account to cover his checks.[9]

In addition, a safe portfolio is necessary to prevent runs. Should depositors learn that a bank's assets are insufficient to meet its liabilities, they will rush to the bank to get back their deposits before the other depositors. As we saw in the last section, this may force the bank to sell off its long-term assets precipitously, causing a further fall in the value of the bank's portfolio.

---

[9] An alternative is to maintain a large enough balance in the account so that there are sufficient funds to cover all checks even with substantial fluctuation in the value of the account (due to fluctuations in the bank's portfolio value). Money market mutual funds, whose value fluctuates with the value of the fund's portfolio, require large minimum balances.

Assets		Liabilities	
Reserves	γH	Deposits	H
Interest-bearing assets	$(1 - \gamma)H + W$	Net Worth	W
Total Assets	$H + W$	Total Liabilities	$H + W$

Figure 13.4. A bank's balance sheet.

Banks can protect themselves from risk in a number of ways. Most obviously, they can choose to hold a large fraction of their portfolios in safe assets.

Depositors can be protected from losses even when bank assets are risky if the bank attracts investors as shareholders in the bank in addition to depositors. Banks organized this way have a positive net worth, W, as illustrated by the balance sheet in Figure 13.4.

Deposits are protected from changes in the value of bank assets by the positive net worth of a bank. The equity holders of a bank put up W dollars in return for a share of a bank's value after depositors have been paid. Depositors have the first claim on the assets of a bank and must be repaid before any shareholders. The priority of depositors' claims implies that any changes in the value of bank assets affect net worth first. If a bank suffers a sudden loss, it will be subtracted from the bank's net worth and not from deposits. Only after net worth falls to zero will depositors lose anything. Of course, if the bank's assets rise in value, the net worth of the bank will rise by that amount. The depositors are entitled only to their deposits and to the interest promised on those deposits.

The shareholders of the bank therefore are heavily exposed to risk. Consider, as an example, the bank described in Figure 13.5, with $20 million (or $20 M) of deposits, a reserve requirement of 10 percent, and an initial net worth of $4 M. Suppose this bank loses 5 percent of its interest-bearing assets ($1.1 M) because of an unexpected surge in loan defaults. The financial position of the bank is now described in Figure 13.6. Although the bank lost only 5 percent of its interest-bearing assets, the shareholders lost 27.5 percent of their investment in the bank, because the entire loss is subtracted from net worth. If shareholders are risk averse, the possibility of these magnified losses will induce the bank to avoid investing in risky assets.

Assets		Liabilities	
Reserves	$2 M	Deposits	$20 M
Interest-bearing assets	$22 M	Net Worth	$4 M
Total Assets	$24 M	Total Liabilities	$24 M

Figure 13.5. A hypothetical bank's balance sheet. Baseline settings.

Assets		Liabilities	
Reserves	$2 M	Deposits	$20 M
Interest-bearing assets	$20.9 M	Net Worth	$2.9 M
Total Assets	$22.9 M	Total Liabilities	$22.9 M

Figure 13.6. A hypothetical bank's balance sheet. Decline in value of interest-bearing assets compared with baseline settings. Here we see how the decline in asset value affects the bank's net worth.

6 The Moral Hazard of Deposit Insurance

If a bank is not insured, it must choose its assets carefully, weighing the risks and average returns of assets, in order to attract shareholders and depositors. A bank that takes on too much risk will be unable to attract shareholders or depositors (who bear the risk after net worth has fallen to zero). The careful consideration of risk and return is distorted, however, if a bank is fully or partially insured against losses.[10]

If the government insures depositors against all losses, depositors will no longer care about their bank's exposure to risk. A high rate of return then is the only thing they care about.[11] Banks seeking depositors must therefore offer the highest rates of return they can find.

Where can they find high rates of return? The rate of return on risky assets must be high (on average) in order to induce risk-averse people to hold them. Banks can therefore increase the average rate of return of their portfolios by holding risky assets. This pleases depositors, who like the high rates of return and do not care about the risk because their deposits are insured. In this way, deposit insurance will induce banks to take greater risks than they would if all the risks were borne by the shareholders and depositors of the bank. This is the "moral hazard" problem of insurance: insuring people against losses removes the incentives for the insured to act to reduce the risk of these losses.

How can the government limit the risk taking deposit insurance encourages? The most direct approach is to limit banks legally to safe assets.[12] There are many projects worth funding, however, that are risky. A way to allow more risk taking without actually subsidizing risk is to charge insurance premiums that depend on the bank's exposure to risk so that the bank, and not the taxpayer, bears the cost of the risk. The difficulty with such a policy lies in establishing a proper method

---

[10] See Kareken (1983) for a clear warning about the dangers of deregulating insured financial intermediaries, written before the wave of savings and loan failures. For a detailed study of the problems associated with deposit insurance in Canada, see Carr, Mathewson, and Quigley (1994).

[11] A high rate of return may be paid to depositors either in the form of a high interest rate on their deposits or as a high level of convenience and service. Both are expensive for the bank.

[12] To some extent, regulation of the types of assets that a bank can hold currently exists. For example, banks in the United States are prohibited from holding shares of stock. The establishment of this regulation was clearly an attempt to reduce the exposure of banks to risk.

to evaluate the riskiness of a bank's portfolio. An alternative to basing insurance premiums on the riskiness of bank assets is to allow banks to choose between being insured but regulated in the assets they may hold and being unregulated but uninsured.

7 The Importance of Capital Requirements

The imposition of capital requirements on banks is another way to reduce risk-taking behavior by banks. A "capital requirement" forces banks to maintain a net worth no less than some fraction of their assets. This provides a larger cushion to absorb asset losses before depositors or the insurer of the deposits suffers any losses. Shareholders will exercise more care in their selection of assets the greater their exposure to risk.

Consider some examples. Look again at the bank in Figure 13.3. Would the bank shareholders have any interest in a \$4 million bet on a coin flip? No (if they are risk averse). Although they would double their net worth if they won, they would lose their entire net worth of \$4 million if they lost. Now suppose the bank's original net worth was only \$1 million. Would the bank's shareholders now be more interested in the coin flip? If they won, they would get \$4 million, as before. If they lost, however, they would lose only \$1 million, because shareholder liability is limited to the net worth of the bank. Their potential gain is four times their potential loss. Certainly, the shareholders will be more inclined to take this risky proposition.

7.1 Capital Requirements for Insured Banks

If shareholders can lose only their \$1 million net worth, who stands to lose the other \$3 million? If depositors are uninsured, they do. As a result of their greater exposure to risk, depositors will be reluctant to make deposits at a bank with a small net worth.

If deposits are insured, depositors will no longer care about the net worth of the bank and its propensity to take risks. It is the insurer (the government) that stands to lose when banks take risks and lose. In this case, it is the government that will be interested in requiring banks to have a net worth large enough to discourage shareholders from taking large risks.

Reacting to the United States' experience with intermediary failures in the 1980s, recent U.S. legislation has taken steps toward addressing these issues. The Financial Institutions Reform, Recovery, and Enforcement Act of 1989 increased core capital requirements of savings and loans from 3 percent of total assets to 8 percent. The Federal Deposit Insurance Corporation Improvement Act of 1991 instituted deposit insurance premiums based on capital-asset ratios and recommended the establishment of capital requirements based on the riskiness of a bank's portfolio. Risk-based capital requirements on commercial banks were fully phased in as of December 1992. The Financial Institutions Reform, Recovery and Enforcement Act stipulated that savings and loans must eventually be subject to the same risk-based capital requirements as those imposed on banks.

7.2 *Closing Insolvent Banks*

Similar reasoning explains why the government is interested in uncovering and shutting down insolvent banks (banks with negative net worth or deposits that exceed their assets). Think of the reactions of the depositors and shareholders of an insured bank if they see that it is insolvent. Depositors do not care because they are insured. The shareholders of the insolvent bank will lose everything if they close down. Investing in safe assets will slowly reduce their already negative net worth, because they have fewer assets paying interest than they have deposits on which interest must be paid. What is the alternative? The shareholders' only chance to regain a positive net worth is to gamble big. If they win enough to make their net worth positive, their shares again have value. If they lose, the bank's net worth falls even further – but shareholders do not suffer any further losses. Shareholders' liability is limited to the amount invested in the bank, the bank's original net worth. When this has been lost, shareholders can lose no more. With nothing to lose and everything to gain by making risky loans and investments, insolvent banks will gamble more and more desperately until they either win enough to regain a positive net worth or are forced to shut down.

This scenario sounds all too familiar in light of the crisis involving savings and loans (S&Ls) in the United States. The Depository Institutions Deregulation and Monetary Control Act of 1980 and the Garn-St. Germain Act of 1982 made it possible for these intermediaries to hold riskier assets than previously.[13] When many of the loans made by savings and loans went sour, savings and loans experienced losses of $4.6 billion in 1981, and a large number of them became insolvent. This, as we have noticed, increased the incentive for those insolvent intermediaries to assume even riskier assets.

Figure 13.7 illustrates the growing number of insolvent savings and loans during the early 1980s. The decline in the net worth of savings and loans is also apparent in Figure 13.8, which shows the ratio of net worth to assets for the thrift industry.

The Federal Deposit Insurance Corporation Improvement Act of 1991 took steps toward dealing with financial institutions that hold inadequate capital. This act stipulated that the FDIC must take action to close banks that have capital-asset ratios of less than 2 percent. This act also introduced provisions that require the FDIC to intervene more quickly in the case of a troubled institution. Furthermore, the act severely limits the FDIC's ability to impose its "too big to fail" policy.

---

[13] Reversing this deregulatory trend, the Financial Institutions Reform, Recovery, and Enforcement Act of 1989 reinstituted stricter regulations on the types of assets that S&Ls could hold.

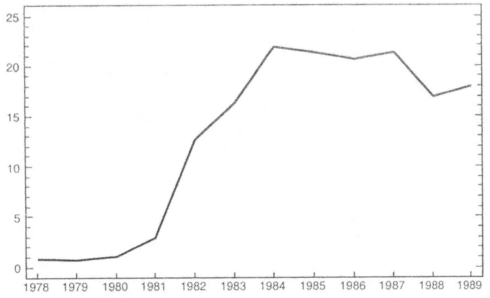

Figure 13.7. Tangible-insolvent thrifts as a percentage of all thrifts. This figure illustrates the increase in the percentage of thrifts that became tangible insolvent during the early 1980s. Thrifts include savings and loans associations (S&Ls) and mutual savings banks, with S&Ls being the main component. A thrift is tangible insolvent if its net worth, excluding goodwill, is negative. *Source:* Federal Home Loan Bank Board and Office of Thrift Supervision data cited by White (1991, Table 2-6, p. 20).

Under this policy, which was adopted during the 1980s, the FDIC automatically excluded the largest banks in the country from being closed in the event of inadequate capital. This policy will be invoked only under special circumstances in the future.[14]

8 Summary

In this chapter, we examined two sources of bank failures – runs on banks and bank holding of risky assets.

A reason for the existence of banks is that, through banks, people can invest in illiquid long-term assets yet be able to withdraw funds when needed. This service – whereby a bank's liabilities are payable on demand, although its assets are not – is also the source of bank instability. If a bank is forced to liquidate its assets prematurely because of an unexpected withdrawal of deposits, it may be forced to sell those assets at a loss. Realizing that their deposits may be at risk, depositors may attempt to withdraw their deposits before the resources of the bank are exhausted.

---

[14] Invocation of the "too big to fail" policy by the FDIC requires approval of a two-thirds majority of the Federal Reserve's Board of Governors and the directors of the FDIC as well as the Secretary of the Treasury.

Figure 13.8. Tangible net worth as a percent of assets for Federal Savings and Loan Insurance Corporation (FSLIC)-insured thrifts. Declining net worth for S&Ls is reflected in the ratio of net worth to assets. During the early 1980s, tangible net worth as a percentage of total assets fell below one percent. FSLIC-insured thrifts are those thrifts whose deposits were insured by the FSLIC. The Financial Institutions Reform, Recovery, and Enforcement Act of 1989 replaced FSLIC with a new insurance fund. *Source:* Federal Home Loan Bank Board and Office of Thrift Supervision data cited by White (1991, Table 2-5, p. 19). The observation for 1989 is for thrifts insured by the newly founded Savings Association Insurance Fund.

Realizing the problem associated with these bank runs, we analyzed a variety of actions that may aid in their prevention. These include interbank lending, identifying unnecessary withdrawals, suspension of withdrawals, and government deposit insurance.

If banks can invest in risky assets, government deposit insurance gives rise to a situation of moral hazard. With deposit insurance, customers no longer monitor the riskiness of bank asset holdings. Banks, in order to attract depositors, have the incentive to take on risky assets that pay higher average rates of return than safe assets. To deal with this moral hazard problem, governments must either regulate the types of assets that banks can hold or charge insurance premiums that are risk related.

Capital requirements may also reduce a bank's incentive to take on risk by providing shareholders with a reason to monitor the bank's selection of assets. The larger this capital requirement, the more shareholders stand to lose in the event of poor returns on a bank's asset holdings. We have seen that, when the net worth of a bank falls to zero, shareholders have nothing more to lose and may be willing to gamble heavily in the bank's acquisition of risky assets.

9 Exercises

13.1. Suppose you are the sole shareholder of a bank with deposits of $1,200,000 and assets of $1,000,000. There is no reserve requirement. Your liability in the bank is limited by law to your investment (if it fails, you needn't make up losses to depositors). You are risk neutral.

   a. What is the net worth of the bank?

   b. Suppose you may reinvest your assets into one but only one of the following projects before the examiners audit your books:

      Project A: pays a certain return of 7 percent

      Project B: has a 50 percent chance of a 21 percent net return and a 50 percent chance of a net return of −21 percent

      Project C: has a 10 percent chance of doubling your assets and a 90 percent chance of losing everything

      Rank the three projects according to which will benefit you personally.

   c. How would your ranking change if the assets of the bank were $1,200,000?

   d. How would your ranking change if the assets of the bank were $2,000,000?

   e. If you have the chance to abscond with $100,000 at the cost of losing ownership in the bank, would you do it (setting aside questions of morality)? How does your answer depend on the net worth of the bank?

   f. If banks are covered by government deposit insurance, why should the government take an active role in closing down failed banks as soon as they can be discovered? Answer with references to the examples in this exercise.

13.2. Suppose there are 200 young people born each period. Each young person receives 200 goods, but nothing when middle-aged or when old. There is a storage technology. For each good put into storage in the current period, a person will receive one unit of consumption good next period. In addition, capital is available. For each unit of capital acquired in date t, 1.25 units of the consumption good will be received at date $t + 2$. If the person liquidates capital after one period, then only 0.8 units of the consumption good can be obtained date $t + 1$. Assume that 10 percent of the people want to consume when middle-aged and the remainder want to consume when old.

   a. How many goods will the bank hold in the form of storage? How many in capital?

   b. If there is no bank run, how many goods will middle-aged people consume? How many goods will an old person consume?

13.3. Suppose there are 100 young people born each period. Each young person receives 250 goods, but nothing when middle-aged or when old. People can access a storage technology that yields one good next period for every good put in storage in the current period. Alternatively, there is a capital good. For each unit of capital acquired in date t, 1.2 units of the consumption good will be received at date $t + 2$. If the person liquidates capital after one period, then only 0.75 units of the consumption good can be obtained date $t + 1$. Assume that ten percent of the people want to consume when middle-aged and the remainder want to consume when old. Now, consider a case in which the bank does not expect a bank run to occur, but everyone withdraws when middle aged. Old consumers simply take their withdrawals and acquire the storage good themselves.

    a. Suppose the first 10 percent of people in line receive the full value of their deposit. How much these people be able to consume?

    b. Suppose the next 90 percent of people receive an equal split of remaining assets. How much will these people be able to consume?

13.4. Use the same data as put forward in problem 13.3.

    a. Suppose the bank liquidates all of its assets and equally splits the value of the bank portfolio among the depositors. What would each depositor be able to consume in this case?

    b. If the bank anticipated a bank run and held everything in storage, what would each depositor be able to consume?

Chapter 14

Liquidity Risk and Bank Panics

1 Roadmap

In Chapter 13, we examined a model economy in which bank insolvency can arise. But there is nothing in the model that looks like money in the sense that there are no explicit trades. What banks holds are real assets as a young person deposits goods to withdraw at a future date. A bank chooses from either a storage good or capital. Yes, storage is more liquid than capital in the sense that it matures in one period instead of two periods, but there is no reason for intergenerational trade between people in Chapter 13.

Here, we go back to a model economy in which there intergenerational trade and money is the means of executing those trades. By having valued fiat money, monetary factors can play an explicit role in bank failures. Our motivation is based on the observation that in actual economies, money is often associated with banking failures. In other words, liquidity shortages, in the form of too little currency, are frequently associated with widespread bank failures, which can turn into banking panics. In this version of the model economy, currency and bank panics are clearly linked. In building this model so, we can examine the roles different regulatory structures play; specifically, we offer an explanation that can account for why some countries experience banking panics and others do not. A key regulatory feature seems to be the restrictions on the issue of currency by private banks.

In addition, we can revisit the issue of optimal monetary policy. In Chapters 4 and 6, we spoke of optimal policy. In both chapters, there was no competing store of value. With capital, we know from Chapter 7 that there is opportunity cost to holding money if the return on capital is greater than the return to fiat money. Is this the only consideration when setting long-run monetary policy?

2 Money with Limited Communication

Though the physical environment is altered in this chapter, there are some clear similarities. Instead of waiting an extra period for capital to mature, here illiquidity is captured in terms of spatial separation that leads to capital to be being illiquid relative to fiat money.

The physical setting consists of two distinct locations. The economy is populated by two-period-lived agents. Capital is illiquid because we restrict it from moving across these two locations. Because capital is immobile – that is, capital cannot be physically relocated – and because there are limited communication problems that arise across the two islands, capital is not a perfect substitute for fiat money.[1] People are identical at birth and their preferences are the same over their lifetime. What distinguishes people is that before they become old, they are divided between movers and nonmovers. As soon as a person receives a moving order, everyone else knows who is a mover and who is not. Hence, unlike the model economy in Chapter 13, there is no private information in this model economy. We will give a more detailed explanation to account for why people are better off when a competitive bank is present than when people allocate portfolios on their own. The key reason is that the bank can use the law of large numbers to choose the efficient portfolio, just as we did when banks were initially introduced.

2.1 A Model with Random Relocation

We begin by building a model in which currency is needed by those depositors who withdraw first. Here, currency is the medium of exchange. Because people are moved from one location to another, they need fiat money to execute trade.[2] The physical environment is depicted in Figure 14.1, including the travel patterns by movers across islands.

Assume that there are two islands. On each island, N (a large number) of two-period-lived people are born in each period. In the first period, each island also has N people (the initial old) who live only in the first period.

Each person born is endowed at birth with y units of a perishable consumption good when young and with nothing when old. Each person wants to consume during both periods of life. Goods also perish if they are transported between islands.

To provide for old-age consumption, each person must use an asset. Fiat money and capital are available. Capital matures in one period, but it cannot move across locations. Moreover, limited communication across locations renders claims against capital worthless. In other words, capital located on island 1 cannot be used to finance consumption on island 2. For each unit of consumption good stored in the current period as money, a person will realize $\frac{v_{t+1}}{v_t}$ units of the consumption good next period. Similarly, for each unit of the consumption good stored in the current period as capital, a person will realize x units of the consumption good next period. We assume that $x > \frac{v_{t+1}}{v_t}$.

---

[1] See Townsend (1979) for description of model economies in which money is useful because of limited communication.

[2] This model economy is a modified version of one developed by Champ, Smith, and Williamson (1996).

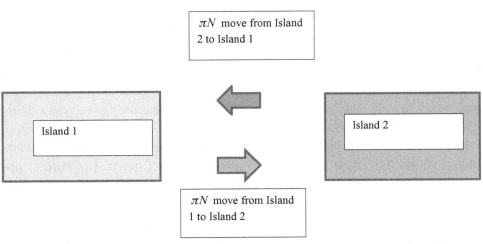

Figure 14.1. A depiction of the physical environment in the random relocation model economy. With the same number of young born on each island and with the number of movers being equal, the population on Island 1 is always equal to the population on Island 2.

On each island, there is a central bank office that controls the money stock. There is a central monetary authority, like the Board of Governors of the Federal Reserve System, that orchestrates identical actions at each office. Changes to the money stock are used to finance a lump-sum transfer to young people. The government's budget constraint is $v_t(M_t - M_{t-1}) = N\tau_t$. If the money supply expands, each young person receives a lump-sum transfer equal to τ units of the consumption good. Conversely, if the money supply contracts, each young pays a lump-sum tax equal to τ units of the consumption good. In other words, when the money supply expands, the value of the expansion, measured in goods, is distributed to each young person. If the money supply contracts, the contraction is collected from each young person, and τ, which is negative in this case, measures the value of the money supply contraction in goods. Money is identical across the two islands so that limited communication problems do not apply with respect to money; it is accepted in exchange on both islands.

With two distinct islands, movement across islands is possible. This model economy is referred to as a random-relocation model precisely because, when born, each person born faces a risk that he will spend old age on the other island. The sequence is as follows: (i) a young person is born on a home island; (ii) the endowment is received; (iii) the consumption-saving decision is irrevocably made; and (iv) each young person is notified whether he will spend old age on the home island or on the foreign island. Once notified, movers will be relocated, beginning their old age on the new island. Let π be the probability that a young person just born will realize that they will be relocated. We assume that the relocation probability is the same on both islands. With so many young people on each island, the probability that one person will move is also used to compute the number of movers between the two islands. Formally, πN is the number of people that will move from island 1 to island 2 and vice versa.[3]

Note that limited communication provides a rationale for why fiat money is valued. Suppose, for example, that communication were costless across the islands. With open communication, each young person could purchase only capital. If a young person were relocated from island 1 to island 2, he could carry a paper claim. The claim would say that the island 1 mover has possession of k units of mature capital. Because it is costless to verify this claim, the old island 1 mover would be able to access the k units of capital of some old island 2 mover. In contrast, suppose communication is limited. Now communication is too costly to permit people living on separate islands from verifying that the claims are accurate. To be more concrete, old island 1 movers would like to offer a claim that says, "I have goods on the other island. I would like to use the claim to acquire an old island 2's return on capital." Our limited communication assumption prohibits island 2 nonmovers from verifying the claim. Hence, claims are useless.

Together, random relocation and limited communication explain why money is valued. Because movers cannot carry acceptable pieces of paper from one island to the next – cannot use claims to finance old-age consumption, there is room for money to be used as a means of payment for old-age consumption. There is a transactional role for money. Money serves the role as a generally acceptable medium of exchange because it can be transported across islands. Now movers from island 1 can use money to purchase goods left behind by movers from island 2.

2.2 The Person's Portfolio Decision

We start by revisiting a question addressed initially in Chapter 8. How does a bank improve welfare? In Chapter 8, recall that capital was illiquid because it did not mature for two periods. We showed that a bank was beneficial because it allocated its portfolio to meet the needs of depositors better than if depositors were on their own. Here, capital is illiquid because it cannot be moved from island to island. We go through the process of verifying that a person's welfare is higher with a bank than without to demonstrate illiquidity defined by spatial frictions at a point in time are often another way to capture illiquidity defined by frictions that exist across time periods.[4] The key feature is that there is no way to trade private claims against the capital a person holds.

---

[3] This is an application of the law of large numbers, meaning that N is large enough to satisfy two conditions. First, the number of people is large enough that not one person has any market power. Second, the number of people is large enough that the probability that any one person will move also pins down the number of people moving. Bencivenga and Smith (1991) use the law of large numbers in their analysis of the random-relocation economy.

[4] With this reasoning, we are developing economic principles that were presented in model economies studied by Arrow and Debreu (1954). In their analysis, a person could purchase Arrow-Debreu securities, which guaranteed delivery of a unit of a future consumption good. In such a setup, all trades occurred in period 0 and then the securities were settled by delivering goods. In an economy with all the necessary Arrow-Debreu securities, the equilibrium in the spot-trading economies is equivalent to sequential trading economies. Thus, a subtle

Now that we have the environment in which people live, it is possible to represent a young person's decision problem. When people are born, they have y units of the perishable consumption good that will be divided into consumption, money, or capital. Thus, the budget constraint when young is represented as

$$y + \tau = c_1 + v_t m_t + k_t.$$

An old person's budget constraint, however, depends on his relocation status. If, for example, a young person is relocated, we assume that capital is left behind and rots. This means that old movers must seek young people on the foreign island, exchanging accumulated money for units of the consumption good. The amount of old-age consumption by a mover is represented as

$$c_2^m = v_{t+1} m_t,$$

where c_2^m represents the amount of goods consumed by old movers. Finally, non-movers can realize the return to any capital investment made when young plus exchange any accumulated money balances for consumption goods sold by young people. Let c_2^n denote the quantity of goods consumed by old nonmovers. Thus, the old nonmovers budget constraint is represented as

$$v_{t+1} m_t + x k_t = c_2^n.$$

The young person's problem is to choose how much to consume when young, how much money to accumulate, and how much capital to purchase. In other words, each young person seeks to maximize expected lifetime utility subject to the three budget constraints – one applies to the young person and the other two apply to the old person as mover and as nonmover, respectively. After choosing the amount to consume when young, each person faces a decision regarding how to divide his saving between money and capital. Each young person chooses a combination of money and capital. It is useful to illustrate the trade-off that exists for the typical young person. As young people make a plan for lifetime consumption, they are subject to risk that they will be moving. The risk is associated with this portfolio choice because movers must forego the returns to any capital investment.

We begin by illustrating a case in which a young person chooses zero-capital investment. Suppose a young person chooses to hold only money to finance old-age consumption. That person is guaranteed to be able to consume whether he moves or not. Indeed, the old-age budget constraint is represented by $v_{t+1} m_t = c_2$. If the return on capital is greater than the return on fiat money, there is an opportunity cost associated with holding only money. With $x > \frac{v_{t+1}}{v_t}$, there is a cost to putting all of your savings into money. For example, if the person is designated a nonmover, old-age consumption could have been higher. Indeed every unit of saving put into capital would have yielded x units of old-age consumption.

---

point made here is that there is an equivalence between frictions that occur in the same period across space and frictions that occur in the same space across time.

Alternatively, consider the case in which the young person puts all of his savings into capital. If that person is a nonmover, then he gets to consume xk_t. However, if the draw is such that the person must move, his old-age consumption is zero. Hence, there is a cost to putting all of your savings into capital.

The young person thus faces an asset decision that coincides with a risky outcome. If I acquire capital and I move, I get no return. There is no such risk if I acquire money, but I forego some consumption if I do not move by holding the lower-returning asset. Naturally, a risk-averse young person will balance the risk against the reward of greater old-age consumption, acquiring some capital and some money.

A young person is then assessing two kinds of trade-offs. One is the trade-off between consumption when young and consumption when old. This is standard for the overlapping generations model. A young person gives up a little consumption today to obtain future consumption.

The other trade-off is storing goods as money or as capital. Capital offers a higher return but is risky. Hence, the marginal decision balances the return on money times the expected marginal utility of consuming a little bit more on either the home island or the foreign island against the return on capital times the expected marginal utility from consuming a little bit more on the home island. Each young person equates the expected marginal value from each asset in deciding how much to save in the form of money and how much to save in the form of capital.

The total supply of consumption goods in the home market is determined by the aggregate endowment and the number of nonmovers. These goods will be consumed by young people, by movers and by nonmovers. Thus, for a particular island, the market-clearing condition in the goods market is represented as

$$Ny + (1 - \pi)Nxk_{t-1} = Nc_1 + \pi Nc_2^m + (1 - \pi)Nc_2^n,$$

where the first term on the left-hand side of the equation is the aggregate endowment and the second term is the aggregate returns on capital realized by nonmovers. The first term on the right-hand side is aggregate consumption by young people, followed by aggregate consumption by old movers and old nonmovers, respectively. We also need a money market clearing condition. Money is demanded because it is the risk-free asset that can be used in transactions by movers. The market-clearing condition for the money market is represented as

$$v_t M_t = N(y - c_1 - k),$$

which indicates that the real value of money supply is equal to the aggregate savings less capital investment.

2.3 Portfolio Allocation with a Bank

Let us reconsider the basic random-relocation model and allow for a third party to exist on each island. You are familiar with the basic operations of the bank. It accepts deposits and uses the proceeds to acquire assets. Thus, in our model, there is either money or capital.

Timing is important. A young person is born on one of the two islands. The endowment of the perishable consumption good is received, and the young person chooses between consuming and saving. Now with a bank, the young person's savings are deposited with the bank. For now, we assume that the bank is a better option than self-saving.

After the deposits are received, the bank chooses how much money and capital to acquire. Banks accepting deposits compete against all other banks. The competition results in rates of return on deposits being the same across all banks. Hence, for each island, competition results in the returns being identical across locations. There is no information problem, so every bank can identify who is a mover and who is a nonmover.

Young people are notified about whether they must move. Upon learning that they must move, movers will go to the bank and withdraw their deposits under the rules established between the bank and the depositor. Unlike the model in Chapter 13, the bank can see who is a mover and who is not a mover. There is no identification problem, as there was with early-type and late-type consumers. The young person will accept money, be relocated, and purchase goods on the foreign island. The bank holds capital that nonmovers will seek to withdraw when they are old. If we assume that old movers consume after the bank has accepted deposits from the young, then the transaction sequence is quite simple. When old, movers will take their money to the bank and acquire units of the consumption good. Nonmovers will withdraw their deposits from the bank and consume.

The bank's problem is straightforward. It must choose to hold enough money to meet the liquidity needs of the movers with the remaining goods stored. The bank's asset allocation must be done to maximize the expected utility of the young depositor. The bank has one major advantage: it does not face any uncertainty. Because it can costlessly distinguish between movers and nonmovers, the bank knows exactly what number of people will need money and what number will not withdraw early. The absence of uncertainty means that the bank will do two things: First, deposit contracts will distinguish between movers and nonmovers. Those needing liquidity are keeping society from acquiring capital. Consequently, movers will not receive the same return as nonmovers because of this social cost.

Second, the bank is not subject to risk and therefore does not require insurance against risk. Indeed, the bank is providing liquidity insurance for young depositors. Without any risk, the bank will put more goods into capital.

People born in period t will take some of their endowment for consumption and deposit the remainder. Thus, the budget constraint for the first period of a person's life is written as

$$y + \tau = c_1 + d,$$

where d stands for the quantity of goods deposited with the bank.

The bank knows that some depositors will have to withdraw early and others will withdraw in the next period. Moreover, the bank can identify who is who. In other words, the bank does not face an identification problem; no person will seek to withdraw early, hoping to fool the banker. The banker can freely look at the person's moving notice and refuse to honor withdrawals made by nonmovers.

It is valuable for the bank to be able to distinguish between movers and non-movers because it removes all uncertainty from the bank's perspective. The bank can then offer different contracts to movers than to nonmovers. Because the contracts are entered into before the young people know whether they are movers or not, the contracts are state contingent. This simply means that the contract is designed to maximize a young person's expected utility with a specific with-drawal amount if the person is a mover and another payout if the person is a nonmover.

With the goods deposited at the bank, there are three decisions to be made. The first is how to divide the deposits between capital and money, the second is what return to pay to depositors who must withdraw when young and the third is what return to pay to depositors who withdraw in the next period. We begin by characterizing the bank's balance-sheet constraint, which is represented for period t as

$$d_t = v_t m_t + k_t.$$

The next two problems help us see what is feasible for the bank. In other words, what can the bank afford to pay movers and nonmovers. To make matters simpler, it is useful to define the reserve-to-deposit ratio. Let γ stand for the amount of money the bank holds as a fraction of deposits, or $\gamma_t = \frac{v_t m_t}{d_t}$. The bank can afford to pay movers up to the amount of real money balances the bank possesses. The return to these money balances depends on the value of money over time. The returns on deposits may depend on whether a person is a mover or a nonmover. Therefore, the notation r^m and r^n is the deposit return for movers (superscript m) and non-movers (superscript n), respectively. The deposit contract for movers is represented as

$$r^m \pi d_t = \frac{v_{t+1}}{v_t} m_t.$$

The left-hand side is the return to movers times the volume of deposits that will be withdrawn by movers. The most the bank can afford to pay is the return on money balances.

Banks also face a separate constraint for nonmovers. Here, the quantity of deposits withdrawn in the next period by nonmovers will be $(1 - \pi)d_t$. Thus, the constraint is represented as

$$r^n(1 - \pi)d_t = xk_t.$$

If we substitute for the reserve-to-deposit ratio, these two constraints can be rewritten as

$$\pi r^m = \frac{v_{t+1}}{v_t}\gamma$$

$$(1 - \pi)r^n = (1 - \gamma)x.$$

The bank then chooses the reserve-to-deposit ratio, the return paid to movers, and the return to nonmovers to maximize the expected utility of the young person.

Each young person takes the returns on deposits as given and seeks to maximize expected utility over his lifetime. When old, a mover's budget constraint is represented as

$$r^m d = c_2^m$$

and nonmovers face the constraint

$$r^n d = c_2^n.$$

The market-clearing conditions are unchanged. The market for goods clears when $Ny + (1 - \pi)Nxd = Nc_1 + \pi Nc_2^m + (1 - \pi)Nc_2^n$, and as always, the money market clears when $v_t M = \gamma Nd$.

What are the properties of the equilibrium in the random-relocation model with a bank? First, the bank permits each young person to avoid old-age disaster. There is no longer an outcome in which a portion of the person's portfolio yields zero return. The expected return for the young person is $\pi r^m + (1 - \pi)r^n$. We can go even further with our analysis. Suppose the reserve-to-deposit ratio is equal to the probability that a young person is a mover, or $\gamma = \pi$. In this case, $r^m = \frac{v_{t+1}}{v_t}$. If the government follows a constant-money-stock rule, then we know that $r^m = 1$. Movers will be guaranteed the return on money. nonmovers will realize the return on capital so that $r^n = x$. It follows that for this special case, the expected return on deposits is $\pi + (1 - \pi)x$.

Compare this with the model in which no bank exists. With a bank, the expected return for each young person's portfolio is $[\pi + (1 - \pi)x]d$. In contrast, when no bank exists the expected return is $\pi m + (1 - \pi)(m + xk)$. Even if deposits were equal across the two economies, the expected consumption enjoyed by old people would be greater with the bank. To see there are losses when banks are absent, note that $\pi m < \pi d$ and $(1 - \pi)(m + xk) < (1 - \pi)xd$. Clearly, total expected returns are greater with a bank. The math confirms that, holding deposits constant, the expected return is greater with a bank than without banks. Remember that banks do not face any aggregate uncertainty. Consequently, a bank provides insurance against a person's idiosyncratic (person-specific) risk by offering a higher return especially for movers. The bank can gather returns from capital. The bank provides this insurance because it does not face any uncertainty. It knows how much liquidity is needed for movers and is free to invest the remainder in capital.[5]

Because of the insurance feature, young consumers will actually deposit more goods with the bank than they would save on their own. Total saving increases, resulting in more goods being placed into capital. Total goods increase in the banking economy compared with the nonbanking economy.

More importantly, each young person realizes an increase in expected lifetime utility. There is a change in the price of consumption when young relative to the price of consumption when old when the bank is present. The change makes old-age consumption relatively cheaper, leading to more consumption when old and less consumption when young. On the surface, the impact on welfare appears ambiguous. However, the budget set expands; that is, combinations of consumption when young and consumption when old are feasible when the bank is present that are not affordable when no bank exists. The upshot is that the young person will realize greater expected lifetime utility because of the liquidity insurance provided by the bank.

This result builds on the previous results regarding the role of banks. Here, the bank plays a specific role in providing liquidity insurance that is not available from another source. In addition, we show that expected welfare is higher in an economy with a bank than in one without a bank. Thus, the bank plays a pivotal role in terms of making people better off; indeed, it serves as the mechanism that yields the same allocation that the planner would achieve in this economic environment. In previous chapters, the bank is endowed with special powers that explain its existence. Here, in contrast, the bank arises endogenously as an entity that increases welfare.

Note also that the bank holds reserves against deposits without any legal restriction. In Chapter 8, we studied a model economy in which bank reserves were held against deposits because a reserve requirement was present. Indeed, this legal restriction was necessary for fiat money to be valued in an economy in which capital pays a higher rate of return than fiat money. In this model economy, money, by assumption, overcomes the limited-communication friction. In the absence of legal restrictions, bank reserves are held to meet expected liquidity needs for people facing exchange frictions. Thus, in economies like Canada's in which reserve requirements are absent, banks will hold reserves against deposits.[6]

2.4 With Only Second-Period Consumption

In the model, the competitive bank is acting on behalf of each young person. The problem is a bit more complicated because the decision problem is made along two dimensions. First, there is the decision of whether to consume when young or when

---

[5] Bencivenga and Smith (1991) provide a formal version of this argument in a growth model.
[6] See Bhattacharya, et al. (1997) for a detailed discussion of bank reserves.

old. Second, there is the decision regarding how to allocate the young person's portfolio, choosing between money and capital. Here, we strip away the decision between consumption when young and consumption when old. By doing so, we see more clearly how the bank improves the lifetime welfare for young people.

Consider an economy in which young people do not value consuming goods when young.[7] Thus, the budget constraint when young simplifies to

$$y + \tau = s,$$

where $s = v_t m + k$ when there is no bank. With a bank, the budget constraint is

$$y + \tau = d.$$

Clearly, the quantity of goods saved by the young person is exactly equal to the quantity of goods deposited into the bank by a young person in the two economies. The question is, which environment – the one with a bank or the one without – will, on average, produce the highest level of old-age consumption? With capital offering a higher return than money, will putting more goods into capital offer greater old-age consumption and thus higher expected lifetime welfare?

We approach this problem by looking at two critical questions. First, is there sufficient liquidity for movers? Second, provided there is sufficient liquidity, which portfolio has the greatest proportion of capital? The answer to the first question is related directly to whether movers will have money to buy the consumption good when old. The answer to the second question is related to the total quantity of goods available for old consumers.

When born, all young people receive their endowment, and any lump-sum transfer is received. When no bank is present, young people will divide their savings between capital and money. Money is acquired by selling some of their endowment to old people. Remember that both movers and nonmovers will carry some money forward to old age to insure against the risk of moving. Before reaching old age, all young people receive notice of their moving status. Movers are relocated and nonmovers stay. When old, movers exchange money for goods, whereas nonmovers exchange money for goods and reap the returns from their capital investment. The point is that everyone faces risk and must choose their portfolio in the face of that risk.

With a bank, each young person deposits the after-transfer amount of consumption goods in the bank. The bank does not face any risk. Because there is a large number of depositors and because the bank has knowledge of the number who will move and the number who will not move, the bank chooses the quantity of money and capital to hold. Another important feature is that banks can costlessly distinguish a mover from a nonmover. This identification process makes it easy for the

---

[7] This version of the random-relocation model has been examined by Bhattacharya, Haslag, and Martin (2005).

bank to write deposit contracts that offer returns tied to a person's type; that is, movers will get a different return on their deposits than will nonmovers.

After accepting the deposits, the bank also serves a retail consumer-good function. Old movers arrive at the bank, seeking to exchange money for consumer goods. This is how the bank acquires the money portion of its portfolio. The deposits less the amount traded with old movers will be invested in capital. Next, all young people are notified about their moving status. Movers will go to the bank, withdraw money balances, and wait to be relocated to the foreign island. Money worth $v_t m_t$ units of the consumption good for a young person born on date t will be worth $v_{t+1} m_t$ units of the date $t+1$ consumption good on the foreign island. Thus, movers effectively receive $v_{t+1} m_t$ goods for the d_t goods they deposited at the bank when young. When old, nonmovers will withdraw their deposits worth $x d_t$ units of the consumption good. The movers are physically relocated, become old, and spend the money, now worth $v_{t+1} m_t$ units of the date $t+1$ consumption good.

With a full description of the events transpiring in this economy, we can answer our two critical questions. A competitive bank will have liquidity to its depositors, and the process of competition will ensure that the return to movers will be the highest amount the bank can afford. The answer to the first of our two questions then rests principally on the nature of the competition in the banking industry.

Regarding the portfolio, people will always put a larger fraction of their savings into money than a bank would on their behalf. Everyone faces a risky situation at the time they choose between capital and money. As long as people are risk averse, they will insure their future consumption by putting more saving into the risk-free asset: money. The bank, in contrast, does not face any risk. Because of the large number of depositors, it knows how to maximize the expected utility of the depositor. In doing so, the bank invests a larger amount into capital, producing a greater quantity of aggregate goods and thereby permitting greater expected consumption by the young depositor.

3 Optimal Consumption Bundles

Recall that in Chapter 2 and again in Chapter 6, we considered what optimal monetary policy would be. In both model economies, a constant money stock was the optimal monetary policy. By holding the money stock constant over time, the return on money was equal to the marginal rate of transformation; that is the rate at which a planner could transform a good at date t into a good at date $t+1$. With productive capital in the model economy, however, the marginal product of capital is now the marginal rate of transformation. Does the presence of an additional store of value affect the optimal monetary policy?

To understand what monetary policy is best, we begin with a benchmark that is the planner's problem. Because it is easier to work with, we continue to use the model economy in which people value consumption only when they are old.

In this case, the planner's resource constraint consists of the sum of endowments and the returns to any capital from the previous period. Those resources will be allocated over consumption by movers, consumption by nonmovers, and goods put into capital this period. We focus on stationary allocation so that consumption and capital quantities are constant over time.

The planner knows the distribution of people. In other wrods, the planner knows the fraction of the population moving and the remaining fraction not moving. So for a person born in this period, the objective is to maximize

$$\pi U(c^m) + (1 - \pi)U(c^n)$$

subject to the resource constraint

$$\pi c^m + (1 - \pi)c^n + s = y + xs,$$

where πc^m is the total quantity consumed by movers and $(1 - \pi)c^n$ is the total quantity consumed by nonmovers.[8] In other words, the resource constraint tells us that consumption by movers (the first term) plus consumption by nonmovers (the second term) plus total saving is equal to the total endowment plus goods produced from capital accumulated one period before. Here, the planner is not engaged in market activities and therefore, does not need to acquire money for movers. The planner is only interested in providing goods. So it makes sense for the planner to take all savings, putting the goods into this period's capital, obtaining goods next period.

After rearranging the resource constraint and the collecting terms, we get $\pi c^m + (1 - \pi)c^n = y + (x - 1)s$.

The comparison is made easier by focusing on people who just want to consume when old. In choosing the quantities to give to movers and to nonmovers, it is critical to understand that the planner does not have a preference of one type over the other. Both are equal in the eyes of the planner. Furthermore, there is no cost difference in treating movers and nonmovers in the planner's point of view. As such, the planner will treat them equally and set $c^m = c^n = c^*$. In other words, the planner allocates goods so that perfect **risk sharing** is achieved. Here, perfect risk sharing refers to an equilibrium in which both movers and nonmovers consume exactly the same quantity when old. No matter what type you are when old, the planner will give you the same amount of consumption.

It is very easy to see how much capital will support this level of consumption. After substituting the quantity of consumption into the resource constraint, we get $c^* = y + (x - 1)s$. If we were to plot the combinations of old-age consumption associated with every level of saving, we would get a straight line as depicted in Figure 14.2. Each point on the line represents a quantity of consumption that could

---

[8] Because people only consume when old, we have dropped the subscripts on consumption. Lifetime consumption and old-age consumption are equivalent in this setup.

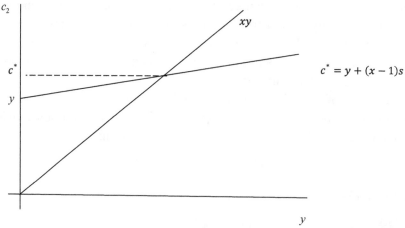

Figure 14.2. The optimal consumption allocation for movers and non-movers. When each person's saving are invested in capital, then we can find the amount of 2nd period consumption by each old person. It will be a point on the line $y + (x - 1)s$. This line plots combinations of consumption that affordable. We include the line xy because indicates the maximum level of consumption that could be achieved if the entire endowment were invested in capital. The intersection of these two lines indicates where the maximum risk-sharing bundle is.

be supported by a given level of capital. At the vertical axis, if we set capital to zero ($s = 0$), then $c^* = y$. Because $x > 1$, the straight line is upward sloping.

Of course, there is a limit to much capital could be invested. The planner's capital cannot exceed the size of the endowment. Doing this would violate the basic resource constraint. Therefore, we include in Figure 14.2 combinations of goods in which the endowment equals the quantity of capital. The xy line represents the maximum quantity of consumption conditioned on the entire endowment being placed into capital. As Figure 14.2 shows, the maximum quantity of consumption that is feasible occurs where the c^* intersects the xy line. Thus, the planner's allocation will have $c^m = c^n = c^*$ and $s = y$. In the efficient allocation, movers and nonmovers will receive the same quantity of consumption from the planner, and the planner will take people's endowment, store it all, and use the gross return on that capital to supply the movers' and nonmovers' consumption.

Example 14.1 Consider the random-relocation model economy represented in this chapter in which old-age consumption solely provides utility to each generation. People are endowed with 50 units of the consumption good when young and nothing when old. The gross real rate of return on capital is 1.25. Suppose 10 percent of the young are relocated in each period t.

a. Calculate the maximum amount a planner would put into capital for each young person.
b. What would old movers consume in the planner's allocation?
c. What would old nonmovers consume in the planner's allocation?

3.1 Optimal Monetary Policy

What would monetary policy have to be to achieve the planner's allocation? Recall that movers will consume the amount the deposit contract offers – that is, $r^m d = c_2^m$. Similarly, nonmovers will consume $r^n d = c_2^n$. To achieve perfect risk sharing, we know that $c_2^m = c_2^n$ if and only if $r^m = r^n$. Monetary policy can achieve rate of return equality by setting the return to money equal to the return to capital. The return to money is, $\frac{v_{t+1}}{v_t}$, equals the rate of money growth in the stationary equilibrium. Accordingly, if $M_t = z M_{t-1}$, then the gross real return to money is $\frac{1}{z}$. With $x = \frac{1}{z} > 1$, the implication is that the money must contract over time to achieve the full risk-sharing level of consumption.[9] Otherwise, $x > \frac{1}{z}$ results in less consumption by the movers; if money grows "too fast" then movers consume less than nonmovers.

As we just demonstrated, the planner would implement a full risk-sharing allocation. The open question is whether the optimal policy is the risk-sharing equilibrium in the decentralized economy.[10] By letting the money supply contract over time, the opportunity cost of holding money is zero. However, the government is collecting a lump-sum tax from each young person as the money supply shrinks over time. Across all the current and future generations, the value of the lump-sum tax is offset by the increase in the value of money balances held by the initial old, who are the only money holders. By contracting the money supply, the rate of return on money increases. So, the demand for money increases and the initial old see the value of their money balances increases. Who is paying for the initial old's increased wealth? Each member of the current and future generations is paying a tiny bit. So, in effect, the choice of the monetary policy that achieves full risk sharing also creates a transfer from the current and future generations to the initial old. Unless this transfer is undone by, say, a corresponding fiscal policy that taxes the initial old and transfers the resources to the current and future generations or an open-market sale that reduces the initial old's money holdings to match the increase in the value of money, the Friedman rule is not the optimal policy.

To put things more succinctly, the monetary authority faces a tradeoff. If it eliminates the opportunity cost of holding money, it transfers goods from people not holding money to those who do hold money.[11] If the monetary authority holds the money stock constant, for example, there is the opportunity cost of holding money but no transfer cost. In general, the monetary policy that maximizes utility of all generations – the initial old and the current and future generations – is to keep the

---

[9] The monetary policy that achieves rate of return equality is referred to as the Friedman rule. See Friedman (1969).

[10] See Haslag and Martin (2007) for the complete arguments on optimal monetary policy in the random-relocation model.

[11] Bhattacharya, Haslag, and Martin (2005) show that the transfer is a generic attribute in model economies in which the distribution of money holdings is not uniform across people. Suppose there are two types of people: those with small money holdings and those with large money holdings. Following the Friedman rule will transfer goods from those holding small money balances to those holding large money balances.

money stock constant. This is true even though the value of the transfer by each generation is small.

Example 14.2 Consider the random-relocation economy in which each person receive an endowment of 100 goods when young, and their preferences are such that they only wish to consume when old. Let the gross real rate of return on capital be 1.1; that is, $x = 1.1$. What would a nonmover be able to consume when old in this economy? What would the rate of change in the money supply have to be (the value of z) to achieve full risk sharing in this economy?

The monetary policy that will maximize welfare for current and future generations is the one that keeps the money stock constant. The rationale is the same as in Chapter 2 of this textbook, although here it is possible to amplify the reasoning. When the money stock is constant, the price level is unchanged, meaning that the initial old do not receive any transfer from the current and future generations. Current and future generations prefer the risk to their old-age consumption associated with relocation to paying the transfer to the initial old.

4 Bank Risk

In the previous sections, we have focused on a model in which there is no aggregate uncertainty. Each person is subject to uncertainty regarding their relocation. This kind of personal risk is called idiosyncratic risk. You can insure against idiosyncratic risk and indeed, the bank's portfolio using the law of large numbers effectively eliminates any risk to people when the return on money is equal to the return on capital. In contrast, aggregate risk involves outcomes that affect every person, like productivity shocks or droughts. There is no insurance against aggregate uncertainty.

So we consider aggregate shocks to the demand for money. In the case in which the fraction of movers is known, the total demand for money by movers is known. And the bank provides the right amount of liquidity. However, if the fraction of movers can take on either high or low values with some positive probability of each event, then our analysis must address outcomes in which the total demand for money is uncertain.[12] In this section, we assume that the return to capital is greater than the return to money; that is, $x > \frac{p_t}{p_{t+1}}$.

The key difference is that the fraction of people who move is now drawn from a distribution of possible outcomes. In other words, π is a random variable. This version corresponds more closely to the environment that banks face. Banks must make decisions regarding the level of money to hold for withdrawals. The realized level of withdrawals is subject to random variation as people's liquidity needs respond to variety of shocks.

---

[12] This section follows Champ, Smith, and Williamson (1996).

The bank's decision problem remains the same. The bank chooses a quantity of reserves in the face of this uncertain demand. Because capital offers a higher rate of return, there is an opportunity cost associated with holding too much money. It is true that the bank will choose a larger quantity of money balances compared to the environment in which the demand for reserves is certain, but it will hold fewer reserves than the amount associated with the highest possible fraction of movers. The marginal condition balances the value of the extra money balances against uncertain demand with the opportunity cost of holding low-return money instead of high-return capital. The upshot is that, under some realizations, the money holdings will be too small to meet the realized liquidity demands because an unexpected large number of depositors will withdraw money. When this event occurs, the bank is insolvent. Remember that there is no bank equity. So unexpectedly large withdrawals require that capital must be liquidated at less than par value. In this case, nonmovers suffer lower returns. Alternatively, the bank may simply not honor withdrawals that exceed the expected level, so that movers, at least the ones at the end of the line, suffer lower returns.

To illustrate the problem faced by the bank, consider a version in which the fraction of people moving is either high or low. Let π^H denote the case in which the high fraction of people are designated as movers and π^L represents the case in which the low fraction of people are designated as movers. The probability is ϵ that the high-fraction mover event is realized, and $1 - \epsilon$ is the probability that the low-fraction mover event is realized. We assume that the expected fraction of movers is equal to the fraction in the deterministic setting; that is, $\pi = \epsilon\pi^H + (1 - \epsilon)\pi^L$. As constructed, the random number of movers means that the stochastic environment is a mean-preserving spread of the deterministic setting.[13] With a constant money stock, it is possible to compare equilibrium in the deterministic model economy and the stochastic one. There is one important implication of adding uncertainty: expected welfare is lower as the distribution of movers is transformed. The bank attempts to hold larger money balances to self-insure against the risk that a larger fraction of movers will occur, meaning that the reserve-to-deposit ratio will be higher than it was in the deterministic case. In terms of expectations, each young person sees a portfolio shifted away from the high-return capital to the low-return money. As such, fewer total goods are available for old-age consumption.

There is a second implication that pertains to the realization of the random fraction of movers. How will the bank meet its contractual obligations to depositors – that is, to movers – if the fraction of movers is greater than the reserve-to-deposit ratio? For one thing, when the fraction of movers is larger than the reserve-to-deposit ratio, the bank can suspend withdrawals or liquidate capital. We refer to a

---

[13] A mean-preserving spread is a transformation of a distribution of uncertain outcomes. In the transformed distribution, the expected value, or mean, is the same as for the original distribution. However, the variance of the transformed distribution function is greater than the variance of the original distribution function.

bank panic as a case in which deposits are insufficient to meet the quantity of withdrawals over a short period of time. Hence, a bank run is just an extreme version of a bank panic. We turn to special cases of this analysis in the next two subsections.

4.1 Regulation and Bank Panics

A bank panic is defined as a series of sudden withdrawals that is widespread. In Chapter 13, we defined a bank panic as a case in which depositors all withdraw at once, because a bank must borrow or sell its assets to pay them off. If the bank is unable to borrow or sell quickly without losses, it may not have enough resources to meet its promises, even if it has the resources to pay off depositors if they withdraw gradually. If all depositors fear that the rush of others to withdraw will leave them with nothing, all will rationally join the rush. Two differences are evident in this model economy. First, liquidity is tied to the holding of fiat money or bank reserves. Second, the bank must realize substantial withdrawals to exhaust its resources and to fail. In other words, a number of banks in the economy realize withdrawals that draw down the liquid assets held by the banks. The withdrawals have to be large enough so that the bank's liquidity evaporates, and even the sale of other bank assets does not assure that the withdrawing people will be paid.[14] One way to deal with a bank panic is to suspend payments. In doing so, the bank staunches the outflow of liquidity, at least temporarily. Suspending payments, however, does not address the underlying factors that caused the bank panic.

Researchers, especially contemporary writers, have offered several different explanations to account for bank panics. There is documented evidence that bank panics have different characteristics in different regulatory environments. The Canadian and U.S. experiences were frequently cited as examples of the role of regulatory structure in bank panics.[15] During the 1930s, Canada enjoyed greater financial stability than the United States. One reason was that Canada put fewer restrictions on bank branching; that is, a single banking firm could open branches at any geographic spot deemed appropriate by bank management. Branching restrictions existed in the United States until the 1980s. Contemporary writers have argued that with more funds concentrated in fewer banks, there was greater cooperation and collusion between branches directed toward maintaining the health of the banking firm. Accordingly, less restrictive branching has been offered as an important regulatory feature contributing to the Canadian experience.

Interestingly, there is no role for currency in these explanations. The model economy developed in this chapter features a mechanism in which money creation and provision of liquidity by banks are related. Insofar as random relocation corresponds to liquidity needs, we can modify this model economy to explore how

---

[14] We adopt the definition from http://financial-dictionary.thefreedictionary.com/Bank+Panic.
[15] See the work by Williamson (1989) and Haubrich (1990).

regulatory structure, the bank's liquidity provision, and bank panics are linked. In addition, there are at least four reasons one might want to study the relationship between bank panics and the role of money. First, most operational definitions of panics identify currency as playing a central role. For instance, depositors have greater difficulty liquidating their accounts when payments are suspended. Payments are suspended because of shortages of cash reserves and premiums on currency. With these and other emergency actions taken to curtail liquidity outflows from banks, it follows that currency issues play a central role in the bank panic definition.

Second, many proposals for U.S. banking and monetary system reforms rest on the belief that the monetary system is related to the panic. Following the Banking Crisis of 1893, the Baltimore Plan proposed concrete measures to address liquidity problems. In particular, note circulation was restricted during the 1893 crisis. The Baltimore Plan would have given banks greater freedom to issue currency. With more elastic currency, designers believed that the crisis would have been much less severe. Making currency supply more elastic found traction in other reform writings at that time. Because the Canadian experience seemed less volatile, some proposals sought to make changes so that the U.S. banking system was closer in form to the Canadian structure. A key aspect was that the Canadian structure adopted a far more elastic currency. These views gained legislative force with the adoption of the Aldrich/Vreeland Act and the Federal Reserve Act. Both expressly identified elastic currency supply as an important component of monetary and banking reform.

Third, contemporary writers stressed that relative importance of banknote issue was critical to any regulatory reform. Many viewed banknote issue as far more important to the reform than bank branching. Branching is valuable as a means to diversify risks, but these reformers' viewed liquidity as the fundamental problem. Bank branching could not address the liquidity problems.

Fourth, empirical evidence points to monetary variables and their relationship to the realization of bank panics. Friedman and Schwartz (1963b) and Miron (1986), for example, cited the behavior of money, credit, the reserve-to-deposit ratio, currency-to-deposit ratio, and nominal interest rates during panic episodes. The empirical evidence suggests that monetary factors are correlated with panic episodes. Thus, the evidence further motivates us to integrate monetary factors into model economies that explain bank panics.

4.2 Inelastic Currency Supply

There are two components that characterize an **inelastic currency regime**. One involves fiat money. In an inelastic regime, there is a fixed supply of fiat money. Even with a fixed supply of currency, banknote issue could provide the liquidity people need. In the United States, banks could not issue notes against general assets. Furthermore, federal government bonds, used as reserves, serve as the chief operational constraint on note issue.

Let η denote the real value of banknotes issued per depositor. In the inelastic currency regime, we assume that $\eta = 0$. The only available liquidity is that which the bank accumulates in the form of fiat money balances. With the fraction of movers being either π^L or π^H, the bank must make its liquidity decision before the fraction of movers is realized. Let γ^* denote the fraction of deposits per deposit by banks in this model economy. Then for $\pi^L < \gamma^* < \pi^H$, there is risk to depositors.

Suppose that the high fraction of movers is realized. Total liquidity demanded by movers will be $\pi^H N r^m d$. However, the liquidity available from the bank is $\gamma^* N r^m d$. There is not enough liquidity to meet the needs of the high fraction of movers realized in this economy. In other words, the bank will exhaust its cash reserves. This event corresponds to the notion of a bank panic. There are simply too many movers presenting deposit claims that exceed the quantity of currency available. Because capital is illiquid, an inelastic currency supply combined with the high realization of currency demand satisfies one of the key conditions of a bank panic.

In this model economy, depositors are served sequentially. The bank panic does not require that currency actually be exhausted. Payment suspension is one way to keep the liquidity from being exhausted.

Currency premiums were also observed in bank panics. Such premiums could emerge in the model economy with a slight modification. Suppose nonmovers are permitted to withdraw their deposits at any time. With the high realization of currency demand at date t, nonmovers are capable of withdrawing currency at date t. With inelastic currency, the bank will not have sufficient currency to meet the needs of all depositors seeking to withdraw. Thus, nonmovers are willing to offer the currency to movers who arrived at the bank after liquidity was exhausted in exchange for deposit claims held by currency-seeking movers.

To further illustrate this point, note that nonmovers withdrawing at date t will receive r^m, which is less than r^n. An arbitrage condition must be satisfied for the nonmover to be willing to withdraw at date t; namely, the nonmover will offer currency to movers at a premium. As long as the currency premium satisfies the arbitrage condition, the nonmover will be willing to withdraw deposits early. If the currency trades at q units of the consumption good, then the arbitrage condition must satisfy $q = \frac{r^n}{r^m}$. With $\frac{r^n}{r^m} > 1$, currency is trading at a premium.

4.3 Elastic Currency Supply

In this regime, banks are permitted to issue banknotes. By permitting banknote issue, the bank panic is averted. Bank note creation is referred to as an "elastic currency regime."

Consider the case in which the high fraction of movers is realized. Instead of exhausting fiat money when too many depositors withdraw, the bank issues banknotes to meet the mover's currency needs. After the relocation, movers use the banknotes to trade for units of the consumption good. Thus, banknotes are redeemed one period after issue. Because banks can redeem all deposit claims by movers, the bank panic does not occur. More concretely, all movers realize the return r^m upon redeeming their deposit claim. In contrast, in the high-mover state, some movers either will not be able to redeem their deposit claims because of the liquidity shortage or will receive less than r^m because there is a premium on currency. Thus, banknote issue holds the key to insuring people against liquidity risk.

The two different currency regimes produce very different implications for banks and bank panics. More importantly, we observe regimes in practice with Canada adopting a more elastic currency regime and the United States implementing a more inelastic currency regime. As developed in this chapter, an inelastic currency regime can result in banks facing liquidity shortages. The shortages are not the result of poor bank management but of unexpected liquidity demands and no coping mechanism. In contrast, elastic currency regimes provide a mechanism – banknote issue – to deal with unexpected currency demand. In other words, when there is a liquidity problem, banks either have to rely on central banks to provide liquidity or have the power to temporarily issue banknotes to satisfy the liquidity needs of depositors.

To summarize, the regulatory regimes matter because of the possibility of bank panics. The model economy developed in this chapter can account for historical episodes in which currency, in its role as medium of exchange, plays a critical role in the bank panic.

5 Money, Banking, and the Zero Lower Bound

In Chapter 12, we discussed how the 2007 Financial Crisis disrupted the settlement process. The institutions operated, but settlements were disrupted as creditors were not capable of obtaining liquidity needed to repay their IOUs.

In this chapter, the model economy is capable of offering a broader overview of the 2007 Financial Crisis. In a setting with an uncertain fraction of movers, the model economy can be used to characterize events in the 2007 Financial Crisis. In particular, the 2007 Financial Crisis was marked by declines in asset values, increases in liquidity, and approaches to the zero lower bound.

A complete description of the 2007 Financial Crisis is beyond the scope of this book. However, this is one of the most important economic events. Economic theory plays an important role in helping us organize our thoughts regarding this event. So a brief overview of the facts is critical if we want to use economic models to describe the 2007 Financial Crisis.

To understand the 2007 Financial Crisis, it is important that we understand this was not a bank run in the same sense that we observed bank runs during the Great Depression. In 2007, the bank run was still about liquidity mismatch and one group trying to obtain liquidity. However, the lines formed in what is called the Shadow Banking industry. We understand how runs occur in commercial banks; liquid deposits are transformed into a combination of liquid securities and illiquid loans. Shadow banks operate primarily in the realm of repurchase agreements, which is also a liquidity transformation. Suppose Bank A offers a security, one that is less liquid than fiat money, in exchange for money provided by Bank B. The repurchase agreement says that Bank A will repurchase the security from Bank B at a slightly higher price on a prespecified future date. Bank B is happy because it earns interest on the liquidity it possesses. Like any deposit relationship, Bank B deposits liquidity and Bank A accepts the deposit with a promise to repay. In other words, Bank B's deposit is transformed into a less liquid asset by Bank A. Because this operation is between banks and because the industry is less regulated than commercial banks, the term shadow bank has been applied. In the shadow banking industry, a run occurs when there is an unexpected large withdrawal of liquidity. Or, in our case, banks cease entering into repurchase agreements with other banks needing liquidity.

In terms of this chapter, the model economy is silent as to why housing values declined. For the purposes of this illustration, we consider an exogenous shock as responsible for the decline in housing prices. However, by tracing the shock through the financial intermediary, it is possible to describe how the initial exogenous shock could be amplified. For this setting, it will be useful to think of each period as having two moving dates. A person can be assigned an early move or a late move time.

The backdrop is that there was a decline in housing prices, causing the value of mortgage-backed securities to fall. In the language of the model economy, the exogenous shock resulted in an initial decline in the value of capital and a decline in the measured return on capital. Let us continue to assume that the gross return on the housing, or the capital stock, is x units of the consumption good paid next period. After the shock, however, the value of capital declined. Let the initial (preshock) value of the capital stock be represented by k_0 and the postshock value is k_1, where $k_0 > k_1$. The return on capital purchased before the shock is measured by the gross return, x, plus the capital loss $k_1 - k_0$. With $k_0 < k_1$, the realized return on capital is less than x. This step alone can partially account for the net interest rate approaching the zero lower bound.

As the financial crisis unfolds, consider what is happening to our representative Bank A and Bank B. Bank A sells a mortgage-backed security to Bank B and promises to repay a dollar amount at the end of the early move period. So a late mover could cash in and take the money to the other island. Bank wants to turnaround and use the mortgage-backed security to enter into a repurchase agreement, promising to pay at the end of the first period. Bank B sees that mortgage-backed securities are worth less in light of the housing price decline. In this case, Bank B refuses to repurchase the mortgage-backed security from Bank A at the end of the early-move period. In effect, Bank B withdraws and chooses to hold liquidity rather than the mortgage-backed security. So at the end of the early move period, there is essentially a run on Bank A.

In terms of the model economy, we can think of Bank B's actions as an unexpected increase in the fraction of movers; the amount of liquidity sought is larger relative to the size of the capital held. Bank B's decision means that for Bank A to acquire liquidity, it will need to liquidate more capital. The liquidation value of capital is φk_1, where $0 < \varphi < 1$. Here, φ tells us that when Bank A, for example, liquidates capital before production, it is converted into units of the consumption good at less than a one-for-one rate. Now the realized return on capital, which initially was $x + (k_1 - k_0)$, is now even lower, falling to $x + (\varphi k_1 - k_0)$. Bank B's decision, therefore, amplifies the effect of the initial shock on the value of capital, and the realized return takes another step toward the zero lower bound.

So what we observe is that the value of houses resulted in a decline in the value of mortgage-backed assets. Asset values decline and the returns on these assets declined. Compared with our discussion in Chapter 12, we now allow for the value of assets to decline. In this setting, shadow banks responded to the risk that the mortgage-backed security was not worth as much as previously believed. There was a run in the shadow banking industry as those depositing goods into a bank withdrew early.

During the 2007 Financial Crisis, the Federal Reserve addressed the liquidity demand – that is, the bank run – by providing fiat money. At the same time that massive liquidity injections were implemented by the central bank, interest rates approached the zero lower bound. One view is that the Federal Reserve, by supplying so much fiat money, is keeping the interest rate on assets near the zero lower bound. This is the classic liquidity trap view. The trap persists because the return on money is essentially the same as the return on capital. Hence, there is no incentive for capital accumulation to occur.

Another view is that return on capital is close to the zero lower bound and has stayed there. The zero lower bound, thus, reflects underlying fundamentals. An exogenous increase in the return on capital will end the current zero-lower-bound experience. The Federal Reserve did not cause the interest rate to approach the zero lower bound by increasing the quantity of fiat money. Rather, the increase in the quantity of fiat money was a response to liquidity needs that coincided with the return on capital approaching the zero lower bound.

6 Summary

In this chapter, we developed a model economy that examined the role of fiat money in the intermediation process, focusing particularly on how money withdrawals are associated with banking panics. The model economy is quite similar to the one developed in Chapter 13. In this case, we change the notion of liquidity; in Chapter 12, capital is illiquid in a temporal sense insofar as its value changes when it's evaluated at two different points in time whereas in this chapter, capital is illiquid in a spatial sense insofar as its value changes when it's evaluated at two different locations in space. In this model economy, we take away the private information that people had about their consumption types. We explain the need for fiat money as a means of executing exchange across locations. By including bank reserves, we show an explicit link between unexpected changes in currency demand and bank insolvency.

By integrating currency's role into the financial system, we see the link between liquidity risks and bank panics. As in Chapter 12's model economy, intermediation plays a role in providing insurance against risk borne by people. Because the bank does not face any aggregate uncertainty, the existence of a bank permits people to realize higher utility; the bank allocates the aggregate portfolio in such a way that liquidity needs are satisfied without sacrificing consumption. In other words, people can enjoy higher expected lifetime consumption when a bank exists than when one does not.

To consider unexpected currency demand increases, we extend the basic model economy to examine the role of liquidity uncertainty. At the country level, banks are permitted to respond to unexpected liquidity needs in different ways. As we saw during the Great Depression, for example, Canada permitted banks to create banknotes when liquidity demand was unexpectedly high. In this way, bank panics were largely averted, and people consume more in the high-liquidity-demand event.

In contrast, with inelastic currency, such as the United States practiced in the 1930s, the liquidity shortage can adversely affect the goods consumed by depositors in the high-liquidity-demand event.

7 Exercises

14.1. Consider the random-relocation economy developed in this chapter. Each person receives an endowment of 500 goods when young and nothing when old. People only want to consume when old. Let $M_t = 1.1M_{t-1}$ for every period t. The net rate of return on capital is 15 percent.

    a. Write down the contract that a competitive bank would offer to a mover.

    b. Write down the contract that a competitive bank would offer to a nonmover.

    c. Does this represent perfect risk sharing? Briefly explain your answer.

    d. What would the growth rate of the money supply have to be in order to achieve perfect risk sharing? Is the monetary policy associated with perfect risk sharing the optimal policy setting?

14.2. In that simple random-relocation model, each person is endowed with 50 goods when young and nothing when old. The money stock is constant and equal to $1,000,000. Each island has a constant population, with 500 people born in each period t. Suppose the fraction of movers takes on either of two values. In the small-fraction event, with probability of .5, 5 percent of the population must move to the other island. In the high-fraction event, with probability of .5, 20 percent of the population must move.

a. Calculate the total currency needed by movers in the event that the small fraction of movers is realized.

b. Calculate the total currency needed by movers in the event that the high fraction of movers is realized.

Suppose the bank holds 15 percent of the deposits in the form of currency. In other words, $\gamma^* = 0.15$. Will the bank have enough in currency to meet the needs of the movers in the high-fraction event?

c. Describe how an elastic currency regime would address the answer to part b.

14.3. Consider a model economy in which each young person receives 200 units of the consumption good. There are 50 young people born each period. The total stock of fiat money is constant and equal to $10,000. Suppose a person's preferences are such that they only want to consume when old. We assume the probability that a person moves is 10 percent. The gross return on capital is 1.10. A bank accepts deposits from all young people.

a. Write down the money market-clearing condition for this economy.

b. Compute the equilibrium value of money for this economy.

14.4. Use the same model economy as described in 14.3.

a. How many goods would each young person deposit? How many deposited goods would be held in the form of money? How many in capital?

b. Write down the budget constraint for a mover. What would old-age consumption be for a mover?

c. Write down the budget constraint for a nonmover. What would old-age consumption be for a nonmover?

Part III

Government Debt

Chapter 15

Deficits and the National Debt

1 Roadmap

The models we have presented to this point have had a government creating fiat money and taxing or providing transfers to people in the economy. Although these are important aspects of government finance in today's world, we have neglected one critical factor. Governments frequently finance current deficits by borrowing.

In this chapter, we ask two questions. First, what gain is there to the government from having multiple types of financial securities? The answer is simple: with different types of people, the combined government – that is, the central bank and the treasury – can use price discrimination to raise more revenue. Second, what effect does the existence of national debt – which is treated as a perfect substitute for capital – have on equilibrium outcomes? We focus on two: the effects that national debt has on government revenue and the effect of monetary policy on the national debt.

2 High-Denomination Government Debt

We observe in most of today's economies that governments often issue two forms of debt – assets held by the public – one called money (e.g., currency) and one called government bonds (e.g., Treasury bills). Although they seem equally safe and negotiable, they have different rates of return. The net nominal rate of return on currency is zero, whereas that on Treasury bills held to maturity is positive. Clearly, Treasury bills dominate currency in rate of return. Why would anyone hold currency if an equally safe asset offers a higher rate of return? What difference in the nature of these two assets can explain the observed disparity in rates of return?

One difference in the two assets is the denominations in which they are offered. Currency is issued in small denominations easily usable in exchange, whereas

Treasury bills are supplied only in large denominations. Imagine the expression on the face of a checkout clerk if you presented a $10,000 Treasury bill in payment for your $50 grocery bill!

There is a gap today between the rate of return of currency and that of interest-bearing $10,000 Treasury bills. As always, a gap in rates of return leads one to wonder if there might not be some way for a financial intermediary to make a profit through arbitrage. This intermediary could purchase the large-denomination bonds and issue small-denomination notes. If the return from the bonds exceeded the cost of issuing the notes, then the intermediary would profit from the enterprise.

Suppose it costs a negligible amount to engage in such intermediation. What will happen to the two rates of return? Let us attempt to answer that question by asking a few more. Suppose you can buy bonds that currently display a 20 percent rate of return. As the manager of an intermediary, you attempt to raise funds to purchase those bonds by attracting depositors. You begin by offering a zero rate of return on deposits. Given that many potential depositors also can purchase the same bonds and receive a much higher rate of return than you are offering on deposits, you have few customers. As an incentive to attract more deposits, you begin to offer higher and higher interest rates on deposits. As your intermediary (and presumably other intermediaries) enters bond markets, bond prices are bid up, and rate of return on bonds fall. Note that the spread between the rate of return on bonds and deposits begins to narrow. As long as there is a difference, profits can be made by engaging in this process. Hence, over time, rates of return on bonds fall as prices are bid up, and rates of return on deposits rise as intermediaries attempt to attract depositors. If this intermediation process is costless (or inexpensive), we expect it to continue until there is no (or little) difference between the rates of return on bonds and deposits.

Can intermediation costs plausibly explain the rate-of-return difference? If so, we have to believe that nominal interest rates soared in the inflationary 1970s because the wages of tellers or some other cost of operating a bank dramatically increased, only to fall again in recent years.

If intermediation is not a plausible explanation for high interest rates on government debt relative to that on currency, then what are other possible explanations? One possibility is that legal restrictions on governing intermediaries have led to this difference. The prohibition on privately issued bank notes is an example of such a regulation.[1]

But why might the government wish to issue this high-denomination asset that requires it to pay interest and, at the same time, regulate intermediation? The awkward denomination on this asset and limits on its intermediation indicate that the asset is not being issued in order to provide a convenient medium of exchange.

---

[1] Wallace (1983) presents a discussion of related issues that is accessible to undergraduates.

2.1 A Model of Separated Asset Markets

Let us now consider a simple model in which the government may wish to issue high-denomination bonds in addition to fiat money in order to finance a deficit.[2] Imagine an economy in which there are two types of people – rich people who are endowed with Y when young and poor people who are endowed with y when young. Let Y be much larger than y. No one is endowed when old. The number of young rich and young poor both grow over time at the rate n.

We assume the following linear capital technology: If k units of the consumption good are invested in capital in period t, $x \cdot k$ units will be produced by capital in period $t + 1$. However, to utilize this technology, a person must invest more than k^* units. On the one hand, we assume that the amount k^* is so much less than Y that the rich are effectively unconstrained in investing in capital. On the other hand, k^* is greater than y, so no individual poor person is able to invest personally. Investment in capital cannot be observed by the government if the investment is done by a person.

There is a supply of fiat money that increases in each period according to the rule $M_t = zM_{t-1}$, where $z > 1$.

First, suppose we allow the formation of an intermediation industry that pools the endowments of the poor so that they can invest in capital. This intermediation process also operates costlessly. Through intermediation, all people in the economy have access to capital that yields a rate of return of x.

Consider the case of a monetary equilibrium. People have a choice of two assets – capital and fiat money. Recall that if the rate of money creation is z and the growth rate of money demand (from population growth) is n, then the rate of return on fiat money will be n/z. For people to be willing to hold money voluntarily, the rate of return on fiat money must be at least as large as the rate of return on the alternative, capital. In other words, for a monetary equilibrium, we must have

$$\frac{n}{z} \geq x.$$

If this were not true, then fiat money would be an inferior asset. People would do better if they invested in capital. Note that the previous equation implies that

$$z \leq \frac{n}{x}.$$

This places an upper bound on the rate of fiat money creation in the absence of legal restrictions. If fiat money is created at a rate that exceeds n/x, then people will refuse to hold fiat money. We see that a monetary equilibrium will not exist if z is greater than n/x. Of course, if z is strictly less than n/x, then holding fiat money

---

[2] The model is adapted from one presented by Bryant and Wallace (1984).

will provide a greater rate of return than holding capital. In that case, people will not invest in capital.

Now let us consider the imposition of a set of laws that effectively bans any intermediation that would enable people to pool their endowments to invest in capital. Recall that this implies that the poor will not have access to the capital technology. In such a case, the poor will have only one asset available to them – fiat money. In this case, fiat money can be created at a greater rate than n/x. Regardless of the rate of return on fiat money, the poor will still hold it, because it is the only means of providing for second-period consumption.

The rich, however, will invest in capital if $z > n/x$, because it yields a higher rate of return. Because the rich do not hold fiat money, the government obtains no seigniorage revenue from them. Note that the rich have an alternative unavailable to the poor – they can invest in capital individually, unobserved by the government. If the government could observe all investments, it could eliminate this option of the rich and force them, too, to hold fiat money.

2.2 *Introducing Government Bonds*

We see that, by pushing the rate of fiat money creation beyond n/x, the government may have increased the seigniorage it takes in from the poor, but it has lost all seigniorage from the rich. Is there some means by which the government might take in revenue from both rich and poor?

Suppose the government issues bonds intended to substitute for capital in the portfolios of the rich. We will assume that these government bonds have a one-period maturity. In other words, a given issue of bonds is retired with interest after one period. At that point in time, the government may issue additional bonds.

For the rich to be willing to hold government bonds, the bonds must pay a rate of return at least as large as that of capital. Hence, x is a lower bound for the rate of return on government bonds intended as substitutes for capital.

But if bonds pay the rate of return of capital, won't the poor, who otherwise are stuck with low-return fiat money, use bonds rather than fiat money to consume in the second period of life? If the poor do use only government bonds, then the government will lose all revenue from seigniorage. How can the government use the bonds to raise revenue from the rich without foregoing the seigniorage raised from the poor? A revenue-hungry government must find a way to make the bonds available to the rich but not the poor.

Suppose, then, that the government issues bonds with a minimum price of k^* goods while banning all intermediation. The minimum price effectively prevents any poor person from buying these bonds because a poor person's endowment y is less than k^*, and the ban on intermediation prevents anyone from pooling the funds of the poor to buy bonds. Now perhaps we can see why the government may take actions that reduce the liquidity of its debt. The bonds are designed to be a

Table 15.1. *Government bond issuance and revenue with x = 0.9*
and n = 1.

Period	Real bond issue	Real bond repayment	Real net revenue
1	1,000	.	1,000
2	1,000	900	100
3	1,000	900	100
4	1,000	900	100
.	.	.	.
.	.	.	.
.	.	.	.

substitute for capital but not for fiat money, so the government can raise revenue from the bonds without losing revenue from seigniorage on fiat money holdings.

3 Continual Debt Issue

It is apparent that the government can induce the rich to lend to the government, adding to the government's revenue in that period. Unlike fiat money, however, these bonds must be repaid with interest in a future period. In this way, government debt may defer rather than permanently answer the need to raise revenue.

Is it possible that the government can defer the payment of debt forever? To do so in every period, the government must borrow enough to pay off its debt from the previous period. If this is possible, government bonds can be used to raise revenue permanently – that is, without ever using future taxes to pay off the debt or the interest on the debt.

Let us first address this question with a numerical example of government debt issuance and repayment. Suppose there are 10 young rich people in each generation and the government issues bonds worth 100 goods per young rich person in each period. This implies that in every period, the government issues bonds worth a total of 1,000 goods. As reasoned previously, the government must pay the real rate of return x on these bonds. This means that the government must pay back $100x$ units of goods to each old person, for a total of $1,000x$ goods. The government again issues bonds worth a total of 1,000 goods. Clearly, if $x < 1$, the government's new issuance of bonds will enable it to retire the old bonds and generate real revenue of $1,000(1 - x)$ goods. For example, if $x = 0.9$, the government repays the 900 goods $(= 1,000x)$ and obtains real revenue equal to 100 goods $[= 1,000(1 - x)]$. Table 15.1 details the government's bond issuance and revenue for these parameter values.

It is evident that the government can sustain this level of debt issue forever and obtain 100 units of real revenue each period. Hence, bond issue can provide a source of revenue for a government.

Table 15.2. *Government bond issuance and revenue with* $x = 1.1$
and $n = 1.2$.

Period	Real bond issue	Real bond repayment	Real net revenue
1	1,000	.	1,000
2	1,200	1,100	100
3	1,440	1,320	120
4	1,728	1,584	144
.	.	.	.
.	.	.	.
.	.	.	.

We can also see why a revenue-maximizing government would want to issue bonds with a minimum denomination of k^*. This enables a government to generate revenue from bond issue and money creation. Given the high denomination of government debt, the poor have no alternative but to use fiat money. This enables the government to obtain revenue by taxing its money holdings. If, contrary to our setup, government bonds are issued in small denominations and paid the rate of return x, the poor will choose to hold government bonds instead of fiat money (if $z > 1/x$). The government will be severely constrained as to its rate of fiat money creation, and, hence, its amount of seigniorage revenue.

However, it is clear from the numerical example that revenue is raised from bonds because we have assumed a rate of return on capital; indeed, the net rate of return, $x - 1$, is negative. Is it possible for the government to permanently generate revenue by repeatedly issuing bonds in the more realistic case in which the real net rate of return is positive (i.e., $x > 1$)? In this case, the government will have to issue an increasing amount of bonds in each period just to repay the old debt.

It is still possible to raise revenue permanently by continually issuing government debt but only if the population is growing at a sufficiently high rate. To return to our numerical example, suppose now that $x = 1.1$ and $n = 1.2$. As before, there are 10 young rich people in period 1. The government still issues bonds worth 100 goods per young rich person in each period. Now, however, total bond issue will grow in each period, because the population is growing. In this case, the government will issue a total amount of bonds equal to $1,200$ [$= (10)(1.2)(100)$] goods in period 2. It will have to repay a total real amount of $1,100$ [$= (10)(100)(1.1)$] goods. This implies the generation of 100 units of goods in real revenue. Table 15.2 details the results for these parameter values. Note that from period 3 on, the government's real revenue from the bond issue grows at the rate n, the rate of population growth. Clearly, total government borrowing and real debt repayment grow at the same rate.

Table 15.3. *Government bond issuance and revenue with x = 1.1 and zero bond revenue.*

Period	Real bond issue	Real bond repayment	Real net revenue
1	1,000	·	1,000
2	1,100	1,100	0
3	1,210	1,210	0
4	1,331	1,331	0
·	·	·	·
·	·	·	·
·	·	·	·

It is important to note that the preceding examples always assume that $x < n$. We will see that if $x \geq n$, the government cannot permanently obtain revenue from the issuance of bonds.

3.1 Rolling Over the Debt

To see the limitation on the government's ability to raise revenue permanently, let us look at one more numeric example. Suppose that instead of generating revenue by a bond issue, the government merely issues enough bonds in each period to make the repayments (including interest) on the previous period's bond issue. We call this practice "rolling over the debt." Using the same parameter values from the previous example, we obtain Table 15.3.

In the case in which the government obtains zero revenue from a bond issue, the total amount of government bonds issued grows at the rate x. We have offered a theory that can account for the presence of government debt and how government debt alters the government budget constraint. We found that issuing government debt today changes the options that are available to the government tomorrow. Perpetual debt financing is not sustainable in the sense that an increase in the government's debt forces an eventual decrease in government expenditures or increase in future taxation.

One of the taxation options is to monetize the debt. When the central bank does not pay interest to the holders of its money, it earns profits that are handed back to the fiscal authority (Treasury). In this case, the net effect of the two steps of printing bonds to cover government expenditures and then monetizing the bonds is exactly the same as having the government simply print money to pay for the expenditures without bothering to issue bonds.

Let us compare the time path of government debt with the government's ability to borrow. The most the government could ever borrow would be the entire endowment of the rich. Let us now determine the time path of this upper limit on bonds. Note that, if the population is growing at the rate n, the total endowment of the young rich people obeys (for simplicity, we denote the total number of young rich people in period t as N_t) the following rules:

$$N_1Y = nN_oY$$

$$N_2Y = nN_1Y = n^2N_oY$$

$$N_3Y = nN_2Y = n^3N_oY$$

$$\vdots$$

$$N_tY = n^tN_0Y \tag{15.1}$$

If we take the natural logarithm of both sides of this equation, we obtain

$$\ln(N_tY) = t\ln(n) + \ln(N_0Y). \tag{15.2}$$

Let us denote the total real amount of the government bond issue in period t as B_t. We know that, when the government obtains no revenue from issue, B_t grows at rate x. Following the techniques used to derive Equations 15.1 and 15.2, we find that

$$B_t = x^tB_0 \tag{15.3}$$

$$\Rightarrow \ln(B_t) = t\ln(x) + \ln(B_0). \tag{15.4}$$

The reason we took natural logarithms of Equations 15.1 and 15.3 is that the resulting equations, Equations 15.2 and 15.4, are linear equations in t that are easy to graph. Figure 15.1 illustrates the time paths of $\ln(B_t)$ and $\ln(N_tY)$. The graph is drawn for the case where $x > n$. What is the importance of this graph? At time T, the total amount of real government bond issue exceeds the total real endowment of the young rich people in the economy. This is infeasible.[3] If the growth rate of the population (n) is less than the growth rate of the bond issue (x), then eventually the government will be unable to find holders for its bonds. The supply of government bonds will outstrip the demand for them. In the case where $x > n$, perpetual government debt issue will become impossible. Eventually, the government will have to issue more bonds than people are willing to hold. Note that this will actually occur before time T, because the young rich will not be willing to save their entire endowment. More generally, we obtain the important conclusion that if the real interest rate on government bonds exceeds the growth rate of the economy, perpetual debt financing becomes impossible.

---

[3] This result was emphasized by Sargent and Wallace (1981).

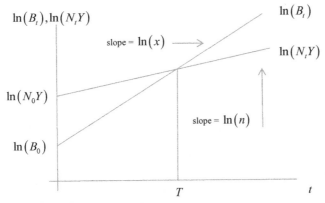

Figure 15.1. The time paths of government bond issue and the economy's endowment ($x > n$). When a government rolls over its debt, the total amount of debt outstanding grows at the rate x, the interest rate it must pay on its debt. When expressed in logarithms, this translates into a straight-line time path, $\ln(B_t)$, with slope of $\ln(x)$. On the other hand, the economy's total endowment grows at the rate of population growth n and is represented by the line $\ln(N_t Y)$. Beyond time T, the real value of the government debt exceeds the total endowment of the economy. This is infeasible, demonstrating the eventual impossibility of rolling over the debt if $x > n$.

It is equally important to note that if $x \leq n$, perpetual government bond financing will be possible. In Figure 15.2, the line representing the total endowment of young rich people has a greater slope than the line representing the total bond issue, so that no period of reckoning T is ever reached. Indeed, the rolled-over debt shrinks as a fraction of the endowment.

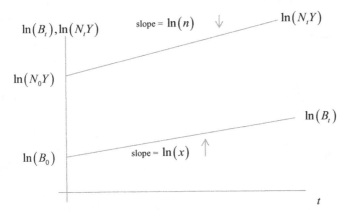

Figure 15.2. The time paths of government bond issue and the economy's endowment ($x \leq n$). When the real interest rate x is less than the growth rate of the economy, n, the total stock of government debt grows at a slower rate than that of the economy. Under these conditions, perpetual bond financing is possible because the growing economy has sufficient resources to absorb the growing quantity of bonds.

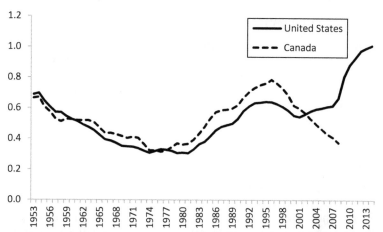

Figure 15.3. The ratio of government debt outstanding to GNP for Canada and the United States. *Sources:* The U.S. data are taken from the Federal Reserve Bank of St. Louis FRED database (http://www/stls.frb.org/fred/index.html). The Canadian data are from various issues of the *Bank of Canada Review*. The data are quarterly observations for each country. For the United States, FRED series gap was divided into FRED series *gfdebt*. For Canada, series *D20056* (GNP) was divided into Cansim series *B2400* (Government of Canada bonds outstanding).

Example 15.1 Suppose that, in addition to population growth, there is growth in the endowment of each young rich person so that $Y_t = \alpha Y_{t-1}$ where $\alpha > 1$. Graph the time path of the log of the total endowment of the rich. For which values of x, n, and α can the government roll over its debt?

From this discussion, we recognize two important facts about the feasibility of rolling over the government debt. First, we realize that the ability of a government to place its debt is related to the economy's ability to absorb it. In the first case considered, where $x > n$, we note that the amount of government debt relative to the total endowment (total gross domestic product [GDP]) of the economy rises over time. In fact, if we were to measure a debt-GNP ratio for this economy, it would go to infinity. However, in a case where $x < n$, the debt-GDP ratio would fall over time. We may then view the debt-GNP ratio as an important determinant of how large a burden that debt is for the economy. An economy with a high debt-GNP ratio would find it much more difficult to retire its debt than an economy with a low debt-GNP ratio. In light of this, we may wish to look at some data.

Figure 15.3 plots the ratio of government debt outstanding to GNP for the Canadian and U.S. economies. The debt-GDP ratios for the two economies look quite similar. Immediately after World War II, both countries had debt-GNP ratios in excess of 1 because of the large issuance of government debt to finance wartime expenditures. Although both countries display falling debt-GDP rations in the

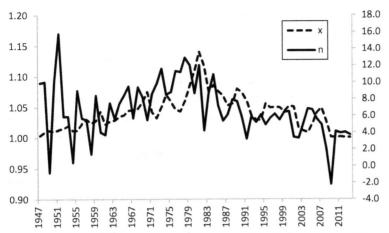

Figure 15.4. The real interest rate and the growth rate of the U.S. economy. Examination of quarterly U.S. data on real interest rate (*x*) and the growth rate of the economy (*n*) indicates a changing relationship between these two variables over time. During the Great Recession, the real interest rate was greater than the economy's growth rate, but most recently the economy growth rate has exceeded the real interest rate. *Sources:* All series are from the FRED database of the Federal Reserve Bank of St. Louis (http://www/stls.frb.org/fred/index.html). The 3-month Treasury bill nominal interest rate (FRED series tb3ms) is converted to an estimate of the real interest rate by using the GDP deflator price index (series gnpdef). See Equation 7.7 for the method of calculation. The growth rate of the economy is measured by the growth rate of real GNP (series gnpc96).

post-war period, this trend reversed during the 1980s. Since 2000, there has been a rather dramatic departure between the two countries. While Canada has continued to follow a policy in which the debt-GNP ratio has been declining, the U.S. flipped and has recorded an increase in the debt-GDP that climbed above 1 percent in 2014.

We have also seen that the feasibility of rolling over the government debt depends on the relative magnitudes of an economy's real interest rate and its growth rate.

Figure 15.4 illustrates U.S. data representing the economy's growth rate and the real interest rate.[4] Figure 15.4 shows that the two variables tend to move together. Upon closer inspection, however, we see that the relative magnitudes of *x* and *n* have shifted over time. According to the most recent observations, the growth rate of the U.S. economy has often exceeded the real interest rate. However, there are clearly time periods (e.g., the early 1980s and during the Great Recession) when the opposite is true. As we show in Chapter 17, a government that chooses to run

[4] How to calculate a real interest rate for an economy is a difficult equation, one that we are sidestepping here. Such a calculation requires the choice of a nominal interest rate and a price index from which to calculate an inflation rate. Choices of alternative interest rates or price indices would change the appearance of Figure 15.4 but would not alter the basic conclusions in the text.

large deficits may cause real interest rates to rise, a situation that tends to move the policy of perpetual deficit financing toward the realm of infeasibility.[5]

Example 15.2 Recall the model of three-period-lived people described in Chapter 8. In this model, capital paid the rate of return X, but only after two periods. All people had the same endowments – y goods when young but nothing when middle-aged and old. In every period, the population grows at the gross rate n. Assume that intermediation (or IOU issue) is costless but observable by the government and that capital creation is not observable by the government.

a. Describe how the government can earn revenue from both seigniorage and bonds in this economy. Describe in particular the form of the bonds and any legal restrictions on financial markets.
b. For what values of X can the government roll over the debt?

4 The Burden of the National Debt

When discussing government spending, it is useful to introduce the "government budget constraint." Like a person's budget constraint, the government budget constraint simply states that a government cannot use up more goods than it acquires. In Chapter 4, we derived a simple form of a government budget constraint. This constraint stated that government expenditures cannot exceed revenue obtained from seigniorage. However, in this chapter, we have introduced another source of government revenue – the issue of government bonds along with lump-sum taxes. Because of this new source of revenue, Chapter 4's government budget constraint must be revised. The new government budget constraint not only will generalize the results from our numerical examples but also will help carefully set down the choices facing the government.

4.1 The Government Budget Constraint

Bonds affect the government budget constraint in two ways. When issued, they provide a source of revenue to the government. However, when they are retired with interest, bonds represent expenditures for the government. To keep the form of the bonds simple, we assume that each government bond will be worth 1 unit of the consumption good and have a one-period maturity; a government bond issued in period t will mature and be retired in period $t + 1$. At that time, the government will repay the principal of the loan plus interest.

An example, let us find the government budget constraint for an economy in which all the people are alike (unlike the rich/poor economy discussed earlier in

---

[5] For interesting discussions of this issue, see those of Sargent and Wallace (1981), Darby (1984), and Miller and Sargent (1984). These papers present both sides of the issue regarding the feasibility of perpetual deficit financing.

this chapter). Furthermore, in this economy, both bonds and money are held; bonds are a substitute for capital but not for money (e.g., the case of reserve requirements that can be satisfied only by fiat money holdings). We denote the number of bonds issued in period t per young person as b_t and the gross real rate of return (principal plus interest) on bonds as r. The government also collects taxes from each young person. This tax per young person is denoted as τ_t. In addition, in each period, the government purchases g units of the consumption good per young person.

Revenue from the government has three possible sources – bond issue, seigniorage from printing new money, and tax collections. In the aggregate, total tax revenue in period t is $N_t\tau_t$, seigniorage revenue amounts to $v_t(M_t - M_{t-1})$, and the amount of revenue generated by bond issue is $N_t b_t$. This implies that the total government revenue from these three sources is $N_t\tau + v_t(M_t - M_{t-1}) + N_t b_t$.

On the expenditure side, the government purchases $N_t g$ units of the consumption good in period t. In the previous period $t - 1$, the government issued $N_{t-1}b_{t-1}$ bonds. These bonds mature in period t and represent an additional source of expenditures for the government. They must pay back the principal plus interest on these bonds. Hence, expenditures to retire the bonds from the previous period amount to $rN_{t-1}b_{t-1}$.

We are now ready to state the government's budget constraint. This is merely that total government expenditures equal total government revenues. In terms of our notation, the government budget constraint is

$$N_t g + rN_{t-1}b_{t-1} = N_t\tau_t + v_t(M_t - M_{t-1}) + N_t b_t. \tag{15.5}$$

If we divide through both sides of this equation by N_t, we obtain

$$g + r\left(\frac{N_{t-1}}{N_t}\right)b_{t-1} = \tau_t + \frac{v_t(M_t - M_{t-1})}{N_t} + b_t. \tag{15.6}$$

Let z_t denote the rate of expansion of the fiat money stock at time t ($M_t = z_t M_{t-1}$). Noting that $(N_{t-1}/N_t) = (1/n)$ and that $M_{t-1} = (1/z_t)M_t$, we can rewrite Equation 15.6 as

$$g + \left(\frac{r}{n}\right)b_{t-1} = \tau_t + \frac{v_t M_t}{N_t}\left(1 - \frac{1}{z_t}\right) + b_t, \tag{15.7}$$

or

$$g + \left(\frac{r}{n}\right)b_{t-1} = \tau_t + q_t\left(1 - \frac{1}{z_t}\right) + b_t, \tag{15.8}$$

where $q_t = (v_t M_t/N_t)$ is the real value of money balances per young person in period t.

4.2 The Government's Intertemporal Choice

Let us look at the government's position at the beginning of the economy. In period 1, the government's budget constraint is

$$g + \left(\frac{r}{n}\right) b_0 = \tau_1 + q_1 \left(1 - \frac{1}{z_1}\right) + b_1. \tag{15.9}$$

The term $(r/n)b_0$ represents the initial debt of the government, and b_1 represents the debt to be passed on to future generations. To simplify our analysis, suppose the government in future periods ($t > 1$) maintains the debt per young person at this level ($b = b_1$). Furthermore, the government will pursue a constant tax (τ) and seigniorage policy (with $q_t = q$ and $z_t = z$). Future taxes and seigniorage may differ from their present levels but will not change after the first period. This will let us represent the future as a stationary equilibrium that can easily be compared with the present. Then for $t > 1$, the government's budget constraint simplifies to

$$g + \left(\frac{r}{n}\right) b = \tau + q \left(1 - \frac{1}{z}\right) + b$$

$$g = \tau + q \left(1 - \frac{1}{z}\right) + b \left(1 - \frac{r}{n}\right) \quad (t > 1). \tag{15.10}$$

Note that the two government budget constraints (Equations 15.9 and 15.10) are linked in that the b_1 of Equation 15.9 is the b of Equation 15.10. In other words, the bonds that are issued in period 1 are the bonds on which interest must be paid in the future.

By looking at Equations 15.9 and 15.10, we can analyze the effects of changes in government spending decisions. Suppose the government wishes to increase government spending g in period 1 without increasing taxes or the rate of money creation in period 1. How can this be accomplished? Reference to Equation 15.9 quickly reveals the answer. Recall that the value of b_0 was determined in period 0 and is outside the government's control in period 1. In this scenario, the government chooses not to increase τ_1 or z_1. The only choice left is to increase b_1 – issue bonds in period 1 to pay for the increased government expenditures.

Recall that the b_1 of Equation 15.9 is the b of Equation 15.10. In other words, the increase in bond issuance in period 1 affects the options available to the government in subsequent periods. If $r > n$, the increase in b causes the right-hand side of Equation 15.10 to fall (because $[1 - r/n]$ is negative in this case). For equality to be maintained, something must "give" in Equation 15.10. Either τ or z or both must increase. Alternatively stated, if the government is to pursue this policy, either taxes or inflation must increase in the future.

During the 1980s, the United States experienced large budgetary deficits, financed by the issuance of government debt. This increase in debt issue led to corresponding increases in interest payments to service this debt, as illustrated in

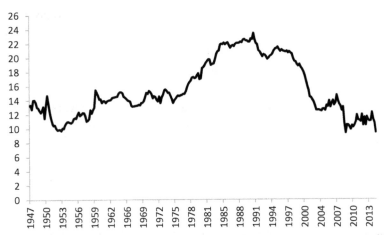

Figure 15.5. Net interest payments as a percent of total U.S. government expenditures. We see here the effect of the U.S. deficits of the 1980s on the fraction of government spending that must be devoted to paying on the national debt. We all see the effects of the surpluses during the 1990s, the wars during the first half of the 2000s. *Sources:* All series are from the FRED database of the Federal Reserve Bank of St. Louis (http://www/stls.frb.org/fred/index.html). U.S. Federal government net interest payments (FRED series afceneti) is expressed as a percentage of total U.S. federal government expenditures (series fgexpnd).

Figure 15.5. By the beginning of the 1990s, total interest payments on the debt amounted to more than 14 percent of total government expenditures. Government surpluses were recorded in the 1990s, and as Figure 15.5 shows, the interest payments began to shrink, falling more than 10 percentage points. The trend then reversed in the early 2000s. The large increase in government expenditures in 2009 actually helped account for the decline in the interest payments as a fraction of total government spending. Even with total spending increasing, low interest rates have helped to keep the ratio from trending upward since the Great Recession started.

This represents an important lesson. Government decisions made today about spending, taxation, borrowing, and money creation affect the options available for the government in the future. In this case, the decision to spend more in period 1 implies higher taxes and/or inflation in the future. If the government decides to spend more currently, it cannot expect to lower both taxes and inflation in the future. The option simply does not exist if $r > n$.

The government may have sensible reasons not explicitly modeled here to defer taxes temporarily by running a deficit even if $r > n$. It may wish to run a deficit to help out an unlucky generation burdened with a war or a recession. It may also wish to make future generations pay for durable government projects like schools and dams that benefit more than one generation. Finally, it may wish to spread over time the distortions that result from non-lump-sum taxes, such as income taxes.[6] The government budget constraint does not say that the government should never

---

[6] See Barro (1989) for a survey on deficit policy.

run a deficit; it says that (if $r > n$) lower taxes or seigniorage today imply higher taxes or seigniorage in the future. The government may rationally choose to run deficits in wartime and recessions, but the government budget constraint requires surpluses in peacetime and prosperous times. The government cannot always run deficits.

Another important lesson is that there are strong links between fiscal and monetary policy – links that cannot be ignored. Decisions about taxation (τ), spending (g), and borrowing (b) are linked through the government budget constraint to monetary policy (z). This provides a strong argument for coordination of fiscal and monetary policy.[7]

Example 15.3 Use the government budget constraints (Equations 15.9 and 15.10) to answer the following questions. In answering these questions, assume that $r > n$.

a. Suppose that every year the government runs the same deficit, $g - \tau$. If the central bank tries to reduce inflation today, what must happen to inflation in the future?
b. Suppose the central bank is very independent and has vowed never to increase the rate of monetary expansion. If the government reduces taxes today, what must happen to taxes in the future?
c. Suppose the government vows to reduce taxes forever, and at the same time the central bank vows to reduce forever the rate of expansion of the money supply. Can both promises be kept without reducing the government expenditures?

5 Open Market Operations

The institutional arrangements defining the seigniorage power of most monetary authorities in economically advanced countries are not quite as straightforward as just presented. The fiscal authority is generally not allowed to print money at will to make government purchases. The authority to print money is generally given to a central bank, which is allowed to issue money only for "open market purchases" of government debt.

The balance sheet of such a central bank is that shown in Figure 11.1 in Chapter 11 of this book, but with government debt serving as the interest-bearing asset, depicted here in Figure 15.6.

What will the effects be of an expansion of the money stock by this type of central bank? Will it be an inflation tax on money holders, as it was when we assumed that the fiscal authority could itself print money to purchase the goods it desires (Chapter 4)? Will it be completely neutral in its effects, as it was when the government printed money to purchase productive assets (Chapter 11)? To answer, we

---

[7] The costs of uncoordinated fiscal and monetary policy are described by Sargent and Wallace (1981) and Sargent (1980b).

Assets	Liabilities
Interest-bearing assets (government bonds)	Central bank money (currency and reserves)

Figure 15.6. A Central bank's balance sheet. The balance sheet for a central bank issuing money backed by government debt.

must first specify what happens to the interest earned from the assets of the central bank.

If the central bank receives interest from its assets but does not pay interest on its liabilities (money), it earns profits. In the United States and elsewhere, these profits are turned over to the government. Under this arrangement, when the central bank prints money to buy up government bonds, it has reduced the burden of the government's debt. It has "monetized" the government's debt. Any interest paid on government debt in the hands of the central bank represents a profit and so is returned to the government's treasury. An increase in the money stock remains a tax on those holding money (seigniorage): wealth is transferred from money holders to the government.

The only difference is that seigniorage from open market operations provides government revenue in the future instead of in the present, because the government uses the expansion of the money stock to buy up assets (reducing the debt on which it must pay interest) rather than to buy current goods. Therefore, if the government does not pay interest on money, we may think of an open market purchase as the combination of two policy actions – the taxation of money balances and the purchase of assets by the government. Remember that, although the central bank carries these assets on its books, the assets are effectively owned by the government because the interest from these assets is turned over to the government (after the central bank expenses). Recalling the government budget constraints for $t = 1$ and $t > 1$,

$$g + \left[\frac{r}{n}\right] b_0 = \tau_1 + q_1 \left[1 - \frac{1}{z_1}\right] + b_1, \qquad (15.11)$$

$$g + \left[\frac{r}{n} - 1\right] b = \tau + q \left[1 - \frac{1}{z}\right] \quad (t > 1). \qquad (15.12)$$

We see from Equation 15.11 that for a given demand for money, q, an increase in the fiat money stock in the first period (an increase in z_1 above) is used to reduce the real debt that must be financed in the future, $b_1 = b$. If $r > n$, this reduction in b reduces the interest that must be paid to finance the debt $[(r/n) - 1]b$ in all future periods in a stationary equilibrium. As a result, in the future, government expenditures may be increased or taxes may be decreased.

Seigniorage that is used to buy goods directly (as we studied in Chapter 4) allows the government to increase government expenditures or reduce taxes in the current period. Therefore, open market operations change only the timing of these effects. Moreover, if a government can count on the central bank to monetize its debt, it can issue debt to increase expenditures or reduce taxes. The net effect of this combination of issuing debt and monetizing it is exactly that of simply printing money to buy goods for the government: the government acquires goods in the current period at the expense of those holding money balances. Although a veneer of respectability may be added by restricting the central bank to open market operations, if the central bank earns profits from its portfolio of government debt and returns them to the government's treasury, the revenue effects of open market operations are essentially the same as those of expanding the money stock to buy goods.

(In Chapter 11 we worked out the implication of monetary expansions if the central bank takes the interest it earns and uses it in turn to pay interest to those who hold its money. In this case, central bank money is a perfect substitute for inside money in the portfolios of money holders. Increases in central bank money then simply cause people to reduce their holdings of inside money to keep their total money balances the same. Specifying that government debt is the interest-bearing asset backing central bank money does nothing to change this analysis.)

6 Political Strategy and the National Debt

We have seen that the decisions a government makes today with regard to fiscal and monetary policies affect the options available for those policies in the future. Could a politician exploit this fact to detrimentally alter the options available for a political party that may come into power in the future?[8]

To answer this question, let's consider an example. For simplicity, assume that the population is constant. Suppose a government faces the following constraints on its ability to raise revenue: in each period, the most the government can raise through all taxes, including seigniorage is 1,000,000 goods. Also assume that the maximum real government debt that the fixed population can willingly hold, given the limitations of their endowments, is 950,000 goods. Government debt pays a real rate of return of 1.2. In period 1, government expenditures are equal to 900,000 goods. Finally, suppose no debt was issued in the previous period ($B_0 = b_0 = 0$).

The current leaders of the government detest government expenditures but know they will not be in power in the next period. Let's see how they can use their power over current taxes and government debt to force their successors to reduce government expenditures.

The government budget constraint facing the current leaders in period 1 is

$$Ng_1 + rNb_0 = N\tau_1 + v_1[M_1 - M_0] + Nb_1$$

---

[8]   See Persson and Svensson (1989) for a more complete discussion of this topic.

or

$$Ng_1 = N\tau_1 + v_1[M_1 - M_0] + Nb_1 \quad \text{(because } b_0 = 0\text{).} \qquad (15.13)$$

According to our assumptions, current government expenditures are $Ng_1 = 900,000$. To severely limit the next government's options, the current leaders choose to raise no revenue from taxes or seigniorage. In other words, they choose to finance the entire amount of government expenditures through issuing debt. From Equation 15.13, with $N\tau_1 + v_1[M_1 - M_0] = 0$, we see that the total amount of debt that must be issued is

$$900,000 = Nb_1, \qquad (15.14)$$

which is sustainable because it is less than the maximum the public is willing to hold. The current leaders have forced the next leaders to inherit government debt, which must be repaid with interest.

Now let us see the options this implies for the new leaders who take power in period 2. We know that if these leaders do nothing about the outstanding debt, it will grow at the rate r. We also know that if $r > n = 1$, which is the case in this example, the government cannot permanently roll over the debt.

The government budget constraint in period 2 is

$$Ng_2 + rNb_1 = N\tau_2 + v_2[M_2 - M_1] + Nb_2. \qquad (15.15)$$

Substituting $r = 1.2$ and $Nb_1 = 900,000$ into Equation 15.15, we obtain

$$Ng_2 + (1.2)(900,000) = N\tau_2 + v_2[M_2 - M_1] + Nb_2$$

$$Ng_2 + 1,080,000 = N\tau_2 + v_2[M_2 - M_1] + Nb_2. \qquad (15.16)$$

If leaders in period 2 choose to raise revenue from seigniorage and taxes up to the maximum, Equation 15.16 becomes

$$Ng_2 + 1,080,000 = 1,000,000 + Nb_2. \qquad (15.17)$$

We also assumed that the maximum amount of government debt the public desires to hold is 950,000 goods. If these leaders choose to issue debt equal to that amount, we see from Equation 15.17 that

$$Ng_2 + 1,080,000 = 1,000,000 + 950,000$$

$$Ng_2 = 870,000. \qquad (15.18)$$

We see that the old leaders have forced the new leaders to reduce government purchases from their period 1 level of 900,000 to 870,000. If the leaders had not chosen to raise taxes or issue debt up to the maximum amounts, government expenditures would have had to be reduced even further.

The political ramifications of this example are clear. The expense of the interest payments on government debt forced the new leaders to lower government expenditures, regardless of what they normally would have wanted to do. In this way, the old leaders were able to force the new leaders to choose a lower level of government expenditures, as the old leaders desired. Of course, future leaders will inherit the debt that the leaders in period 2 issue. This will limit the choices that are available to them in a similar manner.

7 Summary

We began this chapter by noting that there are significant rate-of-return differences between government bonds and fiat money. Chapter 8 investigated one possible explanation for rate of return differentials – the liquidity advantage of fiat money over other assets. The model of this chapter focused on the large denominations of government bonds as the source of their illiquidity. We found that the government may wish to issue illiquid bonds as a substitute for capital but not fiat money. In this way, the government is able to raise revenue from both seigniorage and the issuance of debt.

Another important topic of this chapter was the feasibility of perpetual debt financing, often referred to as rolling over the debt. On the one hand, we found that, if the real interest rate paid on government debt exceeds the growth rate of the economy, perpetual debt financing is infeasible. In such a case, the ever-expanding volume of government bonds would outstrip the economy's limited ability to absorb them. On the other hand, we found that perpetual debt financing is possible when the real interest rate is less than the growth rate of the economy.

This chapter took a detailed look at how the presence of government debt alters the government budget constraint. We found that issuing government debt today changes the options available to the government tomorrow. If perpetual debt financing is infeasible, an increase in the government's debt forces an eventual decrease in government expenditures or increase in future taxation.

One of the taxation options is to monetize the debt. When the central bank does not pay interest to the holders of its money, it earns profits that are handed back to the fiscal authority (Treasury). In this case, the net effect of the two steps of printing bonds to cover government expenditures and then monetizing the bonds is exactly the same as having the government simply print money to pay for the expenditures without bothering to issue bonds.

8 Exercises

15.1. Assume that the maximum revenue that can be collected from all taxes, including seigniorage, is 5,000 goods and that the maximum debt is 6,000 goods. The real gross market rate of return is 1.2. Government expenditures currently equal 4,500 goods.

The current leaders of the country detest government expenditures but know they will not be in power next period. How can these leaders use their control over current taxes, subsidies, and the government debt to force their successors to reduce steady-state government expenditures below 4,500 goods? Use the government budget constraint in giving your answer.

15.2. Consider an overlapping generations economy in which capital pays a 25 percent net rate of return. The population of a generation grows by 10 percent each period. In the initial period (period 1), there are 100 people and a preexisting fiat money stock of $M_0 = \$1$ million. Because of a political impasse, government expenditures exceed (nonseigniorage) tax revenues by 50 goods per young person in every period. Each young person wishes to hold real money balances worth 200 goods regardless of the rate of inflation.[9]

a. Use the government budget constraint to find the rate of fiat money creation that is required to finance the excess of government expenditures over taxes. Find also the fiat money stock and the price level in periods 1 and 2.

b. Suppose that, in the initial period, the monetary authority hesitates to print new money, forcing the government to issue debt at the market rate of interest. In the second period, the monetary authority relents, printing enough new money to pay off the debt as well as to pay for the second period's excess of government expenditures over taxes. Find the fiat money stock in period 2 and compare it with your answers in part a. Explain the difference.

c. Suppose that, in the initial period, you anticipate the actions of the monetary authority described in part b. What rate of inflation do you expect? If (contrary to our assumption) anticipated inflation discourages the use of fiat money, why will the price level rise in period 1 even though no fiat money is printed?

15.3. Suppose there are 100 young rich people born in every period. Government debt and capital both pay real net rates of return equal to 25 percent. The fiat money stock is fixed. Each young rich person wishes to save 50 goods in each period. In period 0, the government issues a total amount of real government debt equal to 2,000 goods. The government attempts to roll over this initial debt in subsequent periods.

a. What are the real holdings of capital and bonds of each young rich person in period 0 and in period 1?

b. In what period does it become impossible for the government to continue to roll over its debt?

c. Now suppose the number of young rich people born in each period grows at the net rate of 10 percent. There are 100 young rich people born in period 0. Recalculate your answer to part b. Explain the difference in your answer.

15.4. Suppose the economy starts with zero outstanding government bonds. Let government expenditures be 100,000 goods per young person each period. Neither taxes nor seigniorage are used in periods 1 and 2. So the entire amount of government expenditures is financed through issuing debt.

---

[9] This exercise illustrates an idea presented by Sargent and Wallace (1981).

    a. Let $r = 1.2$. Write down the government budget constraint, in per-young-person terms, in periods 2 and 3, solving the outstanding quantity of government bonds in periods 1 and 2.

    b. What would taxes per young person have to be in period 3 if only taxes are used to pay for government expenditures and for interest on bonds?

    c. What would seigniorage have to be, per young person, if only seigniorage were used to pay for government expenditures and for interest on government bonds?

15.5. For a stationary economy, suppose the gross real interest rate on government bonds is equal to the population growth rate; that is, $r = n$. Assume that the government purchases 1,000 goods per young person. The outstanding stock of government debt is equal to 250 goods per young person. Taxes are used to pay for government expenditures.

    a. What would taxes, per young person, be in this economy?

    b. At some date t in the future, suppose $r = 2n$. Assume the change in the interest rate is permanent. If taxes stay constant, compute the amount of seigniorage that would be necessary to meet the government interest payments in date $t + 1$. (Assume the demand for real money balances per young person is always 100 goods.)

    c. Using your answer from part b, what would the money growth rate need to be the following period.

Chapter 16

Savings and Investment

1 Roadmap

In earlier chapters, we used the overlapping generations model as a model of money. People needed money, whether fiat, commodity, or inside money, to acquire a market good. We did not interpret this good literally as consumption in old age, because money balances are a trivial source of savings for retirement. We used the overlapping generations structure as a simple way to model exchange without taking the age of the model's people very seriously.

In this chapter, we use the age structure of the overlapping generations model more seriously as we turn to studying the factors that determine aggregate saving and investment. By doing so, we focus our analysis on government bonds and capital. These two stores of value are important parts of people's lifetime savings.

In this chapter, we analyze the basic consumption-saving decision from the perspective of real goods and services. By focusing on the real side of the economy, we can look at the myriad events that occur over a person's lifetime and how these changes affect consumption-saving outcomes. We can include taxes as a means of affecting after-tax wealth. With the age profile structure in the overlapping generations economy, it is straightforward to analyze whether changes in the timing of tax collections affect consumption and saving behavior or affect lifetime welfare.

One way that is particularly interesting is when the government offers a pension program to provide resources for old-age consumption. Pensions can be funded by having young people taxes as a kind of forced saving. The other way is to tax current young people to pay for consumption by current old people, also known as a pay-as-you-go scheme.

2 The Savings Decision

Let us look now at how individuals choose their level of savings. We do this in the context of the overlapping generations model of two-period-lived people who

321

must choose how much to consume when young and when old. In one particular way, we consider a more general setting in which have endowments of y_1 goods when young and y_2 goods when old. We may think of the endowments as labor income. We assume that young people face a gross real interest rate, r, and choose accordingly the number of goods they wish to save, s_t.

We now can describe the budget of someone born at t. When young, this person has y_1 goods from her labor, which she can either consume or save. We express the individual's budget constraint when young as

$$c_{1,t} + s_t \leq y_1. \tag{16.1}$$

When old, she can consume both her old-age endowment/labor income and the return (principal and interest) from her saving, implying the following old-age budget constraint:

$$c_{2,t+1} \leq y_2 + rs_t. \tag{16.2}$$

Solving Equation 16.2 for s_t and substituting into Equation 16.1, we find the lifetime budget set:

$$c_{1,t} + \frac{c_{2,t+1}}{r} \leq y_1 + \frac{y_2}{r}. \tag{16.3}$$

This budget set is graphed in Figure 16.1. Note that the budget line goes through the point (y_1, y_2) because individuals could always choose merely to consume their endowment in each period and zero savings.

For a given budget, the savings s^* that allows the highest utility (reaches the highest possible indifference curve) is found where the line defining the budget set is just tangent to an indifference curve. As shown in the diagram, the utility-maximizing choice of savings satisfies $s^* = y_1 - c_1^*$. It should be noted that the relative positions of c_1^* and y_1 depend on individual preferences. As drawn, $s^* = y_1 - c_1^*$ is positive. With a different set of preferences, the indifference curve could be tangent to the budget line so that c_1^* would lie to the right of y_1, implying a negative value for savings. Try drawing such a diagram on your own. We interpret a situation of negative savings later in the chapter.

2.1 Wealth

Note from Equations 16.1 and 16.2 that without saving ($s_t = 0$), an individual's consumption in each period would be completely determined by her current "income" (her endowment). Saving allows a person to choose a combination of consumption constrained only by her "wealth," a measure of her income over her entire lifetime $y_1 + y_2/r$.

Note that an individual's wealth is not simply the sum of income in both periods of life. Income in the second period of life is divided by the interest rate. To explain

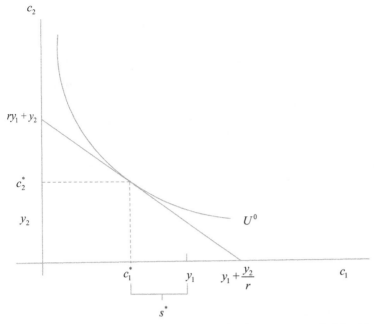

Figure 16.1. The savings choice. A person endowed when young and old, able to save at the real interest rate, r, faces the lifetime budget line portrayed here. The level of savings, S^*, is determined by the difference between the person's first-period endowment and the utility-maximizing choice of first-period consumption.

why income in the second period of life is treated differently from income in the first period of life in the determination of wealth, we must understand the concept of present value.

2.2 Present Value

Is the value of goods independent of time? Would you rather own 10 goods today or 10 goods in the future? To answer this question, suppose you have 10 goods today. You can transform these current goods into future goods by saving them. If saving pays a positive net real interest rate (gross rate r greater than 1), 10 goods saved today will yield more than 10 goods in the future. In this way, 10 goods today are more valuable than 10 goods in the future.

The analysis applies also to the problem of a borrower. If the individual borrows 100 units of the good and r equals 1.10, $(1.10)(100) = 110$ units of the goods will be repaid in the following period. In other words, given this interest rate and our scheme of borrowing, 100 units of the good today are worth 110 units of the good tomorrow.

Now reverse the direction of this analysis. If an individual is to repay 110 units of the good next period, what is the amount that must be borrowed? The answer, of course, is 100. This is obvious in this simple example, but it is useful to realize how it is derived. The 100 is obtained by taking 110 and dividing it by the gross real interest rate to obtain $110/r = 110/1.10 = 100$. The 100 units of the good obtained today via the loan is often termed the "present value" of the loan. Correspondingly, the 100 units representing the loan repayment in the *next* period is called the "future value" of the loan. The two concepts of value in this simple example of a one-period loan are related by

$$\text{present value} = \frac{\text{future value}}{r}. \tag{16.4}$$

Alternatively, we could write the relationship as

$$\text{future value} = r(\text{present value}). \tag{16.5}$$

In many of our model economies, people live for only two periods, so the simple version of the concept of present value just presented is adequate. Here, loans are made only over a one-period horizon.

However, what if a loan is made for a larger number of periods? Assume that a person who lives for three periods borrows 100 units of the consumption good at a one-period gross interest rate of $r = 1.10$. In the following period, the loan must be repaid and the total repayment, as before, is 110 units of the good. Suppose the person borrows 110 units at the same interest rate to repay the first loan. What is the total loan repayment in the following (third) period? It is, of course, $(1.10)(110) = 121$. Note that this amount is $(r)(r)(100) = (r^2)100$. Alternatively stated, the present value of the loan (100) is the future value (121) divided by r raised to the number of periods over which the loan ex10ds. In general, we can write that

$$\text{present value} = \frac{\text{future value}}{r^T} \tag{16.6}$$

or

$$\text{future value} = r^T(\text{present value}), \tag{16.7}$$

where T represents the number of periods that transpire before the loan is repaid or matures (often called the "duration" of the loan). In general, to convert a future value to a present value, we say that we "discount" the future value by a discount factor (r^T). Note that Equations 16.6 and 16.7 are consistent with Equations 16.4 and 16.5 because, in those equations, T was equal to 1.

Armed with our knowledge of the concept of present value, we can now understand the presence of r in the lifetime budget constraint. Look again at the lifetime budget constraint (Equation 16.3)

$$c_{1,t} + \frac{c_{2,t+1}}{r} \le y_1 + \frac{y_2}{r}. \tag{16.8}$$

The terms divided by r are y_2 and $c_{2,t+1}$. Because the old-age consumption and endowment occur one period in the future, we must discount by $r^1 = r$ to convert them into a present value. Because $c_{1,t}$ and y_1 occur in the first period of life, they are already present values and there is no need to discount them.[1]

Because all variables are now expressed in present value terms, we call the left-hand side of Equation 16.8 the present value of a person's lifetime consumption. The right-hand side of Equation 16.8 is the present value of her lifetime endowment. We refer to the present value of lifetime endowments as a person's measure of wealth, or simply her **wealth**.[2] We denote the wealth of a person born at t as w_t.

$$w_t = y_1 + \frac{y_2}{r}. \tag{16.9}$$

Example 16.1 Suppose a three-period-lived person is constrained to receive an endowment in only one period of her life. She may choose between receiving 90 goods when young and 100 goods when middle-aged or 115 when old. Which will she choose if the net real interest rate is 10 percent? If the net real interest rate is 20 percent? *Hint*: Generalize the definition of wealth in Equation 16.9 to three periods.

2.3 Wealth and Consumption

If we apply our definition of wealth to the lifetime budget constraint graphed in Figure 16.1, we find that a person's consumption bundle will be entirely determined by her wealth w_t and the interest rate r. Let us now ask how her consumption bundle will respond to an increase in her wealth. An increase in a person's wealth enables her to consume more over her lifetime. The breakdown of this extra consumption depends on her relative preferences for consumption when young and when old.

If a person responds to an increase in wealth by consuming less of a certain good, we say that the good is an "inferior good." Hamburger and bus transportation may be examples of inferior goods. When our wealth rises, we buy fewer of these items and replace them with steak and sports cars.

Consumption when young and consumption when old do not seem likely to be inferior goods. We expect a person faced with an increase in wealth to consume more when young and when old. Goods whose consumption rises with wealth are called "normal goods." We assume that consumption when young and consumption when old are both normal goods. An increase in wealth induces a person to increase both c_1 and c_2, as illustrated in Figure 16.2. We see from Figure 16.2 that when people may freely choose their level of saving, the consumption pattern they choose depends uniquely on their wealth and the interest rate. In particular, note that for a

---

[1] The astute student may very well ask: Why have we waited until this chapter to worry about the discounting of quantities that occur in the future? In fact, we have been appropriately discounting all along. For example, in Chapter 1, the only asset available was fiat money, and people were endowed only when young. In that chapter, the lifetime budget constraint was $c_{1,t} + (v_t/v_{t+1})c_{2,t+1} = y$. There we discounted the future value of $c_{2,t+1}$ by the rate of return of fiat money v_{t+1}/v_t.

[2] The true measure of an individual's wealth is utility she can afford, but we need a measure of wealth denominated in goods.

Table 16.1. *Endowment combinations for which wealth is 100 (when $r = 1.1$). So, for Combination C, income when young is 70 and income when old is 33 so that lifetime income or wealth is 100. Formally, $70 + \frac{33}{1.1} = 100$.*

Combination	y_1	y_2	Wealth $= y_1 + \frac{y_2}{r}$
A	50	55	100
B	100	0	100
C	70	33	100
D	0	110	100

given level of wealth, the consumption pattern chosen does not depend on when that wealth is received. Suppose, for example, that a person's wealth is 100 goods and the real (gross) interest rate is 1.1. Many different combinations of the endowments y_1 and y_2 are consistent with this wealth of 100 goods. Four such combinations are given in Table 16.1.

In all four combinations listed in Table 16.1, wealth is the same. Thus, people will choose the same consumption bundle, (c_1^*, c_2^*) based on the level of lifetime wealth. It does not matter when the income is received, but the present value of that income since we assume that a person can borrow or lend freely. In each of the four cases, the lifetime budget set would be the same. It is important therefore to

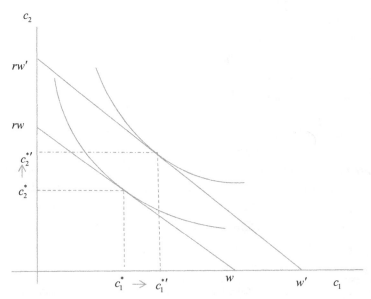

Figure 16.2. The effect of an increase in wealth on lifetime consumption. When a person's wealth increases from w to w', the lifetime budget constraint shifts to the right. Assuming that c_1 and c_2 are normal goods, consumption increases in both periods of life.

distinguish between income and wealth. "Income" represents the goods a person produces or receives in any single period. In contrast, wealth is the present value of a person's lifetime income stream. Wealth can be measured at a point in time whereas income is measured over a unit of time.[3] It is wealth, not income, that determines consumption.

Example 16.2 Suppose a three-period-lived person is constrained to receive an endowment in only one period of her life. She may receive 95 goods when young, 100 goods when middle-aged, or 105 when old. Assume that the net real interest rate is 10 percent and that all goods are normal goods. For which endowment will she consume the most when middle-aged?

2.4 Income and Saving

What happens if a person's income in some period is not sufficient to support her desired consumption in that period? She can adjust her savings to allow her consumption to exceed her income in that period.

Suppose, for example, that when the net real interest rate is 10 percent ($r = 1.1$) and a person's wealth equals 100 goods (in present value terms), she receives the highest utility by consuming 50 goods when young and 55 goods when old. (Check that this consumption bundle satisfies the person's lifetime budget constraint [Equation 16.8].) Note that all four endowment patterns of Table 16.1, despite their very different timing, represent wealth of 100 goods. It follows that an individual with any of the four endowment patterns will wish to consume 50 goods when young and 55 goods when old. How can the person arrange this consumption pattern?

If a person has the endowment pattern A in Table 16.1, she can simply consume her endowments as they arrive. What if, however, she has endowment pattern B, where y_1 is 100 and y_2 is 0? Her endowment income exceeds her desired consumption when young and is less than her desired consumption when old. How does she reconcile her income with her consumption? She simply saves 50 goods when young, which, when she is old will yield the 55 goods she wishes to consume. (Recall that a person's budget when young is $s_1 = y_1 - c_1$, which in this case equals $100 - 50$.) A person with endowment pattern C ($y_1 = 70$, $y_2 = 33$) will save only 20 goods to arrive at the desired consumption pattern ($s_t = 70 - 50$). Note that the level of savings adjusts to the level of income when young to achieve the desired consumption bundle. Consumption does not adjust to income; it is determined by wealth (and the interest rate).

Consider finally the endowment pattern D ($y_1 = 0$, $y_2 = 110$), in which the person has an endowment only when old. In this case, using the young person's budget

---

[3] Because wealth can be measured at a particular instant, it is referred to as a "stock variable." Alternatively, things that are measured over an interval of time, like income, are called "flow variables."

Table 16.2. *Consumption and saving when wealth is 100 and* $r = 1.1$. *To illustrate how the table works, consider the third row, Combination C. Here income when young is 70. The person wishes to consume 50 goods when young, so saving is the difference between income when young and consumption when young. In Combination C, a young person saves 20 goods. In the fifth column, we compute old-age consumption. If the person receives 70 goods when young, we know from Table 16.1 that old-age income is 33 goods, which is* $1.1 \times (100 - 70) = 33$. *So, old-age consumption is* $(1.1 \times 20) + 33$.

Combination	y_1	c_1	$s = y_1 - c_1$	$c_2 = rs + y_2$
A	50	50	0	55
B	100	50	50	55
C	70	50	20	55
D	0	50	−50	55

constraint, $s_t = y_1 - c_1$, suggests that saving must be equal to −50 to arrive at the desired consumption bundle. Can a person save a negative number of goods? Yes, if she borrows.[4] Borrowing 50 goods is the same as saving −50 goods (sometimes referred to as "dissaving"). Table 16.2 summarizes the behavior of saving for the endowment patterns listed in Table 16.1.

At this point, let us summarize what we have learned about the determination of consumption and saving.

1. Consumption is determined by wealth. In particular, an increase in wealth brings about an increase in consumption in each period of life (assuming normal goods).
2. Saving adjusts to income. The saving of the young will equal the difference between their current income and their desired consumption.

3 The Effects of Taxes on Consumption and Savings

Let us now apply these lessons to study the effects of some tax policies on consumption and savings. To focus on the effects of taxes on savings, we will look only at two lump-sum taxes – a tax of τ_1 goods on each young person and a tax of τ_2 goods on each old person.

To see how these taxes affect a person's wealth, let us incorporate them into her budget constraints:

$$c_{1,t} + s_t \leq y_1 - \tau_1, \tag{16.10}$$

$$c_{2,t+1} \leq y_2 - \tau_2 + rs_t. \tag{16.11}$$

---

[4] Although an individual can save a negative amount by borrowing, the economy as a whole cannot do so because an individual can borrow (save a negative amount) only from another individual willing to lend (save a positive amount).

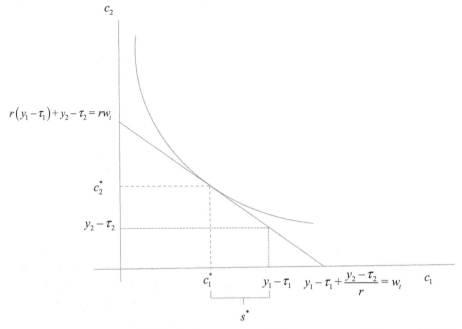

Figure 16.3. The savings decision in the presence of lump-sum taxes. When an individual is subject to lump-sum taxes in both periods of life, the lifetime budget constraint is as shown in the diagram. The lifetime consumption pattern is determined by preferences, the real interest rate, and the present value of the after-tax income stream.

Solving Equation 16.11 for s_t and substituting in Equation 16.10, we find the lifetime budget set represented in the following equation and graphed in Figure 16.3:

$$c_{1,t} + \frac{c_{2,t+1}}{r} \leq y_1 - \tau_1 + \frac{y_2 - \tau_2}{r} \equiv w_t. \qquad (16.12)$$

The right-hand side of Equation 16.12 represents the present value of a taxpayer's *after-tax* endowments. This is the limit on the present value of the taxpayer's (private) consumption (the left-hand side of Equation 16.12) and thus the true measure of the taxpayer's (private) wealth.[5] Note that taxes paid when old are future values and therefore are discounted by the gross interest rate (r).

3.1 Wealth-Neutral Tax Changes

We would like to analyze the effect of taxes on personal decisions about consumption and saving. Consider first changes in taxes that do not affect a taxpayer's wealth.

---

[5] We insert the adjective *private* here to emphasize that we are ignoring any benefits the individual may receive from government expenditures paid from tax revenues.

Let τ_1^* and τ_2^* represent the initial taxes on the young and old, respectively. Now suppose we increase the taxes on the young by 10 (to $\tau_1^* + 10$) but decrease the taxes on the old by $10r$ (to $\tau_2^* - 10r$).

Has this change in taxes affected the taxpayer's wealth? To find out, let us substitute the new level of taxes into the measure of wealth defined in Equation 16.12:

$$y_1 - \tau_1 + \frac{y_2 - \tau_2}{r} = y_1 - (\tau_1^* + 10) + \frac{y_2 - (\tau_2^* - 10r)}{r}$$

$$= y_1 - \tau_1^* - 10 + \frac{y_2 - \tau_2^*}{r} + \frac{10r}{r}$$

$$= y_1 - \tau_1^* + \frac{y_2 - \tau_2^*}{r}. \tag{16.13}$$

We see from Equation 16.13 that the taxpayer's wealth has not changed. In present-value terms, the decrease in taxes paid when old exactly offsets the increase in taxes paid when young. Because this tax change did not affect the taxpayer's wealth, her desired consumption combination will also be unaffected by the change. A person's consumption is determined by the present value of her lifetime taxes but not by the timing of those taxes. In this case, the present value of lifetime taxes has not changed. This is analogous to the earlier result that a person's consumption pattern is not affected by the timing of the endowments.

Note that the taxpayer's after-tax income when young has fallen by 10. What then happens to the savings of a young person? Look at the budget constraint of the young (Equation 16.10). She can maintain the same consumption when young only if she reduces her savings by 10 to offset the tax increase. How will this affect her when old? Look at the budget constraint of the old (Equation 16.11): her income from savings will fall by $10r$, but that is exactly the amount by which her taxes are reduced, leaving her consumption when old unchanged.

3.2 Wealth Effects

Suppose our taxpayer now faces an increase in taxes when young without an offsetting tax decrease when old. How will this affect consumption and saving? As always, we first determine her desired consumption, then look back at how she can save to achieve this consumption.

The rise in the taxpayer's lifetime tax burden reduces her wealth. As a result, she must consume less over her lifetime. If, as we assume, consumption in each period of life is a normal good, she will spread the reduction in consumption over her entire life; that is, she will consume less in each period of life.

How must her saving adapt to these changes? The taxpayer wishes to reduce consumption in both periods of life, but her income has fallen only in the first period of life. To reduce her consumption when old, she must reduce her savings.

In this way, young people split their reduction in income between consumption and savings.

4 Social Security

With its generational structure, this model of saving and investment is well equipped to address one of the more important issues of the day: the effects of government-run pension plans, such as the U.S. social security system or the social insurance program of Canada.

A hotly debated policy issue involves the structure of old-age pension programs. In the United States, the question is what to do with Social Security, which promises payments to people after they reach a certain age. There are two types of funding approaches. A fully funded approach taxes young people, stores them on their behalf and uses the proceeds to make payments to people when old. Fully funded programs are similar to a kind of government-sponsored, or forced, saving. Alternatively, a pay-as-you-go approach collects taxes from young people and uses the proceeds to make payments to current old people. The United States' Social Security is an example of a pay-as-you-go plan. We analyze the effects of each plan.

4.1 Fully Funded Government Pensions

A "fully funded" pension plan pays a pension to old people financed by the forced contributions they paid when young. We represent this plan in our model as a tax of τ goods on each young person to pay a pension of σ goods when she is old. The plan is considered fully funded, because payments of the young are saved at the market rate of return r and then used to finance the pensions of the same people who made the payments. For simplicity, we assume that there are no other sources of government revenue or other government expenditures. This is represented by the following government budget constraint:

$$N_t \tau r = N_t \sigma \quad \Rightarrow \quad \tau r = \sigma. \tag{16.14}$$

The budget constraints of a person when young and old, respectively, are

$$c_{1,t} + s_t \leq y_1 - \tau \tag{16.15}$$

$$c_{2,t+1} \leq y_2 + r s_t + \sigma. \tag{16.16}$$

If s_t is free to take any value, positive or negative (negative savings representing borrowing), we can solve Equation 16.16 for s_t and substitute into Equation 16.15 to find the lifetime budget set:

$$c_{1,t} + \frac{c_{2,t+1}}{r} \leq y_1 + \frac{y_2}{r} - \tau + \frac{\sigma}{r}. \tag{16.17}$$

The right-hand side of Equation 16.17 is the person's wealth in the presence of the fully funded social security plan.

From the government budget constraint (Equation 16.14), we know that $\sigma = \tau r$, implying that wealth

$$y_1 + \frac{y_2}{r} - \tau + \frac{\sigma}{r} = \frac{y_2}{r} - \tau + \frac{r\tau}{r} = \frac{y_2}{r} \tag{16.18}$$

is unchanged by the government pension plan. Because wealth is unchanged, people are free to choose the same consumption combination they would have chosen without the government's pension plan. The government's pension plan has no effect on people's consumption and welfare.

What is the reaction of saving to this fully funded pension plan? If the government increases the tax contributions of the young from 0 to some positive number τ, how can the person still reach her desired consumption pattern? Look at the budget constraints (Equations 16.14 and 16.15). To keep consumption when young unchanged, savings must fall by τ, reducing the returns from saving by $r\tau$ when old. But this reduction of the returns from saving exactly matches the increased income when old from the government pension, leaving consumption when old also unchanged. The effect of the government's pension plan is illustrated in Figure 16.4. The government here is acting like a private pension. Therefore, when the government tells people to increase their contributions to the government plan, people can still arrive at their desired consumption pattern by reducing their voluntary contributions to their private pension plans (in our notation, by reducing s). In this way, a fully funded pension plan merely causes a shift from one pension plan to another, this one run by the government. If both offer the same rate of return, people really don't care which plan manages their pensions, only the total matters.

4.2 Pay-as-You-Go Pensions

An alternative way to finance government pensions to those who are old in period t is to tax those who are young in that period, a "pay-as-you-go" system. The government undertakes no investment on behalf of the old, relying instead on intergenerational transfers, as depicted in Figure 16.5.

The government budget constraint under a pay-as-you-go system requires that the total subsidies paid to the old in each period t equal the total taxes paid by the young at t:

$$N_{t-1}\sigma = N_t \tau \tag{16.19}$$

or

$$\sigma = \frac{N_t}{N_{t-1}}\tau = n\tau. \tag{16.20}$$

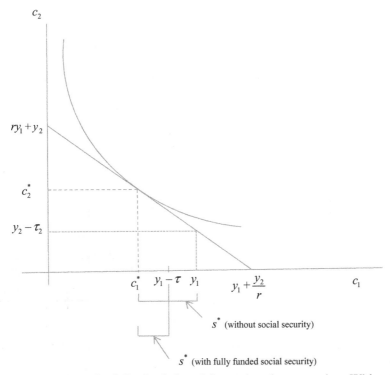

Figure 16.4. The effect of a fully funded social security plan on saving. Without a social security plan, the person's choice of saving is determined by the gap between the first-period endowment, y_1, and the person's first-period consumption choice, c_1^*. This level of saving is represented by s^* in the diagram. As we have seen, personal wealth and choice of consumption are identical under a fully funded social security plan. However, from the person's first-period budget constraint (Equation 16.15), saving under the social security plan is different between the after-tax endowment and first-period consumption. This lower level of saving is denoted by $s^{*\prime}$ in the diagram.

Note from the government budget constraint (Equation 16.20) that a growing population ($n > 1$) implies that there are more young people than old, so that each of the old can receive more for any given tax paid by each young person. The total tax paid by the young is spread over a smaller number of old people.

Substituting this new government budget constraint (Equation 16.20) into the person's wealth as found in the lifetime budget constraint (Equation 16.17), we find

$$y_1 + \frac{y_2}{r} - \tau + \frac{\sigma}{r} = y_1 + \frac{y_2}{r} - \tau + \frac{n\tau}{r} = y_1 + \frac{y_2}{r} + \left[\frac{n}{r} - 1\right]\tau. \quad (16.21)$$

Do future generations like a pay-as-you-go system? From Equation 16.21, we see that a pay-as-you-go system increases the wealth of future generations only if $n > r$; in that case, the last term in Equation 16.21 is positive and, hence, adds to personal wealth. If $n < r$, why don't the future generations like pay-as-you-go government pensions? To understand, suppose the young were allowed to opt out of

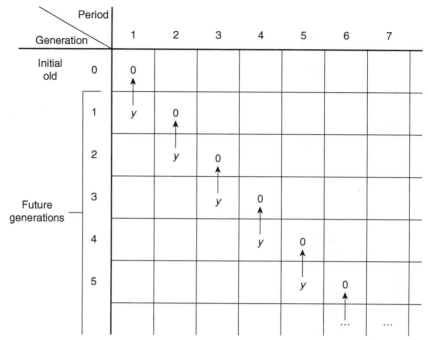

Figure 16.5. A pay-as-you-go social security system. Arrows depict intergenerational transfers in a pay-as-you-go government pension plan.

the plan, eliminating both their tax contributions and their benefits. If a young person then invested what she would have contributed in taxes (τ), she would receive a return of $r\tau$ from her investment while losing $n\tau$ in benefits. Clearly, she is better off investing on her own if $r > n$, and she is worse off if $n > r$.

So who would object if the government allowed young people to opt out of a pay-as-you-go government pension system? The current old, those who are old when the pay-as-you-go system is dropped. Whether or not these people made payments when they were young themselves, they favor the largest possible pay-as-you-go transfers from this point forward because the days of their contributions (if any) are in the past.

5 Summary

In this chapter, we have taken the age structure of the overlapping generations model more literally to study economic decisions related to saving and investment. Our goal was to understand the factors that influence those variables.

On the one hand, we found that wealth – the present value of the lifetime income stream – is an important determinant of consumption. An increase in wealth generates higher levels of consumption in both periods of life. On the other hand, savings responds to income. A shift of income from one period to another does not alter consumption but does alter savings.

We also explored the effects of taxes on consumption and savings. A change in the timing of taxes that leaves wealth unaltered has no impact on the lifetime consumption pattern. Savings adjusts in order to maintain consumption. However, tax changes that cause changes in wealth generate changes in savings and consumption. These results will prove to have important implications with respect to the economic effects of government debt issue, a topic we take up in Chapter 17.

6 Exercises

16.1. Consider an increase in the lump-sum taxes paid by old people. Find its effect on wealth consumption when young and old and on saving by the young. Assume that capital is the only asset in the economy. What effect does the tax increase have on output?

16.2. Suppose people live three-period lives. If the government cuts taxes on the middle-aged, what will happen to the consumption and saving of the young? To the consumption and saving of the middle-aged?

16.3. Suppose we introduce the following fully funded government pension system in an overlapping generations economy where capital pays the fixed gross rate of return x. The government taxes each young person τ goods and invests the tax payments in capital (and only in capital). When old, each person receives the full return from her tax payments.

    a. Find the budget constraints for a person endowed with y when young and nothing when old. Argue that, for small values of τ, the value of τ has no effect on the equilibrium consumption path.

    b. Use the budget constraints of the person and the government to show that the sum of private and government capital does not change if consumption does not change.

    c. Describe the values of τ for which the consumption is affected.

16.4. Consider a pay-as-you-go social security plan that would collect 10 goods from each young person and distribute these goods evenly to old people. Find the effect of this plan on the wealth of future generations, consumption when young and old, private saving by the young, and investment by the young in each of the following cases. Specify as much as possible about the magnitude of the changes.

    a. Population is constant and $r = 1$.

    b. Population is constant and $r > 1$.

    c. Population grows at the rate $n > r$.

16.5. Consider an overlapping generations economy in which endowments increase over time. Let $y_t = \alpha y_{t-1}$, where $\alpha > 1$. Endowments are received by young people while old people receive no endowment. Preferences are such that a young person always wants to consume half of their endowment. The government's only activity is to run an old-age pension plan. The government chooses a pay-as-you-go pension system in which taxes are collected from the young to pay the old-person's pension. Assume the population is constant.

    a. Write down the budget constraint for a young person.

    b. Write down the budget constraint for the old person.

    c. Derive the lifetime budget constraint.

    d. Write down the government budget constraint. Assume the government runs a balanced budget each period.

    e. Will an old person prefer a pay-as-you-go pension plan to an equilibrium in which no pension plan is operated?

Chapter 17

The Effect of the National Debt on Capital and Savings

1 Roadmap

In 2009, the United States passed the American Recovery and Reinvestment Act. The goal was stimulate the U.S. economy during the Great Recession. With declining tax revenues, the U.S. government relied on deficits in order to finance the spending increase. The attention from the media, politicians, and economists focused sharply on deep divisions regarding the efficacy of such spending packages to stimulate economic activity. Researchers continue to develop our understanding of how changes in government expenditures affect economic activity. During economic downturns, for example, governments have relied on government debt issue to finance expenditure increases. We need to understand whether spending combined with possible future tax liabilities affects the current and future levels of GDP, for example. Clearly, the answers are important and the topic is worthy of attention.

In this chapter, we hope to clarify the relevant issues. To do so, we will apply what we learned about wealth, consumption, and saving in the previous chapter to study the effects of the national debt. Suppose that the government cannot simply roll over its debt forever because $n > r$. In order for the government to settle its debt, future taxes must be paid. We learned from Chapter 16 that higher taxes result in less lifetime after-tax wealth. Therefore, for people living for 75 years, say, it matters whether the future taxes will increase during their lifetime. In other words, an analysis of the effect of national debt on people's behavior depends critically on how quickly the government will settle the debt obligations and whether the government's plans fit into the planning of forward-looking people.

We start by using the approach of lifetime budget constraints developed in Chapter 16. We then extend the basic framework to analyze an economy in which nominal money can affect people's decisions. In addition, we extend a person's planning

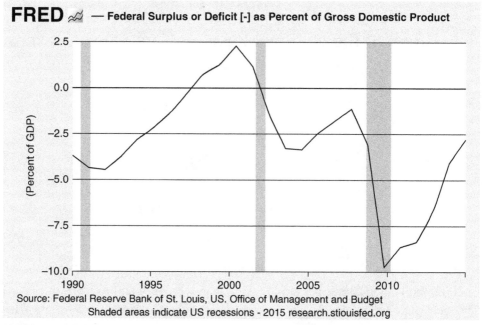

FRED 〰 — Federal Surplus or Deficit [-] as Percent of Gross Domestic Product

Source: Federal Reserve Bank of St. Louis, US. Office of Management and Budget
Shaded areas indicate US recessions - 2015 research.stlouisfed.org

Figure 17.1. The ratio of federal surplus/deficit $(+/-)$ to GDP, 1990–2015. During this 25-year period, you can see an emerging cycle. The upswing lasted from 1990 to 2001, followed by a downswing that lasted until 2009. Since then, the ratio appears to be on an upswing.

horizon by having them care about future generations. Even if you live only two periods, you act as if your planning horizon extends out forever.

2 The National Debt and the Crowding Out of Capital

Government bonds and capital are both assets through which people save. If the government increases the stock of bonds, does this mean that people will invest in less capital? We address this question by examining two cases: one in which government deficits cause a reduction in capital investment and one in which the deficits have no effect on capital. The two cases differ only in a single assumption. This assumption therefore will prove to be the key to understanding when the size of the national debt is important to the size of the capital stock.

It is easy to see why the policy analysis is important. Figure 17.1 plots the surplus and deficit for the United States as a fraction of GDP. Since 1990, you can see eras of spending. There is a clear period in which the deficit-to-GDP ratio was shrinking and even switched signs to become a surplus. The surplus was short lived as the deficit spending increased in the early 2000s. We see a period in which the deficit-to-GDP ratio has been increasing. After staying around 2.5 percent of GDP during the first half of the 2000s, we see a sharp decline as the deficit approached

10 percent of GDP in 2009. At the time of this writing, the deficit-to-GDP ratio had fallen to 2.5 percent.

In both cases, we examine the overlapping generations economy developed in Chapter 16 of two-period-lived agents, each endowed with y_1 goods when young and y_2 goods when old. For simplicity, assume a constant population. Capital in this economy will pay the one-period rate of return r, a constant. There will be no money, but if the government chooses, it may issue bonds paying the same rate of return as capital. At time t, each young period pays a lump-sum tax of τ_1 goods, and each old person pays a lump-sum tax of τ_2 goods. The after-tax lifetime wealth is used to make lifetime consumption purchases. The lifetime budget constraint is

$$c_{1,t} + \frac{c_{2,t+1}}{r} \leq y_1 - \tau_{1,t} + \frac{y_2 - \tau_{2,t+1}}{r} \equiv w_t. \tag{17.1}$$

Each period, the government budget constraint is represented as:

$$g_t + rb_{t-1} = \tau_{1,t} + \tau_{2,t} + b_t. \tag{17.2}$$

Equation 17.2 tells you that the government buys goods worth g goods, makes principal and interest payments on debt issued last period. To make these payments, the government collects taxes from young (τ_1) and from old (τ_2), borrowing the remainder so that the constraint is satisfied each period.

Consider now the effect of a cut in taxes of 100 units per young person in period t with no change in government expenditures. From the government budget constraint, we see that this can be accomplished only with an increase of 100 goods in government debt per young person. We assume that the debt will be paid off at some future date by some other generations. This will prove to be a critical assumption.

How will people change their lifetime consumption plan, $c_{1,t}$ and $c_{2,t+1}$, in response to this tax cut? People who receive a tax cut with no later increase in taxes experience an increase in their (after-tax) wealth. If, as we assume, $c_{1,t}$ and $c_{2,t+1}$ are normal goods, then the consumption of each will rise with the increase in wealth.

How does this affect the savings of a member of this generation? To provide more consumption when old, each person's savings must rise. However, to consume more when young, her savings will rise only by a number less than 100. In other words, for first-period consumption to rise, the person cannot save the entire tax cut.

Now that we know what happens to savings, we can determine what happens to capital. There are two assets with which one can save in this economy – capital and government bonds. Therefore

$$s_t = k_t + b_t. \tag{17.3}$$

Let us use the symbol Δ to represent changes in a variable that result from the policy change. To make this more formal, let $\Delta x_t = x_t - x_{t-1}$. Then it follows from

Equation 17.3 that

$$\Delta s_t = \Delta k_t + \Delta b_t. \tag{17.4}$$

To finance the tax cut, government bonds have increased by 100 ($\Delta b_t = 100$), but savings has increased by some number that is less than 100 ($\Delta s_t = 100 - \Delta c_{1,t} < 100$, because $\Delta c_{1,t} > 0$). From Equation 17.4, capital must have fallen:

$$\Delta s_t = 100 - \Delta c_{1,t} = \Delta k_t + 100$$

$$\Rightarrow \Delta k_t = -\Delta c_{1,t} < 0. \tag{17.5}$$

We see that capital would fall by the increase in consumption when young. Although the stock of assets increased by the number of bonds issued – that is, by the size of the tax cut – people did not wish to increase their savings by the full amount of the tax cut. Therefore, the bonds could be held only if people reduced their holdings of capital. The reduction of capital due to the increase in government debt is often called the crowding out of capital because bonds are substituting for capital in personal savings.[1]

Example 17.1 Consider an economy of two-period-lived people in overlapping generations. Let there be capital paying the rate of return x. Assume for simplicity that there is no fiat money.

What will the effects on a young person's wealth, saving, consumption, and capital investment be of a tax cut of 100 goods per young person in period t financed by an equal increase in the government debt? Assume that in the following period ($t + 1$), the debt will be paid off with a tax on the young of the next generation. Use the lifetime budget sets in your answer.

2.1 Deficits and Interest Rates

By rate-of-return equality, the (real) interest rate equals the marginal product of capital, which for simplicity was assumed to be fixed. If we assume instead that capital has a diminishing marginal product, we can determine the effects of government debt on the interest rate. As we discussed in Chapter 6, rate-of-return equality and a diminishing marginal product of capital imply an inverse relation between the capital stock and the interest rate. Therefore, it follows directly that if an increase in government debt reduces the capital stock, it will increase capital's marginal product and thus the interest rate.

A second interpretation of the model may help us understand the relation between the debt and interest rates. In the previous example, an increase in the national debt increases desired savings by less than the increase in bonds. In other

---

[1] Any reduction of capital will also reduce wages if the marginal product of labor is an increasing function of the capital stock. See Diamond (1965).

Table 17.1. *Comparison of government financing alternatives. Plan A is a balanced-budget plan in which the government runs neither a deficit nor a surplus. Plan B is a deficit-financed plan in which the government borrows and repays the debt one period later.*

Plan A	Plan B
$\tau_1 = g_t$	$\tau_1 = 0$
$b_t = 0$	$b_t = g_t$
$\tau_2 = 0$	$\tau_2 = rb_t$

words, for any given interest rate, the supply of savings has risen by less than the demand for those savings by capitalists and the government. In a free market, supply cannot exceed demand, so how can the government (or any other "demander" of savings) induce people to hold its bonds? It can offer a higher interest rate. The higher interest rate on government bonds will entice savers away from capital with a marginal product lower than the interest rate, thus crowding out capital.

3 Neutral Government Debt

With one key change in this policy, we can find an example of a deficit that does not crowd out capital. Assume now that the debt created at t will be repaid not by taxing generations in the future but by taxing the old at $t + 1$. Under this assumption, the tax to repay the debt falls on the generation that enjoys the tax reduction. We analyze this case by comparing the lifetime budget constraints under two fiscal plans that provide the same level of government expenditure per young person g_t. In plan A, each member of generation t simply pays a tax equal to g_t goods when young. No government debt is issued, because government expenditures are completely financed by taxes. In plan B, the generation pays no taxes when young; instead, the government spending is covered by an issue of government debt worth g_t goods per young person so that b_t is equal to g_t. This debt is then retired with interest by a tax on the old at $t + 1$. Because government bonds pay the gross rate of return r, each old person has to pay a tax equal to the amount rb_t.

Recall that the lifeline budget constraint in general is

$$c_{1,t} + \frac{c_{2,t+1}}{r} \leq y_1 - \tau_{1,t} + \frac{y_2 - \tau_{2,t+1}}{r}.$$

By substituting the particulars of each plan listed in Table 17.1 into this constraint, we can compare the budgets of people under the alternative plans (see Table 17.2).

Table 17.2. *Comparison of a person's lifetime budget constraint under alternative government financing schemes.*

Plan A	Plan B
$c_{1,t} + \frac{c_{2,t+1}}{r} = y_1 + \frac{y_2}{r} - g_t$	$c_{1,t} + \frac{c_{2,t+1}}{r} = y_1 + \frac{y_2 - rg_t}{r}$

Table 17.2 reveals that the lifetime budget set is the same under the two plans. The deficit-funded tax cut does not change the wealth of the generation, because the increase in income from the tax cut when young is exactly offset in present value by the decrease in income from the tax to retire the debt. Generation t pays for the entire government expenditure in both plans. It doesn't affect their wealth when they are taxed to pay for it.

Because wealth is the same with or without the deficit, people will choose the same consumption in both periods of life. People do not consume any part of their tax cut when young; they save the entire tax cut in anticipation of the forthcoming tax hike that will be required to pay off the deficit. By saving the entire tax cut, they will have just the right amount of funds to pay the higher taxes when they are old.

What is the effect of this deficit on the stock of capital? Again, saving equals capital plus bonds, so that changes in savings must equal the sum of changes in capital and government bonds:

$$s_t = k_t + b_t \quad \Rightarrow \quad \Delta s_t = \Delta k_t + \Delta b_t. \tag{17.6}$$

Although bonds rise by the size of the tax cut, so does saving, because the entire tax cut is saved ($\Delta s_t = \Delta b_t$). This implies that there is no change in capital as a result of this deficit ($\Delta k_t = 0$). There is no crowding out of capital. Therefore, there is no effect on the marginal product of capital or the interest rate. The desire to save rose by exactly the amount of the government's issue of bonds, so that the government did not need to offer a higher interest rate to induce people to hold its bonds.

We see that a deficit-financed tax cut has no effect on real variables such as consumption or capital in this case. This result is often referred to as the "Ricardian Equivalence Theorem" after David Ricardo, a well-known philosopher and classical economist, who was the first to consider this case.

We have looked at two cases that have two quite different results. In the first case, the deficit-financed tax cut leads to altered consumption, savings, and capital holdings. In the case just considered, no such effects are found. What is the crucial difference between these two cases?

In the first case, the tax cut alters real variables, because the people who benefit from the tax cut do not have to pay the tax increase that retires the debt. Because of this, these people experience an increase in their wealth, which leads them to higher consumption. In the second case, people pay a higher tax in the second period of life in order to retire the debt. These people experience no change in their wealth and thus do not alter their consumption. Clearly, the effects of bond-financed tax cuts depend on whether the people who receive the tax cut will live to pay the increase in taxes that will retire the resulting debt.

Example 17.2 Answer the question in Example 17.1 assuming that the debt is paid off with a tax on the old in the period immediately after the tax cut. Explain the difference in your answers to the two exercises.

4 Fiat Money and the Crowding Out of Capital

Fiat money, like interest-bearing government bonds, is a form of government debt. The question is how will another type of government paper affect the equilibrium outcomes. Specifically, do changes in fiat money crowd out capital?

To answer this question, let us reintroduce fiat money into our model. Fiat money is held to satisfy a government requirement that each young person must hold fiat money worth φ goods. This is essentially a lump-sum reserve requirement in that each person must hold these reserves, regardless of her total savings or bank balances.[2] In this way, the requirement does not affect the rate of return on savings or bank balances, as did the fractional reserve requirement of Chapter 8. We assume that fiat money is held by requirement rather than to reduce transaction costs or for some other motive so that we can isolate money's effect on wealth from its effect on transactions.

Let there be a constant stock of fiat money. In the initial period, the stock of fiat money is divided equally among the initial old ($m_0 = M/N_0$). Assume, as before, that there is capital paying the gross one-period rate of return $r > n$. Capital and fiat money are the only assets available in the economy.

The budget of a member of the future generations is given by the two equations

$$c_{1,t} + v_t m_t + k_t = y \tag{17.7}$$

$$c_{2,t+1} = v_{t+1} m_t + r k_t, \tag{17.8}$$

which, if k_t is positive, yields the lifetime budget constraint

$$c_{1,t} + \frac{c_{2,t+1}}{r} = y - v_t m_t + \frac{v_{t+1} m_t}{r}$$

$$= y + v_t m_t \left[\frac{v_{t+1}}{v_t r} - 1 \right]. \tag{17.9}$$

---

[2] The reserve requirement in this model economy is a level of money balances. In Chapter 8, we concentrated on money balances as a fraction of deposits. See Champ and Freeman (1990).

The condition for the clearing of supply and demand for money when fiat money is held only to satisfy the legal requirements is

$$v_t M = N\varphi. \tag{17.10}$$

In a stationary equilibrium (as we have seen many times), the constant money stock implies a value of money that grows at the population growth rate n. Therefore, when $v_t m_t = \varphi$, we have $v_{t+1} m_t = n\varphi$. The budget constraints (Equations 17.7 to 17.9) can then be written as

$$c_1 + \varphi + k = y \tag{17.11}$$

$$c_2 = n\varphi + rk \tag{17.12}$$

$$c_1 + \frac{c_2}{r} \leq y + \varphi \left[\frac{n}{r} - 1 \right]. \tag{17.13}$$

We find easily the effect of real money balances on the wealth of future generations, the right-hand side of Equation 17.13. With $r > n$, an increase in the level of real money balances φ, for example, means that lifetime wealth decreases. The second term in Equation 17.13 is negative and a larger value of real money holdings means a smaller number. Or, put another way, people forced to hold fiat money in place of capital receive a lower rate of return on their savings, which reduces their wealth.[3]

Where does this wealth go? If, as assumed, the initial stock of fiat money is owned equally by each of the initial old, the consumption of a member of the initial old is

$$c_{2,1} = rk_0 + v \left[\frac{M}{N_0} \right] = rk_0 + n\varphi, \tag{17.14}$$

where k_0 is some given nonnegative number representing the stock of capital held by a member of the initial old. An increase in the value of a unit of fiat money, v, from an increase in the demand for money, φ, increases the wealth of the initial generation by increasing the value on its initial stock of fiat money.[4]

What is the effect of real money balances on capital and output? Recall that the budget constraint when old for future generations in a stationary equilibrium is $c_2 = n\varphi + rk$ (Equation 17.12).

---

[3] The intuition for result goes back to the concept of present value. Fiat money is both an expense and an income for future generations: it is an expense of φ goods when young because future generations must give up goods to acquire the money instead of capital. Fiat money does generate a flow of old-age purchases equal to $n\varphi$ goods. Because the old-age flow of goods from fiat money is received one period after the expense is incurred, however, it must be discounted by the gross interest rate r. For $r > n$, the present value of the old-age flow of goods is less than the present value of the expense. For this reason, the net benefit of holding fiat money, $\varphi[(n/r) - 1]$, is negative when $r > n$.

[4] Note that this is the same type of transfer that operates between initial old and future generations we saw in Chapter 13.

For any given level of desired c_2, a rise in real fiat money balances φ, by providing more income when old, reduces the need to save through capital. In this way, an increase in fiat money balances crowds out capital. Moreover, if c_2 is a normal good, old-age consumption will fall with the drop in wealth, further decreasing desired saving through capital. Lower steady-state capital implies lower real output.

4.1 Offsetting Wealth Transfers

Policy changes studied in this book have often affected the demand for money and thus the value of any fiat money balances owned by the initial old. A decrease in the reserve requirement, for example, increases the rate of return on deposits, helping future generations, but it also lowers the value of initial fiat money balances, hurting the initial old. If a policy change involves a transfer of wealth between generations, it is difficult to recommend such a policy from an objective standpoint; the desirability of the policy change depends on which generation's welfare is valued more by the one who must make the decision.

We have seen in this chapter that government debt may be used to transfer wealth between generations by altering the incidence of taxes. This suggests that we might be able to use government debt to offset the wealth transfers that occur when a policy changes the value of initial balances of fiat money. Let us consider in particular the suggestion of Auernheimer (1974) that if any policy decreases the value of initial fiat money balances through a decrease in the demand for fiat money, the government can reduce the supply of fiat money by exactly enough to leave the value of fiat money (and hence also the price level) unchanged, thus offsetting any transfer of wealth from the initial old.

Such a decrease in the fiat money stock must of course be financed in some way. An increase in the taxes of the initial old would defeat the purpose of helping the initial old, so consider instead financing the decrease of the fiat money stock through an issuance of government debt. The debt per person is to be held constant, and interest on the debt is to be paid from taxes collected on future generations. The wealth transfer from the initial old to the future generations that was caused by the drop in the demand for fiat money has now been offset by an increase in the national debt, which transfers wealth back from the future generations (who must pay taxes to fund interest payments) to the initial old (who benefit from the reduction in the fiat money stock).

The issuance of debt to reduce the stock of fiat money represents an open market sale of government debt for fiat money. In a similar fashion, an open market purchase of government debt by an expansion of the fiat money stock may be used to keep the value of fiat money unchanged in the face of any policy-induced increase in the demand for fiat money. The purchase of debt by the government reduces the tax revenue needed to pay interest on the government debt. With the wealth of the initial old maintained at its initial level by these open market operations, we are free to judge the effects of monetary policies solely by their effects on future generations.[5]

5 Infinitely Lived Agents

In this book, we have uniformly focused on model economies in which people live a finite number of periods. We use trade between generations as the way to explain why people would be willing to hold a store of value that is also useful as a medium of exchange. In other words, we developed a set of assumptions that are necessary to build a model of money. We showed that intrinsically useless fiat money can have value only in economies with no known terminal date.

To focus on overlapping generations is a modeling choice. For model economies that go on forever, there are two frameworks – models with people (or families) who live forever or models with an infinite number of overlapping generations of finitely lived people. In order to be thorough, we now examine the other framework to learn where our choice has made a difference in the results we have found.

For most of the topics we have studied, whether the decision maker lives forever does not matter. The assumption does matter, however, for the effects of the national debt and money balances on wealth and capital, a subject we take up here.

5.1 A Model of Infinitely Lived People

Consider an economy with a single generation of N identical, infinitely lived people, each of whom owns an endowment of y goods in each period of life. We write the lifetime utility of an infinitely lived person as a weighted sum of the instantaneous utility enjoyed from consumption at each of an infinite series of periods:

$$u(c_1) + \beta u(c_2) + \beta^2 u(c_3) + \cdots = \sum_{t=0}^{\infty} \beta^t u(c_t). \tag{17.15}$$

Here β represents the "discount factor" applied to utility obtained in the future. We assume that $\beta < 1$. This assumption implies that future instantaneous utility does not receive as much "weight" in the measure of lifetime utility as instantaneous utility derived in the present. For example, an additional unit of instantaneous utility in period 1 also causes lifetime utility to increase by 1 unit. However, an additional unit of utility in period 3 causes lifetime utility to increase by only β^2 units, which is less than 1 unit.[6] Notice that because there are no additions to

---

[5] Auernheimer studied open market operations in a model with only a single generation. For applications of his open market operations to models of overlapping generations, see Bacchetta and Caminal (1994) and Freeman and Haslag (1995, 1996).

[6] Without this discounting of future utility (i.e., for $\beta \geq 1$), the infinite sum would would yield infinite utility for any constant level of consumption.

the population in this model, there is only a single type of person. Models in which everyone is alike are called "representative agent models."

Assume that there are capital and government bonds, both paying the gross one-period rate of return $r > 1$.[7]

5.2 *Wealth, Capital, and Interest-Bearing Government Debt*

Recall that a reduction in (lump-sum) taxes financed by an increase in government bonds will have no effect on a person's wealth if the people who pay the future taxes to retire the bonds are those who benefit from the tax cut. If a person's wealth does not change, she will not alter her consumption or investment. In models of a single generation of identical infinitely lived people, those who pay the tax increase are always those who receive the tax cut, regardless of when future taxes are increased. Therefore, deficit-financed tax cuts are always neutral in their effects.

A look at the lifetime budget constraint of an infinitely lived person will confirm this. We build the lifetime budget constraint from the person's period t budget constraint. In any period t, her expenditures to acquire consumption and assets (here, government bonds and capital) cannot exceed her after-tax income, including the return from assets previously acquired:

$$c_t + s_t \leq y - \tau_t + rs_{t-1}. \tag{17.16}$$

Where $s_t = k_t + b_t$ for the first three periods, we have

$$c_1 + s_1 \leq y - \tau_1 + rs_0 \tag{17.17}$$

$$c_2 + s_2 \leq y - \tau_2 + rs_1 \tag{17.18}$$

$$c_3 + s_3 \leq y - \tau_3 + rs_2. \tag{17.19}$$

To construct the lifetime budget for this person, we solve Equation 17.18 for s_1 and then substitute this expression into Equation 17.17 to get

$$c_1 + \frac{c_2 + s_2 - y + \tau_2}{r} \leq y - \tau_1 + rs_0$$

or

$$c_1 + \frac{c_2}{r} + \frac{s_2}{r} \leq y - \tau_1 + \frac{y - \tau_2}{r} + rs_0. \tag{17.20}$$

---

[7] For the discounted lifetime utility (Equation 17.15) to be finite (which is, of course, necessary to allow for a discussion of maximizing utility), r cannot be too large. Exactly what is meant by "too large" is explained by Jones and Manuelli (1990).

Now repeat these steps by solving Equation 17.19 for s_2 and substitute this expression into Equation 17.20:

$$c_1 + \frac{c_2}{r} + \frac{1}{r}\left[\frac{c_3 + s_3 - y - \tau_3}{r}\right] \leq y - \tau_1 + \frac{y - \tau_2}{r} + rs_0. \quad (17.21)$$

Repeating these steps indefinitely gives us the lifetime budget constraint of the infinitely lived person:

$$c_1 + \frac{c_2}{r} + \frac{c_3}{r^2} + \frac{c_4}{r^3} + \cdots \leq y - \tau_1 + \frac{y - \tau_2}{r} + \frac{y - \tau_3}{r^2} + \frac{y - \tau_3}{r^3} + \cdots + rs_0.$$

$$(17.22)$$

The lifetime budget constraint for an infinitely lived person is essentially the same (although longer) as for anyone else; the present value of lifetime consumption cannot exceed the present value of lifetime after-tax income (wealth). Also note that Equation 17.22 appropriately discounts values that occur in the future. For example, fourth-period consumption, which occurs three periods in the future, is discounted by r^3. Because s_0 occurred one period in the past, it must be multiplied by $r^1 = r$.

Consider now a tax cut of 10 goods in period 1 financed by an increase in government debt. This debt is paid off with interest after T periods (in period $T+1$) by an increase in taxes of $10r^T$. In present-value terms, the tax increase is worth $10r^T/r^T = 10$ goods, exactly the present value of the tax cut. Wealth has not been changed, so consumption will also remain unchanged.

What will the effect be on capital? By definition, $s_t = k_t + b_t$ so that $\Delta s_t = \Delta k_t + \Delta b_t$. Because their wealth has not changed, people save the entire proceeds of the tax cut in anticipation of the future tax increase. This increase in saving equals the increase in government bonds ($\Delta s_t = \Delta b_t$), so that capital is not crowded out [$\Delta k_t = 0$].

Example 17.3 Consider an economy of identical infinitely lived people. Suppose that in period 3, taxes are cut by 50 goods per person. The tax cut is financed by an increase in the national debt, which will be repaid with an increase in taxes in period 7. By how much will taxes rise in period 7? How much of the tax cut will be saved and how much consumed in period 3? Explain.

5.3 Wealth, Capital, and Real Money Balances

Models with infinitely lived people also differ from overlapping generations models in the effects of money balance on wealth and capital. To see this, let us examine the effect of a lump-sum reserve requirement on wealth and capital in models of people with infinite lives.

Let there be a constant stock of fiat money. In the initial period, the stock of fiat money is divided equally among all people ($m_o = M/N$). Fiat money is held to satisfy a government requirement that each person must hold fiat money worth φ goods ($v_t m_t = \varphi$).

For simplicity, we assume that there are no government bonds. The budget set of a person in any period t can then be written as

$$c_t + v_t m_t + k_t = y + v_t m_{t-1} + rk_{t-1}. \tag{17.23}$$

The right-hand side of Equation 17.23 tells us that the total sources of funds available to a person at time t consist of the person's endowment, the real value of money held by the person from the previous period, and the return from last period's savings in the form of capital. These sources of funds are used to consume and acquire assets (money and capital). These assets will, in turn, be sources of funds in the following period $t + 1$.

As always, equilibrium requires that the nominal supply of fiat money equal the nominal demand in any period t:

$$M = Nm_t$$

or

$$m_t = \frac{M}{N} = m_{t-1}. \tag{17.24}$$

This simplifies the budget constraint (Equation 17.23) through the cancellation of the two terms that involve money:

$$c_t + v_t \left[\frac{M}{N}\right] + k_t = y + v_t \left[\frac{M}{N}\right] + rk_{t-1}, \tag{17.25}$$

$$\Rightarrow c_t + k_t = y + rk_{t-1}. \tag{17.26}$$

Following the same steps of repeated substitution used to find Equation 17.22, you can verify that Equation 17.26 implies a lifetime budget constraint of

$$c_1 + \frac{c_2}{r} + \frac{c_3}{r^2} + \frac{c_4}{r^3} + \cdots \leq y - \tau_1 + \frac{y - \tau_2}{r} + \frac{y - \tau_3}{r^2} + \frac{y - \tau_3}{r^3} + \cdots + rk_0. \tag{17.27}$$

Note that the value of a unit of fiat money, v_t, does not affect the budget of an average person. An increase in the value of fiat money equally increases the value of the money balances she already owns (m_{t-1}) and the money balances she acquires for the next period (m_t). Because people must acquire new money balances in every period to replace any money balances they spend, an increased value of money does not lead to increased wealth, consumption, or investment. Because a change in the demand for fiat money (from a change in φ) does not affect their constraints on consumption and capital (Equation 17.26 or 17.27), it will not affect their choices of consumption or capital.

For the same reason, there is no Tobin effect in a representative agent model. An increase in the rate of inflation may discourage the use of fiat money, just as it does in the overlapping generations model. In a representative agent model, however, a decreased use of fiat money, whatever distortions it may cause, does not transfer wealth. The constraints on consumption and capital (Equation 17.26 or 17.27) are unchanged and thus will not lead to an increased use of capital. Be aware, however, that increases in the rate of inflation discourage the use of fiat money, reducing utility, whether people are assumed to live finite or infinite lives.[8] Inflation in both cases also discourages intermediation by institutions required to hold reserves in proportion to deposits.

In the overlapping generations models, anything increasing the value of fiat money transfers wealth from the future generations to the initial generation, who own the initial stock. This transfer does not take place in models of infinitely lived people because such models have only one type of person. If people have infinite lives, an increase in the value of money increases income from old money balances by as much as it increases purchases of new money balances, leaving the person's budget unchanged. If there is no change in a person's budget or preferences, there will be no change in her actions, implying that an infinitely lived person's choice of consumption and investment are not affected by changes in the size of real money balances.

Example 17.4 Let the stock of fiat money change according to the rule $M_{t+1} = zM_t$ with $z > 1$. Assume that the increases in the money stock are given to the infinitely lived people as lump-sum subsidies. Show that a person's budget in period t is unaffected by equation. *Hint:* You will need to use the government budget constraint.

5.4 Parents, Bequests, and Infinite Lives

People don't live forever, so one might well ask why we should bother to consider models that assume infinite lives. The exercise is useful if finitely lived people might behave as if they lived forever. Might not people, in a sense, live forever through their children and their children's children? Barro (1974) proposed that if parents care about the utility of their offspring and provide for them by leaving them bequests, these parents behave as if they live forever through their children. The decision-making unit is the family, which goes on forever, even though every individual family member lives a finite life.

In this section, we construct an example of an economy in which mortal people behave as if they will live forever because they value the utility of their offspring. We will do so by specifying a model of infinitely lived people and then constructing a model of finitely lived people who have the same preferences and budgets as the

---

[8] In models with infinitely lived people, deflation is the optimal monetary policy, in contrast to the overlapping generations model's golden rule of a fixed stock of fiat money. The difference is examined by Freeman (1993).

infinitely lived people and thus the same behavior. The example is adapted from Barro's (1974) well known model.[9]

5.5 A Simple Model of Parents

Are there preferences of finitely lived people that would induce them to behave as if they lived infinite lives? Consider an economy of two-period-lived people, each of whom has a single child when old. Each person born in period t cares only about her own consumption when old (c_{t+1}) and about the utility of her child (U_{t+1}).[10] Although each parent is concerned about her child's welfare, we assume that she values the utility from her own consumption at least slightly more than she values the utility of her child. The relative contribution from one's own utility and the future utility of the child is captured by multiplying the child's future utility by the "discount factor" β where $0 < \beta < 1$. We can express this person's total utility U_t as the sum of utility derived from the person's own consumption $u(c_{t+1})$ and the discounted value of the child's total utility βU_{t+1}.

$$U_t = u(c_{t+1}) + \beta U_{t+1}. \tag{17.28}$$

The utility of a member of the initial generation is therefore

$$U_0 = u(c_1) + \beta U_1. \tag{17.29}$$

Her child's utility can similarly be written as

$$U_1 = u(c_2) + \beta U_2, \tag{17.30}$$

and her grandchild's utility can be written as

$$U_2 = u(c_3) + \beta U_3. \tag{17.31}$$

If we substitute the expression in Equation 17.30 into the utility of a member of the initial generation, we find

$$U_0 = u(c_1) + \beta[u(c_2) + \beta U_2]. \tag{17.32}$$

If we now substitute the expression in Equation 17.32 for U_2 into Equation 17.29, we find

$$U_0 = u(c_1) + \beta\{u(c_2) + \beta[u(c_3) + \beta U_3]\}$$

$$= u(c_1) + \beta u(c_2) + \beta^2 u(c_3) + \beta^3 U_3. \tag{17.33}$$

---

[9] A fuller but still accessible treatment of this model can be found in Aiyagari (1987).

[10] For the purposes of this illustration, we assume that people value their own consumption when old. With this assumption, it follows that only one generation is consuming in any given period. This simplifies the analysis but does not alter any important conclusions.

Note that, because the parent cares for the utility of her child, she also cares for the utility of her grandchild because her child does. Substitution continued infinitely along these lines reveals that the preferences of a member of the initial generation may be expressed as an infinite weighted sum of the utilities from the consumption of her offspring:

$$U_0 = u(c_1) + \beta u(c_2) + \beta^2 u(c_3) + \beta^3 u(c_4) + \cdots = \sum_{t=0}^{\infty} \beta^t u(c_{t+1}). \quad (17.34)$$

We find in Equation 17.34 that the member of the initial generation indeed has preferences like those of an infinitely lived person, even though she will not live forever.

A finitely lived person will behave like an infinitely lived person only if she has both the same preferences and the same constraints. Having found that her preferences may be like those of an infinitely lived person, let us now examine her constraints. As previously, we consider people endowed when young with y goods who choose nominal money balances m_t and capital k_t paying the rate of return x. In addition, each old person in period t chooses her personal consumption and a bequest worth ψ_t goods to her child. The budget sets of the young and old alive in period t are, respectively,

$$k_t + v_t m_t = y + \psi_t \quad (17.35)$$

$$c_t + \psi_t = r k_{t-1} + v_t m_{t-1}. \quad (17.36)$$

Recall that people do not consume when young. This explains the absence of a consumption term in the young person's budget set (Equation 17.35). Note that, in these budget constraints, the bequest ψ_t is a source of income for the young and is expenditure for the old.

The old ones are the ones who decide on the size of the bequest. In so doing, they will weigh the utility they derive from their own consumption against the utility they derive from their children's consumption. If they decide to leave a positive bequest, the budget constraint they face can be found by solving Equation 17.35 for ψ_t and substituting that expression into Equation 17.36. The resulting constraint is the same budget constraint for an infinitely lived person (Equation 17.24):

$$c_t + k_t + v_t m_t - y = r k_{t-1} + v_t m_{t-1}. \quad (17.37)$$

Given that altruistic parents face the same constraint and preferences as infinitely lived persons, they will behave in exactly the same way. Note, for example, that because $m_t = M/N = m_{t-1}$, the budget constraint simplifies to

$$c_t + k_t = r k_{t-1} + y, \quad (17.38)$$

in which money balances do not affect a person's budget, just as they did not affect the budget of the infinitely lived person described in Equation 17.24.

5.6 Parents Leaving No Bequest

There is an important exception to the notion that an altruistic parent will behave like an infinitely lived person. Suppose that when weighing her own consumption against the utility she derives from her child's consumption, a parent decides that her child is so well off (or so unlovable) that on the margin she would like to take resources from the child in order to increase her own consumption – in essence, she would like the bequest to be negative.[11] Without some kind of legal restriction, there is no way to force a transfer from one person to another. The best the parent can do for herself in this situation is to simply leave no bequest. In this case, $\psi_t = 0 = \psi_{t+1}$ and the budget constraints for a person born at t are

$$k_t + v_t m_t = y \tag{17.39}$$

$$c_{t+1} = r k_t + v_{t+1} m_t. \tag{17.40}$$

Each generation saves only for its own old-age consumption, leaving nothing for its descendants. In this case, the lifetime budget constraint simplifies to that of a finitely lived person,

$$\frac{c}{r} = y + v \left[\frac{M}{N} \right] \left[\frac{1}{r} - 1 \right], \tag{17.41}$$

in which money balances are a drain on the wealth of a person, as we found earlier in Equation 17.13.

6 Summary

This chapter has examined how the presence of government debt affects decisions about consumption, saving, and investment. The results crucially depend on the timing of debt issuance and retirement. To illustrate this, we considered two distinct cases – one in which government debt issue had real effects and one in which it did not.

We first analyzed a case in which the presence of government debt does have an important impact on economic variables. In this case, we gave people a debt-financed tax cut whereby the resulting debt was retired by a tax on some other generation. This caused an increase in wealth for the people receiving the tax cut, with all of the effects we encountered in Chapter 16. Here, consumption in both periods of life increased and people reduced their holdings of capital. With a diminishing marginal product of capital, the fall in the capital stock would imply an increase in the real interest rate.

---

[11] In a stationary equilibrium, negative bequests are desired by the parent if $r < 1/\beta$, which may result from low rates of return or low degrees of altruism (β).

The second case was similar to the first in that we gave people a debt-financed tax cut. However, this case differed in that the debt was retired by a tax increase imposed on those people who enjoyed the tax cut. We found that if people saved their entire tax cut, they would have just enough to pay the tax increase. The policy had no impact on individual wealth, implying that the lifetime consumption pattern was unaltered. Because savings completely absorbed the tax cut, there was no crowding out of capital. Here, government debt issue was neutral.

7 Exercises

17.1. Suppose the government debt of 100 goods in period t financed not the tax cut of Example 17.1 but a government capital project that will pay off $100r^g$ goods in the following period $(t + 1)$. At that time, the government retires the debt. Assume that the returns from the capital project are used to reduce the taxes of the old in period $t + 1$.

   a. How large must r^g be so that the next generation need not pay extra taxes to retire the debt?

   b. What will the effect of the debt-financed capital project be on the consumption, saving and privately owned capital of the people born in period t if $r^g = r$?

   c. What will the effect of the debt-financed capital project be on the consumption, saving and privately owned capital of the people born in period t if $r^g > r$?

17.2. Consider an overlapping generations economy in which people are endowed with 100 goods when young and with nothing when old. Population grows at the rate n. Capital pays the gross rate of return of x. Utility is given by $\ln(c_{1,t}) + \ln(c_{2,t+1})$. If people have no income when old, this implies that young people want to save half of their after-tax income when young.

   a. Suppose there is no government expenditure, taxation, or government debt. What is the budget constraint of a young person born in period 1? Of an old person in period 2? Combine these to find the lifetime budget constraint of a young person born in period 1.

   b. Using the utility function, find a person's choice of first-period consumption, second-period consumption, savings, and capital holdings.

   c. Find an expression for gross domestic product (GDP) in period 2.

   d. Now suppose that, in period 1, the government decides to issue bonds of a one-period maturity worth 10 goods per young person, the proceeds of which will be offered as a gift to the king of a distant country. In period 2, government expenditure reverts to 0, and the outstanding debt (both principal and interest) is rolled over into a new debt issue. What is the budget constraint of a young person born in period 1? Of an old person in period 2? Combine these to find the lifetime budget constraint of a young person born in period 1.

   e. Compare the consumption pattern of this generation with that found in part b. Compare the savings of this generation with that found in part b. Compare the capital of this generation with that found in part b.

f. Find an expression for GDP in period 2. Why does GDP differ from that found in part c? What will the real value be of debt per young person issued in period 2?

g. Can the policy to introduce the one-time government expenditure be financed in such a way that the consumption of no future generation is affected? For what parameter values is this possible?

h. As an alternative to the bond finance of part d, suppose the one-time expenditure is financed with taxes of 10 goods per young person in period 1. What is the budget constraint of a young person born in period 1? Of an old person in period 2? Combine these to find the lifetime budget constraint of a young person born in period 1.

i. Compare the consumption pattern of this generation with that found in part b. Compare the savings of this generation with that found in part b. Compare the capital of this generation with that found in part b.

j. **(advanced)** Use calculus and the budget constraints found in part a to verify the assertion that, if people have no income when old, young people want to save half of their after-tax income when young.

17.3. Consider an economy of altruistic two-period-lived people who care about the utility of their children. Children do not care about the utility of their parents. Parents currently leave a bequest worth 50 goods. For each of the following policies, find the size of the bequest in period 1 and the effect of this policy on the capital stock.

a. The government decreases taxes paid by each old person in period 1 by 40 goods, running a deficit that will be paid off with taxes imposed on those old in period 3.

b. The government increases taxes paid by each old person in period 1 by 40 goods, running a deficit that will be paid off with taxes imposed on those old in period 3.

c. The government increases taxes paid by each old person in period 1 by 70 goods, reducing a national debt that will be paid off in full with taxes imposed on those old in period 3.

17.4. Consider an economy of identical infinitely lived people. Suppose there is a tax cut in period 1 of d goods per person financed by long-term government debt that is never retired but pays the net real interest rate $i = r - 1$ in every period. Interest payments are financed by lump-sum taxes in each period.

a. Write the government budget constraints for period 1 and for periods $t \geq 2$.

b. Demonstrate that this tax cut and bond issue will not alter the wealth of an infinitely lived person. *Hint:* You need to make use of the fact that

$$\sum_{t=0}^{\infty} i^t = \frac{1}{1-i}$$

or

$$\sum_{t=1}^{\infty} i^t = \frac{1}{1-i}$$

for any constant i so that $0 < i < 1$.

17.5. Consider an economy populated by a large number of identical, infinitely lived people. Suppose the government decides to tax the capital stock, but only at date 1. (The only existing capital stock in this period is k_0.)

    a. How will lifetime wealth be affected if the government tax is used to finance a lump-sum transfer payment to people in date 1?

    b. Demonstrate that the capital tax will not affect lifetime wealth if the proceeds are used to purchase government capital that offers the same return as private capital.

    c. Demonstrate that the capital tax will affect lifetime wealth if the proceeds are thrown in the ocean.

Chapter 18

The Temptation of Inflation

1 Roadmap

In this final chapter, we look into what it means for a central bank to be independent. We demonstrated that people holding nominal debt suffer a real loss in value when there is an unexpected inflation rate increase. So if the central bank operates in cahoots with treasury, we can imagine a government tempted to rid itself of a burdensome national debt by inflating it away. Countries have taken some effort to make the central bank independent of the treasury. But there is no commitment that is so binding that a potential bond holder ever completely trusts the government not to inflate.

To address these questions, this chapter examines the consequences of a default on the national debt and the temptation of the government to default. Then the chapter shows the equivalence of a surprise inflation to a default. Finally, it examines how the monetary authority can convince the public that it will not give in to the temptation of inflation.

2 Defaulting on the Debt

If government debt crowds out capital and obliges the government to raise revenue just to pay the interest on the old debt, why put up with it? Why not simply default on the debt, refusing to pay it off? Certainly this is a tempting idea to any government that wants to lower taxes.

Suppose the government unexpectedly enacted a one-time default on the debt owed in period t. A look at the government budget constraint (Equation 15.8) reveals that this would enable the government to increase its expenditures, reduce taxes or seigniorage, or reduce the debt passed along to future generations. What would be the consequences of this default?

The most obvious consequence is that the default would redistribute resources from the generation that owned the initial debt to the generations that follow, who no longer need be taxed to pay the interest on the debt. In effect, therefore, the default functions like a tax on bond holders.

If the default at t is truly unexpected, it will have the same effect as a lump-sum tax on the generation born at $t - 1$; that is, the default effectively taxes generation $t - 1$ without affecting its behavior. Generation $t - 1$ chose to acquire the bonds in period $t - 1$, before it knew of the default. (If it had known of the default in advance, the generation would have refused to buy the bonds, forcing the government to raise taxes or lower expenditures.) When the default unexpectedly occurs at t, the generation is unable to go back in time to refuse to buy the bonds. In this way, the government induced generation $t - 1$ to contribute revenue by buying bonds at $t - 1$ but does not have to repay that contribution at t.

An income tax on generation $t - 1$ also would have raised revenue. The income tax, however, would have reduced the incentives of the generation to work or invest, because the private return to these income-generating activities is reduced by the tax. A government that must rely on taxes like the income tax that are not lump-sum taxes, therefore may be tempted by the idea of raising revenue by issuing bonds and failing to pay them off. Note that the temptation to default exists even if the government benevolently acts in the best interests of the public. Because a surprise default works like a lump-sum tax, collecting revenue without distorting incentives, even the public will prefer it to an income tax that raises the same revenue from the same people.

2.1 The Inconsistency of Default

A default works as a lump-sum tax only if it takes people by surprise. Could the government make default a permanent means of raising revenue by defaulting on the bonds in every period? Only if people are very stupid or indifferent to their own welfare. Rational people who care about their own welfare would certainly catch on to the idea that the government does not intend to pay off on any bonds it issues. They will refuse to buy the bonds. For this reason, default is not a permanent solution to the revenue needs of the government.

What if the government defaults once and promises never to do so again? Will people believe the government? Suppose the government defaults at t and then issues some new debt. Would you buy this debt? If you know the government was willing to default in the past, you may well believe that it will break its promise and default once again. As soon as you have purchased its debt, the government's temptation to default will be as strong as it was when the government defaulted before.

The incentive of the government to behave in one way today (e.g., to default) but promise not to behave that way in the future is referred to as the **time consistency** problem of government policy.[1] When there is a time consistency problem, the best policy in the short term is not the best long-term policy. The time consistency problem is that, as time passes, the future becomes the present, and the government is tempted to break its promise and follow the best short-term policy. If the government's policy is to default today but not in the future, the government will always default because it is always today.[2]

Though it will be easier to illustrate the incentive problem when the option is to either repay or default, we can see the central bank's incentive problem can impart an inflation bias into the economy. In other words, we observe that across countries, the average inflation rate is positive. Why not zero?

To explain the inflation bias, Barro and Gordon (1983) build on Kydland and Prescott's work and describe a game between the central bank and people. In the model economy, output is determined in the same way as in the Lucas model presented in Chapter 6; specifically, output is positively related to surprise increases in the inflation rate. In addition, the normal level of output is below its desired level so that an output gap is present in the economy. The central bank wants to maximize welfare, facing a tradeoff between the benefits of unexpected inflation, in terms of moving output closing to its desired level, and the cost of inflation. In the model economy, the central bank cannot commit to a particular policy. People understand the tradeoff that the central bank faces and form (rational) expected inflation rates based on the central bank practicing the optimal policy. Indeed, the expected inflation is a function of the output gap, resulting in a positive expected inflation rate. The central bank chooses to set the inflation rate equal to the expected inflation rate. In doing so, the output gap does not get any bigger, but the positive inflation rate – the inflation bias – is costly.

The Barro-Gordon setup shows that a central bank that practices discretion will ultimately generate positive inflation without any benefits in the form of higher output. So how can things be improved? To illustrate the tradeoff, we use the extreme version in which the government either repays its debt or defaults. In this version of the game, we know that people will not purchase government bonds if they know that the government always gives in to an incentive to default. To induce people to buy its debt, the government must therefore convince people that it will not default. Analogously, how can the central bank convince people it not try to use inflation to stimulate the economy.

---

[1] The expression "time consistency" and recognition of the problem it poses for macroeconomic policy making come from Kydland and Prescott (1977).

[2] Exams are a well-used example of time-inconsistency. The objective is to have students master a set of material. At the beginning of the semester, the instructor announces the exam date.

Now, suppose students believe the examination will occur and work diligently. The students' effort pays off and each one masters the material. The instructor knows this to be true. For the instructor, writing and grading the exam takes time and effort. It is not fun. So, on the exam date, the instructor announces no exam.

What was optimal strategy for the instructor at the beginning of the semester is not the optimal strategy after time has passed.

2.2 Commitment

The most effective means of convincing people about one's future actions is to bind oneself in advance to these actions. For example, a person taking a loan can offer the creditor something of value as collateral, to be seized by the creditor if the debtor fails to repay the loan. A contract that makes this arrangement formal can be enforced by the legal system. The debtor now has an incentive not to default on the loan. By making the repayment of the loan in her best interest, the debtor becomes committed to the future action, repayment. The creditor now believes that the debtor will repay the loan not because the debtor is particularly honest by nature but because the creditor knows that the debtor will want to repay the loan in order to avoid the seizure of the collateral.

Commitment is not as easy for the government, because the government is both the debtor and the enforcer of contracts. As such, the government may be able to arrange that it not be punished if it fails to repay its debt. As a result, the government may be unable to commit itself to promised future actions and thus may be unable to secure loans. As an analogy, imagine the consequences of a law that prohibited penalizing debtors who default. Anticipating that debtors will never wish to repay their debts, whatever their promises, creditors will be unwilling to lend. As a result, both creditors and debtors will be worse off under such a law.

To commit itself to its promised future actions, the government must surrender some of its freedom to act in the future. One way to do this is to establish an independent judiciary that can oblige the government to keep its promises. A related way for the government to commit itself in the future is to write the promise into the constitution. If the government is later tempted to break its promise, it will be difficult to do so because changing the constitution is a lengthy process.[3] Consider a constitutional amendment that prohibited default on the national debt. To repeal the amendment would take so long that much of the government debt would already have been repaid.

2.3 Reputation

The government may also try to convince people that it will always repay the debt simply by always repaying whatever it borrows in order to maintain its reputation. You might ask, how would a government bind itself and all future administrations to repay all future bond repayments. Though not a binding commitment, a government

---

[3] Commitment through constitutional guarantees is more effective in nations with long, stable democratic traditions. Politically unstable nations may find it much more difficult to borrow, either internally or externally, because even their constitutional guarantees mean little.

Some have argued that Amendment 14, Section 4 is the constitutional amendment to which we speak. It says, "The validity of the public debt of the United States, authorized by law, including debts incurred for payment of pensions and bounties for services in suppressing insurrection or rebellion, shall not be questioned." A full discussion of the appropriate interpretation is outside the scope of this book.

will try to convince people of its future intentions by developing a pattern of repay its debt.

The government demonstrates that it won't give in to the short-term incentives by always following the best long-term policy. If the government is aware that people are watching its current behavior as a signal of its future behavior, it may rationally decide that the gains from defaulting on today's debt may be outweighed by the costs of the government's inability to borrow in the future because of the public's lack of trust.

A reputation for repayment, however, still requires people to trust that the government will not change its mind and that the government believes the long-term costs of default exceed its short-term benefits. Because of its dependence on the public's trust, a reputation is less certain than commitment as a means of changing people's expectations.

2.4 The Rate of Return on Risky Debt

Suppose you think there is only a change of default. You may then buy this debt if it offers a sufficiently high rate of return. How high? Suppose a perfectly safe asset pays the rate of return x with certainty. If the government promised the same rate of return, would you buy the government debt? No. Because there is a chance that the government will default, the average rate of return on government debt is lower than that of the safe asset. Because of the change of default, the risky government debt must promise a rate of return greater than x to yield the same average rate of return. For example, if there is a 50 percent chance that the government will default on its debt, the government must promise to pay $2x$ to give its debt the same average rate of return as the safe asset.

Will people willingly hold the risky government debt if its average rate of return equals that of the safe asset? Risk-averse people won't, because the debt is riskier than the safe asset. Only if the government debt offers a return that is on average greater than that of the safe asset will risk-averse people accept the debt. Therefore, a government that randomly defaults on its obligations will have to pay a greater average rate of return than a government that never defaults. In this way, random defaults on the national debt do not offer a government a long-term solution to the problem of financing government expenditures.

3 Inflation and the Nominal National Debt

The Treasury securities that comprise the national debt are pledges to pay a specific number of dollars at some future date. Because the Federal Reserve can print dollars at will, one might believe that we need never fear the insolvency of the federal government. At any time, the Federal Reserve can print enough dollars to buy up the entire national debt through open market operations. Let us now evaluate this claim with a look at the effects of unanticipated and anticipated inflation on the real value of the national debt.

3.1 Unanticipated Inflation and the Real National Debt

We start by examining the government's budget constraint at t, measured in dollars, for the case of a total national debt worth D_t, dollars issued at t paying the gross nominal interest rate R_t:

$$p_t N_t g_t + R_{t-1} D_{t-1} = p_t N_t \tau_t + [M_t - M_{t-1}] + D_t. \qquad (18.1)$$

Dividing both sides by p_t, we find the government budget constraint in real terms:

$$N_t g_t + \frac{R_{t-1} D_{t-1}}{p_t} = N_t \tau_t + \frac{M_t - M_{t-1}}{p_t} + \frac{D_t}{p_t}. \qquad (18.2)$$

The second term in Equation 18.2 represents the current real value of last period's government debt.

Suppose now that in period t, the government prints fiat money at a rate unanticipated in the previous period. If this inflation was not anticipated, it cannot have affected variables determined at $t - 1$, in particular, the initial nominal debt D_{t-1} and the nominal interest rate R_{t-1}. For given values of these variables, an increase in the current price level reduces the real value of the principal and interest on last period's national debt. A lower real value of the old national debt on the left-hand side of Equation 18.2 means that the government can reduce the terms on the right-hand side of Equation 18.2 by an equal amount, implying a reduction of taxes, seigniorage, or new government debt. In other words, we now *seem* to have an extra tool with which to manage the government's budget. By increasing the fiat money stock, we can raise the price level, which lowers the real value of what the government owes to others (in addition to its usual effect of raising revenue through seigniorage, which itself represents a lowering of the real value of another government-issued asset, fiat money).

Some claim that the power to print money implies that the government need never default on its debt because it can always print enough money to buy up all the debt, as the debt is denominated in dollars. In fact, an unanticipated inflation is exactly equivalent to a default. Look at who loses with unanticipated inflation. Bond holders purchased the bonds to provide for the consumption of real goods in the future. If unanticipated inflation occurs, nominally denominated bonds will purchase fewer goods than the bond holders expected when they bought the bonds. Aren't the bond holders being cheated? Even if bond holders are paid the explicitly promised number of dollars during unanticipated inflation, they haven't been paid what they really care about – the goods they were implicitly promised. The real effect of unanticipated inflation is exactly that of a default: the government reduces or eliminates its obligations at the expense of the bond holders.

What will the effect be of unanticipated inflation on output? The resulting reduction of the real value of the national debt will reduce the crowding out of capital.[4] This increase in capital, in turn, will increase output in the following period. If capital displays a diminishing marginal product, the increase in capital also results in a reduction of that marginal product and thus (by rate-of-return equality) in the interest rate as well. This analysis suggests that, if the nominal fiat money stock stimulates real output, it may be an indirect effect. Surprise increases in fiat money reduce the real value of the national debt, which increase capital and thus real output.[5]

3.2 Anticipated Inflation and the Real National Debt

Let us now look at the effect of a rise in the price level on the real value of the old national debt if the rise is anticipated. As we found previously, the real value of the old national debt can be written as the second term in Equation 18.2, $(R_{t-1}D_{t-1})/p_t$. Let us write this in terms of the real national debt issued in the previous period, $B_{t-1} = D_{t-1}/p_{t-1}$, or $D_{t-1} = B_{t-1}p_{t-1}$, to get

$$\frac{R_{t-1}D_{t-1}}{p_t} = R_{t-1}\left[\frac{p_{t-1}}{p_t}\right]B_{t-1}. \tag{18.3}$$

The term $R_{t-1}[(p_{t-1})/p_t]$ can be interpreted as the actual real rate of return on bonds (i.e., the current real value of the old national debt must equal its initial real value times its actual real rate of return).

Consider people contemplating the purchase of government bonds at time $t - 1$. At that point in time, people do not know the price level that will exist one period in the future (p_t). Let p_t^e denote the people's expectation (anticipation) of the price level at time t. Keep in mind that this expectation is formed on the information available to people at time $t - 1$.

To attract savers to bonds, the government must offer an anticipated or expected rate of return equal to the rate they can get from alternative assets. We assume that government debt and capital are perfect substitutes. For capital, with the gross return x, government debt and capital will offer the same gross real return; in other words,

$$R_{t-1}\left[\frac{p_{t-1}}{p_t^e}\right] = x,$$

---

[4] See Appendix B in Chapter 16 on "infinitely lived people" for an exception to the crowding out of capital.
[5] See Champ and Freeman (1990) for a formal model of this money/output link.

or nominal returns,

$$R_{t-1} = x \left[\frac{p_t^e}{p_{t-1}} \right]. \tag{18.4}$$

Equation 18.4 tells us that the nominal interest rate will rise (or fall) one for one with an increase (or decrease) in the inflation rate anticipated at $t - 1$. This means that the current real value of the old debt issued at $t - 1$ is unaffected by anticipated inflation because the nominal interest rate charged on debt will include any anticipated inflation.

Is inflation a solution to the problem of the national debt? Can the government issue debt in every period and count on being able to inflate away this debt in the next period? To answer this question, state what will happen to the nominal interest rate if the government always tries to inflate away the debt.

We can use Equation 18.4 to find an expression for the net nominal interest rate, $R_{t-1} - 1$, as we did back in Chapter 7 (Equation 7.7). Here we replace P_t with people's expectation of the price-level equation:

$$R_{t-1} - 1 = (x - 1) + \left(\frac{p_t^e}{p_{t-1}} - 1 \right) + (x - 1) \left(\frac{p_t^e}{p_{t-1}} - 1 \right). \tag{18.5}$$

The net nominal rate of interest equals the net real rate plus the anticipated net rate of inflation (plus a term generally small enough to be safely ignored). If people know the growth rate of the economy (n), then the anticipated net inflation rate p_t^e / p_{t-1} is equal to z^e / n, where z^e is the expected rate of fiat money creation.

Example 18.1 Suppose the government must borrow 10,000 goods in period 1. Let the gross real marginal product of capital equal 1.05. Assume that people always want to hold fiat money balances worth a total of 500 goods and that the fiat money stock in period 1 is $1,000. Suppose people expect the government to increase the fiat money stock by 10 percent and that the population is constant.

a. What will the nominal net interest rate be?
b. What will the real value of the debt in period 2 be if the fiat money stock rises by 10 percent?
c. What will it be if there is no change in the fiat money stock?
d. What will it be if the fiat money stock rises by 20 percent?
e. What will it be if the fiat money stock rises by 20 percent but this rise is expected?

3.3 Rational Expectations

Is inflation a long-term solution to the problem of the national debt? Can the government issue debt in every period and count on being able to inflate away this debt in the next period? Not if people are rational. Consider some examples. If the real net rate of return from capital is 3 percent, what net nominal interest rate is required to induce rational people to hold nominal bonds in each of the following cases?

1. The government inflates at a net rate of 10 percent every year.
2. An election is coming next year, and the government inflates at a net rate of 20 percent in every election year.
3. The government tries to stay ahead of the public by increasing the rate of inflation by 5 percent in each period. The current net rate of inflation is 20 percent.
4. The government flips a fair coin, inflating at a 10 percent net rate if the coin comes up heads but does not inflate if the coin comes up tails. Assume that people are risk neutral.

If you answered 13 percent for case 1, 23 percent for case 2, 28 percent for case 3, and 8 percent for case 4, you have used the concept of "rational expectations." Rational expectations (first introduced in Chapter 5) may be defined as the most accurate expectations possible given the information currently available. This is not simply an assumption that people expect future inflation to equal past inflation, as in case 1. Under rational expectations, people try to anticipate the government's actions, even if they fit a more complicated pattern, as in cases 2 and 3. A government policy based on surprising or fooling the public in any systematic way will not work if people have rational expectations. Rational expectations assume that people will catch on to any pattern of behavior the government follows, because failure to catch on will leave each of these people worse off.

Only if the government behavior is random will rational people fail to infer correctly the government's next move. People with rational expectations can make forecasts of the future that differ from what actually occurs, but this difference can result only from some unforeseeable surprise, some information that was not available in the previous period, like the way the coin lands in case 4. Rational expectations assume only that people will not make preventable mistakes when forming their expectations of the future. But even if policy is unpredictable, the public will set its expectations so that people are correct on average (so that on average they receive the same real rate of return from bonds as from capital).

Example 18.2 If the real net rate of return from capital is 4 percent, what net nominal interest rate is required to induce rational people to hold nominal bonds in each of the following cases?

a. The government inflates at a net rate of 7 percent every year.
b. This is an election year, and the government inflates at a net rate of 20 percent in every election year.
c. The government tries to stay ahead of the public by doubling the net rate of inflation in each period. The current net rate of inflation is 4 percent.
d. The government rolls a fair die, inflating at a 30 percent net rate if a six is rolled but not inflating at all for any other roll. Assume that people are risk neutral.
e. The government rolls a fair die, inflating at a 30 percent net rate if a six is rolled but not inflating at all for any other roll. Assume that people are risk averse.

3.4 The Lucas Critique Revisited

We have previously examined the negative correlation between nominal wages and the unemployment rate, commonly called the Phillips curve (Chapter 6) as well as the related positive correlation between money and output (Chapter 10). We noted in both cases the disappearance of that relation at the time governments sought to systematically exploit it.

This chapter's model of nominal government debt suggests another possible link between monetary surprises and output increases. Suppose that for a century a monetary authority keeps the stock of fiat money and the price level rather fixed. The fluctuations that do occur are unpredictable accidents. As we have seen in our model, if the national debt is nominally denominated, an unanticipated increase in the price level reduces the real value of the national debt, thereby reducing the crowding out of capital and increasing real output.

Suppose these correlations are studied by economists who do not know anything about the structure of the economy that gave rise to these patterns in the data. They would be tempted to speculate that there is a trade-off between price increases and real output. With a leap of faith, they might even suggest to the monetary authority and the public that one can systematically raise output through inflation.

Suppose the monetary authority adopts this suggestion and proceeds on an announced policy of inflating at a variety of rates. What would happen to the correlation of inflation with output? Recall that anticipated inflation does nothing to change the real value of the national debt because the government must pay a higher nominal rate of interest to attract people to the debt; therefore, it has no effect on output.

The monetary authority generates inflation but not the intended increase in output. The trade-off proves illusory.

If the monetary authority adopts this policy secretly, it may succeed in stimulating output for a time. In this period, people may dismiss observed inflation as an aberration, just one of those rare, random bursts of inflation they had observed for a century. If the monetary authority continues to inflate in any systematic way, however, rational people will catch on to the policy and adjust their expectations (and the nominal interest rate) accordingly.

Why did the suggestion of our fictional economists fail? The correlations they observed were generated by unanticipated inflation when the government was following a policy of monetary and price stability. These correlations disappeared when the government followed a policy of inflation designed to systematically stimulate output. Obviously, the data generated when the economy was subjected to inflation under one type of policy regime (price stability) did not help predict its reaction to inflation under another policy regime (systematic inflation).[6]

---

[6] As we learned in Chapter 5, the suggestion that correlations observed under one type of macroeconomic policy regime may not be found under another policy regime is commonly called the "Lucas critique." For further reading, see Lucas (1976, 1981).

What does our example and recent experience tell us about designing monetary policy? They warn us about drawing policy inferences from simple correlations in the data if we do not understand the workings of the economy that generated those data. If our fictional economists understood our model economy, they would have known that only unanticipated inflation would have an effect on real output; any systematic inflation would be anticipated and thus would have no effect. Looking at the data alone, they could not learn this, because systematic inflation had not been tried during the period for which they had data. Only if they had reason to believe the effects of inflation would be the same whether inflation were anticipated or unanticipated should they confidently have advised the monetary authority to deliberately inflate. To give reasonable policy advice is not enough to observe patterns in the data; one must understand how those patterns were caused so that one can be confident about the reaction of the economy to a change in policy.[7]

Example 18.3 Consider the overlapping generations economy with a constant population of two-period-lived people endowed only when young. Suppose the real net rate of return from capital is always 4 percent and young people always save a total of 5,000 goods, including fiat money, worth 1,000 goods. In the last period, the price of a good was \$1, people expected a 10 percent net rate of inflation, the fiat money stock was worth \$1,000, and the national debt (of one-period bonds) was worth \$2,000. In this period, the government will issue bonds equal to the principal and interest on the old debt. Find the current real values of the old debt (principal plus interest), the capital stock, and next period's output from capital for the following three cases:

a. The government inflates at a net rate of 10 percent, as expected.
b. The government unexpectedly inflates at a net rate of 20 percent.
c. The government unexpectedly refuses to inflate.

3.5 Self-Fulfilling Inflationary Expectations

Rational expectations imply that the public will try to anticipate the policy the government will want to follow even before the government begins to implement it.

In this section, we examine the danger that the public's rational expectation of inflation may itself cause or contribute to the inflation it expects.[8]

In every period, the government is tempted to inflate away some of the real value of the national debt. Rational, forward-looking people may therefore anticipate inflation and demand a nominal interest rate, $R_{t-1} = x(p_t^e/p_{t-1})$, high enough to yield at least the real rate of return offered by capital.

---

[7] Of course, if an economist's understanding (model) of the economy is wrong, that economist's advice may be wrong as well. Nevertheless, policy advice is likelier to succeed if it is based on some carefully worked understanding/model of the economy than if it is based on correlations that are observed but unexplained.

[8] See Calvo (1978) and Barro and Gordon (1983).

Now suppose the government in place truly does not wish to use inflation to default on its debt and announces its intentions. Will people be able to distinguish this government from one that wishes to default on its debt through unanticipated inflation? No. The government that plans unanticipated inflation will also announce that it will not inflate. Therefore, if the people cannot distinguish between truthful and deceitful promises to end inflation, they may anticipate inflation and thus require a high nominal interest rate.

Suppose the government refuses to inflate, even though people expect inflation. In this case, the government pays a high real interest rate, and the real burden of the national debt will increase. Consider as an example an economy with a real debt of 1 million goods in which $n = 1.1, x = 1.1$, and $p_t = \$1$. Suppose the people expect the government to double the fiat money stock ($z^e = 2$). To induce people to hold their bonds, the government must offer a nominal interest rate of $x(z^e/n) = 2.2$. This means that the government at $t + 1$ will owe $\$2.2$ million. If the government does not actually inflate, this nominal rate is also the real rate, and the government finds itself with a real national debt of 2.2 million goods. If the government inflates as expected, the nominal debt of $\$2.2$ million is worth only 1.1 million goods because the doubling of the fiat money stock will cause the price level to double to $p_{t+1} = 2$. In this way, the honest government that meant what it said about ending inflation finds itself with a real debt twice the size of the real debt it would have found if it had inflated as expected.

From this example, we see that a government faced with inflationary expectations will have a hard time refusing to inflate. If it does not inflate when expected, it will find itself with a large real debt that eventually must be covered through taxes or government expenditure cuts (assuming $x > n$). It is easy to understand why a government with no deceitful intentions, but faced with the alternative of a large real debt, may choose to inflate as expected.

In such a case, inflationary expectations are self-fulfilling. The inflation occurs because people expect it and thus require a high nominal interest rate, which forces the government to inflate to avoid a large real national debt.

3.6 Hyperinflation

Although most countries have net inflation rates of 5, 10, or 20 percent per year, a few experience hyperinflation, inflation rates that rapidly accelerate to annual rates of a thousand or million percent. What may be the cause the dramatic episodes of hyperinflation that we observed recently in Latin America and even more dramatically in Germany and other central European nations after World War I?

Figure 18.1 presents price-level data from the German hyperinflation of the 1920s. The German case is similar to those of Austria, Hungary, and Poland during the same time period. During the most dramatic part of the German hyperinflation, the inflation rate peaked at almost 15,000 percent per month. Lest one think that

Table 18.1. *Modern hyperinflations. This is short list of hyperinflations occurring across the world since 1980. Note that the Yugoslavian and Zimbabwe cases saw inflation rates that exceeded those during the German hyperinflation after World War I. Source: Hanke and Krus (2012).*

Country	Start Date	End Date	Month with Highest Inflation Rate	Highest Monthly Inflation Rate	Time Required for Price Level to Double
Bolivia	April 1984	Sept 1985	Feb 1985	183%	20.3 days
Argentina	May 1989	March 1990	July 1989	197%	19.4 days
Tajikistan	Jan 1992	Oct 1993	Jan 1992	201%	19.1 days
Yugoslavia	April 1992	Jan 1994	Jan 1994	313,000,000%	1.41 days
Zimbabwe	March 2007	Nov 2008	Nov 2008	$7.96 \times 10^{10}\%$	24.7 hours

hyperinflations are a thing of the past, Table 18.1 provides a list of hyperinflations that have occurred since 1980. Indeed, two of the cases reported inflation rates that exceeded those during the German hyperinflationary episode.

One feature common to countries experiencing hyperinflation is fiscal difficulty. To see why, suppose the government has run up an enormous national debt, one so large that the interest payments cannot possibly be financed through taxes or

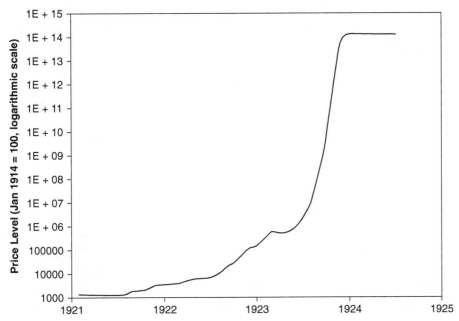

Figure 18.1. The German hyperinflation, 1921–1925. During the first half of the 1920, Germany, Austria, Hungary, and Poland each experience hyperinflations. The German case is illustrated here. By the end of the German hyperinflation, the price level stood at more than one trillion times its pre-World War I level. *Source:* Data from Young (1925) as published by Sargent (1986a, Table 3.18, pp 80–81).

government expenditure cuts. Even if the government has never before inflated, it is easy to anticipate that it must now turn to inflation as its only hope of reducing the real value of its debt. The public will therefore demand high rates of nominal interest before it will agree to hold any bonds of the government. The resulting large nominal interest obligations of the government require the government to print money at a yet faster rate.

We see from Figure 18.1 that the German hyperinflation was stopped and indeed stopped suddenly. How can hyperinflation be stopped when it is fueled by self-fulfilling inflationary expectations? Certainly, the government cannot just announce that it will stop inflating. Who would believe the announcement, knowing the government has a huge debt that it cannot finance in any other way? Only if the government solves its fiscal problems and thus eliminates the need to inflate can rational people believe the government will stop printing money. For this reason, the end of hyperinflation is accompanied by fiscal reforms that reduce government spending or increase government revenue.[9]

3.7 Commitment in Monetary Policy

A binding commitment to avoid inflation is the surest way to convince the public that it will not try to inflate away the national debt. How might the government convince the public that it will be unable or unwilling to inflate in the future?

One way is to index government debt to changes in the price level so that the real value of the national debt does not change when there is inflation. Such indexed government debt removes the government's incentive to inflate as a means to reduce the real value of its debt.

Another approach is to keep the central bank independent of the government and free from political pressure. If an independent central bank is directed by opponents of inflation, such as those who might have much to lose from an inflation (e.g., owners of government debt), the government can convince the public that the central bank will be unwilling to inflate, however much inflation is desired by other branches of government.

Alesina and Summers (1993) investigated the relationship between central bank independence and macroeconomic performance across several countries. Devising a measure of central bank independence is a difficult task, and any proposed measure certainly will be subject to debate. That said, Alesina and Summers build their index using as a starting point other indices of central bank performance presented by Bade and Parkin (1982), Alesina (1988), and Grilli, Masciandaro, and Tabellini (1991). The index focuses on two main areas – political independence and economic independence. Political independence measures the degree of

---

[9] The causes and ends of the hyperinflations of central Europe are carefully analyzed by Sargent (1986a). He identifies in particular the policies implemented to help the central banks commit themselves to noninflationary policies.

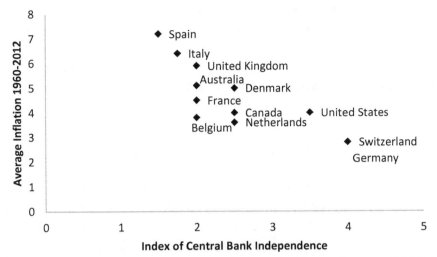

Figure 18.2. Central bank independence and inflation. The Alesina-Summers (1993) index of central-bank independence ranks central banks on a scale of 1 (least independent) to 5 (most independent). The average inflation rate is computed from U.S. Department of Labor data on the Consumer Price Index. As shown in this figure, countries with more independence tend to have lower inflation rates. *Source:* U.S. Department of Labor, Bureau of Labor Statistics, Division of International Labor Comparisons.

separation of the central bank from political influences stemming from the executive and legislative branches of government. Economic independence is an indication of how unrestricted the central bank is in its use of monetary policy tools. (A key component of this is to what degree the central bank is relied on to facilitate the financing of government deficits.) Utilizing this constructed index of central bank independence, we plot the combination of central bank independence index and average inflation in Figure 18.2. The scatter points indicate that countries with less independent central banks, on average, have higher inflation rates.

A more direct way to convince the public that the central bank will not inflate is a constitutional amendment prohibiting expansion of the money stock.[10] As soon as the amendment has been adopted, a government that wished to inflate away the national debt would have to go through the long task of repealing the amendment, signaling the government's intention to inflate. By the time the amendment was repealed, inflation would catch no one by surprise.

4 The Temptation of Seigniorage

Nominally denominated interest-bearing debt is not the only source of the government's temptation to inflate away its budgetary problems. Fiat money is also

---

[10] If there are contingencies under which inflation is desirable, the amendment might specify narrowly defined exceptions for which more money can be printed. Of course, such an amendment eliminates the ability of the central bank to respond to contingencies that cannot be anticipated or defined.

nominally denominated, which allows the government to tax away some of the value of the public's fiat money balances by printing new money, as we learned in Chapter 4.

Seigniorage, like default on the debt, exhibits a time consistency problem because the optimal short-run rate of inflation differs from the optimal long-run rate. Seigniorage in the initial period equals

$$v_1[M_1 - M_0] = v_1 M_1 \left[1 - \frac{1}{z}\right] = N_1 q_1 \left[1 - \frac{1}{z}\right], \tag{18.6}$$

the product of the seigniorage tax rate $[1 - (1/z_1)]$ and the seigniorage tax base $v_1 M_1 = N_1 q_1$. For any given value of fiat money, the government acquires revenue by printing additional units of fiat money ($z_1 > 1$). This expansion of the fiat money stock taxes those already holding fiat money balances. Because these people have already acquired their balances, they cannot change these balances to avoid the tax. The inflation tax is a lump-sum tax on current money holders, the initial old in period 1.

The real value of the seigniorage tax base equation depends on the demand for fiat money, which depends on the expected future rate of fiat money creation (z_2). The government would like people to expect a low rate of inflation in the future so that their demand for fiat money (and thus the seigniorage tax base) is strong. Ideally, then, the government wants to print fiat money today (period 1) while convincing people that it will not inflate in the future (period 2). However, when period 2 arrives, the government will want to inflate, despite any previous promise, while trying to convince people that it will not inflate in period 3. The incentive to inflate today but to promise no future inflation is again the time consistency problem.[11]

5 Inflation and Private Debt

Private debt, when nominally denominated, also may tempt a government to inflate if it wishes to help borrowers at the expense of lenders. If, for example, the government favoring a more equal distribution of wealth sees the poor as borrowers, it may wish to inflate away the real value of the borrowers' debt. As with government debt, the government will be unable to use inflation to help borrowers in any systematic way if lenders anticipate the government's desires. Lenders will expect the government to inflate and thus will lend at only nominal interest rates that take into account the expected inflation.

If a country borrows a great deal from abroad (as a developing nation might well do) or acquires foreign debt to back money issued by a currency board, the government's temptation to inflate is even greater. A surprise inflation would then help the domestic citizens, the borrowers, at the expense of foreigners, the lenders.

---

[11] See Auernheimer (1974) and Calvo (1978).

Lenders, of course, are aware of this inflationary temptation and will be reluctant to sign contracts denominated in the money of the borrowers' country.

Loans denominated in the money of the lender country introduce their own incentive problems. A nation that is a net leader to other nations will wish to have a surprise deflation (price decreases) in order to increase the real value of loans denominated in the lender country's money.[12] Only debt indexed to the price level or denominated in the currency of disinterested third nations is free from the temptations of inflation or deflation.

6 Summary

We began this chapter with a discussion of defaulting on the government debt. Here we encountered the time consistency problem of government policy wherein the best short-term policy (here, default) may not always be the best long-term policy. A government that defaults on its debt may find it difficult to convince people that it will not default again in the future.

This chapter also investigated the effects of inflation on the real value of the government debt. At first glance, it appears that, by inflating, a government can lower the real burden of its debt. However, we discovered that, if inflation is anticipated, nominal interest rates on government debt will rise sufficiently to offset the effect that inflation has on the real value of the debt.

Only if inflation is unanticipated will the inflationary policy succeed in lowering the debt's real value. In this case, the inflation acts as a default on the government debt. The reduction in the real value of the debt lessens crowding out of capital and, subsequently, increases output. However, a government policy that continues to inflate in the hope of further reducing the burden of its debt will eventually fail. Rational people will come to expect inflation and demand higher nominal interest rates on government bonds. The government will be frustrated in its attempt to lower the burden of its debt.

We also found that, if people have come to expect inflation, the government will find it difficult not to fulfill those expectations. Because inflationary expectations are already built into the nominal interest rate, a government that does not inflate will find itself with a larger debt burden; whenever the inflation rate is less than the expected inflation rate, the borrower is harmed.

7 Exercises

18.1. Explain why a government that must run up a large national debt to finance extraordinary spending over the next several years might choose to surrender the power of money creation to a central bank beyond the government's control.

---

[12] The rapid reduction of U.S. inflation from 20 percent in 1979 to 6 percent in 1982 may well have caught heavily borrowing developing nations by surprise, greatly increasing the real value of outstanding debt denominated in U.S. dollars, whether or not this effect was intended.

18.2. What will happen to the demand for fiat money, the nominal interest rate, and the real interest rate if the government tries to use inflation to default on the national debt every other year? In randomly selected years? Explain each of your answers.

18.3. Suppose the government must borrow 1,000 goods in period 1. Let the gross real marginal product of capital equal 1.07. Assume that people always want to hold fiat money balances worth a total of 100 goods and that the fiat money stock in period 1 is \$10,000. Suppose people expect the government to increase the fiat money stock by 100 percent and that the population is constant.

    a. What will the nominal net interest rate be?

    b. What will the real value of the debt in period 2?

    c. What will it be if the fiat money stock rises by 10 percent but this rise is unexpected?

18.4. Consider an economy in which aggregate real money balances is always equal to 1,000,000 goods. What is the maximum amount of seigniorage that a government could generate in this economy in a single period?

18.5. **(advanced)** Consider an economy in which aggregate real money balances is equal to 1,000,000 goods when the money stock is constant. However, the aggregate demand for real money balances is represented by $Nq = 1,000,000 - z$.

    a. Compute the amount of seigniorage that would be generated if the central bank set the money growth rate $z = 2$.

    b. What value of z will result in no seigniorage revenue be collected? In other words, is there a money growth rate at which aggregate real money demand is zero?

8 Appendix: An Activist Monetary Policy

(Calculus and simple statistics – the concepts of expected value and covariance – are used in this appendix. The material in the appendix to Chapter 2 is also a prerequisite to this appendix.)

If it is impossible to fool people in any predictable way, can there be any role for an activist monetary policy, one that occasionally surprises the public with inflation that reduces the real value of the national debt? In a world of certainty, such a policy would seem foolish. It would increase the risk faced by bond holders and thus would also increase the average rate of return (because of the risk premium) the government must offer on its bonds.

To see this, consider an overlapping generations economy in which capital and one-period government bonds are the only two assets. Capital pays the sure real rate of return x, and bonds pay the risky real rate of return r_{t+1}. Let the preferences of each of the model's risk-averse people born at t be described by the utility function $U(c_{1,t}) + V(c_{2,t+1})$, where $U(.)$ and $V(.)$ are continuous, differentiable, increasing, and strictly concave. Each person is endowed with y_1 goods when young and y_2 when old.

The budget constraints of the person may be written as:

$$c_{1,t} + k_t + b_t = y_1 \tag{18.7}$$

$$c_{2,t+1} = y_2 + xk_t + r_{t+1}b_t. \tag{18.8}$$

Substituting these constraints into the utility function, we can express the person's problem as the choice of k_t and b_t to maximize

$$U(y_1 - k_t - b_t) + E_t V(y_2 + xk_t + r_{t+1}b_t), \qquad (18.9)$$

where $E_t V(.)$ refers to the expected value of $V(.)$, given the information known in period t (the period in which the person must choose her asset portfolio). Following the same steps outlined in the appendix to Chapter 2, we differentiate Equation 18.9 with respect to k_t and b_t to find the first-order conditions that identify the maximum expected utility of someone born at t:

$$-U'(c_{1,t}) + xE_t V'(c_{2,t+1}) = 0, \qquad (18.10)$$

$$-U'(c_{1,t}) + E_t\left[r_{t+1}V'(c_{2,t+1})\right] = 0. \qquad (18.11)$$

Together, these imply that

$$x = \frac{E_t[r_{t+1}V'(c_{2,t+1})]}{E_t V'(c_{2,t+1})} \qquad (18.12)$$

$$= \frac{E_t r_{t+1} E_t V'(c_{2,t+1}) + Cov[r_{t+1}, V'(c_{2,t+1})]}{E_t V'(c_{2,t+1})}.$$

by the definition of a covariance.[13]

After canceling terms and rearranging, Equation 18.12 becomes

$$E_t r_{t+1} = x - \frac{Cov[r_{t+1}, V'(c_{2,t+1})]}{E_t V'(c_{2,t+1})}. \qquad (18.13)$$

The covariance between two random variables is a measure of how those two variables move together. Consider an increase in one of the two random variables. If the covariance is positive, then the other variable also tends to increase. If the covariance is negative, then the other variable tends to decrease.

If the random return on government debt is the only source of randomness in the economy, high values of r_{t+1} cause high values of $c_{2,t+1}$ and low values of $V'(c_{2,t+1})$ because of diminishing marginal utility. In this case, $Cov[r_{t+1}, V'(c_{2,t+1})]$ is negative.

Equation 18.13 therefore tells us that, to induce people to hold a risky bond, its expected rate of return must be greater than that of the safe asset. If the government randomizes the rate of return on its bonds, it will wind up paying higher rates of

---

[13] Equation 18.12 follows from the definition of a covariance of two random variables. Suppose two random variables, X and Y, have expected values $E(X)$ and $E(Y)$, respectively. Their covariance (Cov) is defined as

$$Cov(X, Y) = E\{[X - E(X)][Y - E(Y)]\}$$

$$= E[XY - E(X)Y] - E(Y)X - E(X)E(Y)]$$

$$= E(XY) - E(X)E(Y) - E(X)E(Y) + E(X)E(Y)$$

$$= E(XY) - E(X)E(Y).$$

From this, it follows that $E(XY) = E(X)E(Y) + Cov(XY)$. Equation 18.12 is an application of this result, where r_{t+1} plays the role of X and $V'(c_{2,t+1})$ plays the role of Y.

return. This is called the "risk premium":

$$\text{risk premium} = \frac{-Cov[r_{t+1}, V'(c_{2,t+1})]}{E_t V'(c_{2,t+1})} > 0. \qquad (18.14)$$

Note that, if the covariance of r_{t+1} and $V'(c_{2,t+1})$ were positive, this risk premium would be negative, implying that the rate of return that must be offered by government bonds is less than that of the safe asset. Can we imagine such a case?

Suppose there is a second source of randomness in the economy – for example, randomness in the endowment y_2 received by all the old people in a generation. Every old person in a given generation receives the same endowment, but this endowment varies randomly from generation to generation.[14] A below-average endowment when old implies low consumption when old and thus a high marginal utility when old, all other things being equal.

Suppose the government sets bond returns to be slightly higher than average when people receive a below-average endowment when old (and lower when the endowment is above average). Then high rates of return will occur when consumption is low and when the marginal utility of consumption is high. This implies a positive covariance between rates of return and marginal utility and thus, from Equation 18.14, a negative risk premium. People will be willing to hold the risky bonds even if their average rate of return is lower than that of a safe asset. Although in this way the return on the bonds is made random, by paying more when consumption is low, the consumption of bond holders is made less risky. As a result, the average rate of return the government must offer to get people to hold these bonds will actually be less than it would offer if the bonds themselves paid a fixed real rate of return (i.e., the risk premium that must be paid on these bonds will be negative).[15] In this way, the bonds may serve as a form of insurance for bond holders. This is essentially a way in which the government may insure generations against low consumption by paying more to unlucky generations, financed by paying less to lucky generations.

Monetary policy in this case is merely a device through which government bonds can be made to pay real rates of return contingent on shocks. When bond holders receive a good shock, the government inflates to lower the real return on nominal bonds; similarly, it deflates when the shock is bad. With nominal bonds, there still remains, of course, the temptation for the government to announce whatever will justify an inflation with which it can default on its real obligations.

---

[14] If there were randomness in the old-age endowments within a generation, members of that generation could protect themselves against risk through insurance contracts with the other members of their generation. Private insurance contracts will not eliminate risk across generations, given that a generation already knows whether it has won or lost by the time the next generation comes along.

[15] See Lucas and Stokey (1983) for another justification of government bonds paying rates of return contingent on random shocks.

References

Readings marked by "*" are written at a level suitable for undergraduates. Many of the cited publications of the Federal Reserve Banks are now freely available from Bank Web sites.

Abel, A. 1987. "Optimal Monetary Growth," *Journal of Monetary Economics* 19: 437–50.

*Aiyagari, S. R. 1987. "Intergenerational Linkages and Government Budget Policies," Federal Reserve Bank of Minneapolis *Quarterly Review* 11(Spring): 14–23.

*Aiyagari, S. R. 1990. "Deflating the Case for Zero Inflation," Federal Reserve Bank of Minneapolis *Quarterly Review* 14(Summer): 2–11.

Alesina, A. 1988. "Macroeconomics and Politics." In *NBER Macroeconomics Annual*, S. Fischer, ed. Cambridge, MA: MIT Press: 17–52.

*Alesina A., and L. Summers. 1993. "Central Bank Independence and Macroeconomic Performance," *Journal of Money, Credit, and Banking* 25(2) (May): 151–62.

Arrow, K., and G. Debreu. 1954. "Existence of an Equilibrium for a Competitive Economy," *Econometrica* 22(July): 265–90.

Auernheimer, L. 1974. "The Honest Government's Guide to the Revenue from the Creation of Money." *Journal of Political Economy* 82(May/June): 598–606.

Avery, R. B., G. E. Elliehausen, and A. B. Kennickell. 1987. "Changes in Consumer Installment Debt: Evidence Form the 1983 and 1986 Surveys of Consumer Finances," *Federal Reserve Bulletin* 73(10): 761–778.

Azariadas, C. 1981. "Self-Fulfilling Prophecies." *Journal of Economic Theory* 25(December): 380–96.

Bacchetta, P., and R. Caminal. 1994. "A Note on Reserve Requirements and Public Finance." *International Review of Economics and Finance* 3(1): 108–18.

Bade, R., and M. Parkin. 1982. "Central Bank Laws and Monetary Policy." Unpublished manuscript.

Bailey, M. J. 1956. "The Welfare Cost of Inflationary Finance." *Journal of Political Economy* 64(April): 93–110.

Barro, R. J. 1974. "Are Government Bonds Net Wealth?" *Journal of Political Economy* 82(November/December): 1095–1117.

Barro, R. J. 1982. "Measuring the Fed's Revenue from Money Creation." *Economics Letters* 10:327–32.

Barro, R. J. 1989. "The Neoclassical Approach to Fiscal Policy." In *Modern Business Cycle Theory*, R. J. Barro, ed. Cambridge: Harvard University Press.

Barro, R. J., and D. B. Gordon. 1983. "A Positive Theory of Monetary Policy in a Natural Rate Model." *Journal of Political Economy* 91(August): 590–610.

Bencivenga, V., and B. D. Smith. 1991. "Financial Intermediation and Endogenous Growth." *Review of Economic Studies* 58(April): 195–209.

Bernanke, B. S. 1990. "Clearing and Settlement during the Crash." *Review of Financial Studies* 3(1): 133–51.

Bhattacharya, S., and A. V. Thakor. 1993. "Contemporary Banking Theory." *Journal of Financial Intermediation* 3(October): 2–50.

Bhattacharya, J., M. Guzman, E. Huybens, and B. D. Smith. 1997. "Monetary, Fiscal, and Reserve Requirement Policy in a Simple Monetary Growth Model." *International Economic Review* 38(May): 321–50.

Bhattacharya, J., J. Haslag, and A. Martin. 2005. "Heterogeneity, Redistribution, and the Friedman Rule." *International Economic Review* 46(May): 437–54.

Boyd, J. H., and E. C. Prescott. 1986. "Financial Intermediary Coalitions." *Journal of Economic Theory* 38(April): 211–32.

Bryant, J. 1980. "A Model of Reserves, Bank Runs, and Deposit Insurance." *Journal of Banking and Finance* 4(December): 335–44.

Bryant, J., and N. Wallace. 1984. "A Price Discrimination Analysis of Monetary Policy." *Review of Economic Studies* 51(April): 279–88.

Cagan, P. 1965. *Determinants and Effects of Changes in the U.S. Money Stock, 1875–1960.* New York: National Bureau of Economic Research.

Calvo, G. A. 1978. "On the Time Consistency of Optimal Policy in a Monetary Economy." *Econometrica* 46(November): 1411–28.

Canzoneri, M. B., and C. A. Rogers. 1990. "Is the European Community an Optimal Currency Area? Optimal Taxation Versus the Cost of Multiple Currencies." *American Economic Review* 80(June): 419–33.

*Carr, J., F. Matthewson, and N. Quigley. 1994. *Ensuring Failure: Financial System Stability and Deposit Insurance in Canada.* Toronto: C. D. Howe Institute.

Cass, D., and K. Shell. 1983. "Do Sunspots Matter?" *Journal of Political Economy* 91(April): 193–227.

Cass, D., and M. Yaari. 1966. "A Re-Examination of the Pure Consumption Loans Model." *Journal of Political Economy* 74(August): 3563–67.

Champ, B., and S. Freeman. 1990. "Money, Output, and the Nominal National Debt." *American Economic Review* 80(June): 390–97.

Champ, B., B. Smith, and S. D. Williamson. 1996. "Currency Elasticity and Banking Panics: Theory and Evidence." *Canadian Journal of Economics* XXIX(4)(November): 828–64.

Champ, B., S. Freeman, and W. Weber. 1999. "Redemption Costs and Interest Rates under the U.S. National Banking System." *Journal of Money, Credit, and Banking* 31(August, part 2): 568–89.

Cooley, T., and S. LeRoy. 1985. "Atheoretical Macroeconometrics – A Critique." *Journal of Monetary Economics* 16:283–308.

*Darby, M. R. 1984. "Some Pleasant Monetarist Arithmetic." Federal Reserve Bank of Minneapolis *Quarterly Review* 8(Spring): 15–20.

Diamond, D. W., and P. H. Dybvig. 1983. "Bank Runs, Deposit Insurance, and Liquidity." *Journal of Political Economy* 91(June): 401–19.

Diamond, D.W. 1984. "Financial Intermediation and Delegated Monitoring," *Review of Economic Studies,* 51(July): 393–414.

Diamond, P. A. 1965. "National Debt in a Neoclassical Growth Model." *American Economic Review* 55(December): 1126–50.

Fama, E. 1980. "Banking in the Theory of Finance." *Journal of Monetary Economics* 6:39–57.

*Federal Deposit Insurance Corporation. 1998. *Managing the Crisis: The FDIC and RTC Experience.* http://www.fdic.gov/bank/historical/managing/

Feinman, J. 1993. "Reserve Requirements: History, Current Practice and Potential Reform." *Federal Reserve Bulletin* 79(6): 569–89.

Fisher, I. 1926. "A Statistical Relationship between Unemployment and Price Changes." *International Labor Review* 13(June): 785–92. Reprinted as "I Discovered the Phillips Curve." *Journal of Political Economy* 81 (March/April 1973):496–502.

Fischer, S. 1982. "Seigniorage and the Case for a National Money." *Journal of Political Economy* 90(April): 295–313.

Freeman, S. 1985. "Transactions Costs and the Optimal Quantity of Money." *Journal of Political Economy* 93(February): 146–57.

Freeman, S. 1987. "Reserve Requirements and Optimal Seigniorage." *Journal of Monetary Economics* 19:307–14.

Freeman, S. 1988. "Banking as the Provision of Liquidity." *Journal of Business* 61(January): 45–64.

Freeman, S. 1989. "Fiat Money as a Medium of Exchange." *International Economic Review* 30(February): 137–51.

Freeman, S. 1993. "Resolving Differences over the Optimal Quantity of Money." *Journal of Money, Credit, and Banking* 25(November): 801–11.

Freeman, S. 1996a. "The Payments System, Liquidity and Rediscounting." *American Economic Review* 86(December): 1126–38.

Freeman, S. 1996b. "Clearinghouse Banks and Banknote Over-Issue." *Journal of Monetary Economics* 38:101–15.

*Freeman, S., and J. Haslag. 1995. "Should Bank Reserves Pay Interest?" *Economic Review* Federal Reserve Bank of Dallas, Fourth Quarter: 25–33.

Freeman, S., and J. Haslag. 1996. "On the Optimality of Interest-Bearing Reserves in Economies of Overlapping Generations." *Economic Theory* 7(3): 557–65.

Freeman, S., and G. Huffman. 1991. "Inside Money, Output, and Causality." *International Economic Review* 32(August): 645–67.

Freeman, S., and G. Tabellini. 1998. "The Optimality of Nominal Contracts." *Economic Theory* 11(3): 545–62.

*Friedman, M. 1960. *A Program for Monetary Stability*. New York: Fordham University Press.

Friedman, M. 1969. "The Optimum Quantity of Money." In *The Optimum Quantity of Money and Other Essays*. Chicago: Aldine.

Friedman, M., and A. Schwartz. 1963a. "Money and Business Cycles." *Review of Economics and Statistics* 45(February): 32–64.

Friedman, M., and A. Schwartz. 1963b. *A Monetary History of the United States*. Princeton: Princeton University Press.

Greenwood, J., and B. Jovanovic. 1990. "Financial Development, Growth, and the Distribution of Income." *Journal of Political Economy* 98(October, part 1): 1076–1107.

Grilli, V., D. Masciandaro, and G. Tabellini. 1991. "Political and Monetary Institutions and Public Finance Policies in the Industrial Countries." *Economic Policy* 13(October): 341–92.

Gu, C., and J. Haslag. 2014. "Unconventional Open Market Purchases." *Review of Economic Dynamics* 17(July): 543–58.

*Hammond, B. 1957. *Banks and Politics in America from the Revolution to the Civil War*. Princeton: Princeton University Press.

Hanke, S. H., and N. Krus. 2012. "World Hyperinflations." Cato Working Paper, Cato Institute, Washington, DC.

Haslag, J., and A. Martin. 2007. "Optimality of the Friedman Rule in an Overlapping Generations Model with Spatial Separation." *Journal of Money, Credit, and Banking* 39(October): 1741–58.

Haubrich, J. 1990. "Nonmonetary Effects of Financial Crises: Lessons from the Great Depression in Canada." *Journal of Monetary Economics* 25(March): 223–52.

Jevons, W. S. 1875. *Money and the Mechanism of Exchange*. London: Appleton.

*Johnson, J. F. 1910. *The Canadian Banking System*, Washington, DC: U.S. Government Printing Office.

Jones, L. E., and R. Manuelli. 1990. "A Convex Model of Equilibrium Growth." *Journal of Political Economy* 98(October, part 1): 1008–38.

*Kahn, C. M., and W. Roberds. 1999. "The Design of Wholesale Payments Networks: The Importance of Incentives." Federal Reserve Bank of Atlanta *Economic Review* 84(3): 30–9.

*Kareken, J. H. 1983. "Deposit Insurance Reform: or Deregulation Is the Cart, Not the Horse." Federal Reserve Bank of Minneapolis *Quarterly Review* 14(Spring): 3–11.

Kareken, J. H., and N. Wallace. 1977. "Portfolio Autarky: A Welfare Analysis." *Journal of International Economics* 7(February): 19–43.

Kareken, J. H., and N. Wallace. 1981. "On the Indeterminacy of Equilibrium Exchange Rates." *Quarterly Journal of Economics* 96(May): 207–22.

King, R., and C. Plosser. 1984. "Money, Credit, and Prices in a Real Business Cycle." *American Economic Review* 74(June): 363–80.

King, R., N. Wallace, and W. E. Weber. 1992. "Nonfundamental Uncertainty and Exchange Rates." *Journal of International Economics* 32(1): 83–108.

Kiyotaki, N., and R. Wright. 1989. "On Money as a Medium of Exchange." *Journal of Political Economy* 97(August): 927–54.

Kocherlakota, N. 1999. "Money is Memory." *Journal of Economic Theory* 81(August): 232–51.

Krugman, P. 1979. "A Model of Balance of Payments Crises." *Journal of Money, Credit, and Banking* 11(August): 311–25.

Krugman, P., and J. Rotemberg. 1991. "Speculative Attacks on Target Zones." In *Target Zones and Currency Bands,* P. Krugman and M. Miller, eds. Oxford: Oxford University Press.

Kydland, F., and E. C. Prescott. 1977. "Rules Rather than Discretion: The Inconsistency of Optimal Plans." *Journal of Political Economy* 85(June): 473–91.

Lacker, J. 1988. "Inside Money and Real Output." *Economic Letters* 28:9–14.

Laidler, D. 1984. "Misconceptions about the Real-Bills Doctrine: A Comment on Sargent and Wallace." *Journal of Political Economy* 92(February): 149–55.

Leamer, E. 1985. "Vector Autoregressions for Causal Inference?" *Carnegie-Rochester Conference Series on Public Policy* 22: 255–303.

Litterman, R., and L. Weiss. 1985. "Money, Real Interest Rates, and Output: A Reinterpretation of U.S. Postwar Data." *Econometrica* 53(January): 129–56.

Loewy, M. 1991. "The Macroeconomic Effects of Bank Runs: An Equilibrium Analysis." *Journal of Financial Intermediation* 1(June, no. 3): 242–56.

Lucas, R. E. Jr. 1972. "Expectations and the Neutrality of Money." *Journal of Economic Theory* 4(April): 103–24. Also in *Studies in Business Cycle Theory*. R. E. Lucas Jr., ed. Cambridge, MA: MIT Press, 1981.

Lucas, R. E. Jr. 1973. "Some International Evidence on Output-Inflation Tradeoffs." *American Economic Review* 63(June): 326–34. Also in *Studies in Business Cycle Theory*. R. E. Lucas Jr., ed. Cambridge, MA: MIT Press, 1981.

*Lucas, R. E. Jr. 1976. "Econometric Policy Evaluation: A Critique." *Carnegie-Rochester Conference Series on Public Policy* 1: 19–46. Also in *Studies in Business Cycle Theory*. R. E. Lucas Jr., ed. Cambridge, MA: MIT Press, 1981.

*Lucas, R. E. Jr. 1981. *Studies in Business Cycle Theory*. R. E. Lucas Jr., ed. Cambridge, MA: MIT Press, 1981.

Lucas, R. E. Jr., and N. Stokey. 1983. "Optimal Fiscal and Monetary Policy in an Economy without Capital." *Journal of Monetary Economics* 12(July): 55–93.

Maeda, Y. 1991. "Fiat Money in a Pairwise-Trading Multi-Good Overlapping Generations Model." *Journal of Economic Theory* 54:84–97.

Metzler, L.A. 1951. "Wealth, Saving and the Rate of Interest." *Journal of Political Economy* 59(April): 93–116.

*Miller, P. J., and T. J. Sargent. 1984. "A Reply to Darby." Federal Reserve Bank of Minneapolis *Quarterly Review* 8(Spring): 21–26.

Miron, J. A. 1986. "Financial Panics, the Seasonality of the Nominal Interest Rate, and the Founding of the Fed." *American Economic Review* 76(March): 125–40.

Muth, J. F. 1961. "Rational Expectations and the Theory of Price Movements." *Econometrica* 29(July): 315–35.

Persson, R., and L. E. O. Svensson. 1989. "Why a Stubborn Conservative Would Run a Deficit: Policy with Time Inconsistent Preferences." *Quarterly Journal of Economics* 104(May): 325–45.

Porter, R., and R. Judson. 1996. "The Location of US Currency: How Much is Abroad?" *Federal Reserve Bulletin* 82(10): 245–74.

Prescott, E. C. 1987. "A Multiple Means-of-Payment Model." In *New Approaches to Monetary Economics*, W. Barnett and K. Singleton, eds. Cambridge, MA: Cambridge University Press.

*Radford, R. A. 1945. "The Economics Organization of a P.O.W. Camp." *Economica* 12(November): 189–201.

*Rolnick, A. J., and W. E. Weber. 1989. "A Case for Fixing Exchange Rates." *Federal Reserve Bank of Minneapolis 1989 Annual Report*: 3–14.

*Rolnick, A. J., B. D. Smith, and W. E. Weber. 1998. "Lessons from a Laissez-Faire Payments System: The Suffolk Banking System (1825-58)." Federal Reserve Bank of St. Louis *Review* 80(May/June): 105–16.

Romer, D. 1985. "Financial Intermediation, Reserve Requirements, and Inside Money." *Journal of Monetary Economics* 16(September): 175–94.

Salant, S. W., and D. W. Henderson. 1978. "Market Anticipation of Government Policy and the Price of Gold." *Journal of Political Economy* 86(August): 627–48.

Samuelson, P. A. 1958. "An Exact Consumption-Loan Model of Interest With and Without the Social Contrivance of Money." *Journal of Political Economy* 66(December): 467–82.

*Sargent, T. J. 1986a. "The Ends of Four Big Inflations." In *Rational Expectations and Inflation*. New York: Harper & Row: 40–109.

*Sargent, T. J. 1986b. "Interpreting the Reagan Deficits." Federal Reserve Bank of San Francisco *Quarterly Review* (Fall): 5–12.

*Sargent, T. J., and N. Wallace. 1981. "Some Unpleasant Monetarist Arithmetic." Federal Reserve Bank of Minneapolis *Quarterly Review* (Fall): 1–17.

Sargent, T. J., and N. Wallace. 1982. "The Real-Bills Doctrine vs. The Quantity Theory: A Reconciliation." *Journal of Political Economy* 90(December):1212–36.

Sargent, T. J., and N. Wallace. 1983. "A Model of Commodity Money." *Journal of Monetary Economics* 12(July): 163–87.

Schreft, S. 1992. "Transactions Costs and the Use of Cash and Credit." *Economic Theory* 2(April): 283–96.

*Sengupta, R., and Y Tam. 2008. "The LIBOR-OIS Spread as a Summary Indicator." Federal Reserve Bank of St. Louis *Monetary Trends* November.

Sims, C. 1972. "Money, Income and Causality." *American Economic Review* 62(September): 540–52.

Sims, C. 1980. "Comparison of Interwar and Postwar Cycles: Monetarism Reconsidered." *American Economic Review* 70(May): 250–75.

*Smith, B. D. 1985. "American Colonial Monetary Regimes: The Failure of the Quantity Theory and Some Evidence in Favour of an Alternate View." *Canadian Journal of Economics* 18(3)(August): 531–64.

*Smith, B. D. 1988. "The Relationship Between Money and Prices: Some Historical Evidence Reconsidered." Federal Reserve Bank of Minneapolis *Quarterly Review* 12(Summer): 18–32.

Smith, B. D. 1991. "Interest on Reserves and sunspot Equilibria: Friedman's Proposal Reconsidered." *Review of Economic Studies* 58(January): 93–105.

Sprague, O. M. W. 1910. *A History of Crises Under the National Banking System*, Washington, DC: U.S. Government Printing Office.

Tallman, E. W., and J. R. Moen. 1990. "The Panic of 1907: How Trusts Tipped the Scales." Federal Reserve Bank of Atlanta *Economic Review* 75(May/June): 2–13.

Tobin, J. 1965. "Money and Economic Growth." *Econometrica* 33(October): 671–84.

Tobin, J. 1970. "Money and Income: *Post Hoc Ergo Propter Hoc?*" *Quarterly Journal of Economics* 84(May): 301–17.

Tolley, G. 1957. "Providing for the Growth of the Money Supply." *Journal of Political Economy* 65(January): 447–84.

Townsend, R. M. 1979. "Optimal Contracts and Competitive Markets with Costly State Verification." *Journal of Economic Theory* 21(October): 265–93.

Townsend, R. M. 1980. "Models of Money with Spatially Separated Agents." In *Models of Monetary Economies*, J. Kareken and N. Wallace, eds. Minneapolis: Federal Reserve Bank of Minneapolis: 265–303.

*Wallace, N. 1979. "Why Markets in Foreign Exchange Are Different from Other Markets." Federal Reserve Bank of Minneapolis *Quarterly Review* 3(Fall): 1–7

*Wallace, N. 1980. "The Overlapping Generations Model of Fiat Money." In *Models of Monetary Economies*, J. Kareken and N. Wallace, eds. Minneapolis: Federal Reserve Bank of Minneapolis: 49–82.

Wallace, N. 1981. "A Modigliani-Miller Theorem for Open Market Operations." *American Economic Review* 71(June): 267–74.

Wallace, N. 1983. "A Legal Restrictions Theory of the Demand for 'Money' and the Role of Monetary Policy." Federal Reserve Bank of Minneapolis *Quarterly Review* 7(Winter): 1–7.

*Wallace, N. 1984. "Some of the Choice for Monetary Policy." Federal Reserve Bank of Minneapolis *Quarterly Review* 8(Winter): 15–24.

White, L. J. 1991. *The S&L Debacle: Public Policy Lessons for Bank and Thrift Regulation*. New York: Oxford University Press.

*Williamson, S. D. 1987. "Recent Developments in Modeling Financial Intermediation." Federal Reserve Bank of Minneapolis *Quarterly Review* 11(Summer): 19–28.

Williamson, S. D. 1989. "Restrictions on Financial Intermediaries and Implications for Aggregate Fluctuations: Canada and United States, 1870–1913." In *NBER Macroeconomics Annual 1989*, O. Blanchard and S. Fisher, eds. Cambridge, MA: Cambridge University Press:

Young, J. P. 1925. *European Currency and Finance*, vols. 1 and 2, Commission of Gold and Silver Inquiry, United States Senate, Serial 9. Washington, DC: U.S. Government Printing Office.

Author Index

Subject Index

CPSIA information can be obtained
at www.ICGtesting.com
Printed in the USA
LVHW100918270721
693812LV00007B/336